tHe AuthoR

Travel writer and journalist George Cantor worked as a sports writer and city editor for the *Detroit Free Press* before becoming its travel editor in 1973. He's now a *Detroit News* columnist. His travel books include *The Great Lakes Guidebook, Where the Old Roads Go, Historic Black Landmarks,* and *North American Indian Landmarks.*

A TRAVELER'S GUIDE

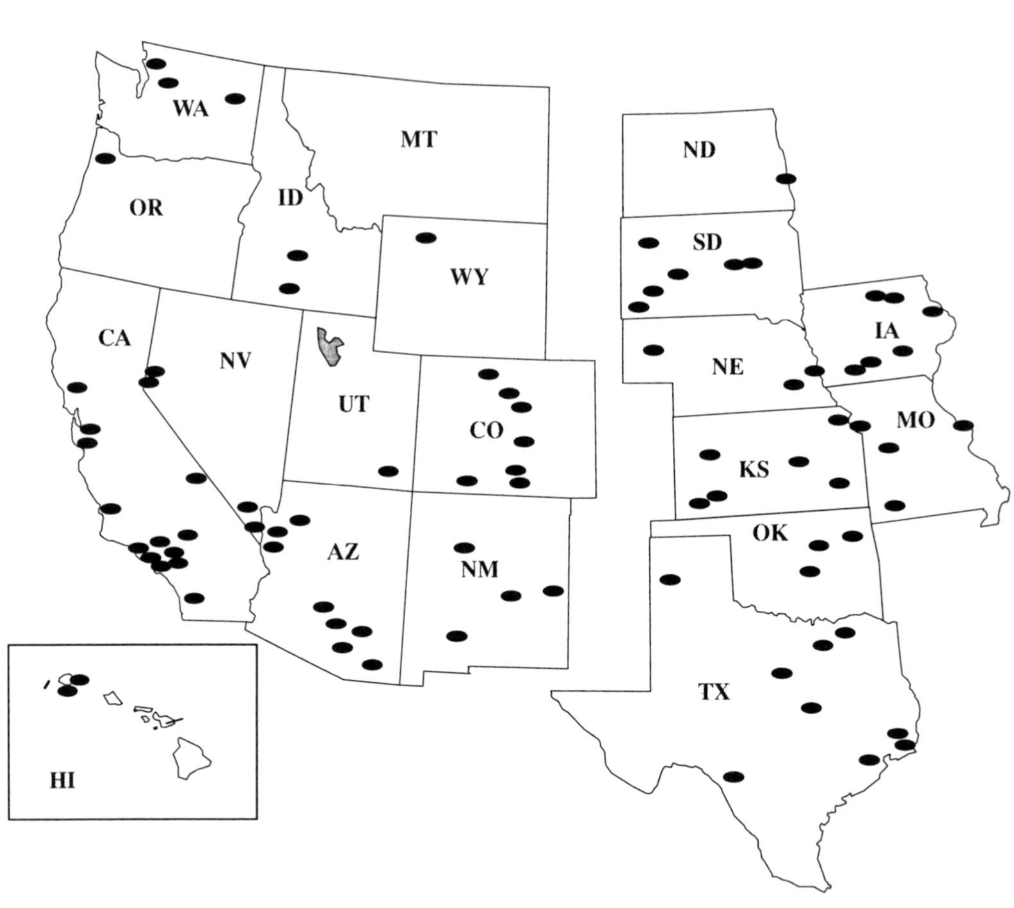
WA
MT
ND
OR
ID
SD
WY
IA
CA
NV
NE
UT
CO
MO
KS
OK
AZ
NM
TX
HI

Lake Superior
MN
Lake Michigan
Lake Huron
MI
Lake Erie
ME
VT
NH
NY
MA
RI
CT
PA
NJ
MD
DE
OH
IN
IL
WV
VA
KY
TN
NC
AR
SC
MS
AL
GA
LA
FL

A TRAVELER'S GUIDE

George Cantor

with foreword by

Ray B. Browne

Director of the Center for the Study of Popular Culture,

Bowling Green State University

DETROIT • WASHINGTON, D.C. • LONDON

POP CuLTURE LANDMaRKS: A TRAVeLER'S GUIDE

by George Cantor

Published by **Visible Ink Press**™
a division of Gale Research Inc.
835 Penobscot Bldg.
645 Griswold St.
Detroit MI 48226-4094

Visible Ink Press is a trademark of Gale Research Inc.

ISBN 0-8103-9899-0

Cover and Page Design: Pamela A. E. Galbreath
Map Design: Sherrell Hobbs
Editor: Rebecca Nelson
With thanks to: Diane L. Dupuis, Amy M. Marcaccio, Kevin Hile, Kelle Sisung, and Jolen Gedridge

FRONT COVER PHOTOS: Wall Drug, *courtesy of Wall Drug Store*; Walk-Thru Fish, *courtesy of National Freshwater Fishing Hall of Fame*; San Francisco cable cars, *courtesy of Roger Matuz*; Carhenge, *courtesy of the Worley Studio*; Grand Ole Opry, *courtesy of Opryland, USA*. BACK COVER PHOTOS: Hollywoodland sign, *UPI/Bettman*; Wrigley Field, *AP/Wide World Photos*; World of Coca-Cola, *photograph by Michael Pugh, courtesy of the Coca-Cola Company*.

10 9 8 7 6 5 4 3 2 1

FOR MIKE CANTOR, TOM HUTH, BOB CROSS, TOM DELISLE, SURLY JEROME, & THE OTHER FRIENDS WHO SHARED THE ROAD WITH ME TO THESE PLACES OVER THE YEARS

Contents

GREAT LAKES/OHIO VALLEY

GREAT PLAINS

WEST AND PACIFIC

LANDMARKS AND POPULAR CULTURE

BY RAY B. BROWNE
DIRECTOR OF THE CENTER FOR THE STUDY OF POPULAR CULTURE,
BOWLING GREEN STATE UNIVERSITY

Popular culture is the way of life of the people—the things they use day-to-day, how they entertain themselves, and what their leisure-time activities are. It is television, movies, music, and transportation. But it is far more, too: Though much of popular culture is disseminated by the media, it is the total culture in which we live—the world around us. It is the everyday culture, what people do while they are awake, how they do things, where they sleep, and what they dream about.

THE WORLD OF LANDMARKS

Landmarks are events, discoveries, decisions, important points in civilization and culture. They mark what people, for one reason or another, consider significant in their lives. They can be emotional events like Paul Revere's ride through the Massachusetts countryside at the beginning of the American Revolution. More likely they are places, like the Empire State Building in New York City or the Professional Football Hall of Fame in Canton, Ohio.

Every community has created landmarks. Big or small, they are used to focus attention on an event or a person, to attract people to a place, to get the public to linger for a while, and to learn from or just remember what the landmarks represent. There are far more landmarks than can be covered in a single book. And some are only important to a small group of people.

One such place is the tomb of Reuben "Rube" Houston Burrow, who was known as one of the country's leading bank robbers before he was killed in 1890. Though his fame may be limited now, many in Lamar County, Alabama, still regard him as one of America's great outlaws. Some souvenir seekers even chip away at his tombstone. Landmarks need not be large to hold value for some people.

Landmarks, like those in this volume, are increasingly places of group participation. As such, they satisfy a growing need in our society: They pull us from the comfort of our homes and out into the world where we must react to the environment and participate in society. As landmarks draw us together, they make strong our social bonds. We get to know one another better, to see that our apparent differences are less important than are our similarities. Thus landmarks can help create community spirit.

Our political landmarks, such as the Lincoln Memorial and the Vietnam Veterans Memorial in Washington, D.C., are becoming increasingly valued, as

Americans seem to become more passionate about preserving history. Social and cultural landmarks are significant because they set the shape of society to come.

One major social landmark is the shopping mall. As malls draw commercial and community activities from the heart of our cities, shifting them to the outskirts and suburbs, the malls take on a life of their own, becoming cities unto themselves. Some, like the Mall of America in Bloomington, Minnesota, attract weekend tourists from as far away as Great Britain.

Perhaps more important as social landmarks are the four Disney theme parks in California, Florida, France, and Japan. Walt Disney realized that people wanted clean, safe amusement parks where they and their children could be entertained. When Disneyland opened in Anaheim, California, in July 1955, it established an entirely new approach to amusement parks: It fused entertainment and education. "Disneyland," says the official brochure on the Disney theme parks, "combines fantasy, history, adventure, and learning." Roy Disney summarizes the purpose of Florida's Walt Disney World in similar terms: "May Walt Disney World bring joy and inspiration and new knowledge to all who come to this happy place . . . to laugh and play and learn together." Max Rafferty, California's superintendent of education, called Walt Disney "the greatest educator of the twentieth century."

As democratic cultures develop throughout the world, landmarks take on added significance. Rising interest in tribalism, ethnicity, and nationalism, engendering the desire to get back to roots, compel us to identify new landmarks. Every community needs some physical, spiritual, emotional, commercial, or historical place around which to settle its energies. If such a place does not exist, the group may create one, often from nothing. But landmarks, once created and nurtured, often take on a life of their own and reach an importance out of all proportion to their real value or to the hopes of the people who created them. Such might be said about the Mirror Lake Shuffleboard Club in St. Petersburg, Florida, or of Waikiki Beach in Honolulu, Hawaii, which, after all, is just a long beautiful sandy beach.

Some landmarks grow by association. For example, Carhenge in Alliance, Nebraska, would never have been created and would not be noticed except for its association with Stonehenge, on the Salisbury Plains in England, site of old Druid culture and religious practices for at least five thousand years. In fact, Stonehenge is only one of several hundred Druid remains throughout England and owes its importance to clever development by interested parties.

The sports halls of fame in America have achieved their hoped-for importance, and new ones will probably also flourish. The Rock 'n' Roll Hall of Fame in Cleveland, Ohio, is also expected to succeed.

There is no doubt that popular culture landmarks will continue to be created. Already the three hundred or so sites described in this book could be expanded to several thousand.

THE FUTURE OF LANDMARKS

New creations, regardless of size, demand the public's time and money. As more landmarks are created, more of the nation's resources will go into sustaining them. Some might argue that indulgence in landmarks is a waste of resources. This is true only if landmarks are misinterpreted as places of passing or of only incidental importance. But by definition, landmarks are significant places or activities. They are benchmarks, high-water marks, they are something out of the ordinary. If we look upon today's and tomorrow's landmarks as opportunities for learning, we can realize a great deal about our communities, about our society, and about life in general.

June 1994

The Walt Disney quotes are from the essay "Instruction and Delight: Theme Parks and Education," by Margaret J. King, in *The Cultures of Celebrations,* edited by Ray B. Browne and Michael T. Marsden, Bowling Green: Popular Press, 1994.

PREFACE

On the very first overnight trip I ever took with my family, my father drove us to Niagara Falls. We posed for still pictures and home movies with the falls in the background, marveled at the rush of water, peered through curbside telescopes at 10 cents a pop, and listened to my little brother complain that he wanted lunch. It wasn't until many years later that I understood I'd had my first popular culture travel experience.

The falls were, of course, familiar before I ever saw them. From the front of the Nabisco Shredded Wheat box. From the classic Marilyn Monroe movie *Niagara.* From the hundreds of television jokes I'd heard—and just dimly understood—about honeymoons. That, I think, is the purpose of traveling to a landmark of popular culture. You know what you're going to see before you even get there. But, in the best cases, it turns out to be more than you'd expected.

Many of the places in this book I first saw as a child, thirty-five years ago and more. They have changed, some of them for the worse. Many are now surrounded by the franchises and tourist traps that have themselves passed into the popular culture in the years since. Others have sadly deteriorated because time has diminished the stature they once held.

But so many of them still have the power to awe—to make the traveler say to himself, "I am actually standing here in front of this place I have heard about all my life." To me, that is the essence of travel. Once you lose it, you may as well stay home.

During the writing of this book, the movie *Sleepless in Seattle* came out. One of its stars is the Empire State Building. It plays a central role as the symbol of American romance. Other buildings are now taller. But the Empire State wore the title for so long, during a time when early movies and pioneer television were fixing their images indelibly on our memories, that it still packs a tremendous emotional kick. It is more than a skyscraper. It is a symbol of dreams.

Some of the places in this book were similarly chosen for their symbolic power in our lives. Others were picked for historic interest, illustrating the fading popular culture of an earlier part of the century. And still others, such as Carhenge in Nebraska and Roadside America in Pennsylvania, for what they tell us about the odd compulsions that give this country so much of its individuality and unexpectedly bind us.

This book was great fun to research and write, more fun than a writer probably should have while he works. I hope that comes across in these pages, and that this guide will be read and used in the same spirit.

George Cantor
June 1994

CONNECTICUT

MAINE

MARYLAND

MASSACHUSETTS

NEW HAMPSHIRE

NEW JERSEY

NEW YORK

PENNSYLVANIA

RHODE ISLAND

VERMONT

WASHINGTON, D.C.

Macy's, the store that practically invented the Christmas shopping season. *(AP/Wide World Photos)* *See* page 43.

NORTHEAST

CONNECTICUT
1 Gillette Castle, East Haddam
2 Goodspeed Opera House, East Haddam
3 Louis' Lunch, New Haven
4 Monte Cristo Cottage, New London

MAINE
5 L. L. Bean Sporting Goods, Freeport

MARYLAND
6 Babe Ruth House, Baltimore
7 Eubie Blake Cultural Center and Museum, Baltimore
8 H. L. Mencken House, Baltimore

MASSACHUSETTS
9 Bull and Finch Pub, Boston
10 Faneuil Hall Marketplace, Boston
11 Fenway Park, Boston
12 Cruises and Kennedy Memorial, Hyannis
13 Jack Kerouac Memorial, Lowell
14 Cranberry World, Plymouth
15 Plymouth Rock, Plymouth
16 Thornton Burgess House, Sandwich
17 Marconi Wireless Station, South Wellfleet
18 Basketball Hall of Fame, Springfield
19 Norman Rockwell Museum, Stockbridge

NEW HAMPSHIRE
20 "Peyton Place," Gilmanton

NEW JERSEY
21 The Boardwalk, Atlantic City
22 Sunnyside, Albert Payson Terhune Memorial, Pompton Lakes
23 Edison National Historic Site, West Orange

NEW YORK
24 Rod Serling Exhibit, Forum Theatre, Binghamton
25 Anchor Bar, Buffalo
26 QRS Piano Rolls, Buffalo
27 National Baseball Museum, Cooperstown
28 American Kazoo Co., Eden
29 Apollo Theatre, New York
30 Carnegie Hall, New York
31 Coney Island, New York (Brooklyn)
32 Ellis Island and the Statue of Liberty, New York
33 Empire State Building, New York
34 General Grant National Memorial, New York
35 Macy's, New York
36 Museum of the Moving Image, New York (Queens)
37 Museum of Television and Radio, New York
38 New York Stock Exchange, New York
39 Plaza Hotel, New York
40 Rockefeller Center, New York
41 St. Patrick's Cathedral, New York
42 Times Square, New York
43 Yankee Stadium, New York (Bronx)
44 Maid of the Mist Boat Trips, Niagara Falls
45 International Museum of Photography, Rochester

PENNSYLVANIA
46 First Turnpike Tourist Town, Breezewood
47 Tom Mix Birthplace Park, Driftwood
48 Pearl Buck Home, Dublin
49 Chocolate World, Hershey
50 James Stewart Birthplace, Indiana
51 Jim Thorpe Mausoleum, Jim Thorpe
52 Sesame Place, Langhorne
53 Honeymoon Resorts, Mount Pocono
54 Mario Lanza Museum, Philadelphia
55 Statue of "Rocky," Philadelphia
56 Roadside America, Shartlesville
57 Amish Village, Strasburg
58 Little League Stadium, Williamsport
59 Harley-Davidson Plant and Museum, York

RHODE ISLAND
60 International Tennis Hall of Fame and Museum, Newport
61 "Rosecliff," Newport

VERMONT
62 Grandma Moses Exhibit at the Bennington Museum, Bennington
63 Frisbee Memorial, Middlebury
64 *Newhart's* Waybury Inn, Middlebury
65 Trapp Family Lodge, Stowe
66 Ben & Jerry's Ice Cream Factory, Waterbury

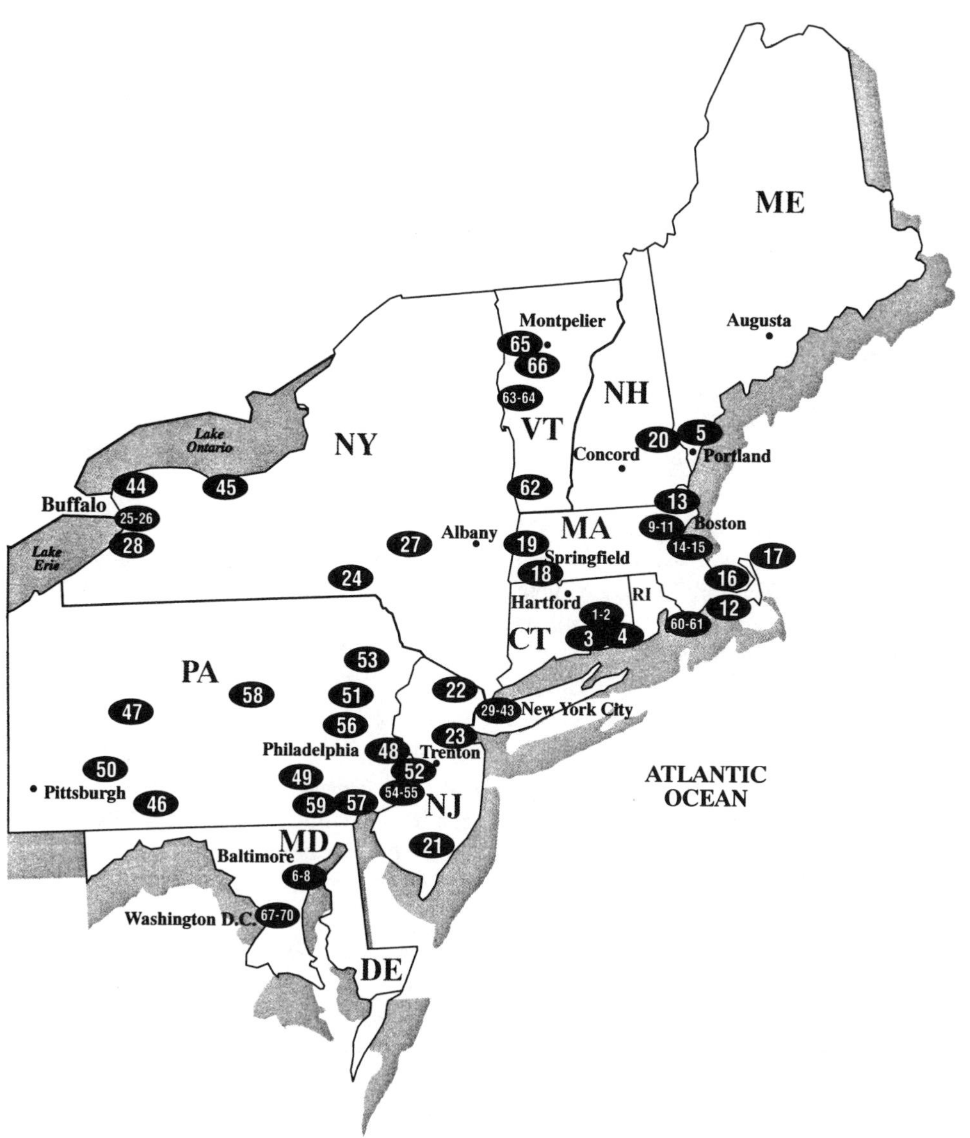

WASHINGTON DC

67 FBI Headquarters

68 Lincoln Memorial

69 National Museum of American History

70 Vietnam Veterans Memorial

Connecticut

EAST HADDAM

GILLETTE CASTLE

To contemporary Sherlock Holmes fans, the definitive picture of the famed detective is Basil Rathbone, who portrayed him in the movies in the 1940s. But to an earlier generation of Americans, the image of Holmes was supplied by William Gillette, the first actor to transfer the fictional detective from print to stage.

He collaborated with Holmes's creator, A. Conan Doyle, as playwright, and then assumed the title role when the first production of *Sherlock Holmes* opened in New York in 1899. Gillette was already an established dramatist and actor, but for the next thirty years his appearances in revivals of this play filled theaters around the country. His tall, gaunt form and hawk-like face seemed to be taken directly from the illustrations of Doyle's short stories. Critics wrote that all subsequent portrayals of Holmes were merely imitations of Gillette's, so firmly had he fixed the detective's image in the public mind.

He was the son of a U.S. senator, and his aristocratic bearing was more than a stage image. A reclusive man, Gillette built this limestone castle in 1919 on a crag overlooking the Connecticut River. He spent most of his time there, surrounded by art work, cats, and the miniature railroad that he delighted in running across the estate.

At his death in 1937, his will stipulated that the castle not fall into "the possession of some blithering saphead who has no conception of where he is or with what surrounded." The castle, accordingly, is operated as a state park, although it is not clear if that would have satisfied Gillette's request. Much of the actor's art collection and memorabilia have been preserved and are on display.

■ **LOCATION:** The Castle is reached by an access road running west from Connecticut 82, south of the town of East Haddam. ■ **HOURS:** Daily, 10–5, Memorial Day to Columbus Day; weekends only, 10–4, until December 19. ■ **ADMISSION:** $4 ■ **TELEPHONE:** (203) 526-2336

Great musicals from the past are staged at the Goodspeed Opera House.
(UPI/Bettmann)

GOODSPEED OPERA HOUSE

Every so often, the American musical theater is written off as an endangered species or an outworn relic of the past. But in this tiny river town, three hours from Broadway, it is stunningly restored to life.

For ten months every year, this old theater, built in 1876, stages new versions of great, sometimes forgotten, American musicals from the past. Some involve extensive dramatic detective work, tracking down lost scripts and choreography from shows that were written merely to entertain. No one had ever dreamed they would come to be regarded as precious pieces of American culture. The Goodspeed favors productions that enjoyed popularity when first staged but are seldom seen today. Since the 1960s, it has mounted revivals of several of the Jerome Kern and P. G. Wodehouse Princess Theatre shows from the century's second decade, regarded by many stage historians as the musicals that shaped the form. The Goodspeed also has restored the Roaring Twenties shows of the team of DeSilva, Brown, and Henderson–supposedly outdated but very well received by audiences here.

Many Goodspeed productions make the trip back to Broadway for successful runs. Shows that actually originated here, *Man of La Mancha* and *Annie,* became two of the greatest successes in the history of the musical theater.

■ **LOCATION:** The Goodspeed is on Connecticut 82, at the eastern end of the Connecticut River bridge. ■ **HOURS:** The theater is open for tours, Monday, 1–3, in July and August. Otherwise, it can only be seen during production in its March–December season. Tickets should be reserved several weeks in advance because there are fewer than 400 seats. ■ **ADMISSION:** Ticket prices vary. ■ **TELEPHONE:** (203) 873-8668

NEW HAVEN

LOUIS' LUNCH

There are several places across America that claim to have been the birthplace of the definitive national dish, the hamburger. Louis' Lunch, which has been serving them up since 1903, has about as good a case as any. Even if it wasn't actually the first, it certainly looks the part. This small brick building in downtown New Haven is in the fourth generation of ownership by the Lassen family. When the place was threatened with demolition, the local historical association sponsored its move to a new location.

The aroma of grilled meat seems permanently embedded in its dark interior. Patrons, including hungry Yalies from the nearby campus, sit at school desks to wolf down the specialty of the house, cooked vertically and served on toasted bread.

■ **LOCATION:** 261 Crown Street, southwest of The Green in downtown New Haven. ■ **HOURS:** Monday through Friday, 9–5:30. ■ **TELEPHONE:** (203) 562-5507

NEW LONDON

MONTE CRISTO COTTaGE

This little house was the boyhood home of playwright Eugene O'Neill and, as one of his biographers put it, he returned to it, again and again, throughout his career. Most notably, it was the dark setting of *Long Day's Journey into Night,* the lacerating drama drawn from his own family's history, which he wrote near the end of his career.

His father, James O'Neill, was an actor who built a career out of playing the title role in the romance *The Count of Monte Cristo.* So it was natural for him to call the house after his greatest success. James O'Neill was a vain, tyrannical man while his wife was hopelessly addicted to morphine, prescribed for her after a difficult labor with Eugene.

But Eugene O'Neill also returned to this setting for his only comedy, *Ah, Wilderness,* a nostalgic portrait of small town life written in 1933. The cottage contains O'Neill family memorabilia and a good multimedia introduction to his life and work.

■ **LOCATION:** Monte Cristo is south from U.S. 1, at the southern edge of the city, at 325 Pequot Avenue. ■ **HOURS:** Monday through Friday, 1–4, April to mid-December. ■ **ADMISSION:** $3 ■ **TELEPHONE:** (203) 443-0051

MAINE

FREEPORT

L. L. BEAN SPORTING GOODS

When Leon L. Bean opened his doors on Main Street (U.S. 1) in this town on the southern Maine coast, he only wanted to sell boots. He had developed something called the Maine Hunting Shoe, a rubber boot on which he sewed a leather top. It seemed like a good idea in 1912. He hadn't the slightest notion that it was going to turn him into a symbol of Maine.

But Bean had built a better boot. It became the base of a sporting goods empire and the world soon was marching to his door. Shortly before his death, in 1967, he received an official commendation from the state for enhancing its national image.

The beginning was not terribly promising. Bean's first batch of Maine Hunting Shoes literally came apart at the seams, leaving his customers wet and irate. But as irritated outdoorsmen descended upon the store, Bean hit upon the policy that became his trademark: Unconditional returns, no questions asked.

Bean built a reputation for reliability by catering to the demands of society sportsmen. There was something right about his honest Yankee craftsmanship, something that seemed to create a mystique in the minds of his wealthy customers. In his 1985 book, *In Search of L. L. Bean,* writer M. R. Montgomery argued that Bean shrewdly cultivated the image. He understood that selling the image of L. L. Bean was more important than selling anything he was stitching in his boots.

He was able to transfer his reputation for reliability and his Down East persona into a booming mail-order catalog business. The store in Freeport became known nationally as a purveyor of quality goods from the true north. Mail customers made the town a mandatory stop on visits to Maine. This, in turn, brought so much traffic into Freeport, that the entire center of town has been transformed into a factory outlet mall. Nearly one hundred discount stores are clustered here. Tour buses disgorge their loads of shoppers every weekend and the central business district is ringed with parking lots.

It is the Bean store that remains at the center, however. It is open twenty-four hours a day, 365 days a year, selling everything from hunting boots to mosquito netting, as well as an image that has come to mean Maine in the national mind.

■ **LOCATION:** U.S. 1, 15 miles north of Portland. ■ **HOURS:** Always open. ■ **TELEPHONE:** (207) 865-4761

MaryLanD

BALTIMORE

BABE RUTH HOUSE

He is the single-most dominant figure in the history of American sports. Most of his records have been broken. Only a dwindling number of people survive who ever saw him play. In the old newsreels, with his speeded-up trot around the bases, he seems to belong to another, far distant time.

And yet the influence of Babe Ruth remains an indelible part of athletics. He practically created the image of the sports hero; bigger than life with a face as familiar as a movie star's. He recast baseball from a mere sport to a metaphor for American life. His celebrity became bigger than the game and his salary bigger than the president's. He healed the sick with promises of home runs. One season he hit more home runs by himself than any *team* in the American League. In the 1932 World Series, it was said that he stepped up to the plate and called his shot, but later research has indicated that this is just a myth. Still, the actual achievements of the man make it seem plausible.

In reality, he was something of a lout. Overweight, crude, a philanderer of Olympic proportions. But that isn't the Babe Ruth the public wanted to know about, then or now. When a movie debunking his myth was made in 1991, it was a flop at the box office.

When Roger Maris pursued Ruth's single season home run record, the tension was so great that most of his hair fell out. When Henry Aaron went after Ruth's career record, he received hate mail. But The Babe always had a good time and was universally beloved. It is what makes his image so appealing even now, sixty years after his retirement.

Ruth grew up in Baltimore. While not an orphan, as early sentimentalized versions of his life reported, it was still a childhood spent in poverty and in unsavory surroundings. Maybe part of the reason he remained an overgrown kid ever afterward was an attempt to reclaim this lost childhood. The house where he was born in 1895 is now preserved as a museum. Along with three adjoining row houses it contains exhibits about both The Babe and the Baltimore Orioles. Displays and memorabilia relating to his life and the history of the ball club fill the rooms of the museum. Other exhibits salute baseball stars from Maryland.

■ **LOCATION:** Immediately west of central Baltimore, off Pratt Street, at 216 Emory Place. ■ **HOURS:** Daily, 10–4. ■ **ADMISSION:** $3 ■ **TELEPHONE:** (410) 727-1539

EUBIE BLAKE CULTURAL CENTER AND MUSEUM

Eubie Blake's career spanned the entire course of show business in the twentieth century. He was one of the creators of the ragtime tradition and lived long enough to see the music, which once had been considered depraved, elevated to the concert hall.

Blake and his partner, Noble Sissle, co-wrote the 1921 revue, *Shuffle Along,* the first Broadway production staged by African-Americans and incorporating jazz in its score. From that show came "I'm Just Wild about Harry," his best-known song, and later, the theme for Harry S Truman's presidential campaign of 1948.

Blake, who published his first song in 1898 when he was fifteen years old, faded into obscurity when the Jazz Age ended. But he was rediscovered by serious musicians in the 1970s when a new appreciation of ragtime developed. He became regarded as a national treasure, a piece of living history. The last decade of his life was spent giving lectures and concerts and explaining how American popular music was born. He died in 1983, shortly after his hundredth birthday.

He always regarded Baltimore as his home and stipulated in his will that any exhibits about his life be located here. The Eubie Blake Cultural Center is the result. Musical memorabilia and many personal belongings are displayed.

■ **LOCATION:** Just north of downtown, at 409 North Charles Street. ■ **HOURS:** Monday through Friday, 12–6. ■ **ADMISSION:** Free ■ **TELEPHONE:** (410) 396-1300

H. L. MENCKEN HOUSE

He was called the "Sage of Baltimore." He was called a lot of other things, too, not all of them printable and not many of them polite. But Henry Louis Mencken gave as good as he got, and as an essayist and journalist he is remembered for his cheerfully vicious attacks on some of the most sacred of the twentieth-century cows.

He gave us the term "Bible Belt" and described his fellow citizens as belonging to the species "Boobus Americanus." He went into hotel rooms and signed Gideon Bibles "with the compliments of the author." He disliked almost everything he saw, and railed against virtually every ethnic and religious group in the country. When his diaries were published posthumously they contained remarks that were interpreted as bigoted toward Blacks and Jews. But in his

H. L. Mencken's house: The journalist is probably best remembered for his vitriolic essays. *(UPI/Bettmann)*

personal dealings with all people he was regarded as the most tender-hearted of men and the best of companions. His published rantings only arose out of a conviction that people urgently needed to be informed about the errors of their beliefs and the foolishness of outworn traditions.

He reached the peak of his popularity in the 1920s, when his irreverence matched the spirit of the time. His essays in *The American Mercury* were required reading on college campuses. His attacks on Prohibition and religious fundamentalism delighted the "Smart Set," which was also the name he gave to another of his magazines. He discovered and encouraged many young writers of the period, among them Willa Cather and F. Scott Fitzgerald.

But when the party ended and the Depression began, Mencken found himself suddenly dated. He seemed merely mean-spirited in troubled times, his bitter attacks on the New Deal only the fulminations of a sourpuss. When asked to list his occupation then, he put down "retired six-day bicycle rider." This reference to the 1920s fad was Mencken's own caustic way of saying he was out of date. But he embarked on a second career, as a scholar of the language.

His monumental *The American Language* and three-volume autobiography are probably of more lasting influence than all the vitriolic essays he had written before.

Mencken died in 1956 in the house he had occupied for sixty-eight years. This row house on Baltimore's west side is virtually unchanged from the time when a sage dwelled there. An audio-visual display sums up Mencken's long career and other exhibits in the house and garden illustrate his life.

"If you ever remember me and have some thought to please my ghost," he once wrote in a self-epitaph, "forgive some sinner and wink your eye at a homely girl." Those who bridle at that statement as politically incorrect probably wouldn't like much else about Mencken either.

■ **LOCATION:** The Mencken House is at 1524 Hollins Street, west of the central business district by way of Lombard Street. ■ **HOURS:** Wednesday through Sunday, 10–5 ■ **ADMISSION:** $1.75 ■ **TELEPHONE:** (410) 396-7997

Massachusetts

BOSTON

BULL aND FINCH PUb

In September 1982, a television landmark passed with hardly anyone noticing. A comedy show called *Cheers,* set in a basement bar in Boston, debuted on NBC. Within three months, the show itself had fallen to the basement, the very bottom of the audience ratings.

But favorable reviews and great word-of-mouth among its tiny core of intensely loyal fans encouraged network executives to stay with this apparent failure. Eleven years later, when the final *Cheers* episode aired, in May 1993, it was the media event of the year. Magazines and newspapers gave it space usually reserved for the signing of peace treaties. Even the other TV networks acknowledged that a significant slice of American culture was passing from the scene.

The place "where everybody knows your name" had become the longest-running, most successful prime time series in TV history. Its scripts were brilliantly written. But more than that, the show touched an American moment in time. As urban residents felt increasingly estranged from their environment, this odd bunch of bar flies, losers all, reminded viewers of the simple human attachments and pleasures that only city life can bring. The neighborhood bar as a comedic meeting ground has long been a staple of popular entertainment, going back to William Saroyan's *The Time of Your Life* on the stage and radio's *Duffy's Tavern.* But *Cheers* outdid them all.

The model for its interior set, and the site of its exterior shots, was this tavern near downtown Boston. (Its name is a pun on that of colonial Boston's leading architect, Charles Bullfinch, who designed the State House, a few blocks up Beacon Street from the bar.) As the show's popularity grew, The Bull and Finch became a major attraction in its own right. People came here from around the world to identify the barstools corresponding to the ones where the show's characters sat and to reconstruct favorite episodes. After the final show aired, the identity was made complete when NBC's *Tonight Show* broadcast live from the bar, with cast members showing up for interviews.

Everyone may not know your name here, but they share the same bar room memories.

Almost ten thousand people converge on the Bull and Finch Pub after *Cheers'* final episode. *(AP/Wide World Photos)*

■ **LOCATION:** The Bull and Finch is located at 84 Beacon Street, opposite the Boston Public Gardens. ■ **HOURS:** Daily, 11:30 A.M.–2 A.M. ■ **TELEPHONE:** (617) 227-9605

FANEUIL HALL MARKETPLACE

Once it was called the "Cradle of Liberty." But two centuries later, this Boston landmark was reborn as the gateway to a festival marketplace and a new vision for remaking urban centers.

Named for merchant Peter Faneuil, the first hall on this site was built in 1742. When fire destroyed that structure twenty years later, it was rebuilt to the original plan, with market stalls on the ground floor and an assembly hall one flight up. It was here that some of the most dramatic meetings of the Revolutionary Era were held, with impassioned orators stating the case for independence. The quartering of British troops here was one of the acts that heightened resentment toward Parliament. After the war, a third story was added to the hall by architect Charles Bullfinch, and the old building, with its grasshopper weather vane, became one of Boston's most beloved symbols.

Quincy Market was built adjacent to the hall in 1826. At that time, the waterfront docks extended all the way to this area and it was the center of Boston's food distribution system. By the 1970s, however, the old buildings

In August 1978, Faneuil Hall officially opened after a $30-million redevelopment of the historic marketplace. *(AP/Wide World Photos)*

were in disrepair and serious thought was given to tearing them down. A committee of businessmen and preservationists fought stubbornly for years to save the market and integrate it with the historic hall next door.

It was then that architect James Rouse was contacted. Rouse had developed several theories about downtown restoration but had yet to find the right project for their use. He did not believe in artificially recreating the past, but in incorporating elements of past design in a contemporary mode. Rouse's plan for remaking Quincy Market into a festive gathering place, while retaining its historic economic function, became the prototype for dozens of other preservationist projects around the country. Ever since its 1979 reopening, Faneuil Hall Marketplace, with its produce stands, restaurants, and street performers, has been one of the most popular and active places in Boston.

The latest renovation of Faneuil Hall was completed in 1992 and new displays relating to the building's long history were added.

■ **LOCATION:** Faneuil Hall is on Congress Street, near State Street, one block from the Old State House, along the Freedom Trail Walking Tour, in downtown Boston. Quincy Market is to its immediate rear. ■ **HOURS:** Faneuil Hall is open daily, 9–5. Its museum is open Monday through Friday, 10–4. Quincy Market is open daily, 10–9. ■ **ADMISSION:** Free ■ **TELEPHONE:** (617) 635-3105

The Red Sox prepare to host the New York Mets in game three of the World Series at Fenway Park, October 1986. *(AP/Wide World Photos)*

FENWAY PARK

It is the smallest stadium in major league baseball. Unquestionably, the oddest. Probably the most beloved. There is simply nowhere else the game is played quite like it is at Fenway Park, home of the Boston Red Sox.

The ballpark's best-known feature is The Wall. Shaped by the contingencies of urban geography, this thirty-seven-foot high barrier in left field turns simple fly balls into home runs and converts thundering line drives—homers in any other park in existence—into singles.

The constricted space into which the park was squeezed in 1912 dictated that this left-field barrier was situated only 315 feet from home plate. Until 1920, baseball was played with a ball that couldn't be hit as far as the one used since, so in those early days, a ten-foot high wall was deemed sufficient, although a terrace that sloped an additional ten-feet up from the field was also part of the landscape. In 1933 the park was redesigned and the first version of The Wall was erected.

The Wall makes Fenway a uniquely exciting venue for baseball. No lead is secure, not with the always-present possibility of home runs in abundance sailing over The Wall or into the netting above it. Games are usually entertaining, high-scoring, see-saw affairs and the Red Sox have developed some of the most loyal supporters in the game. The park seats only 33,583 people and most games, aside from those at the very beginning and end of the season, are sold out, making the Red Sox among the league's leaders in attendance.

"I know it's irrational," said biographer Doris Kearns Goodwin, in trying to explain the park's mystique. "But you get such a feeling of belonging to the place. I can forget everything else. If I go to the theater or the concert, I can still think of other things. But not at Fenway Park."

The Wall is now made of fiberglass, which has reduced the chances of unpredictable caroms. But it remains the signature of Fenway Park and the most identifiable feature of any stadium in American sports.

■ **LOCATION:** Fenway Park is located just off Kenmore Square, 1 mile west of Boston Common. ■ **HOURS:** The park is open only during Red Sox home games. Tickets should be secured several weeks in advance. Summer weekend games are usually sold out months ahead of time. ■ **TELEPHONE:** (617) 267-1700

HYANNIS

CRUISeS AND KENNEdY MEMORIAL

The images of Camelot at play are among the most enduring from the John F. Kennedy administration. The public was captivated by the photos of Kennedys sailing, swimming, and playing touch football along the beach. They reinforced the aura of youthful vigor that surrounded the president. A few months after Kennedy's death, a collection of photographs in *Life* magazine, showing him walking alone among the Cape Cod dunes, seemed to provide the perfect signature to his life.

The Kennedy associations with this resort town remain very strong in the American mind. Cruises from Hyannis harbor, which offer a glimpse of the Kennedy family compound of summer homes, are consistently popular. No other access is permitted. In the town itself, a small Kennedy memorial, with a fountain and wall bearing the presidential seal, is situated on the main business street.

■ **LOCATION:** Hyannis harbor tours leave from Pier 1, Ocean Street Dock. The Memorial is located a few blocks away, on Ocean Street. ■ **HOURS:** The cruises run from 9–8, June to mid-September; 10–2:30, in April, May, late

September, and October. ■ **ADMISSION:** Fare is $7. ■ **TELEPHONE:** (508) 778-2600

LOWELL

JACK KEROUAC MEMORIAL

Sometimes it all seemed to baffle the man. This movement, this upheaval in American life that he was supposed to have initiated with the publication of one book. For the last twelve years of his life, Jack Kerouac seemed to veer between impatience and confusion over the credit and blame heaped upon him for being the founder of "the beats."

"We're beat, man," he said in an interview with *Playboy* magazine in 1958, the year after his landmark novel *On the Road* was published. "Beat means beatific, it means you got the beat, it means something. I invented it."

But a few weeks before his death in 1969, at the peak of the love-and-peace movement of the sixties, he wrote about his resentment at being considered the spiritual antecedent of Abby Hoffman, Jerry Rubin, and the rest of the hippie crowd. He wasn't establishment, he said, but he didn't feel any kinship to the New Left. Kerouac didn't know quite where he fit in anymore. "I'm not a tax-free and I'm not a hippie-yippie," he wrote with some acidity. "I must be a bippie in the middle."

Kerouac grew up in this mill town before going on the wanderings that helped define a generation. Repelled by materialism and the values system of the fifties, he described a mobile existence, amoral and spontaneous, laced with drugs and liquor and bop. The beats scandalized the America of their day and, although Kerouac may not have liked it, were indeed the cultural forerunners of the more politically-minded hippies who would follow.

Even thirty years after *On the Road* appeared, there was some reluctance in Lowell about placing a memorial to this local boy who got out. "As long as it is understood that we are saluting the man," said the dissenting voice on the town council, "and not the life he stood for."

■ **LOCATION:** The Kerouac plaque, commemorating his birthplace, is located near Lowell National Historic Park, in East Canal Plaza.

PLYMOUTH

CRANBERRY WORLD

There is no actual documentation that cranberries were served at the first Thanksgiving. It is just an educated guess. A pretty good one though

Third-graders pay a visit to the Plymouth Rock in November 1966. Whether or not it's the rock where the pilgrims landed in 1620, it looks the part. *(AP/Wide World Photos)*

considering the native fruit, called *sassamanesh* by the Wampanoag people, was a staple of the Indian diet. Once the Pilgrim settlers found that the berries helped ward off shipboard scurvy, they enthusiastically adopted them, too.

Even if the berries were on the menu at the feast, they weren't called cranberries. The Pilgrims referred to them as fenberries, because of their swampy habitat. Settlers from Holland gave them the lasting name because the fruit's stamen reminded them of the beak of a crane (*kran* in Dutch).

It is also certain that whatever form the fruit may have taken on Thanksgiving Day 1621, it wasn't cranberry sauce. That wasn't devised until almost three hundred years later, when Marcus Urann, founder of the Ocean Spray Cooperative of cranberry growers, hit on the preparation as a way to expand sales.

Until that time, cranberries were regarded as a seasonal item, served only around the traditional holiday. Cultivation of the berries began in 1816 when Cape Cod farmers found that covering the vines with loose sand expanded productivity. But the market grew slowly and was almost wiped out in 1959 when the first pesticide scare contaminated a large part of the crop. Trying to recover from that setback, Ocean Spray initiated large-scale marketing promotions, coming up with new products (juices, muffins, jellies) and plugging their use as a year-round food.

Cranberry World is part of that promotional effort. While the fruit is widely grown in New Jersey, as well as the Pacific northwest, it is still Massachusetts with which it is most closely identified in the public mind, probably because of Thanksgiving. Americans are in a cranberry mood when they arrive in the Pilgrims' home town and Ocean Spray is only too happy to serve them.

There are displays on modern cultivation, cooking, and how cranberries were used by both Indians and Pilgrims.

■ **LOCATION:** Cranberry World is at the northern entrance to the waterfront historic area, at 225 Water Street. ■ **HOURS:** Daily, 9:30–5, May to November. Demonstrations are given every two hours on the half hour after opening. ■ **ADMISSION:** Free ■ **TELEPHONE:** (508) 747-2350

PLYMOUTH ROCK

The first permanent settlement in what would become the United States was made at Jamestown, Virginia, eleven years before the Pilgrims set foot in Massachusetts. But it is Plymouth Rock that is regarded as America's doorstep and this settlement as the "real" beginning of the nation's history. The reason probably goes back to sectional politics during the Civil War. Until that time, there was no national consensus on a Thanksgiving holiday. In an 1863 proclamation, President Lincoln established the November date, giving the Massachusetts site primacy in American lore over its chief rival, which was then the Confederacy.

Pilgrim Hall, the oldest public museum in America, was founded in 1820 to house the personal items of the founding families. But people wanted more. The story of Plymouth Rock had its origin in the century that followed the original landing. No boulder was given the designation until 1741, when a ninety-five-year old man identified the rock as one that was pointed out to him by his father. It turned out, however, that the father hadn't arrived until 1623 and received his information second-hand. But it was a good, big rock and looked the part, so it officially became Plymouth Rock.

In 1834, the rock was moved to Pilgrim Hall, where some doubts arose over its authenticity. So for several years it was stored in a warehouse. It wasn't returned to the waterfront and a protective portico erected above it until 1921, as part of the 300th Thanksgiving celebration. By that time, no one was sure whether this was even its natural location. But here it sits and until a better rock turns up, it will have to do. And to generations of Americans, it looks the way Plymouth Rock ought to look.

■ **LOCATION:** Water Street, central Plymouth ■ **HOURS:** Always accessible. ■ **ADMISSION:** Free

SANDWICH

THORNTON BURGESS HOUSE

For almost half a century, he charmed newspaper readers around the country with tales of Peter Rabbit and his friends in the Great Meadow. But Thornton Burgess was also working on a secret agenda. He was attempting to give children an appreciation of the natural wonders that lay just beyond their backyard, right at their feet.

Burgess was probably the most prolific writer of children's literature that America ever produced: His newspaper bedtime stories ran daily and he also found time to write seventy books. He seemed amazed at his own production. "But if someone asks you to do something and you say no, the door is closed," he said, following his retirement in 1960. "If you say yes and do your best, you will usually surprise yourself."

The stories began in 1910, when Burgess was a thirty-six-year-old widower trying to entertain his young son. The boy was off on a visit and Burgess sent him a daily letter containing a story. The animal tales, mostly concerning Reddy Fox's relentless and inept pursuit of Peter Rabbit, were collected and published as *Old Mother West Wind.* Two years later, he began his syndicated feature and he kept it up for forty-eight years.

He wrote with a naturalist's eye. Burgess's animals remained in character, behaving the way creatures actually would in the natural world, aside from possessing the gift of speech. But in his books, which sold eight million copies, nature was always benign. "Tragedy comes into real life too soon," he said, "and I can't let anything happen to Peter because I'll need him in the next story."

An unassuming man, although he had become a millionaire with his writings, Burgess always expressed a reluctance to return to his birthplace in Sandwich, for fear that old neighbors would believe "I thought myself better than they were." But after his death in 1965, the town, the oldest on Cape Cod, converted one of its historic homes into a museum of Burgess's work. Mementoes, including personal items and copies of his books, are on exhibit.

■ **LOCATION:** Near the center of town, across from the Congregational Church, at 4 Water Street. ■ **HOURS:** Monday through Saturday, 10–4; Sunday, 1–4. ■ **ADMISSION:** Donation asked. ■ **TELEPHONE:** (508) 888-6870

SOUTH WELLFLEET

MARCONI WIRELESS STATION

When the twentieth century began, the concept of messages sent over electrical wires was a well established feature of daily life. But most people still had trouble grasping how messages could arrive by wireless.

Guglielmo Marconi had demonstrated that radio waves could be transmitted across the Atlantic, from Britain to Newfoundland. Still, the feat was regarded as a novelty, with no practical application to daily life.

On January 19, 1901, Marconi set up his first wireless station on American soil on this empty stretch of Cape Cod beach, facing out to the Atlantic with nothing in the way between here and Europe. Before long, Morse code messages were beamed here, as well as faint scraps of music and voices. Marconigrams, messages picked up at this station and then transmitted by telegraph to points around the country, became a part of national life. By 1910 they were called radiograms.

The company Marconi formed to set up operations here eventually grew into the Radio Corporation of America (RCA). Within a generation, radio would bring great events and the voices of the famous into almost every home. This stretch of empty beach was actually the birthplace of the electronic Global Village that transformed communications and defined the century's final years.

Memorabilia from this station is also displayed at the Historical Museum, on Main Street, in the town of Wellfleet.

■ **LOCATION:** The remains of the Marconi Wireless Station are now part of the Cape Cod National Seashore. The access road from South Wellfleet and U.S. 6 is well marked. The site also commands one of the finest ocean views on the Cape. ■ **HOURS:** The station site is open daily, dawn to dusk. The Historical Museum is open Tuesday through Thursday and Saturday, 2–5; Friday, 10–1. ■ **ADMISSION:** To the station site, free; to the museum, $1. ■ **TELEPHONE:** The station is (508) 349-3785; the museum is (508) 349-3346.

SPRINGFIELD

BASKETBALL HALL OF FAME

All James Naismith wanted to do was devise a new activity for his Springfield College physical education students—one that would be a bit more entertaining than calisthenics and tossing around a medicine ball. A graduate of a Presbyterian theological school in his native Canada, Naismith was a firm believer in building character through sports. This was also the mission of the college, which produced staff for most of the nation's YMCAs. He obtained a job there in 1891 and immediately set about to work out a new game. He called it, with some lack of originality, The Game.

It had to fit inside the confines of a gym, have no physical contact, use a soft ball, and give everyone who participated a chance to handle the ball. One century later, aside from the physical contact part, it would still be recognized as basketball. It was given that name when peach baskets found in a storeroom were hung on the gym wall as the first targets.

Naismith's students began playing the game after returning from Christmas break that year. Within two years, it was played across the United States and was responsible for an explosive growth in YMCA memberships, the local Y usually being the only place in town with a gym. By the end of the decade, basketball had caught on in Europe. Soon afterward Naismith would depart for the University of Kansas to establish the first college basketball power.

The sport's official hall of fame and museum returned the game to the place of its inception. Springfield College is in the central part of the city, while the museum occupies a more prominent location downtown, where it houses displays on the game's history and development, tributes to its greatest players, and interactive exhibits that enable visitors to test their shooting and jumping skills. This is a high-tech facility.

■ **LOCATION:** The museum is at 1150 West Columbus Avenue; follow the exit signs from Interstate 91 in downtown Springfield. ■ **HOURS:** Daily, 9–5. ■ **ADMISSION:** $6 ■ **TELEPHONE:** (413) 781-6500

STOCKBRIDGE

NORMAN ROCKWELL MUSEUM

He is the most familiar, the most comforting of all American artists. His covers for *The Saturday Evening Post* and other popular magazines were a running commentary on the country's popular culture for half a century. His very name became synonymous with a certain view of America—gentle and optimistic. Just as Currier and Ives defined the visual image of America for the nineteenth century, Norman Rockwell did it for the twentieth.

Most of the familiar illustrations are here: The flat-chested teenage girl unhappily comparing her profile with the star in the movie magazine. The grandmother saying grace in the apparently profane truck stop. The young couple nervously filling out the marriage license application as the clerk fidgets about closing his office. There is also *The Four Freedoms,* the famous wartime work that, more than any political declaration, defined the values that most Americans want to believe this country is all about. They are displayed here like old friends. So familiar and yet so much larger than anticipated when seen hanging on the museum walls.

Much of Rockwell's best-known work was done while he was living in Vermont. But he moved to Stockbridge, a resort village in the Massachusetts Berkshires, in 1953 and spent the last quarter-century of his life here. His painting of Main Street at Christmas time, done for *McCalls* magazine in 1962, has become a symbol of the town, especially since the view has changed so little.

"He still has a kind of wistfulness," said his wife, Molly, in an interview published just before his death in 1978. "He always wanted to paint a 'great work,' something that would get him recognition as a fine arts artist. It was always just ahead of him, but he never felt he made it. But he had a lot of fun trying."

There are other Rockwell museums, but this has the largest collection of original works and is by far the most extensive. Formerly situated near the middle of town, it had to move to expanded quarters in 1991 because the number of visitors was so large.

■ **LOCATION:** West of town by way of Massachusetts 102, then south on Massachusetts 183. ■ **HOURS:** Daily, 10–5, May to October. Weekday hours are 11–4, rest of the year. ■ **ADMISSION:** $8 ■ **TELEPHONE:** (413) 298-4100

New Hampshire

GILMANTON

"PEYTOn PLACE"

There had been other books that told nasty secrets about small town life. But none of them caused the commotion that the publication of Grace Metalious's novel *Peyton Place* did in 1956.

In the placid 1950s, this sex-besotted tale of passion in Podunk raced straight to the top of the best-seller lists. It led to a major motion picture and then to a long-running television series. The name became a synonym for rural romping. Even twelve years after the book appeared, a hit song called "Harper Valley P.T.A." contained a line that said: "This is just another Peyton Place," and every listener knew immediately what that meant.

Americans had been fleeing small towns in growing numbers since the 1890s and literature reflected the move. The Naturalist writers of that time were the first to strip away the romantic myth of small town life and reveal the poverty and desperation that underpinned it. In the 1920s, Sinclair Lewis caused a sensation with *Main Street* and its depiction of small town tedium and small-mindedness. Sherwood Anderson wrote *Winesburg, Ohio,* which tossed the vague, formless longings of repressed sexuality into the mix. But that was just prologue to the overt sexual passages that made *Peyton Place* such a hot commodity.

Metalious, the wife of a high school teacher, had written about three hundred short stories, by her estimate, without any publishing success. Her novel seemed fated for the same failure until it crossed the desk of a small New York publisher, Julian Messner Inc. Recognizing a spark of appeal, Messner bought the rights and had a phenomenon on its hand. The book sold 250,000 copies in hardcover, one million more in paperback.

A big part of its success was the gender of its author. While sexually explicit literature was slowly becoming mainstream in the 1950s, it was still almost unheard of for a woman to write it. Metalious was a plain-spoken person who favored a wardrobe of flannel shirts and jeans and proved tremendously appealing in newspaper and television interviews. In later years, she regarded herself as a pioneering feminist, whose viewpoint gave a rare look into the sexuality of women.

Gilmanton, where she made her home, was less than thrilled. Her husband lost his job and Metalious was sued by the local high school principal for slander and defamation. His name was Thomas Makris; the principal in the book was called Tomas Makris. He settled out of court. The author denied, however, that the book was based on this town, maintaining her work was a composite picture.

"You live in a small town and there are patterns," she said, shortly before her death in 1964. "The minute you deviate from the pattern you are a freak. I wrote a book and that made me a freak."

Metalious never regained that level of writing success and died of a liver ailment at the age of thirty-nine. While Gilmanton may have forgiven over time, don't expect to see any signs of recognition here. But this, indeed, was the model for the steamiest little town in American popular culture.

■ **LOCATION:** Gilmanton is located about 20 miles northeast of Concord, by way of eastbound Interstate 393 and northbound New Hampshire 106.

New Jersey

ATLANTIC CITY

THE BOARDWALK

The railroad from Philadelphia to a salt water marsh on the New Jersey shore opened in 1854. By summer of that year, what would soon become the East Coast's most popular beach resort began rising from the sand at the end of the tracks.

Newport had the swells and, later on, Coney Island had the subway riders. But Atlantic City took all the customers in between; affluent enough to pack up the family and spend a few days in the healthful ocean breeze, but not affluent enough to do it too often. They came here for a brief respite from the sweltering cities and, after 1870, to stroll the boardwalk.

This four-mile long promenade immediately put Atlantic City in a different category than its competitors. The word boardwalk became virtually synonymous with the resort. The wooden walkway was devised by local businessmen to give visitors something to do on cloudy and chilly days and was an immediate success. Hotels turned their entrances around to face it. Refreshment stands and amusement arcades soon filled the spaces between the hostelries.

In 1884, the next great advance was made. M. D. Shill, a manufacturer of baby carriages, came up with the idea of the rolling chair, which became the preferred means of boardwalk transport. The first of the amusement piers was built about the same time and that was soon followed by salt water taffy and the picture postcard—all American institutions that originated here.

In the 1920s, promoters decided to extend the resort's summer season beyond the traditional Labor Day closing and so they invented Miss America. The beauty pageant began in 1921 and, except for a brief interruption during the Depression years, has celebrated the traditional image of the ideal American girl ever since. Criticized by feminists, the pageant, nonetheless, remains another national symbol.

The resort was so well known by the late 1920s, that when a new parlor game was introduced it borrowed the street names of Atlantic City for its playing board, giving "Monopoly" an immediately recognizable setting.

After World War II, when air travel brought warm weather resorts within reach of the mass market, Atlantic City began a long period of decline. But in

The Atlantic City shoreline in 1978: Now gambling casinos dot the boardwalk that gave birth to amusement piers, salt water taffy, and the picture postcard. *(AP/Wide World Photos)*

1979, with the introduction of casino gambling, the boardwalk area revived. Unfortunately, the glitzy facades of the new luxury hotels conceal terrible poverty in the blocks immediately behind them. But the rolling chairs are still rolling and the taffy is as sticky as ever.

■ **LOCATION:** Eight miles along the beach, through the heart of the resort.

POMPTON LAKES

SUNNYSIDE: ALBERT PAYSON TERHUNE MEMORIAL

In his youth, Albert Terhune traveled among the Bedouin tribes of the Middle East, risking his life in strange surroundings and then writing books about his experiences. The books sold moderately well and gave him the income to retire to this New Jersey estate, built by his father, a clergyman. Here Terhune was able to devote himself to his true avocation, raising collies.

The books he wrote about his dogs were huge national best-sellers in the 1920s. A generation before *Lassie Come Home* turned the collie into the canine equivalent of superstar, Terhune's books had already convinced thousands of readers that the collie was the noblest breed placed upon the Earth. He did not hesitate to ascribe human motivations and characteristics to his collies, and while his books stretch the credulity of today's reader quite a bit, they were seriously regarded in their time.

His first book *Lad: A Dog* appeared in 1921 and through the next ten years it was followed by a series of tales. Terhune was a master of the heart-tugging ending and celebrated the loyalty of his dogs through a variety of lightly fictionalized situations.

Before his death in 1942, Terhune expressed the wish that his country estate not be sold off for a suburban development. Although Sunnyside lies in the middle of northern New Jersey's suburban growth belt, his wishes have been respected. His estate and onetime breeding grounds have been preserved in a park-like setting.

■ **LOCATION:** North of Wayne, on U.S. 202. ■ **HOURS:** Daily, dawn to dusk. ■ **ADMISSION:** Free ■ **TELEPHONE:** (201) 694-1800

WEST ORANGE

EDISON NATIONAL HISTORIC SITE

By the time Thomas Edison moved here in 1887 he was known as the "Wizard of Menlo Park." It was at that site, twenty miles south of here, that he had invented the electric light, which already was illuminating big cities. He had also perfected the "factory" system of invention, setting up teams of subordinates to systematically deal with the problem of turning concepts into products.

At Menlo Park, Edison had begun work on the devices that would eventually become the phonograph and the motion picture. But he needed more space, especially for the work on movies. The West Orange site gave him some elbow room.

Edison was closely following the progress of fellow inventor George Eastman in finding a paper medium that could be rolled through a camera (*see* Rochester, New York). In anticipation of that discovery, in 1888 he filed for a patent on what he called a Kinetoscope.

In the application, Edison compared his motion picture camera to a phonograph. To him, the principle was exactly the same. Just as sound was recorded by engraving electrical impulses on a rotating cylinder, motion could be captured by continuous photography on a moving spiral of film. Eastman began producing film on celluloid in 1889 and immediately sent Edison a fifty-foot strip of the new material, with the length and flexibility required for Edison's new camera. As soon as Edison saw the film, the inventor told his assistants: "That's it. We've got it. Now work like hell."

He set up his famous studio, the tar-paper-covered Black Maria, the true birthplace of the American movie industry. By 1891, he had come up with the first peep-show apparatus, a viewing device for one person at a time. He then made the crucial link between cameras and projectors. With both camera and projector running film of the same width, the movie screen was made possible. The final touch was the introduction of perforated-edge film, which allowed it to be rolled through the camera and projector continuously, reproducing a sense of motion.

The Laboratory Complex here is concerned primarily with the invention of movies, although other devices worked on by the great inventor at this place are also displayed. Next to the lab is Glenmont, Edison's home until his death in 1931. It is furnished just as it was when he lived there, including his "thought bench," where he sat to think through many of his most successful ideas. It would be difficult to name two inventions that were more essential to the growth of American popular culture than the phonograph and the movies.

■ **LOCATION:** Main Street and Lakeside Avenue. Exit 9 from Interstate 280 and follow signs. ■ **HOURS:** Tours are given every half hour, 9:30–3:30, Wednesday through Sunday. Access is only through tours. ■ **ADMISSION:** $2 ■ **TELEPHONE:** (201) 736-5050

New York

BINGHAMTON

ROD SERLING EXHIBIT, FORUM THEATRE

He wrote award-winning dramas during the pioneering years of television, the brief period in the 1950s now referred to as "the Golden Age." But that's not how Rod Serling is remembered.

Instead, just whistle the four urgent musical notes that have come to symbolize the advent of something weird and unsettling and you have his legacy. You have entered *The Twilight Zone.*

The TV anthology of half-hour dramas dealing with the paranormal, the supernatural, and the very odd, originally aired in the 1960s. They have been rerun countless times and Hollywood reworked some of the best episodes as a movie.

Serling, who wrote and hosted most of the shows, found terror in the ordinary. Long before novelist Stephen King, Serling took the Gothic tale from the realm of dark castles and windy graveyards and plunked it right down on Main Street. Time stops, history is rewritten, legends come to life, and all of it is placed in a setting that looks like a scene right out the front window. That's what made *The Twilight Zone* so scary and why the shows retain their power to terrify.

Many of those pleasantly ordinary settings looked a lot like Binghamton, the industrial and college town where Serling grew up and went to high school. When its old downtown movie palace, The Forum, was restored, the town placed in its lobby an exhibit honoring Serling, with memorabilia of his life and work.

■ **LOCATION:** The Forum is in downtown Binghamton, at 228 Washington Street, just off U.S. 11. ■ **HOURS:** Monday through Friday, 8–4. ■ **ADMISSION:** A donation is asked for upkeep of the theater. ■ **TELEPHONE:** (607) 778-2480

BUFFALO

ANCHOR BAR

For many years, Buffalo wings were strictly a local delight, a treat that was a distinct part of this city's culinary character. According to legend, they were devised in 1964 at this neighborhood bar by the Bellisimo family. Some locals indignantly dispute the claim, declaring that Buffalo was munching on wings long before. All Teresa Bellisimo did, they say, was dress them up a little, with celery stalks and blue cheese dressing. Whatever the case, the Anchor is celebrated as the apotheosis of this dish, the Wing Victory.

In the 1980s this chicken delicacy suddenly started appearing on appetizer menus all over the country, as franchise restaurants picked up on them and began serving them to a grateful nation. However, their natural habitat, the Anchor, is regarded as the historically proper place to go for the spicy drumettes with attached bone.

The Anchor's fame hasn't changed it much. It's still just a neighborhood joint in a pretty dreary neighborhood. While there are other items on its menu, wings are what it's all about.

■ **LOCATION:** The Anchor Bar is at 1047 Main Street, New York 5, about two miles northeast of downtown. ■ **TELEPHONE:** (716) 886-8920

QRS PIANO ROLLS

During the 1920s, when families were still expected to provide their own entertainment, player pianos outsold regular pianos. By some accounts, they took over eighty percent of the market. But with the spread of the radio and phonograph, player pianos slowly lost their appeal. They were also expensive and difficult to repair. By the early 1950s, the pianos were mere novelties, nostalgic curiosities, although they did enjoy a brief revival thanks to the 1950 hit song "The Old Piano Roll Blues."

The presence of a piano in the living room was a sure sign of a turn-of-the-century family's cultural status. Getting the kids to take lessons to play the thing was another matter. So the mechanical piano—a device that filled the same room space as a regular piano but demanded no more musical talent than the ability to pump one's legs—entered the scene. The Imperial Industrial Company of Buffalo was among the first to take advantage of the fad by creating its QRS piano rolls, perforated to activate the right keys through the transmission of air pressure.

When the player piano craze crashed, QRS was the only company to stay in business. It still sells more than 750,000 rolls each year. Some of them are the old standard "let's-stand-round-the-piano-and-sing" kind of tunes. But a surprising number of items in its catalog are classical compositions and newly-pressed versions of contemporary hits. Still others are rare finds—like George Gershwin playing his own music on a master roll cut in the 1920s.

The tour explains how piano rolls are manufactured and there are displays on the history of player pianos. The visitor can also play a bit himself.

■ **LOCATION:** QRS Music Rolls is at 1026 Niagara Street, just north of the Buffalo plaza of the International Peace Bridge. ■ **HOURS:** Tours are given at 10 A.M. and 2 P.M., Monday through Friday. ■ **ADMISSION:** $2 ■ **TELEPHONE:** (716) 885-4600

COOPERSTOWN

NATIOnAL BASEBALL MUSEUM

Why baseball's shrine happens to be situated in this lovely lakeside town is the result of a legend chasing a shadow. But no one really minds the historical inaccuracy anymore. Even if baseball really wasn't invented in Cooperstown by Abner Doubleday in 1839 the place is so charming, so consistent with the nostalgic America the game evokes, that everyone is inclined to go along with the story and enjoy it.

The Cooperstown myth was invented by a commission headed by Albert G. Spalding, one of the great pitchers in the sport's early days. He was later the founder of the sporting goods company that was a leading supplier for the major leagues. Around the turn of the century, baseball had a certain credibility problem. It attracted the rougher element in the big cities and many of its players were not likely material for the clergy.

It was in this environment, in 1908, that Spalding's commission was organized and instructed to track down the sport's "true" origin. The commission came upon some material mentioning that Doubleday, who went on to become a Civil War hero, taught a game that featured balls and bases to his class of military school students in Cooperstown. That slim mention was good enough for Spalding. He officially declared Cooperstown baseball's birthplace.

Actually, the game was a variant of ball and stick games that were played in Britain as early as the eighteenth century. In New England, by the 1920s, it was identified as town ball. It was probably this game, using a soft ball (because base runners were retired by being hit with a thrown ball), that Doubleday played. The real father of the game is now acknowledged to be Alexander Cartwright, a sports journalist who, in 1846, drew up the first generally accepted rules for hardball for the New York Knickerbocker Ball Club. Nonetheless, in 1939, the supposed centennial of Doubleday's invention, the Baseball Hall of Fame was opened in Cooperstown, adjacent to the field on which the spurious origin occurred.

The true origin doesn't really matter. The museum has built a legitimacy of its own. It is a vast, magical compendium of baseball fact and lore, filled with great names and stirring deeds. The very mention of the name Cooperstown has become the universally recognized way of referring to greatness in a ballplayer. Since both Spalding and Cartwright are now enshrined there, the historical quibbles are settled forever. And during the first weekend of every

August, when the town comes alive to honor a new class of inductees, the perfection of the setting makes the facts of history irrelevant.

The museum has quadrupled in size since its inception and now covers nearly ever facet of the game's history in its displays—from ballparks to announcers to minorities to women's leagues.

■ **LOCATION:** The museum in on Main Street, near the center of town. Cooperstown is 27 miles south of New York Thruway Exit 30 (eastbound) by way of New York 28, and 32 miles south of Thruway Exit 29 (westbound) by way of New York 80. ■ **HOURS:** Daily, 9–9, May to October; 9–5, rest of the year. ■ **ADMISSION:** $6 ■ **TELEPHONE:** (607) 547-9988

EDEN

AMERICAN KAZOO COMPANY

There are some people who are quite serious about their kazoos. When American Kazoos, which has been making the musical device in this Buffalo suburb since 1915, changed its vibrators, kazoo enthusiasts were outraged. The vibrator, the part that gives the kazoo its unmistakable timbre, had been made from animal gut since the instrument's inception. But by the 1980s demand was running faster than the guts were coming in, so the switch was made to synthetics.

"You had some angry purists who wrote us saying they could get a better sound with the other one [the original]," said Maurice Spectoroff, then president of the company, in a 1984 interview. "Because it isn't the very young that is our market any more. To me, that's a mistake. The fastest way to find if a child has musical talent is to give him a kazoo and see what comes out."

Ultimately, though, the kazoo is a perfect instrument for those with no musical talent whatsoever—except the ability to hum. In some cities, kazoo parades have been held with all participants humming "Louie, Louie." In Detroit, free kazoos used to be distributed at one Tigers ball game annually so bleacher fans could salute the memory of radical labor leader Eugene V. Debs with a chorus of "Solidarity Forever." In Rochester, New York, students from the Eastman School of Music formed the Kazoophony, which recorded classical compositions with the instrument. Billed as "the world's largest kazoo quartet," it had six members. Who can concentrate on counting when you're playing a kazoo?

■ **LOCATION:** The American Kazoo Factory and Museum is located at 8703 South Main Street (U.S. 62), about 20 miles south of Buffalo. ■ **HOURS:** Monday through Saturday, 10–5; Sunday, 12–5. Tours of the factory are given. ■ **ADMISSION:** Free ■ **TELEPHONE:** (716) 992-3960

NEW YORK

APOLLO THEATRE

"Playing the Palace" was the show business cliché for reaching the top. In black America, for much of this century, the equivalent was "playing the Apollo." This theater in the heart of Harlem represented the pinnacle for performers who could not appear in the top showplaces of white America.

The Apollo opened as a burlesque house in 1913. Its clientele was predominantly Yiddish-speaking, the black portion of Harlem still located several blocks north of 125th Street until late in the 1920s. The theater's most celebrated era began in 1930, when its owners switched to black musical revues. Bessie Smith was the first headliner. After her came the vaudeville tap dancers and comics, the swing bands of the 1930s and 1940s, the great blues singers, the first rock 'n' rollers.

Many of America's leading entertainers learned their craft on this stage. Bojangles Robinson, Cab Calloway, Ella Fitzgerald, Screamin' Jay Hawkins—virtually the entire roster of African-American stars, either got their start at the Apollo or returned there in triumph.

The changing economics of the business closed the theater for a time. But after a multi-million dollar renovation, partially underwritten by black entertainers as a gesture of gratitude, it reopened in 1989 to assume a place, not only as a venue for showmanship, but as an historical landmark.

■ **LOCATION:** The Apollo is at West 125th Street and Adam Clayton Powell, Jr., Boulevard (7th Avenue). ■ **TELEPHONE:** For hours and attractions, call (212) 749-5838.

CARNEGIE HALL

Opening night was May 5, 1891, and featured a program of works by Peter Ilitch Tchaikovsky—conducted by Peter Ilitch Tchaikovsky. The great Russian composer had been brought to New York especially for the occasion. That's the caliber of performance that has marked Carnegie Hall throughout its history.

Andrew Carnegie, the steel magnate and philanthropist, who contributed $2 million to the hall's construction, spoke prophetically at its opening. "It is built to stand for the ages," he said, "and during these ages it is probable that this hall will intertwine itself with the history of our country." The thought was repeated by violinist Itzhak Perlman at the hall's rededication, ninety-five years later. "Whoever plays Carnegie—the great or the not-so-great—becomes classier."

It was first called Music Hall because Carnegie felt that the public should financially support the place and might be less inclined to do so if his name were attached to it. But the hall was a consistent money-loser and, eventually, its chief benefactor was honored with the naming. The opening season also saw the first American concert of Polish pianist and composer Ignace Paderewski and two years later, it heard the premiere of Anton Dvorak's *New World* symphony. Through the years, it has been acknowledged as the ultimate showcase for serious music in America.

The hall resulted from an accidental shipboard meeting between Carnegie and Walter Damrosch, conductor of the New York Symphony. The millionaire took the young musician into his circle of closest friends and became inspired by Damrosch's idea of building a great concert hall for New York. The hall's decor was quite plain for that period. But decor was never the attraction. Although acoustical science was then in its infancy, the sound of Carnegie Hall has seldom been surpassed.

It was intended as a bastion of high culture. But it has since become emblematic of any musical performer's rise to eminence to play Carnegie Hall. The swing concert given there by Benny Goodman's band in 1938 was a watershed event. It offended the purists, who felt it was sacrilege for such music to be performed in these hallowed precincts, with jitterbugs dancing in the aisles. Since then, however, a Carnegie Hall concert has been the showcase of excellence in both the popular and high cultures.

Nonetheless, the hall was almost lost in 1960, when a developer proposed tearing it down for an office building. Only a massive publicity and fund-raising campaign led by dozens of top musicians and Governor Nelson A. Rockefeller managed to preserve it. "When you stand on that stage to play," said Isaac Stern, one of the prime movers of the preservation effort, "and feel all that has happened before, you share the special privilege of becoming, for a moment, a small part of a continuing stream of great beauty."

■ **LOCATION:** Seventh Avenue at 57th Street. ■ **HOURS:** Policies vary about admission into the hall. The best bet is to call in advance, or better yet to buy a ticket for a performance. ■ **TELEPHONE:** (212) 247-7800

CONEY ISLAND

It is a synonym for fun on the cheap. A day at a crowded beach paved with baking bodies. A honky tonk boardwalk. A hot dog. A roller coaster ride. All of that is what Coney Island represents.

This Brooklyn sand spit on the ocean, named by early Dutch settlers for the rabbits (*konijn*) found there in profusion, is the working man's wonderland, Bermuda on the BMT. It started off, however, as a resort for swells. The first bathhouse was erected in 1844, and elegant hotels soon followed. Boats made regular trips from Manhattan with wealthy vacationers aboard.

By the end of the century, the sporting crowd had moved in. Coney Island was known as a place for prizefights and horse races. In 1897, the first amusement area,

A slow day at Coney Island in August 1953 (the Cyclone roller coaster is on the right). *(AP/Wide World Photos)*

Steeplechase Park, opened, and New York's first Ferris wheel and roller coaster were in operation. Barbershop quartets sang the new hit song "Goodbye My Coney Island Baby." A mandatory stop was Feltman's, the first establishment to serve sausages, named after the German city of Frankfurt, on a roll. This sandwich was generally referred to as a "coney" by 1913.

But Coney Island didn't really acquire its most enduring reputation until the subway was extended in 1920. That made the island accessible to the steaming masses of New York City, who swarmed here to swim and swelter. The images of that six-mile-long beach, jammed from boardwalk to surf with blankets and bodies, is the most familiar picture of Coney Island.

Celebrated in song, movies, and gastronomy, Coney Island lives on. The neighborhood around it has deteriorated. Its waters are murkier, its boardwalk seedier. But the classic roller coaster, the Cyclone, still has the customers screaming and the hot dogs at Nathan's taste like no place else.

■ **LOCATION:** Coney Island is in Brooklyn, at the end of the BMT Sunway Line from Manhattan. By car, it is reached from the Brooklyn Battery Tunnel by way of westbound Interstate 278, Prospect Expressway and Ocean Parkway. ■ **HOURS:** The beach facilities are generally open from mid-April to mid-October. The Cyclone is part of Astroland Amusement Park, which is open daily, noon to midnight, June to Labor Day. ■ **ADMISSION:** Free to the beach and boardwalk. Astroland rides are priced individually or $12 for unlimited rides in a five-hour time span. ■ **TELEPHONE:** The park is (718) 266-1234; Astroland is (718) 265-2100.

ELLIS ISLAND AND THE STATUE OF LIBERTY

It has been described as the "second Plymouth Rock," where more than one hundred million Americans trace their family's landing in America. It was also known as Gibbet Island when a pirate was hanged, and Oyster Island when Dutch colonists used it for picnics. But in the eighteenth century, when Manhattan merchandiser Samuel Ellis bought it, he gave the island in New York Harbor its most enduring name.

Ellis Island passed through the merchandiser's heirs to the State of New York and then to the federal government for use as an arsenal. But as the flow of immigration to America steadily swelled through the 1880s, it became apparent that the Castle Garden facility at the southern tip of Manhattan could no longer handle the numbers involved. So Ellis Island was transformed into a great processing center. The size of the island was increased nine-fold with landfill, and a series of buildings, some of them almost Byzantine in appearance, were erected.

The new immigration center opened in 1892. By that time, the Statue of Liberty had been lifting her torch in the harbor for six years. The sculpture, the work of Frédéric-Auguste Bartholdi, had languished in packing crates in Paris since 1884. Fund-raising efforts in the United States had fallen short of securing a suitable pedestal for the 151-foot-high statue, a gift commemorating a century of friendship between France and America. After the *New York World* editorialized for a solid year about the embarrassing situation, the money was raised by public contribution and a 156-foot-high base was erected for *Liberty Enlightening the World* on Bedloe Island.

For millions of immigrants, the statue was their first view of America. For decades afterward, memories of the emotions this symbol of freedom stirred could still bring tears to their eyes. When Hollywood mogul Harry Cohn was seeking a corporate symbol for his newly-formed Columbia Pictures in the 1920s, he chose the Statue of Liberty because "nobody would dare make fun of that."

The actual experience at Ellis Island was not quite as uplifting. The immigration process could be dehumanizing and brusque. Processing delays of several days were common and there was always the possibility that one would be turned away. In 1907, when the human flood reached its peak of 1.3 million immigrants, it was a crowded, unhealthy, squalid place. European immigration slowly receded, though, and after restrictive laws were put in place in the 1920s, immigration slowed to a trickle. In 1954, the Ellis Island facility shut down; not many mourned its passing.

In the next generation, a new current of ethnic awareness began to run through American life. Instead of surrendering to the melting pot, more and

To the millions who passed through its portals, Ellis Island represented a new beginning *(left, AP/Wide World Photos)*. Lady Liberty offers many their first view of America *(right, courtesy of National Park Service)*.

more people became interested in exploring their family origins and celebrating the immigrant experience. Its grimy realities misted over by memory, Ellis Island was hailed as a place of great beginnings.

A fund-raising effort, headed by Chrysler Corporation chairman Lee Iacocca, the son of immigrants, was coordinated for the 1986 centennial of the Statue of Liberty. Part of the program involved a renovation of Ellis Island into an immigration museum, with a special focus on the Great Hall, where the immigrants awaited processing. A tremendous outpouring of grass roots involvement enabled the National Park Service to restore the island as a monument to those who arrived as "huddled masses" and went on to secure the blessings of liberty for their descendants.

■ **LOCATION:** Boats that stop at both the Statue of Liberty and Ellis Island leave from Castle Garden, at the southern tip of Manhattan. ■ **HOURS:** Boats leave daily, every half hour, June–Labor Day; every 45 minutes, rest of the year. ■ **ADMISSION:** Free. Boat fare is $6. ■ **TELEPHONE:** (212) 363-3200

EMPIRe STATE BUILdING

The first true skyscrapers—towers constructed around a steel frame—were built in Chicago in the 1880s. Within half a century, every major American city had one, as a matter of civic pride. But it was in New York that they were brought to their finest realization. The skyscraper is New York's signature, one of the most powerful symbols of twentieth-century America. Manhattan's towers have come to signify wealth, power, hope, excitement. Viewed from a ship

The Empire State: Still the center of attention and object of affection even though it's no longer the country's tallest building. *(Courtesy of Howard J. Rubenstein Associates)*

arriving in New York Harbor, the skyline is a stunning statement of the New World's purpose and promise.

For most of the century, the Empire State Building was the tower that rose above them all. Its very construction was something of an expression of hope. The old Waldorf-Astoria Hotel, which previously occupied the site, was torn down just three weeks before the Stock Market crash of 1929. It was squarely in the face of the Great Depression that the Empire State went up, opening its doors on May 1, 1931.

The sheer power of this unbroken, 1,250-foot-high limestone wall captured the public imagination like no other building. It was hailed from the beginning, its designers awarded the Architectural League's gold medal for 1931. Within two years of its construction, the Empire State became the setting for the closing scene of the film *King Kong*. The unforgettable image of the giant ape clinging to the side of the proudest of all man-made structures, marked the building in the minds of a generation. When the film was remade half a century later, the World Trade Center had replaced the Empire State as New York's tallest building. So the producers gave it the role of Kong's monkey bars. The film was a dud. The new tower had none of the power to awe that the Empire State possessed.

New Yorkers and tourists alike still flock to its observation deck for a view of Manhattan. The midtown setting like nothing else brings home the sweep, scope, and physical diversity of New York. Some early observers compared it to a giant lighthouse. The Empire State has always touched a core of romance. In popular entertainment, from the 1944 musical *On the Town* to the 1993 movie *Sleepless in Seattle,* it is the refuge in the sky where lovers rendezvous.

By the 1990s, the Empire State was, officially, the third tallest building in the country, behind the Sear's Tower in Chicago and the World Trade Center. Third tallest as the hand measures, perhaps, but not the heart.

Elevators run to observatories on the 86th and 102nd floors. On the ground floor is the Guinness Book of Records Museum.

■ **LOCATION:** The main entrance to the Empire State Building is on 5th Avenue at 34th Street. ■ **HOURS:** Daily, 9:30 to midnight. Most impressive time is dusk when the lights of the city come on. ■ **ADMISSION:** $3.75 to the observation tower. ■ **TELEPHONE:** (212) 736-3100

GENERAL GRANT NATIONAL MEMORIAL

It isn't very respectful, but this edifice became a local joke almost from the day it opened in 1897. Raised by public subscription, the tomb honors the eighteenth president and Civil War general Ulysses S. Grant, and his wife. Architectural critics immediately sneered at it because of its careless mix of styles. Nonetheless, in the early years of the twentieth century it became a must-see attraction for out-of-towners coming to the big city. In fact, the old joke went that no New Yorker had ever been to the place and no visitor had ever missed it.

The ultimate indignity came during the 1950s, however, when it became the punch line on one of radio and television's most popular quiz shows. Groucho Marx, a native New Yorker, always had a final question to ask a contestant who had failed to win any money on his show, *You Bet Your Life.*

"Who is buried in Grant's Tomb?" Groucho inquired and everyone had to know the answer to that. Mostly because of the show, the memorial remained a popular tourist attraction. But when the tomb was taken over by the federal government, it fell victim to cutbacks in parks funding. Newspaper articles in the early 1990s described it as fallen into disrepair, with graffiti smeared on the exterior and many of its windows broken. Apparently shamed into action, the National Park Service began a program of restoration. While the tomb is no longer the attraction it was to earlier generations, it is, at least, again a fitting memorial to a president and his lady.

■ **LOCATION:** The Tomb is located at Riverside Drive and 122nd Street. ■ **HOURS:** Wednesday through Sunday, 9–5. ■ **ADMISSION:** Free ■ **TELEPHONE:** (212) 666-1640

MACY's

There are other Manhattan merchandisers who are more innovative, more prosperous, more trendy, more favored by the city's taste-makers than the big store near Herald Square. But it is Macy's that shaped the definition of the words department store in America.

The store was founded in 1858 by a former whaling captain from Nantucket. R. H. Macy understood the significance of several important developments that were then coming together. The elevator made it possible to expand over several floors, enabling merchandisers to carry a greater variety of goods and yet display them in a relatively compact area. Plate glass allowed imaginative store owners to draw customers in from the street with window displays. Mass circulation newspapers enabled them to reach a far wider audience faster through advertising. Macy's was, in fact, one of the first to leave white space in its ads and to spread them over more than one column, making them stand out from the dull, cramped type of its competitors.

Macy's practically invented the Christmas shopping season. It daringly kept its doors open until midnight on Christmas Eve, 1867 and set a store record for receipts. Seven years later, it presented the first window displays with a Christmas theme, and by the end of the decade December had become its most profitable month of the year. Its annual Thanksgiving parade, in which the arrival of Santa Claus officially signalled the start of the holiday season, has become an institution, imitated by dozens of stores nationally. The classic film *Miracle on 34th Street* was based on the excitement of the holiday season at Macy's.

The store was also a pioneer in setting fixed prices for its goods, giving everyone who entered the same values. The policy revolutionized the business and set off the most competitive era in merchandising history. "Would Macy's tell Gimbels?" became a nationally-known catch phrase, symbolizing the intense rivalry between New York's two leading department stores.

Gimbels is gone, but Macy's is still doing business at the same stand, the square block it has occupied since 1902. A victim of the leveraged buy-out frenzy of the 1980s, the store had to shield itself from creditors by going into bankruptcy in 1992.

■ **LOCATION:** Broadway at 34th Street. ■ **HOURS:** Daily, 10–5. Weekend and evening hours vary. ■ **TELEPHONE:** (212) 695-4400

MUSEUm OF THE MOVING IMAGE

Before anyone had ever heard of Hollywood, New York City was the center of the movie industry. Many early features and serials were shot right across the Hudson River, at Ft. Lee, New Jersey. It is from the New Jersey palisades that Pearl White dangled in *The Perils of Pauline* serials and created a new word for filmed excitement, the cliffhanger.

Another unlikely base of the infant industry was in the Astoria section of Queens. Paramount Studios shot its earliest features there after 1912. Within a few years, the bulk of the industry had moved on to southern California, transported by its own success. The public's appetite for greater spectacle and natural settings could only be satisfied by the California climate, which permitted a greater number of days for exterior shooting.

But the Astoria studios remained open until World War II, with both Paramount and independent producers shooting there. Some of the Marx Brothers features were also filmed, as were many other films with New York locales. The studios were then used by the U.S, Army Signal Corps for thirty years as a production facility for training films. In more recent years, *The Cosby Show,* one of the big TV hits of the 1980s, was taped here. So were sequences of *Sesame Street* and the film *Glengary Glenross.*

Since 1988, a portion of the studios has been set aside as a museum of film and television technology. Early cameras, mikes, tape recorders, and other apparatus are exhibited. The visitor can chart the progression from their bulky beginnings to the high tech models of today.

■ **LOCATION:** The museum is in Queens, at 35th Avenue and 36th Street, three blocks from the Steinway stop on the BMT subway. ■ **HOURS:** Tuesday through Friday, 12–4; weekends, 12–6. ■ **ADMISSION:** $5 ■ **TELEPHONE:** (718) 784-0077

MUSEUm OF TELEVISION AND RADIo

The Museum of Television and Radio is the historical showcase of the broadcasting industry, a place for casual channel-surfers and serious scholars alike. Its library of forty thousand tapes of early and classic programs in both mediums is regarded as the finest in existence and at peak hours there will be a wait for a viewing or listening booth.

There are some other mild disappointments, too. The most avid fans may be disappointed to learn, for example, that there are only two episodes of *Our Miss Brooks* on file. But in terms of a broad cross-section of the history of broadcasting, and a first-hand glimpse of how it changed American life in the twentieth century, this is the best place going. The museum also holds special programs in its auditorium, featuring rare and historic shows.

■ **LOCATION:** The museum is at 25 West 52nd Street. ■ **HOURS:** Tuesday through Sunday, 12–6; until 8 on Thursday. ■ **ADMISSION:** $5 ■ **TELEPHONE:** (212) 621-6800

NEW YORK STOCK EXCHANGE

The promise of America was always wealth. The chance to get rich, no matter who you were or where you came from. The epicenter of American wealth, the focus of millions of dreams of avarice, was Wall Street. The Stock Exchange's formal address actually is Broad Street. But its activities, its market, its endless buying and selling is what everyone means when they use the term "Wall Street" to stand for the riches made by American business.

The street itself was named for the wall erected by Dutch Governor Peter Stuyvesant to protect his tiny seventeenth-century colony from hostile Indians. In 1790, with the city grown far beyond its boundary, the U.S. Congress, then based in New York, issued $80 million in bonds to finance the operation of the federal government. To handle the transaction, three large banks set up a market under a buttonwood tree on Wall Street. Two years later, the first formal trading agreement was drawn up and the stock exchange opened for business, at what is now 40 Wall Street.

It was in the decades after the Civil War, with American expansion at its zenith and tycoons eager to raise capital to finance these imperial dreams, that Wall Street came to dominate the country's economy. Outgrowing its old quarters, the Stock Exchange moved to its present location in 1903. Several additions have been added since then.

While Wall Street and the Stock Exchange are symbols of America's riches, at other times they also serve as images of greed. The financial "panics" that swept through the country once a generation throughout the nineteenth century were blamed on the Street. The collapse of the Stock Exchange in 1929 was popularly supposed to have brought on the Great Depression (although the actual causes were far more widespread and intricate than that). Again in the 1980s, during the takeover frenzy and junk bond scandals, Wall Street came to be associated with the worst excesses of business. A film called *Wall Street* was a major success during that time. The title was all that was needed to describe its content.

A symbolic buttonwood tree still stands at the entrance to the Exchange. The visitor's gallery enables onlookers to see the trading that occasionally reaches peaks of chaos. The brightly jacketed traders on the floor below appear to be engaged in some sort of mysterious and loud ritual, unintelligible to the casual onlooker. That, too, is part of Wall Street's allure.

■ **LOCATION:** The Exchange is at 20 Broad Street, just south of Wall Street. ■ **HOURS:** Monday through Friday, 9:15–4. ■ **ADMISSION:** Free ■ **TELEPHONE:** (212) 656-5167

Skyscrapers now shadow two Fifth Avenue landmarks: The Plaza Hotel *(left, AP/Wide World Photos)* and St. Patrick's Cathedral *(right, AP/Wide World Photos).*

THE PLAZA HOTEL

It opened its doors in 1907 and the first name to be entered in its guest register was Vanderbilt. Right from the start, the Plaza was New York's grandest. Its location at the southern edge of Central Park. Its patronage by the extraordinarily rich and the very famous. Its celebration in books and films. All of it has given the Plaza a special cachet among Manhattan's hotels.

The hotel was built as a home for the wealthy. Ninety percent of the rooms in the French Renaissance palace were originally private apartments, rented by the year to New York socialites. By the 1920s, it had become a symbol of the Jazz Age. F. Scott Fitzgerald was so fond of the place that Ernest Hemingway once suggested he will his heart to it. The fountain in front became a place for late night splash parties for the rich, famous, and inebriated. Royalty preferred it as its New York address.

Oddly enough, the Plaza's most famous resident was a fictitious little girl. *Eloise,* a children's book written in 1956 by entertainer Kay Thompson, chronicled the adventures of a precocious tot who lived in the hotel. It was a surprise best-seller and even spun off a modest hit record, convincing a new generation of customers that there was no hotel like the Plaza. Playwright Neil Simon reinforced the notion with his 1970s hit, *Plaza Suite.* Those suites, by the way, rented for $25 a night when the hotel opened, or about one-eighth the cost of the least expensive room in the Plaza by the 1990s.

The hotel fell on hard times in the early 1970s, as a wave of newer luxury inns opened in New York. "A big part of the problem is that every time we try to modernize or make changes, we have to do it surreptitiously," said a manager at the time. "It's a case of the regular customers saying 'Touch not a hair on yon gray head.'" However, when real estate magnate Donald Trump bought the

Fountains play on a statue of Prometheus in the sunken plaza at Rock Center. Derided by critics, it turned out to be the epitome of New York sophistication. *(UPI/Bettmann)*

hotel in 1989, it was given a complete facelift—although it still remains very much The Plaza.

■ **LOCATION:** The Plaza is at the corner of 5th Avenue and 59th Street. ■ **TELEPHONE:** (212) 759-3000

ROCKEFELLER CENTER

"They all laughed at Rockefeller Center, now they're fighting to get in." So ran the Ira Gershwin lyric from a song hit of the 1930s and so ran the facts as well. Derided by critics as a hideously expensive mistake at its opening, Rockefeller Center turned out to be the epitome of New York glamour and sophistication. When it was purchased by Japanese investors in the late 1980s, Americans reacted as if part of the national heritage had been sold off and that the entire country had somehow been diminished.

When John D Rockefeller, Jr. announced plans for this "city within a city" in 1929 it was regarded as too far uptown, impossibly removed from the existing business and shopping district, to ever attract tenants or customers. Instead, it remade the map of Manhattan by pulling business to it. It wasn't the first privately financed center situated away from the traditional downtown. That distinction belongs to Detroit's New Center (*see* Michigan). But no other development had the immediate impact of this one. Rockefeller Center's mix of entertainment and commerce, its incorporation of art work in public space, its use of open space, made it the marvel of its time.

Rockefeller Plaza especially captured the popular imagination. Approached from Fifth Avenue, through a narrow hedge-lined walkway, the view of the former RCA Building (now the General Electric Building) and the sunken Plaza, with the Art Deco sculpture of Prometheus at its far end, is quintessential New York. Visitors who have not been in Manhattan for a while come to this spot to fully experience the rush of being in the city again.

The former RCA Building has been the home of the National Broadcasting Company since the 1930s. The tour of its studios is among the most popular attractions in the city. The glamour never seems to wear thin. When a newsmagazine show debuted on the network in the summer of 1993, opening segments were televised live from Rockefeller Plaza, to bring home the New York state of mind like no other setting. The Rainbow Room, on the building's 65th floor, continues to look like the set from Fred Astaire's last musical. Dancing cheek-to-cheek with the lights of Manhattan shining below is the sort of sophistication that doesn't go out of style.

It may be, however, that the Radio City Music Hall is the best known of all the Center's attractions. The magnificent Art Deco showplace, home of the precision-dancing Rockettes, was the largest indoor theater in the world at its opening in 1932. It was, originally, a flop. Samuel "Roxy" Rothafel insisted on operating it as a vaudeville house. When his losses mounted, he had to sell out to Rockefeller and the policy was changed to a blend of movies and live entertainment. Long after other movie theaters had dropped live acts, the elaborate shows, always featuring the Rockettes, continued to pull in the patrons. Eventually, however, it became too expensive to operate as a full-time cinema and in the late 1980s it switched to a schedule of holiday extravaganzas and live headliners.

■ **LOCATION:** Rockefeller Center occupies the area between 5th Avenue and Avenue of the Americas and 48th to 51st streets. The Plaza is west of 5th, between 49th and 50th. The NBC Studio tours leave from inside the GE Building. The Radio City Music Hall is at the corner of Avenue of the Americas and 50th Street. ■ **HOURS:** NBC Studio Tours are conducted Monday through Saturday, 9:30–4:30. Radio City Musical Hall tours leave from the theater lobby, daily, 10:15–4:45, when there is no show scheduled. ■ **ADMISSION:** Both tours charge $8. ■ **TELEPHONE:** (212) 664-4000 for NBC Studio Tour information; (212) 247-4777 for the Music Hall.

ST. PATRICK'S CATHEDRAL

Rockefeller Center was criticized, in 1929, for moving too far uptown, to 5th Avenue and 50th Street (*see* previous entry). Imagine the sneers that went up a full seventy years prior, when the site was announced for the location of the new St. Patrick's Cathedral—the Center's neighbor on the east side of 5th Avenue.

It was called "Hughes Folly" by the experts of 1858. At the time, St. Patrick's stood at a downtown location, on Mott and Prince streets, in a facility it had outgrown. When Archbishop John Joseph Hughes laid the cornerstone for New York's new cathedral, churchmen predicted that he had committed the future of the city's Roman Catholic life to a cow pasture. The first major Gothic religious structure to be built in America, St. Patrick's instead developed into a much loved symbol of the city, treasured by Catholics and non-Catholics alike.

It took twenty-one years to finish the work, with a long interruption occasioned by the Civil War, at a cost of $2 million. Modelled on Germany's Cologne Cathedral, St. Patrick's is 398 feet long, with a height of 112 feet at the central nave. Its twin spires rise three hundred feet and were the dominant feature of the Manhattan skyline before the coming of the skyscrapers.

The cathedral has been added to and renovated many times. Its exterior was completely restored in 1948 at a cost exceeding that of its entire construction. St. Patrick's has also been bombed in protest against the Vietnam War, and invaded by activists who disrupted a Mass in anger over Church opposition to homosexuality. Even the St. Patrick's Day Parade, where the reviewing stand is set in front of the cathedral, has become an occasion for protest by gay activists. The fact that the cathedral has become such a potent political symbol is probably the best testimony to its position in America's cultural life.

■ **LOCATION:** Fifth Avenue at 50th Street. ■ **HOURS:** Daily, 6:30 A.M.–8:45 P.M. ■ **TELEPHONE:** (212) 753-2261

TIMES SQUARE

From its beginnings, New York's theater district had continually moved north along the route of Broadway. By the time it reached 42nd Street, at the start of the twentieth century, another new star was illuminating the Manhattan sky—the electric sign. And in 1903, the New York Times built its new editorial offices at this same intersection, giving its name to the vast square it faced.

All these developments combined to create Times Square, or the Great White Way, as it was quickly dubbed. This was the heart of show business, and every night hundreds of thousands of people crossed the square on their way to the theater and other places of entertainment. It was a natural arena for advertisers to capture an audience.

The first illuminated sign in New York, extolling Heinz Pickles, had been placed on 5th Avenue and 23rd Street in 1900. O. J. Gude is credited with being the marketing genius who predicted how these signs, unlike any other, could create a commercial impact. By the end of the century's first decade, the Times

Times Square in 1952 *(left, The Bettmann Archive)* and in 1982 *(right, AP/Wide World Photos)*, keeping the promise that it's "brighter at midnight than most cities are at noon."

Square area was filled with them. "Brighter at midnight than most cities are at noon," was the proud boast.

During the 1912 World Series, a huge electric scoreboard giving inning-by-inning rundowns of the games was erected. That led directly to the custom of gathering in Times Square for memorable occasions, most notably New Year's Eve. It is not clear when the New Year's observance began but it was already in full swing during World War I and has continued unabated—except for the odd holiday blizzard—through the years. The televised countdown of the illuminated ball dropping from the former Times building at midnight has become an integral part of the season. It's doubtful that a new year could begin without it.

By the 1970s, the area had degenerated into a tawdry sink of porno movies and penny arcades. But a determined cleanup campaign by the city reversed the decay in at least some parts of Times Square and the lights of Broadway are still shining.

■ **LOCATION:** The usual delineation of Times Square is given as Broadway and 7th Avenue between 42nd and 47th streets.

YANKEe STADIUM

The New York Yankees are the most successful franchise in baseball history. No team comes close to matching their thirty-three pennants and twenty-one world championships. But it wasn't always this way. For the first two decades of this century, they were the orphans of New York baseball.

They moved to New York from Baltimore in 1903. Since Baltimore had fired John McGraw, who went on to lead the New York Giants to success, there was bad blood between the local franchises from the start. The Giants dominated the game in the city and disdained the struggling American League team, then called the Highlanders because it played in a ballpark located on a slight elevation.

But that all changed in 1920, when the Yankees swung the most notorious deal in baseball history, acquiring Babe Ruth from the cash-strapped owner of the Boston Red Sox. In two years, the Yankees won their first pennant, with Ruth pulverizing every home run record in existence and drawing record crowds to the ballpark. The trouble was the ballpark was the Polo Grounds: The Giants were the primary tenants and the Yankees, who had joined them in 1913, were decidedly guest boarders. With the arrival of Ruth, a jealous McGraw demanded their eviction. So the Yankees picked a site in the Bronx, directly across the Harlem River from the Polo Grounds, and built what was then the largest baseball stadium in the world, with a seating capacity of seventy-five thousand. (It has since been cut back by about twenty thousand seats.)

The two teams had met in the 1921 and 1922 World Series, with all games played in the Polo Grounds. The Giants won both times. In 1923, Yankee Stadium opened its gates. In the only time in baseball history, the same teams met in a third consecutive Series. This time, Ruth, who had been shackled by Giants pitching the previous two years, broke out with three home runs and led the Yankees to their first championship.

The park was tailored to the Babe's power with its short right field and was popularly known as "The House That Ruth Built." In the first forty-two years of its existence, the World Series was played there twenty-seven times. It became a shrine to the game's greatest stars and its most powerful team. Other ballparks may put forth a more nostalgic appearance, but none has the awesome presence of Yankee Stadium. A major remodeling in the 1970s stripped the stadium of much of its historic gingerbread decor. It remains, however, baseball's most hallowed ground.

■ **LOCATION:** 161st Street and River Avenue, in the Bronx. Accessible from Exit 5 of the Major Deegan Expressway, Interstate 87, or by the IRT subway line (Jerome Avenue Express). ■ **HOURS:** Open only during Yankees home games, April to September. ■ **TELEPHONE:** (718) 293-6000

NIAGARA FALLS

MAID OF THE MIST BOAT TRIPS

Father Louis Hennepin was the first European explorer to reach the Niagara Falls. The year was 1678. He estimated that the falls were about six hundred feet high. He was a bit off. The falls are less than one-third that height. But it is easy to understand how Hennepin could have made the mistake. The awe and terror inspired by this wide, violent, torrent of water makes them seem much bigger than they are.

From the beginning, tourists have come here with a touch of terror in their hearts. They built viewing towers at the brink of the precipice. Hewed passageways out of the supporting rock to get close to the base. Packed themselves in barrels and crashed over the top. On the Canadian side of the falls, on a street called Clifton Hill, there is a whole block full of amusement attractions of the "Haunted Castle" and "Dracula" genre, feeding off the fright engendered by the deafening crash of the falls. Even in the supposedly jaded 1990s, a Canadian daredevil got headlines for doing the barrel stunt again; a ride that is, incidentally, illegal.

Niagara Falls is no longer the honeymoon haven it was earlier in this century. That business has moved on to the Poconos (*see* Mount Pocono, Pennsylvania). Still, the falls remain as big a crowd-pleaser as they were when the National Biscuit Company placed them on boxes of shredded wheat as an instant symbol.

One of the best ways of getting close to the waters is aboard the Maid of the Mist, the little boats that chug within a splash of the base. The boat name is based on one of the sentimental legends, wholly manufactured, that so appealed to Victorian tourists; the Indian maiden who threw herself into the falls at the loss of her lover from a warring tribe. You don't need phony legends to enjoy this trip.

You are handed raincoats as you wait in line to board. As the boat moves toward the American falls, the traveler may feel this is an unnecessary precaution. The spray is hardly more than that deposited by a passing drizzle. But once the boat moves to the Horseshoe Falls, on the Canadian side, you'll understand. This is a soaking, drenching typhoon. All sight is blotted out by the ferocity of the waters, pounding against the massive rocks just a few dozen yards away. Theme parks spend millions to create water rides that don't come close to approximating this kind of experience. It is nature at its scariest and best.

■ **LOCATION:** Prospect Point, at the base of the American falls. ■ **HOURS:** Daily, 10–7, mid-June to Labor Day; 10–5, mid-May to mid-June and Labor Day to late October. ■ **ADMISSION:** Fare is $8.65. ■ **TELEPHONE:** (716) 284-8897

ROCHESTER

INTERNATIONAL MUSEUM OF PHOTOGRAPHY

Historian Daniel Boorstin has marked the critical difference between photography and the graphic arts that preceded it. Before the invention of the

George Eastman's house is now the International Museum of Photography.
(AP/Wide World Photos)

camera, an event or a person was commemorated because someone of wealth had commissioned an artist to do just that. After the camera, things were remembered just because somebody happened to take a picture. We had "mass-produced the moment" and made the repeatable experience democratic—the moment of origin of popular culture.

George Eastman was the inventor who put this ability to stop time and re-examine it at leisure in the hands of the public. A Rochester bank clerk fascinated by cameras, Eastman worked for years on finding a substitute for the bulky, expensive, glass plates on which the photographic image was carried. He patented an emulsion for coating the plates in 1880 and then began working on using a similar process on rolling strips of paper. By 1888, he managed to get the first Kodak camera on the market. (He made up the word because of a fondness for the "k" sound. To Eastman, it indicated action.)

Buyers bought the camera for $25 and when they finished shooting a roll of one hundred pictures, they sent the whole thing back to the Eastman factory. It was developed, reloaded for another $10, and sent back to the owner who could then start on his second hundred pictures. It was a long, inconvenient process, although a huge advance on what had preceded it.

Almost simultaneously, Hannibal Goodwin, an Episcopal clergyman, came up with his own kind of paper strip. He used a celluloid base with a chemical coating that he called "film." That was the critical step in making photography quick and cheap. When film came to the attention of Thomas Edison, it led directly to the invention of the motion picture. After a long patent fight, Eastman won control of the celluloid process and the riches of the new invention poured into Rochester.

The Georgian mansion he built and lived in until his death in 1932, is now a museum of photography, with an extensive collection of historic pictures. Part of the home is furnished as it was when Eastman lived there. There are also displays of cameras and equipment from the early days of the medium. The best part of a visit, though, is to simply look at the faces of ordinary people, preserved forever from another time because of Eastman's little Kodak.

■ **LOCATION:** The museum is at 900 East Avenue (New York 96), just east of downtown. ■ **HOURS:** Tuesday through Saturday, 10–4:30; Sunday, 1–4:30. ■ **ADMISSION:** $5 ■ **TELEPHONE:** (716) 271-3970

PENNSYLVANIA

BREEZEWOOD

FIRST TURNPIKE TOURIST TOWN

When the first section of the Pennsylvania Turnpike opened in 1939, most observers were sure that something wonderful was accomplished. Only they weren't sure exactly what.

The first limited access roads, which were called parkways, had been built around New York City in the 1920s. They were seen as a way of easing traffic congestion, which even then was strangling that area. The roads were limited to cars, however, and were not linked to any continuous long-distance routes.

The Pennsylvania Turnpike was different. The mountain ranges that run the breadth of Pennsylvania had made east-to-west travel extremely difficult since colonial times. The first western highway, the National Road, ran to the south of the state, where natural gaps existed in the mountains. The westbound pioneer road developed along mountainous Indian trails. Eventually, it became U.S. 30, the Lincoln Highway. But the drive from Philadelphia to Pittsburgh was still arduous and dangerous, making links between the state's two largest cities difficult to maintain.

The turnpike changed all that. It bypassed towns and traffic lights and tunneled through the mountains on new routes chosen by engineers. It was the prototype of the interstate system that would develop after World War II and transform American auto travel.

The first section of the turnpike ran from Carlisle to Irwin, through the most mountainous part of the route. One unanticipated problem cropped up right away. While the old roads passed through a succession of small towns, the turnpike ran around them. Moreover, much of its route ran across lightly populated areas where sleeping, eating, and service facilities did not exist.

Out of that came Breezewood. Near the mid-point of the turnpike, it was barely a collection of shacks when the highway opened. But after the war, when family car travel resumed, it developed into something brand new—a turnpike service city. It was the model for all the communities that grew up thereafter along the interstates. Franchise motels, fast food restaurants, and gas stations made up Breezewood, and it would become a big part of the entire American travel landscape after the 1950s.

■ **LOCATION:** Breezewood is at Exit 28 of the Pennsylvania Turnpike, at the junction of Interstates 70 and 76.

DRIFTWOOD

TOM MIX BIRTHPLACE PARK

The greatest of the silent screen's western stars, Tom Mix always insisted he was born on a ranch in west Texas. He also said that he saw action in Cuba under Teddy Roosevelt during the Spanish-American War, fought in the Boxer Rebellion and Boer War, that he was a Texas Ranger and a "free-lance" frontier sheriff, and a champion rider with Oklahoma's famous 101 Ranch.

All of that went into his "official" obituary in 1940. The last item may even be true. Otherwise, Mix crafted a colorful past that fit perfectly with his hard-riding, clean-cut screen image. He was actually born in this little town northeast of Pittsburgh and while he did join the Army during the Spanish-American War, he never left the United States. In fact, he went AWOL and headed west to become a ranch hand.

In 1909, he found his destiny when he joined the 101 Ranch touring show and caught the eye of some movie scouts. They were looking for a western hero to compete with the dour William S. Hart character and the personable, good-looking Mix seemed like he could fill the screen.

Mix went on to make four hundred movies, teamed with Tony the Wonder Horse, and thrilled a generation of movie fans with his feats of valor. To Americans who grew up in those years, he remains the personification of the movie cowboy. In the 1920s, he was the highest-paid actor in Hollywood, making $17,500 a week. When his career faded with the coming of sound, he toured with his own western-theme circus for ten years before his death in an automobile accident (*see* Florence, Arizona). The legend went on, though. The Tom Mix Radio Show, with the Ralston Straight Shooters, was an after-school network hit until 1950, introducing an entire new generation to the Mix legend.

Despite his preference for a fictitious birthplace, Driftwood fondly remembers its native son. A museum, historical marker, and original buildings from the Mix Run settlement are preserved here as a memorial park. Mix lived here until the age of nine, when his family moved to DuBois, Pennsylvania. That nearby town puts on a Tom Mix Festival every September.

■ **LOCATION:** Driftwood is a bit out of the way but can be reached on state roads from Interstate 80. Eastbound, take Exit 17, then north on Pennsylvania 255 to Saint Mary's and east on Pennsylvania 120. Westbound, take Exit 22, then north on Pennsylvania 144 to Renovo and west on Pennsylvania

120. Driftwood is about 60 miles from the interstate either way. The Mix Run area is one mile west of town on Pennsylvania 555. ■ **HOURS:** Monday through Friday, 9–5, and weekends, 8 A.M. to 9 P.M., mid-April to mid-October. ■ **ADMISSION:** $2 ■ **TELEPHONE:** (814) 546-2044

DUBLIN

PEARL BUCK HOME

She learned to speak Chinese before she could speak English. The daughter of Presbyterian missionaries, Pearl Buck was raised in China, living there until she was seventeen. Later, she returned to China for another twenty-one years. In the years between the world wars, there was no other American writer who was so equipped to sympathetically and realistically portray that still faraway land.

Her greatest success, *The Good Earth,* was published in 1931 and became an immediate classic, winning the Pulitzer Prize. Its epic sweep, telling the story of a simple Chinese farm couple coping with the modernization of the culture and their love of the land, was written in deceptively simple language. "I am not a 100 percent American writer," she said in a 1969 interview. "My concept of the novel is based on the Chinese novel, which has a simple, direct style. I read Chinese novels almost exclusively until I came to America to go to college."

The Good Earth was turned into a movie in 1936 and its star, Luise Rainer, won an Academy Award as best actress. Two years later, Buck was awarded the Nobel Prize for Literature. She went on to write several books about China, but none approached the influence of *The Good Earth.* After World War II, the Communist authorities, who felt Buck was too reverential to Chinese tradition, barred her from returning. She dedicated the last decades of her life to the Pearl Buck Foundation, which cared for abandoned children of American servicemen in the Far East. Many of them came to live with her in this Bucks County farmhouse and she adopted nine of them.

The house was opened as a museum after her death in 1973, just as diplomatic contacts were reopening China to Westerners. "Through her eyes," said President Nixon in tribute, "millions of readers were able to see the beauty of China and its people at a time when direct personal contact was impossible." The house displays her awards as well as much personal memorabilia.

■ **LOCATION:** About 50 miles north of Philadelphia, just off Pennsylvania 313, at 520 Dublin Road. ■ **HOURS:** Tours are given March-December, Tuesday through Saturday, at 10:30, 11:30, 1:30, and 2:30; weekends at 1:30 and 2:30. ■ **ADMISSION:** $5 ■ **TELEPHONE:** (215) 249-0100

HERSHEY

CHOCOLATE WORLD

Milk chocolate made its first recorded appearance sometime around 1875 in Switzerland. But it remained for a Pennsylvania confectioner, Milton Hershey, to transform a European delicacy into a treat for the mass market.

Americans had been dabbling in chocolate for a considerable time. French style candy, or bonbons, had become popular here just before the Civil War. In 1896, the first penny candy, the Tootsie Roll, made its debut. But the visionary Hershey, a caramel manufacturer in nearby Lancaster, was the first to see the big picture.

He introduced the Hershey Bar, a flat chunk of wrapped milk chocolate, right after the turn of the century. It was received so warmly that by 1903 he built the planned industrial town of Hershey for the sole purpose of supplying candy bars to a grateful nation. He so dominated the market that before World War I, Hershey Bar was almost a generic word for chocolate candy. During that war, chocolate bars were billed as a healthy treat for the Doughboys. That is when the market expanded and other candy-makers rushed into the field.

Hershey, with its trademark chocolate-brown wrapping, still dominates. The aromas from the chocolate plant, one of the largest in the world, make any stroll through this town a delectable jaunt. The factory is no longer open to the public, but Chocolate World is a reproduction of the manufacturing process and a good introduction to the Hershey story. Best of all, there are free samples at the end.

■ **LOCATION:** Hershey is 13 miles northeast of Exit 19 of the Pennsylvania Turnpike, on U.S. 422. Chocolate World is on Park Boulevard. Signs direct you there from any part of town. ■ **HOURS:** Daily, 9–6:45, mid-June to Labor Day; closes at 4:45, rest of the year. ■ **ADMISSION:** Free ■ **TELEPHONE:** (717) 534-4900

INDIANA

JAMES STEWART BIRTHPLACE

In his long Hollywood career, James Stewart played just about every sort of role, from musical comedy to western to the companion of an invisible rabbit. But his most enduring image was that of the ordinary guy who stood up for what he believed was right. Whether he was portraying Charles Lindbergh, the "Man Who Shot Liberty Valance," or Mr. Smith (in *Mr. Smith Goes to Washington*), it was the role in which audiences most wanted to see him. He may have stammered and looked uneasy and had some doubts, but in the end you could count on him to do the right thing.

It also characterized the role with which he became most closely identified, the small town banker in *It's a Wonderful Life.* The story about this Christmas movie has become familiar: It was a flop when it first appeared right after World War II, its open sentimentality too much for a nation just emerging from a fight for its life. But as time passed, the story that celebrates the worth and dignity of every human life touched something basic in a country that had to be reminded of those simple truths. Bedford Falls, the setting of the film, became the sort of ideal small town in which we all wished we could live.

Stewart's actual boyhood home of Indiana has a lot of Bedford Falls in it. Surrounded by hills and rich farmland, with a college campus at its center, Indiana could easily pass itself off as Bedford Falls. In 1983, Stewart returned for his seventy-fifth birthday and the town unveiled a statue of him on the courthouse lawn. There is also a street and an airport named for him, and a plaque marks his birthplace.

■ **LOCATION:** Indiana is about 70 miles east of Pittsburgh by way of U.S. 22 and U.S. 119. The courthouse is at Philadelphia and 6th streets. The Stewart historic plaque is located at 965 Philadelphia Street.

JIM THORPE

JIM ThORPE MAUSOLeUM

The town used to be known as Mauch Chunk and as far as anyone knows the great Native American athlete Jim Thorpe had no connection to it. But in 1954, one year after Thorpe's death, the place changed its name to honor him and was awarded the rights to his burial place. (He was a member of the Sac and Fox tribe and Thorpe's widow originally planned to have him buried near his Oklahoma birthplace. But when plans for an elaborate memorial fell through, she awarded the rights to Pennsylvania.) The town was also promised a museum, an Olympic stadium, and a tourist bonanza, none of which materialized. In fact, a referendum on changing the name back to Mauch Chunk failed by just 150 votes in 1966.

Nonetheless, if any athlete deserves to have a town named for him, it is Thorpe. An All-American running back at Carlisle Indian School, winner of both the pentathlon and decathlon at the 1912 Olympics, a pioneer of professional football, an outfielder with the New York Giants, Thorpe was voted the greatest athlete of the half century by the Associated Press in 1950.

■ **LOCATION:** Jim Thorpe is 11 miles west of the Pennsylvania Turnpike Northeast Extension, at Exit 34. The mausoleum is just east of town on Pennsylvania 903. ■ **HOURS:** Daily, dawn to dusk. ■ **ADMISSION:** Free

LANGHORNE

SESAMe PLACE

Ever since the first show flickered to life on the tube, television has been heralded as a great educational medium. Unfortunately, the promise has rarely been filled. Described as "a vast wasteland" in the early 1960s, commercial TV often went downhill from there. Thirty years later, Congress was threatening stricter regulation unless network executives did something to tone down the violence that permeated TV programming.

One of the major exceptions to that bleak picture went on the air in 1969. *Sesame Street* was a modest experiment by public television to try and give a head start to disadvantaged children. Instead it grew into one of the most powerful educational tools for pre-schoolers ever devised and a commercial giant in its own right. It was the first educational program to understand and use the ground rules of TV: It employed entertainment values, rapid-fire sequences, and music to make its points. A few educators questioned the lasting impact of these techniques and were uncomfortable with the short attention spans and demand for constant change that the program seemed to foster. But most reported strong improvements in understanding letters and numbers, and even in overall intelligence, among its young viewers.

Sesame Street is a star-maker. Big Bird, Cookie Monster, Kermit T. Frog, Bert and Ernie—they all became nationally recognizable figures, even to grown-ups. Joan Ganz Cooney, chairperson of the Children's Television Workshop (CTW), which created the show, says her group was always cautious about making "the quick buck" off its young fans. But in the 1970s, she also realized that the workshop couldn't count on its original funding sources—government and foundations—for the long run. So a commercial arm was set up to license *Sesame Street* characters and make sure CTW's work could continue and expand.

One result is Sesame Place, a theme park with an educational base. There are no thrill rides here, instead there are activities that lead children to develop skills by playing games. The emphasis is on interactive devices dealing with science and technology, although a change of clothing is recommended for the water section. There is also a re-creation of the show's neighborhood-like set and appearances by some of its stars.

■ **LOCATION:** Can you tell me how to get to Sesame Place? North from Philadelphia on Interstate 95 to the northbound U.S. 1 Exit. ■ **HOURS:** Daily, 10–8, mid-June through August; weekday closing time is 5 P.M., mid-May to mid-June and first week of September. ■ **ADMISSION:** $19.95 ■ **TELEPHONE:** (215) 752-7070

MOUNT POCONO

HONEYmOON RESORTS

All the credit goes to Morris Wilkins. He was the hotelier who came up with the idea of the heart-shaped bathtub. The rest is history.

Wilkins's amorous innovation, introduced in the early 1960s, helped transform the Poconos into America's premier honeymoon haven. That title had been held—without challenge—by Niagara Falls for almost a century. But the Poconos had the advantage of being much closer to New York City (less than two hours by car) and it was far more secluded. The heart-shaped bathtubs were just what was needed to put the Poconos over the top.

This had been a ski area and mountain retreat for many years and most resorts still seek family vacationers. But Caesars of Las Vegas purchased the four Wilkins hotels and their theme is love, American style. All of them feature Champagne Suites, with whirlpools shaped like long-stemmed champagne glasses, and bedroom lofts. Many of them also have small, heart-shaped swimming pools in the rooms and, of course, the valentine tubs. No marriage should start without one.

■ **LOCATION:** The most centrally located of the resorts is Caesars Paradise Stream, on Pennsylvania 940, just east of Interstate 380. ■ **TELEPHONE:** Reservations at all four Caesars honeymoon resorts can be made by calling 1-800-233-4141.

PHILADELPHIA

MARIO LANZA MUSEUm

Arturo Toscanini called Lanza's tenor "the voice of the century" and soprano Licia Albanese said it was "the greatest voice I ever heard." When Hollywood made the 1951 film biography of opera legend Enrico Caruso, Lanza took the lead role almost as his birthright.

In the early 1950s, Mario Lanza was one of the great show business draws, a box office winner in movies and the last operatic-style singer whose records made the Hit Parade. Yet he never sang in a real opera and before he reached the age of forty, his body gave out on him.

Lanza was discovered while working as a piano-mover in the south Philadelphia Italian neighborhood where he was born. Hearing that conductor Serge Koussevitzky was in the next room at the Philadelphia Academy of Music, Lanza burst into a wall-penetrating aria. The maestro was impressed and arranged for Lanza's concert debut in 1942. Critics called his voice untrained and undisciplined, but other musicians and Lanza himself regarded it as "a gift from God."

Lanza (his real name was Alfredo Arnold Cocozza) went into the Army during World War II but emerged to go on the concert circuit. His stunning 1947 performance at the Hollywood Bowl brought him to the attention of film producers and he was given the lead in *That Midnight Kiss.* It was a surprise box-office success and other roles followed, although his acting was never a match for his vocal ability.

After Lanza's appearance in *The Great Caruso,* the top movie draw of 1951, his career went downhill. He battled temperament and weight problems, ballooning to three hundred pounds and walking out on contracts. His television debut was marred by revelations that he had lip-synched the words to old records. He pleaded that his voice had been weakened by dieting. Finally, with the IRS pursuing him for millions in unpaid taxes, he moved to Italy. He collapsed and died in Rome in 1959, allegedly after a rigorous stay in a diet clinic.

But south Philly didn't forget. Nick Petrella, owner of a record store in the old neighborhood, founded the Mario Lanza Institute in the 1970s. It preserved the singer's memorabilia and awarded music scholarships to promising youngsters. The institute expanded to become part of Settlement Music School, where Lanza studied as a youth. It displays articles associated with his career, portraits and photographs, and items sent to him by admirers.

■ **LOCATION:** The museum, within the Settlement Music School, is located at 416 Queen Street, south from downtown by way of Fourth Street. ■ **HOURS:** Monday through Saturday, 10–3:30. ■ **ADMISSION:** Free ■ **TELEPHONE:** (215) 468-3623

STATUe OF "ROCKY"

The saga of Rocky Balboa, unknown club fighter who, by a fluke, gets a title bout with the heavyweight champion, became one of the surprise movie hits of 1976. It launched the career of its screenwriter and star, Sylvester Stallone, and spun off several sequels. The hopeless underdog who never gives up, even though matched against men who are bigger, smarter, and more talented than he is, has seldom been brought to the screen more effectively than in the Rocky movies.

Stallone, a Philadelphia native, set the Rocky story in his hometown. The most dramatic sequence in the original film involves Rocky getting into shape. Accompanied by stirring theme music, he is seen running tirelessly through the streets of the city. The sequence climaxes with Rocky pounding up the stairs of the Philadelphia Museum of Art and dancing in triumph, waving his arms high above his head.

A statue of Stallone in that pose was cast for the film *Rocky 2* and placed at the head of the museum steps. But when the film wrapped, museum officials politely requested that it be moved elsewhere. The Spectrum, Philadelphia's largest indoor arena, was happy to oblige. That's where *Rocky* stands now, in front of the main entrance.

■ **LOCATION:** The Spectrum is as the corner of Broad Street and Pattison Avenue, due south from downtown by way of Broad.

SHARTLESVILLE

ROADSIDE AMERICA

As long as people have been traveling by road, there have been roadside shrines offering balm for the weary. The American roadside culture developed its own kind of shrine, influenced by a strange passion for miniaturization. Throughout the country, as the highway system expanded, a cult of the cute grew along with it. Scaled down versions of religious scenes, local landscapes, famous parks, and gardens popped up along the new roads to amaze the traveler. Their creators seemed to feel that by compressing the familiar they made it more compelling.

By far the most ambitious of these projects is Roadside America, a representation of the growth of rural America. Laurence Gieringer spent about half a century assembling this tiny fanciful country. Mechanical figures wave and twirl, model trains race across the countryside, and in the evening the skies darken and the recorded voice of Kate Smith sings "God Bless America." The entire tableau covers 8,800 square feet and is housed in its own roadside structure.

■ **LOCATION:** Roadside America is on U.S. 22, just off the Shartlesville exit of Interstate 78, about 35 miles west of Allentown. ■ **HOURS:** Daily, 9–6:30, July to Labor Day; 10–5, rest of the year. ■ **ADMISSION:** $3.75 ■ **TELEPHONE:** (215) 488-6241

STRASBURG

AMISH VILLAGE

In earlier times, the persistent refusal of the Pennsylvania Dutch to assimilate was an irritant to their neighbors. Now it is almost a badge of pride.

The Amish were among the strictest, most conservative, or in religious terms, the "plainest" of the Mennonite sects that took up William Penn's offer of free land for those seeking religious tolerance. Followers of Jacob Ammon, the Amish broke away from the main body of Mennonites when that group became too worldly for their tastes. The Mennonites had first settled around Philadelphia in 1682 (Germantown is named for their community) and gradually moved west to the rich land east of the Susquehanna River. Most Mennonites are of German origin, a few are Swiss. Since the word for "German" in the German language is *Deutsch,* the Mennonites became known as Dutch.

With their severe clothing and refusal to accept the incursions of the modern world, the Amish and other Mennonite sects sometimes came into conflict with the government. Most of this was over education, with the Mennonite groups flatly refusing to send their children to state-run schools. By the 1930s, these issues had been legally resolved and Pennsylvania began to see what an asset it had in these plain folk. A certain sameness had begun to characterize America's regions. Yet here was a group, close to the country's largest population centers, that looked and behaved in a distinctly different manner. The Amish seemed, in fact, to have stepped right out of a history book.

To their astonishment, by the 1950s the Amish found themselves turned into a tourist attraction. U.S. 30 in Lancaster County became the Pennsylvania Dutch Highway, lined with an assortment of Amish-styled souvenir shops, restaurants, and craft stores. They entered the popular culture in music ("Throw Momma from the Train a Kiss"), in theater *(Plain and Fancy),* and in film *(Witness).* There seemed to be no end to the public's fascination with these horse-and-buggy people who so stubbornly resisted twentieth-century America.

Amish Village (the name is copyrighted) is fairly representative of the area. It includes a typical Amish farmhouse, school, blacksmith shop, and smokehouse, introducing visitors to "the Amish way of life," as it developed from colonial times to the 1920s.

■ **LOCATION:** Amish Village is 2 miles north of Strasburg, on Pennsylvania 896, and 1 mile south of U.S. 30, about 8 miles southeast of Lancaster. ■ **HOURS:** Daily, 9–5, mid-March through October. ■ **ADMISSION:** $5 ■ **TELEPHONE:** (717) 687-8511

WILLIAMSPORT

LITTLe LEAGUE STAdIUM

Kareem Abdul-Jabbar was a Little Leaguer, although he must have been the biggest one ever. So were Baseball Hall of Fame member Tom Seaver and all-time strikeout leader Nolan Ryan. In fact, the Little Leagues, once criticized by traditionalists for taking the spontaneity out of sandlot baseball, have become a summer institution, where many of the game's biggest stars got their first taste of being a hero.

It began on a grassy hilltop in Williamsport in 1939. Carl Stotz, looking for a place for his nephews to play ball, rounded up some neighborhood kids, folded up some old newspapers for bases, and called on local businessmen to help buy equipment and uniforms. Stotz's twelve-player team was the foundation of

Little League fans pack Howard J. Lamade Stadium. *(Courtesy of Little League Baseball.)*

Little League. Within eight years, teams from across the country came here to play a World Series and by 1989 it had 2.5 million players on 140,000 teams.

"I'd tell kids, 'Get your father to start a team,'" Stotz recalled in a fiftieth-anniversary interview. "I wanted to give every kid a chance to play. That was always the secret—parental involvement."

There are some who would say that parents became too involved. The image of the infuriated dad in the stands, yelling at a tearful strikeout victim is one that Little League has worked hard to overcome. And competition sometimes goes over the edge, as it did in 1992 when a team representing the Philippines had to forfeit its first-place trophy when it was found to consist primarily of over-age ringers.

Nevertheless, the annual Little League World Series, held here each August, has become an international gala, dedicated to baseball and the hold the game has on kids. The museum adjoins the World Series stadium and displays memorabilia of the league's past and the famous players who once wore its insignia on their sleeves.

■ **LOCATION:** The stadium and museum are about one mile south of Williamsport on U.S. 15. ■ **HOURS:** Monday through Saturday, 9–7, and Sunday, noon–7, Memorial Day to Labor Day; closes at 5, rest of the year. ■ **ADMISSION:** $4 ■ **TELEPHONE:** (717) 326-3607

YORK

HARLEy-DAVIDSON PlANT AND MUSeUM

"Harleys are everything that American cars used to be," said actor Peter Fonda. "Heavy, big and loud." He ought to know. Fonda starred in one of the classic biking movies, *Easy Rider,* made in 1969, "and I didn't do it just by accident. I love these bikes."

Fonda was interviewed while attending the company's ninetieth anniversary celebration in the streets of Milwaukee in the summer of 1993. He and sixty thousand other Harley owners rode their hogs proudly in the birthday parade. While Harley-Davidson, the last remaining American motorcycle manufacturer is based in a Milwaukee, Wisconsin, its main assembly plant is in York. And it is here that the mystique of this cycle is best felt, at the Harley-Davidson Museum.

The bike was first made in a Milwaukee backyard in 1903, when William Harley and the three Davidson brothers put it together. Within four years, they had sold their bikes to several police departments for traffic enforcement and the legend of the Harley was being built.

It became known as the biggest and the wildest of all the bikes, the one that black leather jackets were made for. The bike Marlon Brando road in *The Wild One* wasn't a Harley but most people thought it was—so strong was the company's identification with the tough biker image.

But things began changing in 1969, when the family firm sold out to a conglomerate. Japanese competitors took away most of the motorcycle market and Harley itself seemed to forget what its image was all about. By 1980 it was on the verge of bankruptcy. That's when some former executives bought the company back and turned it around. They restored Harley's image as the biggest and baddest bike, but also took it upscale—brightening up the showrooms and featuring young executives rather than Hell's Angels in its promotions. The concept worked. By the end of the decade, Harley was selling eighty-eight thousand bikes a year and the income of its typical buyer had gone up by $10,000 annually.

The museum includes a version of the original 1903 model, as well as exhibits on the bike's development over the years, racing trophies, and vintage ads. The plant tour is highlighted by the assembly line, which turns out a new Harley every minute and a half.

■ **LOCATION:** The plant is on U.S. 30, immediately east of Interstate 83. ■ **HOURS:** The museum is open Monday through Saturday, 10–3. Plant hours vary with production schedule. Call in advance. The plant can only be seen on a guided tour. ■ **ADMISSION:** Free ■ **TELEPHONE:** (717) 848-1177

Rhode Island

NEWPORT

INTERNATIONAL TENNIS HALL OF FAME AND MUSEUM

Tennis has privileged origins in Newport. This resort, once the summer playground of the exceedingly rich, was the cradle of the sport in America. The first international polo match in America was held at Newport in 1876, and in 1895 the Newport Country Club was the site of the first National Open Golf Championship. Yachting championships were decided in the nearby waters. These were the aristocratic sports, and only the rich had the time and money for them. Tennis fit right in.

The first lawn tennis court in the country was laid out on Staten Island in 1874. But only seven years later, the first U.S. Open was held at the Newport Casino, built in 1880 by newspaper publisher James Gordon Bennett, Jr. He sold it to the Newport Association for championship matches and afterward, it was regarded as the unchallenged base of the sport.

Tennis did not receive much media coverage then and the names of the Open's earliest winners are almost unknown to contemporary fans. Part of the reason is that the tournament was run under the challenger system. That meant the previous year's winner sat out until a challenger emerged from the field. It was a gentlemanly, if rather dull, way of doing things and helped Richard Sears win the first seven opens. Tennis really didn't emerge as a major sport until the more exacting tournament seeding system was adopted here in 1911.

The period from 1890 to 1914 is known as Newport's Gilded Age. Never again were parties quite so lavish or cottages quite so huge. The annual tennis tournament played a central role in each summer's social season. But the final gilded summer ended with war breaking out in Europe. In 1915, Wimbledon was canceled for the first time, while privileged young men fought in the trenches of Flanders. That same year, the U.S. Open left Newport for its new home at New York's West Side Tennis Club. Newport assumed a subsidiary role in the sport.

In 1954, tennis returned to town when the Hall of Fame opened at the Newport Casino. In 1955, Sears was among the hall's first inductees and its first president was William J. Clothier, the 1906 U.S. Open champion. The annual

The ballroom at Rosecliff. *(Courtesy of The Preservation Society of Newport County)*

Tennis Week celebration in July is the occasion for a professional tournament and the enshrinement of new inductees.

Exhibits include historical displays and memorabilia of the game. There is also a *court* tennis court, with exhibitions on how this fifteenth-century forerunner of lawn tennis was played.

■ **LOCATION:** The casino is at 194 Bellevue Avenue, just south of Memorial Boulevard, Rhode Island 138. ■ **HOURS:** Daily, 10–5. During July's Tennis Week, only tournament ticket-holders are permitted inside the casino. ■ **ADMISSION:** $6 ■ **TELEPHONE:** (401) 849-3990

ROSECLIFF

There are several spectacular oceanfront estates in Newport. Rosecliff merits inclusion in popular culture not because it is one of them, but because of the role it played: It was the setting for the 1974 movie *The Great Gatsby,* portraying one of the most famous mansions in American fiction.

In F. Scott Fitzgerald's novel, Gatsby's estate is on Long Island, but the summer cottages of Newport represent just the sort of locale Fitzgerald describes. Designed in 1902 by Stanford White, high society's favorite architect, and ornamented by sculptor Augustus Saint-Gaudens, Rosecliff features a heart-shaped grand staircase and a forty-by-eighty foot ballroom. New York socialite Hermann Oelrichs built the home as a romantic gesture for his wife, Theresa, whose father hit the Comstock Lode.

■ **LOCATION:** Rosecliff is on Bellevue Avenue, in the midst of the estate district. ■ **HOURS:** Daily, 10–5, April to October. ■ **ADMISSION:** $6 ■ **TELEPHONE:** (401) 847-1000

Vermont

BENNINGTON

GRANDMA MOSES EXHIBIT AT THE BENNINGTON MUSEUM

If "White Christmas" provided the traditional sound of the American holiday season, Grandma Moses supplied the traditional look. Her paintings of rural life were reproduced on an estimated one hundred million Christmas cards, while the story of her own art career was the stuff of fantasy.

She was born Anna Mary Robertson and lived most of her life just a few miles west of Bennington, across the New York state line, near the town of Eagle Bridge. When her husband, Thomas Moses, died in 1927, she went on working the family farm by herself, although she already was sixty-seven years old.

Ten years later, afflicted with arthritis, she was ordered by her doctor to slow down and take up a hobby. She found some paint and brushes in a barn and started to draw her memories. The way the countryside looked when she was growing up—all white churches and neat houses. The landscape filled with busy people—quilting, sugaring, hanging laundry—occupied with hundreds of little tasks. She was fond of old Currier and Ives prints and transposed some of the figures she found in them to settings of her own imagination.

"I paint from the sky down," she once said, "filling in the personal details last. Once I tried to do a landscape without people but it looked so lonely I just had to put some in."

Family and friends encouraged her, and the local druggist in Hoosick Falls, New York, agreed to hang some of her pictures in his window. They were seen in 1939 by vacationing Manhattan collector Louis Caldor who rushed to her home to buy up her entire output. Within a year, three of her paintings were exhibited anonymously at the Museum of Modern Art, and in 1940 she was given a one-woman gallery show.

Her work was described as being in the vanishing tradition of American folk art. Among serious critics it was studied as an echo of a dying genre. But to most Americans, the work of Grandma Moses (she was given the name by a cheeky New York City newspaperman during her first exhibition) struck something much deeper. She showed them an America they wanted to remember. A simpler place of hard-working, happy people who lived by the clearer values of a distant time. For the next two decades, she became the best-known and most beloved of American artists.

At her death, at the age of 101 in 1961, she was saluted by President Kennedy as an artist "whose directness and vividness restored a primitive freshness to our perception of the American scene." The Bennington Museum maintained a close relationship with the Moses family and acquired the largest collection of her work in existence. The museum has an extensive assortment of memorabilia and displays on how she worked. In addition, the one-room schoolhouse she attended in Eagle Bridge is part of the exhibit.

The museum also contains displays of local art and history relating especially to the Battle of Bennington, fought in 1777. The battleground is adjacent to the museum.

■ **LOCATION:** The museum is west of central Bennington, on Vermont 9, West Main Street, in Old Bennington. ■ **HOURS:** Daily, 9–5, March to December; weekends only, rest of the year. ■ **ADMISSION:** $4.50 ■ **TELEPHONE:** (802) 447-1571

MIDDLEBURY

FRISBeE MEMORIAL

About the origin of the name, there doesn't seem to be much doubt. The original frisbees were pie tins, used by the Frisbie Baking Company of Bridgeport, Connecticut, as containers for its goodies. It is after that basic fact that stories vary.

Some say the first collegians to use the tins as missiles were Yale students from nearby New Haven, who sailed them at one another while hollering "Frisbie." By some accounts, this sort of activity may have been going on as early as the 1890s.

According to the Middlebury College version, however, the tins were first sailed by a group of its students, left stranded and bored by car trouble in the middle of Nebraska in 1938. Other campuses have variations of the same tale.

By the late 1940s a carnival worker named Walter Morrison was amusing midway crowds by sailing the tins to an accomplice. He claimed they were being carried along by "invisible string." He didn't sell much of the string but he reasoned that if he could find a safer material he might be able to peddle the pie tins. He hit upon a plastic version and pitched the idea to Wham-O, a California sporting goods company that had struck it rich with the hula hoop.

Wham-O introduced the Pluto Platter in 1957, but it never got off the ground. The company was convinced, however, that with the right marketing the platter would soar. By the time they hit upon calling it Frisbee, the times were right. It was 1967, in the midst of the love-and-peace era, and the idea of

Middlebury College's frisbee monument: The game has become so popular, even dogs know how to play it. *(©Erik Borg)*

this languid, noncompetitive pastime—perfect for love-ins and rock concerts—caught on with the Aquarians. The fad never died out. By 1993 an estimated two hundred million Frisbees had been sold.

Eventually, tournaments were held. A contact sport called "guts" Frisbee was devised. Dogs were trained to catch the gizmos, which became a surefire hit at sporting event half times. It is the canine version of the game, a dog leaping to catch a sailing Frisbee, that is saluted in the memorial at Middlebury. It was unveiled in 1988 at the supposed fiftieth anniversary of its origination.

■ **LOCATION:** The sculpture stands in front of Monroe Hall, near the center of the Middlebury College campus.

NEWHArT'S WAYBURY INN

In the century after the Civil War, Vermont was one of the nation's slow-growth states. There were times, in fact, when it was a net exporter of population. But that began to change in the 1980s. As the big cities of the East were increasingly perceived as less desirable, even unlivable places, predominantly rural Vermont turned into a magnet for younger families. The University of Vermont became the only state school in the country with a majority of students enrolled from outside the state. Its politics changed from rock-ribbed Republican to predominantly liberal.

Many of these demographic movements were reflected in the long-running television hit, *Newhart,* which was on the air from 1982 to 1990. The show depicted the new urban, middle class ideal; moving to a small town and running an old inn. Veteran comic actor Bob Newhart mined the concept for all possible laughs, playing off the Brie-and-Chablis values of its yuppie characters against the eccentric, plain-spoken Vermonters. Although played for comedy, the story line had a very real appeal.

The model for the hostelry depicted in the show was never mentioned. But exteriors were shot at this twelve-room country inn, located a few miles south of the college town of Middlebury. Built in 1810 as a coaching inn, and specializing in traditional Vermont cooking, the Waybury lives up to its televised fantasy image.

■ **LOCATION:** Five miles south of town on U.S. 7, then east on Vermont 125. ■ **HOURS:** The inn is open all year. During summer and color season, its dozen rooms must be reserved months in advance. ■ **TELEPHONE:** (802) 388-4015

STOWE

TRAPP FAMILY LODGe

The critics never regarded it as the best musical the team of Rodgers and Hammerstein ever wrote. But the 1959 Broadway hit, *The Sound of Music,* certainly has been the most enduringly popular with American audiences. After release of the 1965 movie version, starring Julie Andrews and the Austrian Alps, the show became a classic. Its cheery nuns and talented children and villainous Nazis were an irresistible mixture.

The play was based on the experiences of Maria von Trapp, who left a convent at the age of twenty to become governess to the seven children of Baron Georg von Trapp. She later married von Trapp, and in 1938 the family fled Austria after voicing opposition to forced unification with Nazi Germany. Arriving in America destitute, the Trapps (they dropped the aristocratic "von" a few years later) formed a choir that toured for the next eighteen years. Although you would never guess it from the show's score, the Trapp Family Singers presented a heavily classical program and were regarded as serious musicians—although they usually lightened their repertoire with folk favorites. Even after the death of the baron, in 1947, ("He couldn't sing very well," one of his daughters later revealed) the choir continued performing.

In 1941 the Trapps purchased a hilltop property near the ski resort of Stowe as a residence. It reminded them of scenery in the Austrian countryside. Eventually, it became a music camp and in 1962, a few years after the Trapp Family Singers gave up the road, it opened as a ski resort.

"Contrary to what most people believe, I am not swinging in money from that show," said Maria von Trapp (she resumed the aristocratic designation after the musical opened) in a 1967 interview. "I sold the rights for very little. But my story seems to have brought many people closer to God, and that is my reward."

The lodge burned to the ground in a 1980 fire, a few days before Christmas, and most of the family mementoes were lost. It reopened a few years later and was decorated with souvenirs of the Trapps' later years. Maria von Trapp died in 1987, but visitors still flock to the Lodge for its fine Vermont scenery and associations with a musical legend.

■ **LOCATION:** The Lodge is north of Stowe, on Vermont 108. ■ **HOURS:** The Lodge is open year round. Visitors are welcome on the grounds, in the public areas, and in the dining room. ■ **TELEPHONE:** (802) 253-8511

WATERBURY

BEN & JERRY'S ICE CREAM FACTOrY

If there is a single place that illustrates how the tides of pop culture have remade the state of Vermont, this ice cream factory is probably it. Ben & Jerry's has become the state's best-known product and its most visited tourist attraction. It is run by two of the most unlikely entrepreneurs in America, a pair of refugees from the hippie high-noon of the 1960s who learned to make ice cream from a five-dollar correspondence course.

Ben Cohen and Jerry Greenfield were friends in junior high school on Long Island. Like many of their generation, they opted out of the urban grind and moved to New England to seek the alternative lifestyle that the 1960s heralded. The only catch with the lifestyle was that they had to figure out a way to make a living. In 1978, they managed to scrape together $12,000 and opened their first ice cream plant in a converted gas station in Burlington.

Within three years, Ben & Jerry's was being hailed in a *Time* magazine cover story as "the best ice cream in the world." According to company legend, the flavors are especially intense because Cohen has a notoriously weak sense of smell. To get by him, the flavors have to be incredibly rich. They also believe in making sure the consumer always gets a chunk of something with every spoonful of ice cream—be it chocolate chips, candy bits or fruit. But, in 1994, the company introduced a line of "Smooth" ice creams, including flavors such as Aztec Harvest Coffee, Vanilla Bean, and White Russian. The Smooth ice creams cannot hold the promise of a chunk-of-something-in-every-spoonful, but they do deliver on rich taste.

The operation moved to Waterbury in 1985 and has since become something of a shrine to 1960s sensibilities—ice cream with a cultural cachet. One flavor, for example, is called Cherry Garcia, a salute to the leader of the Grateful Dead, a 1960s icon. The containers carry messages about saving the environment and the family farm. The Ben & Jerry Foundation, funded by 7.5 percent of the company's pre-tax profits, goes to help community groups.

All stages of the ice-cream-making operation are on view in Waterbury, Vermont. *(Courtesy of Ben & Jerry's)*

"We never had any intention of becoming business people," said Cohen in a 1988 interview. "We kind of ended up becoming business people. But we believe very strongly that businesses have the ability to improve the quality of life."

Visitors can take tours of the factory, and there is, of course, an ice cream shop on-site.

■ **LOCATION:** Off Interstate 89, at northbound Vermont 100, about 30 miles east of Burlington. ■ **HOURS:** Daily, 9–6; in summer, 9–9. ■ **ADMISSION:** $1 for the tour, which is donated to charitable causes. ■ **TELEPHONE:** (802) 244-5641

Washington D.C.

FBI HeADQUARTERS

The forerunner of the Federal Bureau of Investigation was created in 1908 as an arm of the U.S. Justice Department. But not until sixteen years later, when a twenty-nine-year old bureaucrat, J. Edgar Hoover, was named to head the organization, did it move into a central position in American life.

In 1924, the country was outraged by the lawlessness arising from Prohibition. Armed gangs sprayed streets with machine gun bullets in battles for control of the illegal liquor trade. In places like Chicago and Detroit, it seemed that gangsters were running the city. Criminals used high-powered automobiles to rob banks and cross state lines quickly, thwarting pursuers. There was a public demand for the federal government to step in and get things under control.

There is some argument as to whether Hoover ever really accomplished that. But what he did do, brilliantly, was to harness American popular culture and build the reputation of the FBI as an elite and unstoppable crime-fighting organization. He had an innate sense of how to use movies and radio, and how to cultivate contacts with the powers in the communications industry. He was always ready to cooperate fully with any broadcaster or filmmaker who wanted to enhance the FBI image. Very few were willing to oppose him. In 1962, the studio of Hoover's longtime friend, Walt Disney, produced the film *Flubber,* in which FBI agents were made to look like bumblers. Hoover went into a tirade and declared that enemy agents had managed to get to Disney. Only a long apology and the promise to recut the film to eliminate offensive scenes calmed Hoover.

Hoover originated the "Ten Most Wanted" list, which was broadcast weekly. He always included one or two fugitives on whom he knew the FBI was closing in. When, sure enough, these "most wanted" were captured within a few days, it made the agency seem even more efficient to the public. Incorruptible, staffed entirely by lawyers and accountants who also happened to be expert marksmen, the FBI was the very symbol of law enforcement.

The legend was tarnished over the years. Hoover was seen as less than eager to assist in the struggles of the civil rights era. His alleged "secret files," which contained damning information on most Washington figures including several presidents, was also credited with keeping him in office an unprecedented forty-eight years, until his death in 1972. But his rapport with the public was strong until the end. Part of that was because of the tours he carefully set up through FBI Headquarters in Washington. They became one of the most popular attractions in the capital, always including a dramatic firearms demonstration. The tours were another of Hoover's public relations triumphs. FBI headquarters is now in a building named for him, and the tours continue building the agency's legend on Hoover's foundations.

■ **LOCATION:** The J. Edgar Hoover FBI Building is entered from E Street, between 9th and 10th streets Northwest. ■ **HOURS:** Tours are given Monday through Friday, 8:45–4:15. ■ **ADMISSION:** Free ■ **TELEPHONE:** (202) 324-2447

LINCOLN MEMORIAL

In 1867 the U.S. Congress, still caught up in the tragedy of Abraham Lincoln's assassination, approved construction of a memorial to the fallen president. But it took another forty-four years before it got around to financing the project. The Lincoln Memorial wasn't formally dedicated until Memorial Day 1922, more than fifty-seven years after Lincoln's death.

Many Americans regard this as the most moving monument in the capital. Daniel Chester French's sculpture of the seated president, presumably about to rise after long thought, captures the essence of the country's feelings about the man who most historians rank as America's greatest leader. More than that, the Lincoln Memorial has become a rallying place, in both fact and fantasy, for those who call on the Republic to remember and heed its finer promise.

It was from its steps that Marian Anderson sang on Easter Sunday 1939, after the Daughters of the American Revolution decided not to have a black woman appear in its Constitution Hall. It was where James Stewart went to find courage as he stood up to the forces of corruption in the classic Frank Capra film, *Mr. Smith Goes to Washington.* Most memorably, in 1963 the memorial was the backdrop to Dr. Martin Luther King, Jr.'s "I Have a Dream" address, the high point of the civil rights movement. Over and over again, Americans gather here in times of trouble and gain inspiration from the place. It has become the cultural symbol of, in Lincoln's phrase, "the angels of our better nature."

■ **LOCATION:** The western end of the Mall. ■ **HOURS:** Always open. ■ **ADMISSION:** Free ■ **TELEPHONE:** (202) 619-7222

NATIONAL MUSEUM OF AMERICAN HISTORY

The Smithsonian Institution has been called "America's attic" and none of its facilities fit the description better than this museum. It depicts the entire

The Vietnam Memorial at night: The 58,022 names of the dead and missing are never alone. *(AP/Wide World Photos)*

range of American life, from colonial beginnings to the present. Its displays of popular culture are among the best in existence.

The second floor exhibits on social history include cases full of famous artifacts from movies and television—from Archie Bunker's easy chair to Dorothy's ruby-red slippers. Although only a small portion of the museum's vast collection, this section always seems to draw the largest crowds. As with most of the Smithsonian museums, the best advice is to go during the off season and on a weekday if you really want the time to sample the treasures that are here.

■ **LOCATION:** This museum is at the northwestern corner of the Mall, on Constitution Avenue between 14th and 15th streets Northwest. ■ **HOURS:** Daily, 10–5:30. ■ **ADMISSION:** Free ■ **TELEPHONE:** (202) 357-2700

VIETNaM VETERANS mEMORIAL

When the design for the long-awaited memorial to Vietnam War veterans was first unveiled by architect Maya Lin, there was a sigh of disappointment. It was just a black granite wall inscribed with names. No heroic statue. No stirring words. Just the thousands of names of those who died.

Yet, like nothing else that has been written or shown about that bitter, divisive conflict, the wall has achieved a healing. "It's the parade we never got," said one veteran during the memorial's tenth anniversary celebration in 1992. "It is an astonishing and unprecedented expression of a drawing together of people," said Roger Kennedy, director of the Smithsonian's National Museum of American History (*see* previous entry). "It is not a memorial, but a place in which individuals may come and find an opportunity to state their feelings, and thereby form a community of feelings. This has never happened in our country before."

Because of the depth of emotions it arouses and the way visitors confront it some writers have compared it to the Wailing Wall in Jerusalem. At both places, notes are left—slipped into crevices to try and reach the unreachable. Parts of old uniforms and dog tags are left at the Vietnam Memorial. So are even more personal items—a six-pack of beer with one can missing, a deck of cards, two cans of sardines, a pair of black lace panties. Their significance is known only to the visitor and to one of the 58,183 names on the wall.

Park rangers here are accustomed to dealing with emotional distress. It is a rare visitor who does not cry. And its visitors include both those who marched against the war and those who fought it. Roger Kennedy referred to the wall as a "sacred precinct." It is also the most visited site in Washington.

■ **LOCATION:** Near the Lincoln Memorial between the Reflecting Pool and Constitution Avenue. ■ **HOURS:** Always open. ■ **ADMISSION:** Free ■ **TELEPHONE:** (202) 619-7222

ALABAMA

ARKANSAS

FLORIDA

GEORGIA

KENTUCKY

LOUISIANA

MISSISSIPPI

NORTH CAROLINA

SOUTH CAROLINA

TENNESSEE

VIRGINIA

On February 20, 1962, the Atlas rocket carrying astronaut John Glenn in his Mercury capsule, leaves the launch pad at Cape Canaveral *(AP/Wide World Photos)*. *See* page 93.

SOUTHEAST

ALABAMA
1 Tuxedo Junction, Birmingham
2 W. C. Handy Birthplace, Florence
3 Space and Rocket Center, Huntsville
4 Paul "Bear" Bryant Museum, Tuscaloosa
5 Helen Keller Shrine, Tuscumbia

ARKANSAS
6 Carry Nation House, Eureka Springs
7 Dogpatch USA, Harrison
8 Daisy Air Gun Museum, Rogers

FLORIDA
9 International Museum of Cartoon Art, Boca Raton
10 Kennedy Space Center, Cape Canaveral
11 The Beach, Daytona Beach
12 Hialeah Park Racetrack, Hialeah
13 *The African Queen*, Key Largo
14 Ernest Hemingway Home, Key West
15 Walt Disney World (and EPCOT), Lake Buena Vista
16 Seaquarium, Miami
17 Art Deco District, Miami Beach
18 Fontainbleau Hotel, Miami Beach
19 Museum of Drag Racing, Ocala
20 Gator Land, Orlando
21 Sea World, Orlando
22 Mirror Lake Shuffleboard Club, St. Petersburg
23 Busch Gardens, Tampa
24 Cypress Gardens, Winter Haven

GEORGIA
25 CNN Studio Tour, Atlanta
26 Stone Mountain, Atlanta
27 World of Coca-Cola, Atlanta
28 Uncle Remus Museum, Eatonton
29 Juliette Gordon Low House and Girl Scout Memorial, Savannah

KENTUCKY
30 Corvette Plant Tours, Bowling Green
31 Man O' War Memorial, Lexington
32 Col. Harland Sanders Museum, Louisville
33 Kentucky Derby Museum, Louisville

LOUISIANA
34 McIlhenny Company, Avery Island
35 Bonnie and Clyde Death Site, Gibsland
36 Antoine's Restaurant, New Orleans
37 Bourbon Street, New Orleans
38 Jazz Museum and Mardi Gras Museum, New Orleans
39 Preservation Hall, New Orleans

MISSISSIPPI
40 Delta Blues Museum, Clarksdale
41 Billie Joe's Tallahatchee Bridge, Greenwood
42 Jimmie Rodgers Memorial, Meridian
43 Elvis Presley Birthplace, Tupelo
44 Casey Jones Museum, Vaughn

NORTH CAROLINA
45 *Bull Durham* Park, Durham
46 Furniture Discovery Center, High Point
47 Brown Mountain Lights, Linnville
48 Andy Griffith's "Mayberry," Mt. Airy
49 PGA Golf Hall of Fame, Pinehurst
50 Richard Petty Museum, Randleman
51 Ava Gardner Museum, Smithfield
52 R.J. Reynolds Tobacco Co., Winston-Salem

SOUTH CAROLINA
53 Catfish Row, Charleston
54 Stock Car Hall of Fame and Museum, Darlington
55 U.S. Marine Corps Museum, Parris Island

TENNESSEE
56 Chattanooga Choo-Choo, Chattanooga
57 Rock City, Chattanooga
58 Scopes Trial Courthouse Museum, Dayton
59 Alex Haley House, Henning
60 Loretta Lynn Museum, Hurricane Mills
61 Casey Jones Home and Museum, Jackson
62 Beale Street, Memphis
63 Danny Thomas Pavilion at St. Jude's Hospital, Memphis
64 Graceland and Elvis Up Close, Memphis

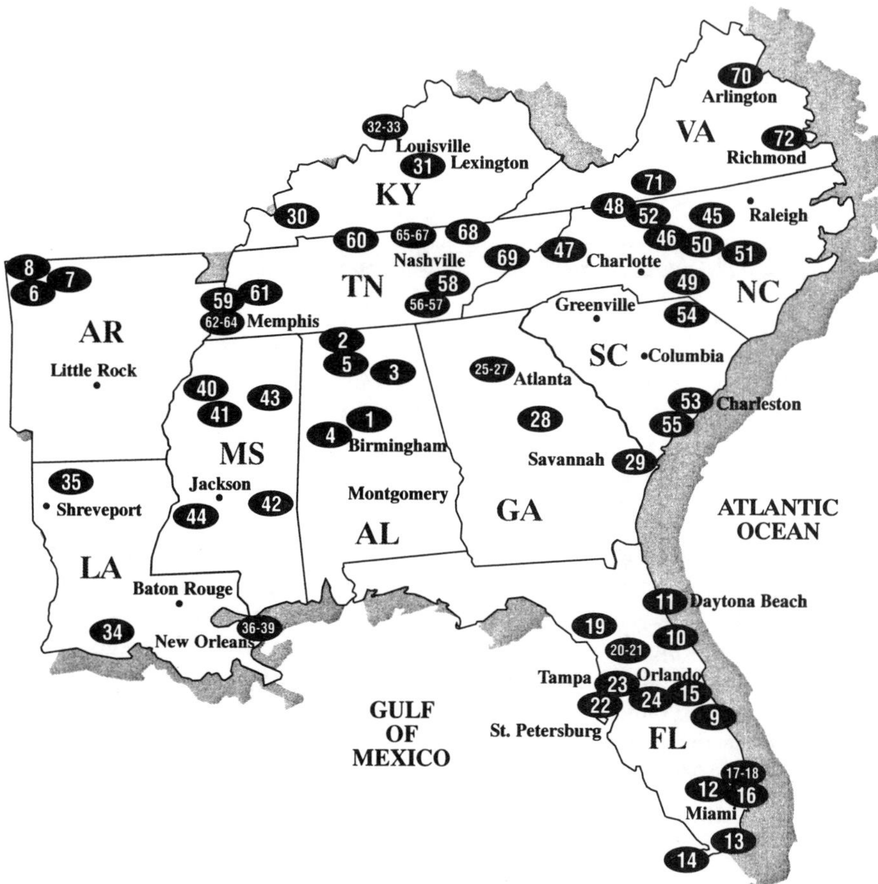

65 Country Music Hall of Fame, Nashville

66 Opryland USA, Nashville

67 Ryman Auditorium, Nashville

68 Sergeant York Memorial Park, Pall Mall

69 Dollywood, Pigeon Forge

VIRGINIA

70 Marine Corps War Memorial, Arlington

71 Wreck of the *Old '97* Memorial, Danville

72 Staircase of the Jefferson Hotel, Richmond

ALabamA

BIRMINGHAM

TUXEDo JUNCTION

One of the classic hits of the Big Band Era was the Glenn Miller recording of "Tuxedo Junction." But not many of the dancers who swung to its lilting beat knew that the song was about an actual placer—a dance hall where the trolley tracks met in Birmingham.

Tuxedo Park was a black community on the west side of this city. The F. N. Nixon Building was built there, at the trolley crossing, in 1922. When a second-floor dance hall was added to the office building it became a favorite stopover for jazz musicians. Among those who hung out at the junction was Erskine Hawkins. Born in Birmingham, this trumpet player fronted his own big band in the 1930s and he penned "Tuxedo Junction" for his own band. Because only the most famous black bands could get network radio air play then he sold the rights to Glenn Miller. Miller's rendition made it one of the Hit Parade's top songs of 1940.

It hasn't been used for dances in many years, but Tuxedo Junction still stands. It now houses a dental clinic. A historic marker attesting to the building's musical past is on the front.

■ **LOCATION:** Tuxedo Junction is at 1728 20th Street. It is immediately north of the 20th-Street Exit of Interstate 20, west of downtown.

FLORENCE

W. C. HANDY BIRTHpLACE

Maybe W. C. Handy didn't invent jazz. A new musical form, after all, is never developed by one person but instead seems to gather in music that is already in the air and present it in a fresh way. There was lots of music in the air in the South at the turn of the twentieth century. The blues. The ragged meter of ragtime. Gospel. Chants that traced their origins to Africa. Handy heard them all, growing up as the son and grandson of ministers in this Alabama river town.

Despite the disapproval of his father, Handy learned to play the cornet while getting a teaching degree. He then left home to wander the South with his brass band for thirteen years, finally settling in Memphis around 1905. While living there, he wrote a campaign song for the city's political boss, Edward H. Crump. Handy would say later that it was the first formally composed tune to incorporate jazz breaks—pauses in the musical line that demand solo improvisation to fill them in. Retitled "Memphis Blues," it is recognized as the earliest example of the music that would come to be known as jazz.

Handy's best-known composition, written about a decade later, was "St. Louis Blues." Breaking out of the traditional blues framework, part of it was written as a tango and part of it borrowed from a church chant he had heard while growing up in Florence. (It is the section that begins: "Got the St. Louie Blues, just as blue as I can be.") Handy formed his own publishing company for this song and it made him a wealthy man: "St. Louis Blues" is one of the most frequently recorded songs in the history of popular music. Handy lived long enough to play it at President Eisenhower's first inaugural in 1953. Handy's life was portrayed on the screen, with a fellow Alabaman, Nat Cole, in the lead.

After his death, in 1958, Handy's heirs donated his personal memorabilia to this museum. His log cabin birthplace, acquired for just this purpose and then stored away, became a museum of his life and work. You can see the piano on which he composed "St. Louis Blues," his cornet, annotated musical scores, and other mementoes of his long life.

■ **LOCATION:** The birthplace is just west of downtown Florence, at 620 West College Street, just off U.S. 72. ■ **HOURS:** Tuesday through Saturday, 9–12 and 1–4. ■ **ADMISSION:** $1.50 ■ **TELEPHONE:** (205) 766-7642

HUNTSVILLE

SPACE AND ROCKET CENTER

In the final days of World War II, American and Russian military units were closing in on the German rocket center at Peenemunde. Its thirty-three-year old technical director, Wernher von Braun, was the mastermind behind the German V-2 project, which, in the first instance of missile warfare had rained rockets and terror on England. In a decision that helped shape the postwar world, von Braun fled west, taking his team of 118 engineers to the American lines.

Regarded as one of the major prizes of the war, von Braun's team was the greatest collection of rocket expertise in the world. The group was first sent to Fort Bliss, Texas, to help the U.S. Army develop its own version of the V-2. In 1950,

Before a group of German scientists arrived in 1949 to work on the moonshot program, Huntsville was a cotton market town. *(AP/Wide World Photos)*

the team found a permanent home at the Redstone Arsenal in Huntsville. In the next decade, it did the research that enabled the United States to overcome Russia's early advantage in the space race. The Jupiter C rocket von Braun developed put the first American astronauts in orbit. It led to the Saturn 5, the rocket that enabled a manned spacecraft to escape Earth's gravity and land on the moon. Von Braun eventually became assistant director of planning for the National Aeronautics and Space Administration (NASA).

Although von Braun became a U.S. citizen in 1955, there were always those who were uncomfortable with scientists who were once employed by the Nazis working for the U.S. He became the model for the fictitious Dr. Strangelove, the classic, dark comic portrait of the scientist who told us to stop worrying and love the Bomb. In reality, von Braun was a deeply religious man, whose family belonged to the Prussian aristocracy and encouraged his scientific interests. "I didn't get a watch and a pair of long pants for my confirmation like most Lutheran boys," he recalled, "I got a telescope." In a 1960 magazine article, he inferred the existence of an afterlife from the scientific principle that matter cannot be destroyed, only transformed. He died in 1977.

His former laboratories have grown into a top space-age attraction, a measure of the deep influence space flight has on popular culture. Visitors can experience the sounds and gravity forces of the Apollo flights and the space shuttle.

This is also the setting for Space Camp, to which hundreds of talented kids come each year to learn about rocket physics. (It is a major training center for authentic space flights as well.) There are more than sixty hands-on exhibits and the Spacedome Theatre features simulated flights on a sixty-seven-foot screen. There are also bus tours of the adjacent NASA Marshall Space Flight Center.

■ **LOCATION:** The Center is located at One Tranquility Base, 15 miles east of Interstate 65, by way of Alabama 20. ■ **HOURS:** Daily, 9–6; 8–7, during summer months. ■ **ADMISSION:** $7.50 ■ **TELEPHONE:** (205) 837-3400

TUSCALOOSA

PAUL "BEAR" BRYANT MUSEUM

For more than two decades, he was college football. No coach ever won more games at the Division 1-A level. Bear Bryant came to stand for more than that in Alabama and throughout the South. When the state's national reputation sunk during the violence of the civil rights years, it was Bryant's University of Alabama teams that managed to restore a measure of self-respect. The Crimson Tide became a regional cult and Bryant a genuine southern hero. He was criticized in later years for not taking advantage of his tremendous popularity and saying more to oppose the Klan and the other forces of segregation. But when Bryant's teams were finally integrated and went on winning national championships, the cause of racial understanding took a step forward.

Bryant won his nickname when he wrestled a bear at a county fair in his hometown of Kingsland, Arkansas. After playing at Alabama, he went on to coach, leading teams at Kentucky and Texas A&M to conference championships and bowl victories. In 1958, as he put it, "Mother called" and he returned to Alabama. He would remain there for the next quarter-century, winning five national championships and building the most honored football program in the country.

"He can take his'n and beat your'n" said one coaching rival in assessing Bryant's talents, "and then take your'n and beat his'n." His teams played with disciplined ferocity, as Bryant preferred smaller, quicker players to brute force. After twenty years, even as the whispers grew that the game had passed him by, he won his final national championship in 1978 with an 11–1 record.

"I always thought of him as The Man," said Grambling State University coach Eddie Robinson, who broke Bryant's mark for total career victories. "To me, he was the John Wayne of football." With his trademark checkered porkpie hat and bass voice, Bryant was a singular presence, and at his retirement, following the 1982 season, he was regarded as one of the most beloved figures in American sports. He died one month after stepping down as Alabama coach, his energy spent with his retirement.

The Paul Bryant Museum is on the Alabama campus. Besides displaying memorabilia of his career, there are also exhibits about Alabama football dating back to 1892. Visitors can also enter a simulated press box, put on a set of earphones, and listen to great plays from the team's past.

■ **LOCATION:** The museum is located at 300 Paul W. Bryant Drive, on the Tuscaloosa campus. ■ **HOURS:** Tuesday through Saturday, 10–4; Sunday, 2–5. ■ **ADMISSION:** $2.50 ■ **TELEPHONE:** (205) 348-4668

TUSCUMBIA

HELEN KELLER SHRINE

This is where the miracle happened. Ivy Green was the home in which Helen Keller grew up and it was here that Anne Sullivan came to teach the blind and deaf child to communicate, starting her off on one of the most inspiring careers of the century. This house was the setting for the celebrated play *The Miracle Worker,* which opened in 1959 and later became a movie.

Stricken with typhoid fever at the age of nineteen months, Keller lost both sight and hearing. Her childhood was spent in a world of complete isolation, "a wild and unruly child" by her own description, unable to make the slightest connection with the external world. Her parents read about Miss Sullivan's work with handicapped children and brought her to Ivy Green in 1887. The long, sometimes brutal battle with her teacher culminated in Keller's comprehending the relationship between words and objects. The word that made the connection was water.

"As the cool stream gushed over one hand," Keller wrote later, "she spelled into the other the word 'water,' first slowly, then rapidly. I stood still, my whole attention fixed upon the motions of her fingers. Suddenly, I felt a misty consciousness as of something forgotten—a thrill of returning thought; and somehow the mystery of language was revealed to me."

She went on to graduate magna cum laude from Radcliffe College and begin her career working for greater opportunities for the blind and for peace. *The Story of My Life* was published while she was still in college. The book brought her to national attention, a place she occupied the rest of her life. She was a tireless traveler and lecturer and was awarded the Presidential Medal of Freedom in 1964, four years before her death.

The cottage at Ivy Green contains many of her personal belongings, including her library and braille typewriter. Visitors can also see the pump at which she first learned the meaning of water. The house itself was built in 1820 by Keller's grandfather. Productions of *The Miracle Worker* are staged here on Friday and Saturday nights during the summer months.

■ **LOCATION:** Tuscumbia is about 6 miles from Florence, on the south side of the Alabama River. Ivy Green is at 300 West North Commons. ■ **HOURS:** Monday through Saturday, 8:30–4; Sunday, 1–4. ■ **ADMISSION:** $2.50 ■ **TELEPHONE:** (205) 383-4066

EUREKA SPRINGS

CARRY NATION HOUSe

Carry Nation's career as a crusader against rum lasted only twelve years. She never lived to see the adoption of Prohibition and its subsequent repudiation. But she made a lasting impression. Dressed in black and wielding a hatchet, she became the very image of the Temperance zealot in the early years of the twentieth century.

She started her campaign in her adopted hometown of Medicine Lodge, Kansas. In the summer of 1899, she and several associates gathered in front of one of the town's saloons. She preached and her friends sang "Those Who Tarry at the Wine Cup." Then she moved toward the saloon, clutching an umbrella. But the proprietor who had been watching all this quickly locked and bolted the door. It was after this frustrating experience that she switched to a hatchet and went national. She referred to herself as the John Brown of Prohibition and felt the violent destruction of saloons and their stock was a justifiable act.

She moved to Eureka Springs in 1908, establishing a home for the families of alcoholics. Although she is regarded as an object of fun-making today, alcoholism was in many ways a more serious social problem in those times: There were no public education campaigns about the dangers of drinking, no medical studies on its hazards to health, and since women had very few legal rights in the face of abusive husbands, the social costs were enormous. Moreover, many men were encouraged to drink on the job and the rate of industrial accidents was horrific.

Carry Nation intended to found a temperance college in this town, but death ended her crusade in 1911. But her spirit of religiosity still pervades Eureka Springs. A remarkably preserved Victorian resort, clinging to the side of the Ozark foothills, it is the site of the American *Passion Play:* The Christ of the Ozarks, a carving that stands on a hilltop outside of town with arms outspread, can be seen across the entire area.

■ **LOCATION:** Eureka Springs is about 50 miles northeast of Fayetteville by way of U.S. 71 and U.S. 62. The Carry Nation House is at 35 Steele Street. ■ **HOURS:** Daily, 10–4, April to October. ■ **ADMISSION:** $2.50 ■ **TELEPHONE:** (501) 253-7324

HARRISON

DOGPATCH USA

For forty-three years, Al Capp worked to expand the newspaper comic strip into a social force. At its peak, the adventures of his hero, L'il Abner, were circulated in nine hundred papers. They were made into a Broadway musical and then into a movie. More important, the characters Capp created and plunked down in the village of Dogpatch, a mythical hamlet somewhere in the southern hills, became national symbols. Pipe-smoking Mammy Yokum. The fearsome Earthquake McGoon. The windy politician, Senator Jack S. Phogbound. The little guy with the eternal black cloud hovering over his head, Joe Btsfplk. The strange little animal called the Schmoo.

Critics said that he had the surest ear for inventing names since Charles Dickens. His satire was also compared to Jonathan Swift, although *Time* magazine cuttingly referred to his work as "Rabelais for the retarded." He began drawing the strip in 1934. "My ambition was not to change the world but to eat regularly," he said. "That may have colored my whole political attitude for the next 30, 40 years."

Known as a political liberal, his attitude changed during the era of Vietnam protests. Put off by the tactics of the New Left, he drew a show business protester named Joanie Phoney, modeled after singer Joan Baez. He created an organization called SWINE (Students Wildly Indignant about Nearly Everything). The strip became bitter. Newspapers dropped it and student hecklers disrupted his personal appearances. He decided to cut it off in 1977. He died two years later.

"Guys are going to be stealing from Capp until the cows come home," eulogized fellow cartoonist Dik Browne ("Hi & Lois" and "Hagar the Horrible"). "He created some characters that will go down in the history of our times," added Charles Addams ("The Addams Family" creator).

That the area he parodied saluted him by creating a park populated with the characters he drew is a measure of Capp's popularity. He never identified the specific location of Dogpatch, so the Arkansas Ozarks are as good a place as any. There is a small railroad in this park, a petting zoo, crafts demonstrations and characters dressed up as the immortal citizens of Dogpatch.

■ **LOCATION:** Dogpatch USA is on Arkansas 7, the scenic highway through Ozark National Forest, 13 miles south of Harrison and the junction of U.S. 62, 65, and 412. ■ **HOURS:** Daily, 9–6, Memorial Day to Labor Day; Saturday only, May and September. ■ **ADMISSION:** $11.95 ■ **TELEPHONE:** (501) 743-1111

DAISY AIR GUN MUSeUM

For more than a century, it was probably the gift more little boys prayed for at Christmas than any other. The Daisy air rifle, or in ruder terms, the B-B Gun, was a coming-of-age present. Advertised universally on the back page of the most popular comic books of the 1940s and 1950s, the Daisy was a fantasy weapon in a far more innocent age. Humorist Jean Shepherd constructed the plot of the film, *A Christmas Story,* about his own longing for such a gun, and his mother's implacable resistance with the warning: "You'll put your eye out."

Daisy was first established in Plymouth, Michigan, in 1887 as a manufacturer of farm implements. It also turned out the air rifle as a novelty item, a giveaway for good customers. But its top salesman, Charles H. Bennett, noted that the demand for the gun was greater than any other product. Within one year, Daisy dropped farm implements and made only B-B guns. Bennett, an astute man, later became president of the company and used much of his income to become an early stockholder in the Ford Motor Company.

Daisy moved to Arkansas in 1957 and continues to turn out the rifles there. The museum has the world's largest collection of non-powder guns, including pneumatic rifles and those that work on a bellows principle. There are also displays on the history of Daisy.

■ **LOCATION:** Rogers is about 20 miles north of Fayetteville, on U.S. 71. The museum is located 1 mile south of town at 2111 South 8th Street. ■ **HOURS:** Monday through Friday, 9–4. ■ **ADMISSION:** Free ■ **TELEPHONE:** (501) 636-1200

FLORIDA

BOCA RATON

INTERNATIONAL MUSEUM OF CARTOON ART

The cartoon has served almost every function imaginable in American culture—from a political weapon that brought down kingmakers to a money machine that built its own Magic Kingdom. The cartoon was an essential feature of the circulation wars that shaped American newspapers in the early twentieth century. In fact, the term "yellow journalism" originated with that era's popular comic strip, "The Yellow Kid." Even in more recent times, a paper that bought the rights to a strip like "Peanuts" felt it was getting a huge advantage over its competition. Repeated reader surveys indicate that comics are one of the major reasons consumers buy a particular newspaper.

The first movie cartoon, "Gertie, the Dinosaur," appeared in 1909. Two years later, Winsor McCay turned his newspaper feature, "Little Nemo," into the movies' first big animated hit. By the 1920s, the cartoon was a familiar part of every movie program. At least two animated stars, Betty Boop and Felix the Cat, were national celebrities. They were also the first cartoons to be drawn on cels, sheets that were lain over pre-drawn backgrounds, which sped the process and enabled the features to run longer. Then came Mickey Mouse in 1928 (*see* Anaheim, California) and cartoons moved into a new dimension.

The political cartoon reached the height of its influence in nineteenth-century New York, when the pen of Thomas Nast toppled Tammany Hall and undid powerful Boss Tweed: Nast's biting and witty cartoons had depicted Tweed and his political machine as a source of graft and corruption. But even in contemporary times, one well-placed cartoon can have powerful echoes. When the *Washington Post's* Herblock drew Barry Goldwater scolding a beggar by saying "If you had any gumption you'd go out and inherit a department store," the laughter effectively stifled the Arizona senator's 1964 run for the presidency. Similarly, the devastating caricatures of a dark-stubbled, sinister-looking Richard Nixon were a powerful force in turning public opinion against him during the mid-1970s.

All these styles of cartoons will be displayed at this new facility, the largest of its kind in the world. For twenty years the museum was located in Rye

Brook, New York, but outgrew its quarters in the late 1980s. Its new home is scheduled to open here in 1995. The galleries will feature original drawings, a cartoonist hall of fame, displays on censorship and freedom of the press, a Toon Town that recreates the sets of famous movie features, and a simulated artist's studio.

■ **LOCATION:** Located in central Boca Raton, in Mizner Park, at 200 Plaza Real. ■ **HOURS:** Call for information. A visitor's center will be open Thursday through Sunday, 1–6, prior to the formal dedication of the museum. ■ **ADMISSION:** A donation is asked. ■ **TELEPHONE:** (407) 361-2090

CAPE CANAVERAL

KENNEDY SPACE CENTER

The place was so remote that when nineteenth-century writer Jules Verne needed a dot on the map for the site of a fictional moon launch he chose Cape Canaveral. Almost a century later the U.S. Defense Department picked the same place for its top secret missile center, and for almost the same reason: It was as out of the way as one could get. When the government quietly began buying up land here in the mid-1950s, the cape was scrub and sand, little changed from the time when Ponce de Leon first saw it in 1513. A tiny land boom during the 1920s had petered out. "Cape Canaveral a Desolate Site," read *The New York Times* headline when reporters were first shown the facility in 1958.

Within months, however, Cape Canaveral had turned into one of the most familiar datelines in the news. More than that, it had become the focus of national pride. The country was trying to rally from the shock of finding itself behind the Soviet Union in the space race. The 1957 launch of *Sputnik,* the first orbiting satellite, staggered America like few events in history. The country feared that Russian control of space would mean their domination on Earth. So Americans had a rooting interest in what they read about and saw at the cape. Television audiences grew familiar with the awesome sight of giant rockets blasting off in a shower of orange flame. We learned the argot of the astronauts. Phrases like "A-OK" and "all systems go" entered the language. Even a veteran newsman like Walter Cronkite could send the big birds up with a heartfelt "Go, baby, go."

Tourists flocked to nearby beaches to observe the historic launches. Alan Shepherd's suborbital ride in 1961 was followed a year later by John Glenn's flight into orbit. In 1969 man walked on the moon. Meanwhile, a Space Age boomtown took shape around the base, whole communities springing out of the ground to serve this high-tech installation.

Now the first flush of space exploration has passed and NASA must struggle for funding like any other federal agency. But the Kennedy Space Center is still one of the symbols of the century's second half. The entire cape was renamed for President John F. Kennedy a few weeks after his assassination. But it was changed back to Canaveral in 1972 upon local request, with the Kennedy designation limited to the space installation itself.

Much of the cape is now a national seashore, with a vast assortment of protected wildlife within its boundaries. But most visitors to the area come to see the Space Center. Tours of the complex begin at Spaceport USA, where tickets for two different two-hour bus trips can be purchased. Areas are open to tourists depending on what operations are in process at the center. (Complete descriptions are available the day of your visit.) Spaceport USA also includes exhibits on the history of the space program, moon rocks, an IMAX Theatre film that features footage shot from space, and displays on the adjacent wildlife refuge. The Astronauts Memorial, a tribute to those who died while serving in the space program, is nearby.

■ **LOCATION:** Spaceport USA and the Kennedy Space Center tours can be reached from Interstate 95 by taking eastbound Florida 405. ■ **HOURS:** Daily, 9–dusk. The tours start at 9:45, the final one leaving two hours before dusk. Make a reservation as soon as you arrive at Spaceport. ■ **ADMISSION:** Spaceport is free. The tours cost $6. IMAX Theatre is $2.75. ■ **TELEPHONE:** (407) 452-2121

DAYTONA BEACH

THE BeACH

Florida was built on its beaches—hundreds of them—down the warm Atlantic and Gulf coastlines and across the Panhandle. But even amid this plenitude of sand, Daytona Beach is unique. It was the "Birthplace of Speed" in the early years of this century. More recently, it has become the "Spring Break Capital of America."

The railroad arrived here in 1888, pushing steadily south down the Florida coast. With it came the first swarm of sun-seekers, the first tourists to discover the hard-packed sand that turned this beach into a Florida landmark.

Fourteen years later, two pioneer automakers were vacationing in the area. Ransom Olds was proud of the cars he built in Michigan, but he met his match in Alexander Winton of Cleveland. A winter-long argument about the merits of their vehicles ended in an agreement to race the following year. In 1903, a one-mile track was laid out on the beach. The two cars finished in a dead heat and the drivers agreed on a rematch.

Winton showed up with Barney Oldfield, the first professional race car driver. Oldfield got the Winton up to 68.19 miles an hour, a new speed record, and so Daytona's legendary races began. The next year, Henry Ford got into the act and several European manufacturers sent race teams, too. The track was extended to twelve miles, using the beach and a blacktop road behind it. In 1928, Malcolm Campbell raced across the sand at 206.95 miles an hour, a land speed record. The racers eventually left for the Bonneville Salt Flats, in Utah, where the sand is just as hard and there is no high tide.

The last auto race on the sand was held in 1958: The crowds had become unmanageable and it was decided to build a permanent oval track inland. The Daytona International Speedway, opened in 1959, has become one of stock car racing's top venues and has kept Daytona at the center of the speed world.

In 1962, the spring break invasion hit the beach. For many years the greatest concentration had been in Fort Lauderdale, the setting for the early fun-in-the-sun flick *Where the Boys Are.* In the 1980s, south Florida decided to change its image and began discouraging the students from showing up. So Daytona became the preferred destination. But the crush of young bodies and their semi-riotous party atmosphere led local residents to complain, especially in 1989 when the annual visitation reached four hundred thousand students. Panama City has taken up much of the slack and Daytona has scaled back to more manageable numbers, although it remains the preferred spring break spot among Canadian students.

Cars are allowed on the beach at Daytona, although the speed limit is ten miles an hour. That may not be the most pleasing arrangement, but it keeps Daytona in touch with its past.

■ **LOCATION:** Daytona Beach runs for about 23 miles, and driving is permitted between Ormond Beach and Ponce de Leon Inlet. ■ **ADMISSION:** The daily toll is $3.

HERNANDO

TED WILLIAMS MUSEUM

His ambition was simple. "When I walk down the street," he once said, "I want people to say: 'There goes the greatest hitter who ever lived.'" If he didn't accomplish that goal, he came very, very close. And if it were not for a couple of wars, there probably wouldn't even be a question about his claim.

Ted Williams joined the Boston Red Sox in 1939 and when he left twenty-one years later, after hitting a home run in his last time at bat, he had stepped across the threshold of legend. He is sixth on the all-time list for lifetime batting average and fourth in home-run frequency. No other player, not even Babe Ruth, could match that combination of consistency and power. Five seasons at the peak of Williams's career were lost to military service in World War II and Korea. Otherwise, he almost certainly would have been among the career leaders in every significant batting category. As it is, his .406 average in 1941 still stands as the last crossing of that hitting divide.

Yet Williams's relationship with the public was often thorny, sharpened by a relentlessly critical Boston media. He was knocked for playing on just one pennant-winning team, although two of his Red Sox teams were eliminated on the very last day of the season. The media found fault in Williams's obsessive approach to hitting, his average defensive skills, even his refusal to wear a tie for any reason. Nevertheless, the record speaks for itself. Williams had remarkable physical gifts, including the most extraordinary eyesight that military examiners had encountered. Added to that was a flawless memory for detail and an analytical approach to hitting that reduced it to a science.

After his retirement from the game, Williams approached sport fishing (especially for Florida bonefish) with the same sort of zeal. The museum is devoted to his careers as both a hitter and a fisherman. Its displays may well make you believe that if he had really put his mind to it, people passing him on the street now would say: "There goes the greatest fisherman who ever lived."

■ **LOCATION:** Hernando is about 75 miles north of Tampa, by way of Interstate 75 and U.S. 41. The museum is located at 2455 North Citrus Hill Boulevard. ■ **HOURS:** Daily, 10–4. ■ **ADMISSION:** $1 ■ **TELEPHONE:** (904) 527-6566

HIALEAH

HIALEAH PARK RACETRACK

By what inspiration Joe Smoot, the founder of Hialeah Park, hit upon flamingos is now unknown. But in 1931 when the track opened, Smoot brought three hundred of the pink birds from Cuba and distributed them around the infield at the racetrack. They quickly became the signature of Hialeah, the very symbol of thoroughbred racing in Florida. The flamingos established the identity of the place.

Smoot also brought in royal palms from Cuba and the everglades, which still line the entry drive. Purple bougainvillea is draped across the grandstand, and the lawns and shrubs are tended as meticulously as any garden. Even those with no interest in racing know about the flamingos and that's what they come here to see. Accordingly, the Flamingo Stakes, a leading event for three-year-olds, is the major race at the track.

■ **LOCATION:** Hialeah is northwest of Miami. Take the westbound 79th Street exit of Interstate 95. The name changes to 25th Street when it enters

Hialeah and the street runs to the track entrance. ■ **HOURS:** Monday through Friday, 9–5, when there is no racing. ■ **ADMISSION:** Free on non-race days. ■ **TELEPHONE:** (305) 885-8000

KEY LARGO

THE AfRICAN QUEEN

In 1952, he won an Academy Award for his portrayal of the profane, boozing riverboat captain in the adventure film, *African Queen.* But four years before that, Humphrey Bogart had turned in another of his career-defining performances in *Key Largo.* He played a disillusioned World War II GI who finds evil as great as that he had fought against during the war when a gangster takes over a resort hotel where he is staying in the Florida Keys. Oddly enough, the two films have come together in this Florida town.

African Queen was actually filmed in Africa under rather difficult conditions. The project, under the direction of John Huston, was later the subject of a best-selling book, *White Hunter, Black Heart.* The title referred to Huston's dictatorial methods in getting the movie done. At one point, he even tried to get mosquitoes to attack on cue, although he eventually had to settle for simulating the event by filming tea leaves settling in an aquarium with buzzing noises on the sound track.

The on-film destruction of the boat that gave its name to the movie was done with a scale model. The real vessel was built in England in 1912 and survived the making of the picture. In 1982 James Hendricks spotted the old boat, rotting away at a dock in northern Florida. It was an odd twist of fate, since Hendricks was the owner of the Holiday Inn at Key Largo. He restored the boat, brought it to Key Largo, and here it remains: One Bogart classic wound up berthed at another.

■ **LOCATION:** The Key Largo Holiday Inn is on U.S. 1, 99701 Overseas Highway. ■ **HOURS:** The owner sometimes takes the boat out on tour, so if you want to see the *African Queen,* it's best to check in advance. On some trips, overnight passengers are accepted. ■ **TELEPHONE:** (305) 451-2121

KEY WEST

ERNESt HEMINGWAY hOME

While he was off covering the Spanish Civil War, Ernest Hemingway's second wife, Pauline, decided to build a salt-water swimming pool behind their home. The cement was still wet when he returned to Key West and asked the price. When told it came in at $20,000, the writer took a penny out

When Hemingway lived here, Key West was a remote place. *(AP/Wide World Photos)*

of his pocket and angrily threw it into the cement. "You took every other cent I have; you may as well have that one, too," he sputtered. He calmed down, eventually, but the penny is still there, encased under glass at poolside.

Hemingway lived here off and on from 1931 to 1940, when he was divorced and moved to Havana. Key West was a world's end sort of place in Hemingway's days. The only land connection to the mainland was the railroad and that was taken out by a hurricane in 1935. The city's economy was also devastated by that storm and for years it was one of the poorest communities in the country.

The Overseas Highway was built before World War II and in the 1950s America began to rediscover this town. It seemed to have been built with the word funky in mind. Dozens of artists and writers, some of them with the stature of Tennessee Williams but most of them obscure, flocked to the place. Old houses were restored, shops reopened, and new developments built. Now the old-timers, or "Conchs" as the natives are called, long for the days when the place was remote.

Hemingway's home continues to be among Key West's top attractions. He worked on much of *For Whom the Bell Tolls* here, while his experiences in Spain were fresh. He kept title to the place until his death in 1961 and the grounds are still inhabited by the descendants of his cats. A high wall encloses the premises, although so many local saloons boast hard-drinking Hemingway associations, it's a bit difficult to understand what he wanted to keep private.

Built in 1851, the house was famous even while the author was living there, and more so now that he has entered the realm of American legend.

■ **LOCATION:** The house is at 907 Whitehead Street, one block off Duval Street, in the historic district. ■ **HOURS:** Daily, 9–5. ■ **ADMISSION:** $6 ■ **TELEPHONE:** (305) 294-1575

MEL FISHER MUSEUM

Late in the summer of 1622, the greatest treasure ship in the Spanish fleet set sail from Cuba, on its way back to the homeland. The galleon was loaded with gold and silver bars, jewelry, coins, and precious gems. But in the Florida Keys it ran into a hurricane. The *Nuestra Señora de Atocha* sank to the bottom, carrying forty-seven tons of riches.

In 1985, 363 years later, Mel Fisher found it. The treasure added up to a $400 million, the greatest bonanza of the century. The Key West-based treasure-hunter had been pursuing the myths and tall tales of the Keys for years, convinced that the shipwrecked riches beneath the Gulf of Mexico were within reach of modern technology. There are few topics that spark the popular imagination more than buried treasure. Yarns of pirate booty and Indian hoards long have been a staple of fiction and folklore. The quest for such riches was one of the engines that drove European explorers to America to begin with. Fisher's find in 1985 seemed to be a fulfillment of this tradition.

It actually took Fisher sixteen years to zero in on the *Atocha,* and it cost the lives of his son and daughter-in-law. They first found the wreck in 1975. But while preparing to dive to it, their ship suddenly started filling with water and capsized. Both Dirk Fisher and his wife, Angel, were drowned. Ten years later to the day, Fisher's younger son, Kane, found the *Atocha* once more and took its treasure.

Riches recovered from the wreck are displayed in the museum here, as are exhibits on the techniques of underwater archeology.

■ **LOCATION:** At 200 Greene Street, near the waterfront. ■ **HOURS:** Daily, 10–5. ■ **ADMISSION:** $5 ■ **TELEPHONE:** (305) 294-2633

LAKE BUENA VISTA

WALT DISNEY WORLD

It was once said of Irving Berlin that he had no place in American popular music. He *was* American popular music. You could say the same thing about Walt Disney World's place in American popular culture.... It *is* American popular culture.

The most successful resort ever conceived, the forty-three square miles of Disney World is the country's top tourist destination. Families find every activity and facility they can imagine here—camping, rafting, golf, beaches, luxury hotels,

Disney opened EPCOT, "the thinking man's theme park," in October 1982.
(UPI/Bettmann)

night clubs, breakfast with Donald Duck, fireworks under the stars, thrill rides, educational exhibits, movie sets, shopping. It is the all-purpose vacation stop. People return year after year because nowhere else can they find a place that combines all the things Americans have come to identify with the ideal vacation.

Disney World is also the essential mainstream American experience. The debate over cultural diversity that tears at the real world is marginalized here. This has become the late twentieth-century version of the melting pot, where everything that goes in emerges wearing strictly U.S.A. middle-class values. It confirms what most Americans want to believe their country is all about. It is secure, decent, and fun.

The park opened a generation after Disneyland (*see* Anaheim, California) had reinvented the amusement park. Although Disney conceived the Florida site and was instrumental in its planning, he did not live to see it open in 1971.

The park's secret is in the planning. Land far exceeding the original requirements was purchased quietly and quickly, beginning in the mid-1960s. It gave the Disney organization the chance to build a modular park, adding on as demand warranted growth and new ideas emerged. First was the Magic Kingdom, an expanded version of the California original. Then EPCOT, the science and international travel theme park. Then the MGM Studios addition in 1992. There is also Discovery Island, a zoological park. River Country and Typhoon Lagoon, two water theme parks. Pleasure Island, an entertainment complex. All of them require separate admission, or the purchase of a special passport. The price options are mind-boggling. (Call in advance for a strategy as well as for room and show reservations.)

To paraphrase what philosopher Jacques Barzun said about baseball: He who would understand the American mind had better study Walt Disney World.

■ **LOCATION:** The main entrance is from the U.S. 192 exit of Interstate 4. ■ **HOURS:** They vary with the seasons, but essentially the Magic Kingdom is open daily, 9–6, and EPCOT is open daily, 9–8. ■ **ADMISSION:** The one-day passport, which covers most of the major park attractions, runs $38 for adults at this printing. A five-day passport costs $189.15 (adults); for children 3–9, a one-day passport is $30.60; five-day passport is $151.10. ■ **TELEPHONE:** (407) 824-4321

MIAMI

SEAQUARIUM

If there was ever an individual animal that influenced an entire country to change its mind about a species, it would be Flipper. In the 1960s this dolphin was the star of its own television series, set at the Seaquarium on Key Biscayne. Flipper (whose real name was Susie) was adorable and smart, repeatedly saving the hide of its human friends. The dolphin also helped introduce Americans to the remarkable intelligence and gentleness of these mammals.

The lesson carried over into the following decade when millions of Americans boycotted Japanese tuna products: The Japanese tuna fishermen were accused of carelessly taking in dolphins in their fishnets and slaughtering them. The outrage resulted in pickets, protests, even destruction of property in some cases. Prospective jury members in one California court case were asked if they had ever watched *Flipper* on TV.

There were also several Flipper movies. The dolphin became a cultural icon. Florida researchers found that swimming with the dolphins was excellent therapy for physically and emotionally handicapped children. The reaction even turned many animal lovers against places like the Seaquarium; they argued that no one had the right to hold captive an animal with reasoning so close to that of humans. Nonetheless, the dolphins are still here where they go through their paces daily.

■ **LOCATION:** The Seaquarium is at 4400 Rickenbacker Causeway, Key Biscayne. Take the Causeway exit from Interstate 95. ■ **HOURS:** Daily, 9:30–6:30. ■ **ADMISSION:** $15.95 ■ **TELEPHONE:** (305) 361-5705

MIAMI BEACH

ART DeCO DISTRICT

It was a mangrove swamp, infested with snakes and mosquitoes. Not a promising beginning for a place that for much of the twentieth century was regarded as the most glamorous resort in America.

John S. Collins had intended to turn the area into an avocado plantation. But when that failed, he decided to sink his money into a residential development, and in 1913 he built a bridge across Biscayne Bay from Miami. Still, the place foundered. Then Collins hooked up with Carl Fisher, a promotional wizard from Indianapolis, who magically transformed Miami Beach into a paradise—all through brochures and newspaper ads.

By 1922 the land rush was on, with formerly worthless lots selling for tens of thousands of dollars. Resort hotels were built the entire length of the beachfront. A cycle of real estate boom and bust followed, but for the next forty years Miami Beach basked in an image of winter warmth, glamour, and excitement. Popular entertainers like Arthur Godfrey and Jackie Gleason telecast their variety shows live from the place and enhanced the city's image. A successful television series helped do the same: *Surfside Six* was about a detective working out of a houseboat on a Miami Beach canal.

Then a number of things happened. Vacationers noticed that the early winter climate was not always reliable, just as package tours were bringing the guaranteed warmth of the Caribbean and Mexico within reach of the average

The Carlyle Hotel: One of the Art Deco district's gems. *(AP/Wide World Photos)*

income. Crime increased. The permanent population grew older. The luxury hotels started looking their age. The glamour had faded. By 1970 the place was in economic distress.

It was then that Miami Beach looked around and discovered its past. The hotels that had been built on the southern end of the resort, during its first rush of riches, were a treasure house of Art Deco, an architectural style that had again become fashionable. The city approved a clean-up of the area and private money began to flow in to help restore some of the Deco masterworks. Miami Beach became a favorite spot for fashion shoots and European tourists looking for bargain rates. A hip young crowd moved in, mingling with Hasidic Jews and Hispanics to form one of the most diverse communities in Florida. The pastel buildings turned Ocean Drive, the beachfront thoroughfare, into a showcase. The economic benefits rippled through the rest of the resort, too. While it hasn't quite recaptured the mystique of its glamorous era, Miami Beach has climbed a long way back to its former place as a cultural symbol.

■ **LOCATION:** The Deco District extends from Ocean Drive west to Washington Avenue and between 5th and 16th streets. The Welcome Center, at 661 Washington, has information and guides for walking tours of the district. ■ **TELEPHONE:** (305) 672-2014

FONTAINBLEAU HOTEL

When it opened in 1954 the Fontainbleau was more than hotel. It was the apotheosis of Miami Beach's greatest era, when the resort was the unchallenged queen of winter glamour in America. Its sweeping S-shaped lines, massive open lobby, gardens, pools, and 1,200 guest rooms were built to be the biggest and best.

In Florida's early days, hotels were usually built in a Spanish colonial motif. The railroad magnates and real estate tycoons who created that Florida were eager to tie their developments to the romantic past. Miami Beach couldn't have cared less about the past. It was a playground of plenty for the present. While the resort began as an exclusive and restricted community, by the end of World War II it had developed a predominantly Jewish texture. Those who came here were onetime immigrants who had spent much of their youth in poverty. They had acquired self-made fortunes and were eager to show them off. So the emphasis was on big, bigger, and biggest. The Fontainbleau was the ultimate, the showcase of a generation's psyche.

The $14-million hotel occupied the most desirable lot on Miami Beach—the former estate of tire magnate Harvey Firestone. Its interior design was French Provincial. A $22,000 chandelier blazed in the lobby. Its nightclub, the Boom Boom Room, was a legend in itself. By 1978, however, the Fontainbleau had fallen victim to the general decline of Miami Beach and was taken over by Hilton. With a massive infusion of funds, the place was completely overhauled and once again is rated as a four-star Collins Avenue showcase.

■ **LOCATION:** The Fontainbleau is at Collins Avenue at 44th Street. ■ **TELEPHONE:** (305) 534-7821

OCALA

MUSEUM OF DRAG RACING

From James Dean to Jan and Dean, drag racing was one of the touchstones of the California youth culture of the 1950s. Restless young men, fast cars, and macho challenges on a deserted highway. It was an activity that seemed to symbolize the estrangement between that decade's cautious adult generation and their brooding offspring.

But it was a young man from Florida who took drag racing to new levels as a sport. Don Garlits was born in Tampa and hung around garages in his hometown, picking up invaluable information about cars and what makes them go fast. He was slight, almost sickly as a youth, so the nickname that was hung on him, "Big Daddy," was an inside joke.

When he first went to California to challenge the top dragsters on their own turf they called him Don Garbage. "They were used to those glittering, chrome-plated, technically perfect dragsters of wealthy guys," he recalled in a 1964 interview. "They took one look at my nightmare and they like to roll over laughing. Actually, they didn't get much of a laugh out of it. I cleaned up on them out there, and they went home shaking their heads."

He dominated drag racing throughout the 1960s and 1970s, just as thoroughly as Richard Petty ruled stock cars (*see* Randleman, North Carolina).

Garlits became the first man to break the two-hundred-mile-an-hour barrier in 1972. To prove it was no fluke he went out the following weekend and broke it twice more in one day.

During the peak of his career Garlits moved to Detroit to be near his automotive sponsors. But after his retirement he moved home to Florida. The museum he opened near Ocala is filled with racing memorabilia and examples of car design and engine developments during the last thirty years of the sport.

■ **LOCATION:** The museum is south of Ocala, just off exit 67 of Interstate 75, then south on county road 475A to 13700 Southwest 16th Avenue. ■ **HOURS:** Daily, 9–5:30. ■ **ADMISSION:** $6 ■ **TELEPHONE:** (904) 245-8661

ORLANDO

GATOR LAND

When tourists first started driving to Florida, the trip was as exotic as a voyage to the moon. The visual images of the state had not yet become familiar. First-time visitors were surrounded by strange plants and animals. Everything was new, unpredictable, and unlike anything they had seen back home.

A variety of roadside attractions dedicated to satisfying that curiosity about Florida's oddities, developed along the state's major highways. Many of the attractions prominently featured alligators. The large, menacing reptiles were especially fascinating to tourists, who shivered at the sight. Native Floridians knew, however, that the gators could be handled if properly approached. The spectacle of gator-wrestling became one of Florida's prime roadside attractions. Gator Land is a newer adaptation of this old tourist standby. Since Florida, especially the area around Orlando, is well-trod ground by now, this is a nostalgic look back to how tourism used to be. There are many varieties of reptiles on view here, as well as a Gator Jumperoo show.

■ **LOCATION:** South of the Florida Turnpike exit to the Orange Blossom Trail (U.S. 17, 92, 441); 14501 South Orange Blossom Trail. ■ **HOURS:** Daily, 8–6. ■ **ADMISSION:** $ 8.95 ■ **TELEPHONE:** (407) 855-5496

SEA WORLD

In the wild, they are among nature's most efficient predators. They can be twenty-seven feet long, weigh nine tons, have rows of sharp teeth, and no natural enemies. But at Sea World, Shamu is transformed into a playful star, and the killer whale, or orca, has grown into one of the most lovable and successful corporate symbols around. "Anyone who hasn't heard of Shamu must be living in an igloo," said one park visitor, in a 1989 newspaper feature.

Shamu enjoys a tail rub from an animal behaviorist at Sea World of Florida.
(AP/Wide World Photos)

Shamu is a generic name, applied to the most talented orcas at every Sea World property. Now the giant mammals are even more popular than Flipper, the dolphin who predated them in show business by about two decades (*see* Seaquarium, Miami). The 1993 hit film, *Free Willie,* further enhanced their popularity. Trained orcas have proven to be about as intelligent as dolphins, with equally lovable personalities. In the real world orcas prey on dolphins but at Sea World the two romp together amicably in the giant pools.

The park also features shows that headline penguins, sharks, sea otters, and a variety of other lovable and terrifying aquatic creatures. But it is Shamu who steals the show. Other Sea World properties are in San Diego, California, San Antonio, Texas, and Aurora, Ohio. The Florida operation is the largest and is also the home of orca research center.

■ **LOCATION:** Sea World is near the intersection of Interstate 4 and Florida 528, about 8 miles east of the main Walt Disney World entrance at 7007 Sea World Drive. ■ **HOURS:** Daily, 9–7. ■ **ADMISSION:** $26.95 ■ **TELEPHONE:** (407) 351-3600

The sport at the peak of its popularity: Club champions compete on the special tournament courts at the Shuffleboard Club at Mirror Lake. *(AP/Wide World Photos)*

ST. PETERSBURG

MIRROr LAKE SHUFFLEBOARD CLUB

Around the beginning of the twentieth century, someone made a study of weather records and declared that St. Petersburg was the healthiest spot in America. It had the mildest climate and the highest incidence of sunshine. The study was widely circulated and within a few years, the city had become known as the retirement center of the state. Ring Lardner celebrated the phenomenon in one of his best-known short stories, "The Golden Wedding." The city propagated the image, even placing green park benches everywhere so that older citizens would never lack a place to sit and pass time. In recent years, St. Petersburg has tried to get away from its reputation as "God's Waiting Room." But some of it still hangs on, most notably in the huge shuffleboard club at Mirror Lake Park.

The sport's connection to Florida has been traced back to 1913 in Daytona Beach. A group of fashionable guests, bored with simply sitting around in the sun, decided to mark out a court on the cement walk of the Lynhurst Hotel. The game was a familiar part of ship voyages, especially on British vessels, but no one had thought of adapting it to land. The game quickly developed from its simple aquatic version, which featured a square placed inside an oval, to a more complicated arrowhead design. That shape put a premium on defensive play—setting up shots to impede the opponent and trying to knock him into the negative zone where points are subtracted from his score.

By the 1930s, shuffleboard was identified as the most widely played seniors game in the country and became a Florida signature. These days, however, you are just as likely to find retirees here on the golf courses, the tennis courts, and softball fields. Nevertheless, shuffleboard continues to have dedicated adherents, who are drawn by its minimal physical demands and the emphasis on strategy. Mirror Lake remains the sport's Yankee Stadium, the testing grounds for the best.

■ **LOCATION:** Mirror Lake is directly west of St. Petersburg's bayfront area by way of 2nd Avenue North Mirror Lake Drive encircles the park and signs direct you to the Shuffleboard Club. Daily memberships may be purchased there.

TAMPA

BUSCH GARDENS

What began as a corporate public relations campaign has turned into a highly successful theme park for the nation's largest beer company. Breweries are not regarded as the most aesthetically pleasing neighbor. They are, in essence, large factories. But Anheuser-Busch made the decision to disguise its Tampa facility by surrounding it with a preserve of African wildlife. What a St. Louis-based brewing company has to do with the fauna of the African veldt is a good question. However dubious the connection, the concept works. Outside of the San Diego Zoo's wild animal park (*see* California), this is the best-attended animal attraction in the country.

The brewery is still there; you can even tour it as part of the visit. But one of Florida's largest tourist attractions, with its monorail-encircled animal preserve, camouflages it. There are also thrill rides, ice skating shows, bird and dolphin performances, and a German festhaus.

■ **LOCATION:** Two miles east of Interstate 275, by way of Florida 580 at 3000 Busch Boulevard. ■ **HOURS:** Daily, 9:30–6. ■ **ADMISSION:** $26.45 (call ahead for further pricing information). ■ **TELEPHONE:** (813) 971-8282

WINTER HAVEN

CYPREsS GARDENS

It began as a swamp—towering cypress trees rising from murky waters. But in the early 1930s, the Pope family started a clearing and planting program, turning the area into a 223-acre tropical garden. They built bridges to arch over the streams and dressed up local girls as Southern belles who would wave and twirl their parasols as the tourist boats went by.

Then in 1942 the owners hit upon the attraction that would set Cypress Gardens apart from all its Florida competitors: pretty girls on water skis. According to company lore, the first show attracted eight airmen from the nearby Air Force base in Lakeland. Next day they returned with about five hundred buddies. Since 1946, the shows have gone on four times a day, rain or shine. Even on winter days, when the smudge pots are out to protect the delicate plants, the skiers hit the water to run through their dazzling repertoire. The flag-waving, high-jumping, somersaulting routines have become a top water attraction.

The gardens figured to be the ideal setting for an Esther Williams movie and MGM made one here in 1954. *Easy to Love,* featuring its chorus line of water skiers, was one of the aquatic star's landmark—better make that watermark–hits. Adjacent to Cypress Gardens, is the Water Skiing Museum, where there are historical displays on both the sport and the park.

■ **LOCATION:** Cypress Gardens are just west of U.S. 27 on Florida 540, southeast of Winter Haven. ■ **HOURS:** The gardens are open daily, 9–6; the museum is open Monday through Friday, 10–5. ■ **ADMISSION:** $18.95 at the gardens; donations at the museum. ■ **TELEPHONE:** (813) 324-2111 for the gardens; (813) 324-2472 for the museum.

Georgia

ATLANTA

CNN STUDIO TOUR

When cable television was in its infancy, not many people were sure what the new technology was good for, besides showing movies in their uncensored form. One man who did have a vision of its possibilities was Ted Turner, owner of a tiny UHF station in Atlanta. But when he described his vision, he was laughed at. A 24-hour a day news station. Showing nothing but news during prime time. With hardly any recognizable names or faces at the anchor desk. The three major networks thought this was hilarious, one of the dumbest ideas they had ever heard. Especially coming from a guy whose station aired one ten-minute newscast a day at 3 A.M. only to satisfy federal regulations.

"I was like that skinny little guy in the comic books who gets sand kicked in his face," Turner said in a 1990 interview, marking the tenth anniversary of his Cable News Network (CNN). "I went to bed gritting my teeth. I said "Someday I'm gonna have news."

CNN went on the air in June 1980, beaming its signal to a minuscule 1.7 million households. The following month when the network went to cover the Republican National Convention in Detroit it was given a booth directly above the band. Every time the band started to play, no one could hear a word being said on CNN.

But things improved. By 1990, it had twenty-one bureaus and satellite links that brought it into ninety countries. In much of the world, CNN had become the window on America. People who had never heard of the major U.S. networks tuned in Turner's operation daily, including, claims CNN, Fidel Castro, who uses it as his chief source of information about America.

Then in 1991 it hit the big time. As the Persian Gulf War began, two CNN staffers, trapped in a Baghdad hotel room with missiles and rockets falling all around them, went on the air live. The world sat transfixed as Bernard Shaw and Peter Arnett described the chaos in Iraq's capital. This was CNN's scoop; no other American network had a camera crew or news team in Baghdad at the time. In one night CNN was transformed into a major player among world news organizations, scoring one of the great news beats of all time.

CNN is still headquartered in Atlanta. The tour through its studios has become one of the most popular attractions in Georgia's capital and a fascinating lesson in how news is beamed to a worldwide audience, twenty-four hours a day. It is a much more intimate look at a news operation than anything available at any other television network.

■ **LOCATION:** CNN is located in downtown Atlanta, at Marietta Street and Techwood Drive, adjacent to the Omni sports complex. Take the International Drive exit from Interstate 75 and turn left on Techwood. ■ **HOURS:** Monday through Friday, 10–5; weekends, 10–4. Tours leave on the hour and are limited to 20 people. ■ **ADMISSION:** $5 ■ **TELEPHONE:** (404) 827-2400

STONE MOUNTAIN

This is the Mount Rushmore of the Confederacy, a symbol of both reverence and defiance. In 1916 when the huge sculpture of three mounted figures—General Robert E. Lee, General Stonewall Jackson, and President Jefferson Davis—was commissioned by the United Daughters of the Confederacy, it was intended as a tribute to the southern heroes of the Civil War. But even while this work was going on, it was also used by the Ku Klux Klan for statewide conclaves. And during the era of the civil rights struggle, Stone Mountain once again became a rallying point for those who opposed racial integration.

The bare granite outcropping, rising sheer from the surrounding plain, has inspired deep emotions from prehistoric times. There is evidence that it was the site of religious ceremonies by Native Americans. The 300-million-year-old mountain commands this degree of awe because of its massiveness and isolation, which makes it seem much higher than 825 feet.

The Confederate Memorial took fifty-seven years to complete. Its original sculptor, Gutzon Borglum, withdrew from the project in disgust when a dispute arose among its sponsors over his design. By then, Lee's head had already been unveiled. The final plan does reflect the heroic southern view of the lost conflict. It has become a part of this region's popular culture.

■ **LOCATION:** Stone Mountain is about 19 miles east of downtown Atlanta, by way of Interstate 20 and Memorial Drive (Georgia 154). The memorial is part of a larger park that contains several other attractions, including a skylift, antebellum plantation, and scenic railroad. Best viewpoint for the memorial is from the Memorial Chapel. ■ **HOURS:** Daily, 6 A.M.–midnight. ■ **ADMISSION:** $5 parking fee. Tickets may be purchased individually for each attraction. ■ **TELEPHONE:** (404) 498-5600

WORLD OF COCA-COLA

"A Coke and a Smile." "Things go better with Coca-Cola." "I'd like to teach the world to sing in perfect harmony."

The World of Coca-Cola. *(photograph by Michael Pugh, courtesy of the Coca-Cola Company)*

Is there any product that has so penetrated the world's consciousness as this soft drink? Invented in and still based in Atlanta, it may be the best known made-in-America product on the globe. Its name has become the generic term for a cola drink, so much so that company inspectors tour the country to make sure that people who ask for Coke are not served something else. Its advertising slogans still ring in the ears thirty years after they have fallen out of use. When the company tried to change the taste of the product in 1985, it touched off a consumer rebellion of such ferocity that it was forced to back down, reverting to its "original formula."

It is the ubiquitous drink, found everywhere from European sidewalk cafes to tropical forests where no one would dream of drinking the water. According to company lore, the first glass was sold in 1886 at Jacobs Pharmacy, Atlanta, when the cola syrup was mistakenly mixed with carbonated water. Until then, its benefits were regarded primarily as medicinal. But the dash of soda water changed all that. It is now consumed 448 million times a day in 160 countries.

Dr. John Pemberton created the original formula but sold it to Asa Candler, owner of a pharmaceutical firm. Candler then founded the Coca-Cola Company in 1892 and steadily expanded it to a dominant position in the soft drink industry. But when Robert Woodruff became company president in 1923, Coke became a marketing legend. With his merchandising tie-ins and ad campaigns, his innovative six-pack, and celebrity endorsements, Woodruff built Coca-Cola into a global colossus.

World of Coca-Cola explores the company's history, development, and the artifacts associated with it. Displays inside the three-story building, with a huge neon sign at the entrance, recap ad highlights, take you on a visit to an old-time soda fountain, and even show off Pemberton's original bottle and notebooks. Its gift shop contains a seemingly endless profusion of Coke items.

■ **LOCATION:** World of Coca-Cola is located downtown, at Martin Luther King Drive and Central Avenue, adjacent to Underground Atlanta. ■ **HOURS:** Monday through Saturday, 10–9:30, Sunday, 12–6. ■ **ADMISSION:** $2.50 ■ **TELEPHONE:** (404) 676-5151

EATONTON

UNCLE REMUS MUSEUm

When Joel Chandler Harris was growing up in this Georgia town he was transfixed by the stories told by George Terrell. A former slave, Terrell sold home-baked cookies on market days and with every treat came a story that he had heard as a young boy. They were stories about animals—rabbits and foxes and bears, constantly trying to outwit each other. Of course, in the rabbit's case he was also trying to avoid becoming the main entree at a dinner party for the other two.

When he became an Atlanta journalist, Harris retold these stories, using black dialect and the voice of a character named Uncle Remus. Harris was an advocate of the New South and spoke out for better treatment for African Americans. He urged his readers to put the romanticism of plantation days behind them. Yet, oddly enough, his Uncle Remus stories had the effect of perpetuating the old images he deplored.

The Walt Disney film version of these stories appeared in 1947, under the title *Song of the South.* It brought the adventures of Br'er Rabbit and his pals to a national audience and made them familiar figures in the comic strips, too. The Uncle Remus museum is made up to resemble plantation cabins, in which the boy in Harris's stories first heard the tales. There are paintings of his characters and first editions of many of his books. Eatonton is also the home of Alice Walker, whose novel, *The Color Purple* won the 1983 Pulitzer Prize and was later turned into a hit film.

■ **LOCATION:** Eatonton is about 80 miles southeast of Atlanta by way of Interstate 20 and southbound U.S. 129 and 441. The museum is three blocks south of the courthouse square, in Turner Park. ■ **HOURS:** Monday through Saturday, 10–12 and 1–5, and Sunday, 2–5. Closed Tuesday, Labor Day to May. ■ **ADMISSION:** 75 cents ■ **TELEPHONE:** (404) 485-6731

SAVANNAH

JULIETTE GORDON LOW HOUSE AND GIRL SCOUT MEMORIAL

She was born to rank and wealth, the daughter of Chicago's founding family, the Kinzies. She later became the wife of a wealthy cotton broker, Andrew Low. Juliette Gordon Low grew up in a tightly corseted Victorian world, where little girls were regarded as delicate ornaments. But she loved cooking out, hiking, and working in leather and other crafts. And if she enjoyed it, Mrs. Low reasoned, why wouldn't other girls, too?

Her husband's business took him to England and while living there she became close friends with Sir Robert Baden-Powell, founder of the Boy Scouts. His sister had founded an organization called Girl Guides and their activities fascinated Mrs. Low. With Baden-Powell's encouragement she resolved to start such a group when she returned to America.

On March 9, 1912, the first group of American Girl Guides met in Mrs. Low's living room in Savannah. Within three years, it had grown so rapidly that national headquarters were moved to Washington, D.C., and the name changed to Girl Scouts. The girls promised to do their duty to God and country, help others at all times, and obey the Girl Scout laws. They also learned to climb mountains, repair machinery, treat snakebites and dozens of other things that helped shatter the old gender molds and pave the way for the feminist movement.

Mrs. Low's birthplace is now preserved as a Girl Scout museum. Its displays relate to her life and to the scouting programs. Her residence, known as the Andrew Low House, where the first troop was actually formed, is also open to the public and is regarded as an architectural showplace of Savannah. Built in 1848, it hosted British author William Makepeace Thackery, who did some writing at the desk in the living room, and also Robert E. Lee, who visited in 1870.

■ **LOCATION:** Both houses are in Savannah's historic district. The Juliette Gordon Low Birthplace is at 142 Bull at East Oglethorpe Street. The Andrew Low House is seven blocks north, at the edge of Lafayette Square, at 329 Abercorn Street. ■ **HOURS:** Juliette Low House is open Monday through Saturday (except Wednesday), 10–4, Sunday, 12:30–4:30, February–November. Closed Sunday, rest of the year. The Andrew Low House is open Monday through Saturday (except Thursday), 10:30–4, Sunday, 12–4. ■ **ADMISSION:** $4 to the Juliette Gordon Low House; $3.50 to the Andrew Low House. ■ **TELEPHONE:** (912) 233-4501 for Juliette Gordon Low House; (912) 233-6854 for Andrew Low House.

BOWLING GREEN

CORVETTE PLANT TOURS

There probably has never been another American-made automobile that inspires the emotions a Corvette does in its owners. It is a different kind of car.

"To many men, their Corvette is their most precious possession," said one Michigan automobile restorer, who specializes in this car. "To some, it even comes before their wives." He quickly added, however, that about 5 percent of his business came from women and "they were the sort of people who were liberated long before women's lib became a movement."

Chevrolet was hoping for something like this when it first showed off the Vette at the 1953 General Motors Motorama. It was the pet project of GM's legendary design chief, Harley Earl. But only three hundred were produced in the first year and, according to its designer, Zora Arkus-Dontov, "it was really a dog. It was supposed to be a boulevard car in the mind of GM, but we turned it into a sports car." That's what it has remained, the quintessential American sports car.

While Ford also introduced a two-seater, its Thunderbird, in 1954 it soon became a standard passenger vehicle. But the Corvette, throughout its twenty-nine-year production history in St. Louis and since its move to Kentucky in 1983, has always been a car for serious drivers.

"The Corvette ranks just one notch below immortality on America's list of mechanical achievements," said a 1968 tribute in *Car and Driver Magazine.* "Like barbed wire and the cotton gin, it borrows from no one. The Corvette is exciting, it's lusty, it stimulates all of the base emotion lurking deep in modern man."

These emotions run so deep that lawsuits are filed over the car. One Texas man sued GM in 1986 for making it a convertible again, claiming that when he bought his Corvette convertible in 1975 he was given certified assurance that it would be the last such model. The thirty-fifth anniversary model in 1988 backed up orders to such an extent that disappointed customers had to wait up to a year for delivery.

Still, the Corvette continues to be made slowly, and publicly. Despite the deliberate pace of its assembly line, about one-quarter the speed of standard production models, the company opens its plant to tour groups. Chevy managers feel it enhances the bonding process between the public and the car.

■ **LOCATION:** The plant is off Interstate 65, exit 28, at Louisville Road and Corvette Drive. ■ **HOURS:** Monday through Friday, at 9 and 1. Closed for a month in summer. Dates vary, so call in advance. ■ **ADMISSION:** Free ■ **TELEPHONE:** (502) 745-8000

LEXINGTON

MAN O' WAR MEMORIaL

They called him "Big Red" and those who saw him run swear that there was never another racehorse like Man o' War. He lost just once in twenty-one starts, sired two Kentucky Derby winners among his 256 foals, and won his final match race by seven lengths over the defending Triple Crown champion. When he died in 1947, at the age of thirty, more than three thousand mourners attended his funeral.

He was a big horse, standing sixteen hands and one and five-eighths inches high. He simply ran his rivals into the turf. His only loss, in the Sanford Memorial at Saratoga, was to Upset, a horse he defeated on four other occasions. He won one race by one hundred lengths and three times went off at odds of 1 to 100. Man o' War became one of the first sports heroes of the Jazz Age and the public enthusiastically looked forward to his running in the 1920 Kentucky Derby. But in a mystery that is still unexplained, Sam Riddle, his owner, refused to enter him at Churchill Downs. He went on to win the Preakness and Belmont, the other two parts of racing's Triple Crown. The Derby itself was won by a horse Man o' War would easily outdistance later.

There were several theories why Riddle chose to follow this course, robbing the horse of the ultimate distinction. There apparently were some questions about the purity of his bloodlines. Riddle had bought him at auction at Saratoga for $5,000 and there were reports that his ancestors included plow horses. Riddle heard about this lapse repeatedly from blood-minded Kentuckians and holding him out of the Derby was his way of getting even. There were also reports that the social-minded Riddle was seeking to win favor with the aristocratic Philadelphia families connected with Pimlico, the Preakness track. He would build up their race by taking a pass on the Derby.

Whatever the reason, the disappointed public demanded a match race with Sir Barton, the 1919 Derby winner. Man o' War won easily. When Riddle was told that he subsequently would have to carry handicap weights of 140 pounds, the horse was retired. For years, a statue of Man o' War stood at the grave site, at Faraway Farm, Riddle's spread outside of Lexington. But with the opening of the Kentucky Horse State Park, the grave and statue were moved there, where they greet visitors at the entrance. The inscription on the base of the statue reads: "Contemporary excellence pales before a legend."

■ **LOCATION:** The Kentucky Horse Park is located just north of Lexington, at the Ironworks Pike exit of Interstate 75. ■ **HOURS:** Daily, 9–5, mid-March to October; Wednesday through Sunday, rest of the year. ■ **ADMISSION:** $5.95 (Since the memorial stands outside the park gate, you do not have to buy a park ticket to visit it. But, there is a $1 parking fee.) ■ **TELEPHONE:** (606) 233-4303

LOUISVILLE

COLONeL HARLAND SaNDERS MUSEUm

When he was sixty-six years old, at a time when most Americans are either retired or thinking seriously of becoming so, a new highway came through Corbin, Kentucky, and put Harland Sanders out of business. He had been cooking up chicken in the back of his gas station and cafe for years. He already had been made an honorary colonel for his contributions to Kentucky cuisine. But he wasn't quite ready to pack it in. So in 1956 he hit the road in a ten-year-old Ford, trying to sell fried chicken franchises with his own secret formula.

"Making money when you're my age is no different from making money when you're young," he said later. "You just have to try harder." He took his pressure cooker and tried hard to hit restaurants just after their rush hour. Sanders offered to feed the help if they let him demonstrate how he made his chicken. If they didn't like it, the meal was free. More often, though, he gained a franchise, getting four cents for every chicken the restaurant sold.

In seven years, he had opened six hundred outlets, but the size of the enterprise was "beginning to run right over me and mash me flat." So he sold out for $2 million, but only on the assurance that the new owners wouldn't mess around with his recipe. They not only promised him that, they kept Sanders on the payroll as a roving ambassador. His white goatee and string tie became one of the best known corporate symbols in American history. Sanders's earnest endorsements of his "finger-lickin' good" chicken turned him into a celebrity. When he died at the age of ninety in 1980, a Coca-Cola executive saluted him as "our last living American symbol."

This museum, at the KFC headquarters, traces the history of the chicken empire and also features a taped interview with the Colonel. It should be known, however, that this famed symbol of Kentucky was actually born in Indiana.

■ **LOCATION:** The museum is just west of Interstate 264, exit 15A. ■ **HOURS:** Monday through Thursday, 8:30–4; Friday, 8:30–1. ■ **ADMISSION:** Free ■ **TELEPHONE:** (502) 456-8353

In the home-stretch at the Derby museum at Churchill Downs. *(Courtesy of Kentucky Derby Museum)*

KENTUCKY DERBY MUSEUM

People with no interest at all in horses or the races they run, know the name of this horse race. The Kentucky Derby is a national event. More money is wagered in office pools on this one race and more people will watch it on television, than any other in the country.

So it may startle most people to learn that for the first 40 years of its existence, the Derby was regarded as nothing special. When it began in 1875, and for the rest of the nineteenth century, the American Derby and the Latonia were regarded as far more prestigious. When the great jockey Isaac Murphy won the Derby three times, between 1884 and 1891, it was not regarded as a great achievement. Only much later, when his record was toted up posthumously, did it become one of the cornerstones of his reputation.

The Derby owes much of its prestige to the showmanship of Matt Linn, who directed the race for forty-seven years. He realized that Kentucky was strongly identified in the national mind with horses, yet the state had no nationally-known race. So he began subsidizing sports writers from the large East

Coast dailies to come out to Louisville and Churchill Downs on the first weekend in May, when the mid-South climate was at its peak, and watch the three-year-olds run. He planted the grounds with tulips and other early-spring blooms. He was also an early advocate of the $2 pari-mutuel bet, the attraction that brought the Sport of Kings down to the level of the ordinary racing fan.

In 1913, a long shot named Donerail won the race and paid off at better than 90-to-1. That got the Derby tremendous publicity. But his biggest break came two years later when one of the leading Eastern breeders, Harry Payne Whitney, entered his filly, Regret. She won the race, the only filly to do so until 1980, and again it became a major national story. "I don't care whether she ever wins another race," said an exuberant Whitney. "She's already won the greatest race in the world." That clinched it. From that time on, the Kentucky Derby has been recognized as "the brightest jewel in racing's Triple Crown," as they say on the sports page.

People throng into the city for the annual week-long celebration. Even those who have never been in the state before in their lives, choke up when the band plays "My Old Kentucky Home" during the parade to the post. The museum, on the grounds of Churchill Downs, summarizes the history of the race and the horses and riders who have won. It also features hands-on exhibits and a 360-degree show that places the viewer right down the middle of the homestretch.

■ **LOCATION:** Churchill Downs is at 700 Central Avenue, south of downtown Louisville by way of 3rd Street, or the northbound Southern Parkway exit from Interstate 264. ■ **HOURS:** Daily, 9–5. Closed on Derby Day. ■ **ADMISSION:** $3.50 ■ **TELEPHONE:** (502) 637-1111

LOUISIANA

AVERY ISLAND

McILHENNY COMPANY

Times were hard in the years immediately after the Civil War. Food was sometimes in short supply and what there was of it wasn't very good. At least, not by the exacting standards of Louisiana. It was in the hungry year of 1868 that Edmund McIlhenny, the owner of Avery Island, decided to liven up his bland diet by concocting a new kind of sauce.

Soldiers who had served in the Mexican War years before had returned with a gift for the McIlhennys. It was an especially inflammatory kind of pepper that the Indians in Mexico had called Tabasco. The McIlhennys grew sugar on their island, but they decided to plant the pepper seeds, too, to see what would come up. According to later measures of spiciness, a jalapeño pepper warms things up at the rate of 1,500 Scoville heat units. The Tabasco pepper comes in at 50,000 units.

McIlhenny took some of these peppers and let them age in a salt mixture for a month. He added wine vinegar and let it all set a bit more, then he drained and bottled it. The result was Tabasco Sauce, one of America's most familiar and original condiments. The distinctive, long-necked bottle with its orange fluid is a staple in most recipes calling for a taste of the Southwest or Creole country. It is still made on the island, essentially in the same manner approved by the McIlhennys. Visitors can watch it being made in the plant here.

■ **LOCATION:** Avery Island is about 10 miles south of New Iberia, off U.S. 90, by way of Louisiana 329. ■ **HOURS:** Monday through Saturday, 10–4. ■ **ADMISSION:** Free ■ **TELEPHONE:** (318) 365-8173

GIBSLAND

BONNIE AND CLYDE DEATH SITE

On May 23, 1934, a squad of six special officers, including a former Texas Ranger, lay in wait in the brush near this northern Louisiana town. Acting on a tip, they were waiting for the arrival of gunman Clyde Barrow and his cigar-smoking companion, Bonnie Parker. The pair were accused of killing twelve people, most of them without warning or provocation, and were the objects of a national search.

When their car appeared, the police shouted a warning. The pair inside reached for their weapons, instead, and were immediately riddled with about fifty bullets. Frank Hamer, leader of the lawmen, said he regretted shooting a woman, "especially while she was sitting," but it was a matter of "either their lives or ours."

In their times, Bonnie and Clyde were regarded as small-timers. Certainly not in the class of the region's most notorious gunman, Pretty Boy Floyd. His contemporaries called Barrow "a punk, a snake-eyed murderer who killed without giving his victims a chance to draw," according to the usually dispassionate *New York Times.* Parker, who accompanied him for two years, was described as being red-haired, slight and tattooed, with a tightly drawn mouth. "Not pretty in the face but she had a beautiful body," said her former seamstress. Both were returned to Dallas for burial, with Bonnie interred wearing a blue negligee. "Her nails again were tinted, as she had worn them for two years since she began her fast life with Clyde," according to a wire service report.

The pair would have remained in obscurity had it not been for a 1967 movie about their lives. The highly romanticized film, *Bonnie and Clyde,* depicted them as glamorous, sensitive individuals, victims of the Depression. The climactic death scene, with their lifeless bodies moving in ballet-like grace under the endless barrage of bullets, was hailed as a masterpiece of stylized screen violence.

■ **LOCATION:** The marker is on Louisiana 154, just south of Gibsland. It is about 60 miles east of Shreveport, by way of Interstate 20.

NEW ORLEANS

ANTOINE'S RESTAURANT

The distinctive Creole cuisine of Louisiana is among the leading attractions of the state's largest city. New Orleans is filled with nationally known eating places. There are some that contemporary food critics rate above Antoine's. But only as restaurants. None has a higher place in American popular culture, where it has become a symbol of the romance of the French Quarter.

The restaurant's history goes back to 1840, when a young man from Marseille, France, Antoine Alciatore, opened his doors. It is still operated by his descendants. It is not an ostentatious place that tries too hard to play up its nostalgic setting. The decor, in fact, is mostly old newspapers and photographs. Through its depiction in numerous novels and films, though, Antoine's stands for old New Orleans.

Oysters Rockefeller (so named because the dish is so rich, not because a Rockefeller had anything to do with it) originated here. So did pompano *en papilotte,* fish cooked in a paper bag. This is the place visiting presidents are taken to dine. When Richard Nixon came, he recalled that he ate here on his honeymoon. Probably the most celebrated presidential visit, though, was made by Franklin D. Roosevelt, in 1937. The mayor of New Orleans, awed by his distinguished guest, inquired: "How'd ja like them ersters, Mr. President?" He said that he liked them just fine.

■ **LOCATION:** Antoine's is located at 713 St. Louis Street. ■ **HOURS:** Monday through Saturday, 12–2 and 5:30–9:30. ■ **TELEPHONE:** (504) 581-4422

BOURBON STREET

The French Quarter has two distinct personalities, sometimes separated by less than a block. The first is charming, historic, mysterious. The other is rowdy, boisterous, and loud, and its address is Bourbon Street. Named to honor the French royal family, on most evenings it seems more inclined to honor the Tennessee whisky. Every kind of music, from jazz to rock, pours from the doors of its bars, while crowds of pedestrians overload the sidewalks and amble down the middle of the street.

This is one of the country's top entertainment districts and Bourbon Street is suitably bawdy in the New Orleans tradition. Jazz, after all, was supposed to have originated in Storyville, the famed city-supervised red-light district that thrived in New Orleans before World War I. The music has long had associations with heavy breathing.

With one or two exceptions (*see* Preservation Hall, further on) you won't hear much classic New Orleans jazz played on Bourbon Street. But this is where Mardi Gras' carnival spirit goes on all year and the music is pretty much drowned out anyway by the sound of inhibitions being thrown aside. The best activity here is just to join the throngs promenading along the street, drinks in hand, and watch the ongoing human circus.

One place where history does meet folly, however, is the Old Absinthe House. This establishment, at 240 Bourbon Street, dates from the early nineteenth century. According to legend, in 1815 Andrew Jackson met the pirate Jean Lafitte here to plan the defense of the city from British attack.

■ **LOCATION:** Bourbon Street is one of the major east-west corridors through the French Quarter, one block north of Royal Street. The Old Absinthe House is at the corner of Bienville Street. Most of the entertainment area is clustered along the west end, closer to Canal Street.

JAZZ MUSEUM AND MARDI GRAS MUSEUM

At about the same time that jazz was first making its appearance, another New Orleans landmark was packing it in. The U.S. Mint, established here in 1838 and also the coin-maker for the Confederacy, was closed down in 1909. It became a Veterans' Bureau office, and later, a prison. Finally, in the 1980s it was taken over by the Louisiana State Museum to become a showcase for two of New Orleans' defining phenomena, jazz and Mardi Gras. Each subject takes up an entire section of the huge building.

The Jazz Museum traces the history of the music in New Orleans (*see* Preservation Hall, further on) with photographs and mementoes of the musicians who created the form. The instruments, bits of clothing, and other equipment associated with these musicians, some almost forgotten and some whose names are now legends, makes this unlike any other museum in the country, the finest of its kind.

It is hard to imagine a celebration as free-spirited as Mardi Gras confined to something as sedate as a museum. This wild explosion of color and noise at the beginning of the Lenten season is the signature of the city. It is the biggest celebration in the country, and its parades, balls, and music are an American original.

The roots of Mardi Gras in New Orleans have been traced all the way back to 1820, when a group of Creole youths returned from France determined to bring a masked parade to their hometown. In 1857, the first of the official parade organizations, the Mystic Krewe of Comus, was formed. But not until 1872 did Mardi Gras assume its present form. According to the story, a Russian Grand Duke came to the city in pursuit of a famous actress, Lydia Thompson. He had seen her perform in New York and sing the song with which she was most closely associated, "If Ever I Cease to Love." New Orleans was enchanted by this romance and decided to shape its celebration to fit the moment. A new figure was introduced: Rex, the Lord of Misrule, was meant to symbolize the Grand Duke. An official holiday was declared and all the krewes agreed to join in the planning. And Miss Thompson's song became the theme music of the parade.

So it has continued, only bigger and wilder every year. No ticket in America, not even the ones to the Super Bowl, are as avidly sought after, and as hard to obtain, as those to the masked balls of Mardi Gras. The museum tries to capture some of the excitement of the floats and costumes that are shown off in the annual parades. But while they are impressively displayed, nothing can really replace the unbridled hysteria of the real thing.

■ **LOCATION:** The U.S. Mint Museums are located at Esplanade at Decatur Street, in the southeastern corner of the French Quarter. ■ **HOURS:** Wednesday through Sunday, 10–5. ■ **ADMISSION:** Combined ticket is $4. ■ **TELEPHONE:** (504) 568-6968

PRESErVATION HALL

Just a few steps from the clamor of Bourbon Street is one of the last bastions of traditional jazz, the sound that originated in this city sometime around

Preservation Hall: One of the last bastions of traditional jazz. *(AP/Wide World Photos)*

1900. Trumpet playing lead, clarinet on harmony, trombone supplying the bass, and everything from tubas to drums to pianos to banjos laying down the beat.

The music had salacious beginnings, getting its name from a local term for the sex act. But it seemed to grow up out of many roots simultaneously—blues and gospel, ragtime and street "spasm" bands. It has even been suggested by one local historian, that the segregation laws of the 1890s provided an impetus: Classically educated musicians of the Creole elite gave structure and form to the improvised music of the streets. Whatever the cause, jazz began here and rapidly traveled north with the great black emigration that began during World War I.

Ideally suited to the new medium of the phonograph, jazz defined the entire decade of the 1920s. Its top artists, such as New Orleans born Louis Armstrong, became nationally recognized celebrities. The form changed as it left its home base though and evolved into swing by the early 1930s. Real New Orleans jazz began to die. By the 1950s, no club in this city played the music. Most of the musicians who grew up in the old traditions had no outlet to perform in their own home town.

Then a group of traditional fans began holding pass-the-hat concerts in the French Quarter and some of the old-timers came out of retirement to perform. A touring band was formed to let the rest of the country hear what the real thing sounded like. Younger musicians were trained to ensure the legacy would be passed on. Preservation Hall was acquired to become their permanent home. Performances here are usually played before standing room crowds and New Orleans jazz once more is a major attraction in the city of its birth.

■ **LOCATION:** Preservation Hall is at 726 St. Peter Street, just south of Bourbon Street. ■ **HOURS:** Nightly performances begin at 8 P.M. and closing time is usually 12:30 A.M. ■ **ADMISSION:** $3 ■ **TELEPHONE:** (504) 522-2841

Mississippi

CLARKSDALE

DELTA BLUES MUSEUM

The most distinctively American forms of music were born and nurtured in the rich soil of Mississippi: The blues, country and western, rock and roll (*see* Tupelo, Mississippi). To some degree, all of them originated here, in the most poverty-stricken of states. If all great music arises from despair the explanation for Mississippi's pre-eminence is apparent.

The Delta is the legendary birthplace of the blues, evolving from the work songs of Black laborers. The musician credited with advancing the form, and inspiring an entire generation of imitators, was Muddy Waters. He was born near Clarksdale and learned to play the blues from men whose musical experience ran back to the slavery era. He was recorded by musicologist Alan Lomax in 1941, which first brought him to public attention. Moving to Chicago two years later, Waters developed the urban blues style, marked by electrical amplification of the guitar. The music he recorded in the postwar years was the genesis of rock. One of his singles, "Rollin' Stone," inspired the name of a British rock group, a Bob Dylan composition, and rock's leading magazine.

The museum pays tribute to all Delta musicians but its exhibits are primarily devoted to Waters, who died in 1983. Housed in Clarksdale's Carnegie Library, the museum was expanded in the early 1990s through the contributions of several rock notables, especially the band ZZ Top, who felt especially indebted to Waters.

■ **LOCATION:** The museum is in downtown Clarksdale, at 114 Delta Avenue. Signs on U.S. 61 and 49 bypass direct the traveler. ■ **HOURS:** Monday through Friday, 9–5. ■ **ADMISSION:** Free ■ **TELEPHONE:** (601) 624-4461

GREENWOOD

BILLIE JOE'S TALLAHATCHEE BRIDGE

The question used to irritate singer Bobbie Gentry. Just what was it that Billie Joe McCallister threw off the Tallahatchee Bridge a few days before leaping to his own death? The song that raised the question was one of the top hits of the 1960s. A mournful ballad about young love and suicide, for one month in 1967 it took the top spot on the charts away from both the Beatles and Motown, and it remains a perennial favorite.

"What was thrown off the bridge really isn't that important," Gentry said in a later interview. "The song is about thoughtlessness, unconscious cruelty. The family sits there, eating their meal and talking about his death, while his girlfriend is right there with them, part of their family."

The riddle was supposedly answered in a 1976 film that indicated Billy Joe killed himself because of an inner conflict over his sexual preference.

Gentry, the song's composer, lived in Greenwood for seven years as a child before her family moved to California. Although there is no indication that she had the town specifically in mind when she wrote the song, the movie was shot here. And it was the local bridge over the Tallahatchee that was shown as the spot of Billy Joe's fatal leap in the film.

■ **LOCATION:** The bridge is north of town, on the highway to Money. Leave downtown Greenwood by way of Grand Boulevard.

MERIDIAN

JIMMIE RODGERS MEMORIAL

Throughout the 1920s, the traditional folk music of the South was slowly evolving into something else. Borrowing elements from the old Appalachian ballad, the blues, and the thirty-two-bar framework of popular songs, a new musical form was taking shape. It talked about the hard realities of life and it told the stories in simple, straightforward language. But while jazz was breaking into the mainstream of American life, this music was rudely categorized as "hillbilly" and limited to a regional market. Not until after World War II did it come to be known as country and western and win respect from the larger musical world.

In 1953, most of the stars of country music came to Meridian to honor the memory of Jimmie Rodgers. On the twentieth anniversary of his death from tuberculosis, this museum was dedicated to him, honoring Rodgers as the father of country music. Wire service reports condescendingly called them "the elite of the hillbilly music world." They included Roy Acuff, Bill Monroe, Hank Snow—musicians who were already legends. They came to pay tribute to the "Singing Brakeman," whose records were regarded as an innovative force.

Rodgers, always a frail man, was the first to employ steel guitar, yodels, and blues-tinged chords in his music. His recording career lasted only six years but he was making records until days before his death and his impact was enormous. Much of his material seemed drawn from life. "When I was a brakeman, working on the rail, You had another daddy in the county jail," went the lyric to one of his early hits "High-Powered Mama." He sang about hard times, cheating women, and leaving home—three themes that remain constant across the sweep of country music. Exhibits include his guitar, original sheet music, concert wardrobe, and some of the equipment used in his railroad job. He took that part of his life seriously. Another of the invited guests at the museum dedication, in fact, was the widow of legendary railroad man Casey Jones (*see* Jackson, Tennessee).

■ **LOCATION:** The museum is at 1725 Jimmie Rodgers Drive, off Exit 153 of Interstate 20, then 2 miles north. ■ **HOURS:** Monday through Saturday, 10–4; Sunday, 1–5. ■ **ADMISSION:** $3 ■ **TELEPHONE:** (601) 485-1808

TUPELO

ELVIS PRESLEY BIRTHPLACE

The first taste of success in the Presley legend came here, when as a fifth-grader he sang "Old Shep," by Red Foley, at a school assembly. His teacher, suitably impressed, entered him in a talent show at the Mississippi-Alabama State Fair. He won second place. It would be interesting to find who finished first.

His mother was so delighted that for a birthday present she bought him his first guitar, for $12.98 at Tupelo Hardware. Three years later, the family moved to Memphis, guitar and all, and the rest is cultural history.

Presley devotees can recite the facts by heart. He was born in this small frame house on January 8, 1935. His twin, Jesse Garon, was stillborn. He was brought up singing gospel music at the nearby First Assembly of God Church, and was deeply influenced by country and Black music, both of which abounded in Tupelo.

The fifteen-acre park here preserves the birthplace and also contains a small memorial chapel. Maps outlining a self-guiding Elvis driving tour of Tupelo can be picked up at the visitors center. (*See* Memphis, Tennessee, for other sites associated with Presley.)

■ **LOCATION:** Exit U.S. 78 at Canal Street and follow the signs to 306 Elvis Presley Drive. ■ **HOURS:** Monday through Saturday, 10–5; Sunday, 1–5. ■ **ADMISSION:** $1.50 ■ **TELEPHONE:** (601) 841-1245

VAUGHN

CASEY JONES MUSEUM

This little village was the scene of the most famous train wreck in American railroad history, the crash of April 30, 1900, that killed Illinois Central engineer Casey Jones (*see* Jackson, Tennessee). Wrecks were not an uncommon event in the America of that time. More than 50,000 people were killed or injured from that cause in the year 1900 alone.

But an engine wiper named Wallace Saunders was a great admirer of Jones. He made up a ballad about the engineer, with a refrain imitating the mournful call of a train whistle. It has become such a part of the American musical tradition, that most people are surprised to learn that it isn't a folk ballad but actually has a composer's credit. Not that it did Saunders much good. He sold all rights to it for a bottle of gin.

The museum, in the town's restored rail station, displays memorabilia relating to the crash and to Jones, as well as early railroading in Mississippi. Some of Saunders's original sheet music can also be seen.

■ **LOCATION:** Vaughn is about 35 miles north of Jackson, on Interstate 55. The museum is at 10901 Vaughn Road. ■ **HOURS:** Tuesday through Saturday, 9–5. ■ **ADMISSION:** $1 ■ **TELEPHONE:** (601) 673-9864

North Carolina

DURHAM

BULL DURHAM PARK

The minor leagues have a place all their own in baseball lore. In the stories, the pitchers are wilder, the fields lumpier, the bus rides longer, and the players loonier than anywhere else in the game.

Ron Shelton, an ex-minor-league-ballplayer turned screenwriter, blended many of these old stories in the 1988 movie, *Bull Durham.* The film was a surprise hit and became a cult favorite among baseball aficionados. It also turned the ballpark in Durham into something of a shrine to the minors. It has become a symbol of bush league baseball and the men who, with no realistic hope of ever reaching "the big show," play it.

Most of the movie's game sequences were shot at this park, home of the Durham Bulls of the Carolina League. It is a flavorful old ballpark, an intimate playing ground that peels away the game's celebrity glitter and replaces it with charm and nostalgia. Even if you cannot see a ball game here, anyone with a feel for the game will enjoy the setting.

■ **LOCATION:** The official name of the Bulls' home field is Durham Athletic Park. It is located north of downtown at 428 Morris Street near the Liggett and Myers headquarters. ■ **HOURS:** The park may be visited daily during daylight hours. ■ **TELEPHONE:** (919) 688-8211

HIGH POINT

FURNITURE DISCOVERY CENTER

Furniture tends to be made where there is plenty of wood. In the 1880s, the wood near some of the country's older manufacturing centers was disappearing, depleted by decades of uncontrolled lumbering. But wood was a commodity with which North Carolina was well supplied. The state also had a labor force that was willing to work for far lower wages than workers in the northern cities.

The Durham Athletic Park. *(Courtesy of Durham Bulls)*

The first furniture-maker to set up shop here came in 1888. By the end of the century, there were two dozen factories in High Point. They transformed the town from a hamlet, named by surveyors for the peak altitude on the Charlotte-Greensboro Railroad, into the center of the American furniture industry. Twice a year, buyers pour into the city for the home furnishings market, one of the country's most influential industry shows. More than 125 plants are now located in the immediate area, and they turn out the bulk of furniture that is found in the homes and hotels of the United States.

The best-known symbol of all this is the Giant Bureau, a 32-foot-high building shaped like a chest of drawers, complete with knobs and a simulated mirror. Formerly the Chamber of Commerce offices, it was built in 1926. It now functions primarily as a subject for photographers.

High Point has added a Discovery Center, where visitors can view the furniture assembly process. The center also has several rooms set up to illustrate changes in furniture design and the Furniture Hall of Fame.

■ **LOCATION:** The Discovery Center is behind the High Point Convention Center, downtown, at 101 West Green Street. ■ **HOURS:** Monday through Saturday, 10–5; Sunday, 1–5. ■ **ADMISSION:** $6 combination ticket to both the museum and Hall of Fame. ■ **TELEPHONE:** (919) 887-3876

LINNVILLE

BROWN MOUNTAIN LIgHTS

Set high in the Blue Ridge Mountains, this little town offers the best viewpoints for one of the South's most enduring legends. The Brown Mountain Lights have been observed here since the late nineteenth century. They can be seen through the nightly mists that hover above Jonas Ridge—flaring up brightly like a fireworks display, then fading away before suddenly reappearing hundreds of yards away.

Scientists and geographers have taken shots at explaining the lights, attributing them to discharges of static electricity or the refraction of headlights from the next valley. But no explanation was ever proven beyond question. According to local legend, the lights come from a ghostly lantern carried by a long-dead slave who is searching for his master who disappeared while hunting. The story was set to music by country artist Scot Wiseman and "Brown Mountain Lights" is a favorite in the Bluegrass repertoire.

■ **LOCATION:** Linnville is on U.S. 221, about 18 miles south of Blowing Rock, just off the Blue Ridge Parkway. The lights can be observed from several vantage points in the vicinity, depending on atmospheric conditions. Best bet is to inquire locally.

MT. AIRY

ANDY GRIFFITH'S "MAYBERRY"

The most famous town in this state is not on any map. It's a Carolina Never-Never Land, where Aunt Bea is at home baking pies, Barney Fife is talking big over at the barber shop, Opie is down at the fishing hole, and unflappable Sheriff Andy is trying to restore an element of calm to the goings-on.

Mayberry was the fictional home of the long-running *Andy Griffith Show,* one of the top network television hits of the 1960s. The place was based on Griffith's memories of his own boyhood home, Mt. Airy. Fans of the show, which plays in reruns and on occasional reunion telecasts, have made Mt. Airy a place of pilgrimage, where they try to recapture the ambience of the ideal, slow-paced southern small town.

There is, indeed, a Snappy Lunch downtown, just as in the show. But for the most part, Griffith's Mayberry was just a broad outline sketch of Mt. Airy, rather than a detailed portrait. There is an Andy Griffith Playhouse, and the star's boyhood home is marked, at 711 East Haymore Street, in the historic district. But Mt. Airy's top physical feature is still the granite quarry that was once the basis of its economy. That is rock-hard reality. The Mayberry that overlays it is as insubstantial as a dream.

■ **LOCATION:** Mt. Airy is just south of the Virginia line, 37 miles northwest of Winston-Salem, by way of U.S. 52. The Chamber of Commerce, at 134 South Renfro Street, is accustomed to answering questions about Mayberry and handing out maps. It also has paintings of Mayberry as imagined by a local artist. ■ **HOURS:** The Chamber of Commerce hours are Monday through Friday, 8:30–5. ■ **TELEPHONE:** (919) 786-6116

PINEHURST

PGA GOLF HALL OF FAME

When Boston philanthropist James W. Tufts acquired five thousand acres of North Carolina property in 1895, his intent was to turn it into a health resort. The winter climate was mild and the summer humidity was low. It seemed the perfect combination for salubrious relaxation.

But that was also the year in which the first U.S. Open Golf Tournament was held. The sport had taken hold in the northeastern states, with the first country club formed in Yonkers, New York, in 1888. Within a very short time golf had become an obsession among wealthy sportsmen. The drawback was that the season was limited by climate. So an intense interest was developing in building golf resorts in the south. That is how the Tufts property became Pinehurst, a colonial-style community built around its country club and golf courses. Famed landscape architect Frederick Law Olmsted was called in to lay out the parks and then golf architect Donald Ross developed the courses. The original four courses now have grown to thirty and several tournaments are held here during the year.

No wonder this is where the Professional Golfers Association has chosen to place its museum and hall of fame. The PGA Museum has memorabilia of golfing greats and of famous tournaments, as well as historical exhibits that trace the sport and its equipment back to their foundations in fifteenth-century Scotland.

■ **LOCATION:** Pinehurst is located off U.S. 1, about 70 miles southwest of Raleigh. The museum is 2 miles east of the village, at the junction of U.S. 15 and North Carolina 211. ■ **HOURS:** The museum is open daily 9–5, March through November. ■ **ADMISSION:** $3 ■ **TELEPHONE:** (919) 295-6651

RANDLEMAN

RICHARD PETTY MUSEUM

There have been few athletes who have dominated their sport as thoroughly as Richard Petty ruled stock car racing in his prime. He won two hundred races between 1958 and 1984, more than twice as many as anybody else. In his peak year, 1967, he won twenty-seven out of forty-eight races, including an incredible ten in a row. There is not an auto racing fan in America who doesn't think those marks will stand forever. Or, at least, hopes they do.

He was called King Richard, and in his trademark feathered hat and dark glasses and wide smile, Petty was every inch racing royalty. His last eight years on the NASCAR circuit, before his retirement in 1992, were winless, but still he was the one who drew the adulation of the fans. "He got three fans for every other driver's one," said one longtime rival.

In the Carolinas, where stock car racing is close to a religion, Petty occupied a place of special adulation. His race car number, 43, is as well known as Babe Ruth's number 3. Pro basketball star Brad Daugherty, who grew up in North Carolina, even insisted on wearing 43 as his uniform number as a tribute to Petty.

One writer once called him "Elvis behind the wheel of a race car," and that's a fair gauge of his position in this state. The museum, operated by the Petty family, contains memorabilia of his thirty-four-year career, including three of his most famous cars.

■ **LOCATION:** Randleman is located off U.S. 220, about 17 miles south of Greensboro. Turn left at the Level Cross exit onto Branson Mill Road and go about a mile; 311 Branson Mill Road. ■ **HOURS:** Monday through Saturday, 10–4. ■ **ADMISSION:** $3 ■ **TELEPHONE:** (910) 495-1143

SMITHFIELD

AVA GaRDNER MUSEUm

One of Hollywood's top stars in the late 1940s and early 1950s, Ava Gardner specialized in playing the role of the sophisticated lady who had paid the price for her corrupted innocence. She was sultry but sad, a combination shown off to best advantage in the cult favorite, *The Barefoot Contessa,* with Humphrey Bogart. She also made headlines during the 1950s with her stormy marriage to Frank Sinatra.

She was born on a tenant farm and brought up in a boarding house in this town. She went to Hollywood as an eighteen-year-old, worked hard to lose her thick southern accent, and finally got her break in the 1946 film, *The Killers.* Her part was short but sensuous and it was a star-maker. She went on to play in everything from the musical comedy *One Touch of Venus* (her singing voice was dubbed) to Hemingway's *The Sun Also Rises.*

After her death in 1989, a collection of personal mementoes and souvenirs from her years as a star were assembled here and shown off in the house in which she grew up. Gardner is also buried nearby, at Sunset Memorial Park, west of town on U.S. 70.

■ **LOCATION:** Smithfield is just west of Interstate 95, at the U.S. 70 exit, or 28 miles southeast of Raleigh, by way of U.S. 70. The museum is east of town on North Carolina 1007. Call in advance because hours and opening dates are subject to change. ■ **TELEPHONE:** (919) 934-5830

WINSTON-SALEM

R. J. REYNOLDS TOBACCO COMPANY

Tobacco has been an American cultural force since the colonial times. It was the economic foundation of early Virginia and cultivation gradually spread southward into North Carolina. It developed slowly here until the 1850s, when the development of the bright leaf variety tripled production and made it the state's leading cash crop, a position it has never lost.

The great tobacco company fortunes, however, were put together immediately after the Civil War. Richard Joshua Reynolds entered the field with cut plug chewing tobacco in 1875. Opening a tiny factory in Winston, he expanded steadily, acquiring competitors along the way. Among them was a small tobacco operation run by the Hanes family, who took their earnings and invested in the underwear and hosiery business, a field it still dominates.

Reynolds itself was acquired by James Duke's tobacco trust in 1899, but then re-emerged under its own identity twelve years later when the trust was broken up by the federal government. By then, plug tobacco was going out of fashion. Trying to create a new market, Reynolds turned one of its pipe tobaccos into a blend, which it then marketed as a milder kind of cigarette. It was called Camels and within four years of its introduction in 1914 it dominated the field, winning 40 percent of the market. The dromedary on each pack, nicknamed Old Joe, became one of the most familiar company symbols in America.

By the 1990s, the climate had changed completely. To some, the cigarette industry is evil incarnate, a threat to everybody's health. Even Old Joe is under fire, accused of being a marketing aide to sell tobacco products to the young. The largest cigarette manufacturer in the country, R. J. Reynolds has been in the forefront of the industry's battle against print advertising bans and the steady spread of smoking prohibitions. Part of a giant corporate conglomerate, RJR was also a leading player in the corporate takeover frenzy of the 1980s, its role profiled in a national best-seller, *Barbarians at the Gates.*

The Reynolds factory here turns out three hundred million cigarettes a day and, despite wide opposition, smoking remains an intrinsic part of our culture. This plant tour is one of the most popular attractions in the state. Visitors see the entire cigarette manufacturing process. Other exhibits display the history of tobacco and the various stages of production, from planting to auction.

■ **LOCATION:** The R. J. Reynolds plant is 3 miles north of central Winston-Salem, by way of U.S. 52 and Akron Drive. ■ **HOURS:** Monday through Friday, 8–6. ■ **ADMISSION:** Free ■ **TELEPHONE:** (919) 741-5718

South Carolina

CHARLESTON

CATFISH ROW

In a city defined by its colonial era heritage, one of the most popular sights is a little alleyway on Church Street, in the midst of the historic district. It once was called Cabbage Row, for the plants its residents displayed in their window boxes. But in his novel *Porgy,* local writer DuBose Heyward renamed it Catfish Row, and so it has come down in the musical classic, *Porgy and Bess.*

Contemporary African-Americans are not especially happy with the characterization of blacks in the folk opera, set in the century's early years. Still, George Gershwin's score, written in 1935, is acknowledged to be a milestone in American musical history. Through countless productions overseas, *Porgy and Bess* has become a national symbol of American culture and has taken Catfish Row into the realm of places that art makes real.

■ **LOCATION:** Catfish Row is located at 89-91 Church Street, several blocks north of The Battery, on the Charleston waterfront.

DARLINGTON

STOCK CAR HALL OF FAME AND MUSEUM

At its opening in 1950, Darlington Raceway was regarded as the fastest and most complete auto racing facility in the South. But the experts doubted it would succeed. Its founder, H. W. Brasington, had chosen to build it eighty miles from the nearest city of any size, and this was in an age before interstate highways. The public was also taken aback when the first motorcycle event held here had to be canceled because two drivers in the first race were killed and the rest refused to participate because it was "too dangerous."

But Darlington survived its critics. It is now a revered venue of racing, the second oldest major track in the country behind Indianapolis. Its Southern 500, held on Labor Day weekend, is a major event on the stock car circuit and the races that have been run here wear the patina of legend. This is an apt location for the Stock Car Hall of Fame, which is said to house the largest collection of race cars in the world. Exhibits, some of them underwritten by the auto companies, trace the evolution of stock cars from 1950 to the present, with special reference to those who were winners at Darlington.

■ **LOCATION:** Darlington is about 80 miles northeast of Columbia, and is easily accessible from either Interstate 20 or 95. The Raceway is 2 miles west of town on South Carolina 34 (west of junction with U.S. 52 bypass). ■ **HOURS:** Daily, 9–5. ■ **ADMISSION:** $2 ■ **TELEPHONE:** (303) 393-2103

PARRIS ISLAND

U.S. mARINE CORPS MUSEUM

"This is no rose garden." That is how Major General Carl W. Hoffman, former commanding general of this Marine Corps training facility, succinctly described it in 1971. Many would call that an understatement. The basic philosophy at Parris Island is that to be a Marine you've got to be tough and so the training has to be tough. "The only pleasure in it is taking a worm and turning him into a man," said one veteran drill instructor. "It's a 24-hour a day job."

The Marines occupy a unique niche in American culture. They are glamorized in Hollywood's war epics. But the rigors of measuring up to the Corps' demands, of being able to become one of "a few good men," is also the stuff of horror stories. Under the tender ministrations of his DI (Drill Instructor), a recruit is badgered, bullied, and browbeaten until he either breaks or makes the grade. In 1956, six recruits drowned on a night punishment march and since then the training has been toned down somewhat. Still, in 1971, thirty-nine trainees had to be hospitalized for kidney damage as a result of excessive exercise ordered by their DI. Parris Island's reputation intensifies the Corps' status as an elite fighting unit.

Parris Island was taken over by the Corps in 1915. But it already had a history of disciplinary disorders. In 1562 French Huguenots under Jean Ribaut attempted to colonize it. When he sailed to Europe for supplies he left a strict disciplinarian in command. The new commander hanged one offender and left another on a nearby island to starve, setting off a mutiny in which the commander was killed and everyone else abandoned the colony and returned to France. During the Civil War, the U.S. Navy used the island as a coaling station and the island remained under the navy's control until becoming a Marine Corps facility. There is a memorial to Ribaut on the base and the War Memorial Building houses a museum of Marine Corps history, from its inception as a special unit to fight piracy in the West Indies in 1798.

■ **LOCATION:** Parris Island is 10 miles south of Beaufort. ■ **HOURS:** The museum is open daily. It is best to check in advance for hours, which can change according to season and special events. ■ **ADMISSION:** Free ■ **TELEPHONE:** (803) 525-3650

Tennessee

CHATTANOOGA

CHATTANOOGA CHOO-CHOO

You may wonder what a song about a city in Tennessee was doing in the middle of a Hollywood musical set in Idaho. Little details like that never seem to bother filmmakers.

Sun Valley Serenade was a 1941 production about the famous ski resort. Reportedly, there was a tie-in deal with the Northern Pacific Railroad, which was eager to publicize its new resort. The studio also wanted to show off the Glenn Miller Orchestra, the most popular of the big bands at that time. Veteran songwriters Harry Warren and Mack Gordon were called in to do the score.

"Chattanooga Choo-Choo" was one of their happy inspirations. It was placed in the film as a specialty number for the Miller band, showing off its singing group, The Modernaires, and its featured sax player, Tex Beneke. After they swung through a couple of choruses, the tap-dancing Nicholas Brothers were also brought in to develop the production even further.

The irresistible rhythm, simulating the movement of a train, and the mellifluous title made the song one of the top hits of the year. It became, in fact, the first certified million-selling record.

Chattanooga grew up as a major rail center, one of the reasons several Civil War battles were fought in its vicinity. When its old railroad station was restored and turned into an entertainment complex and rail museum, it seemed quite natural to call it the Chattanooga Choo-Choo. An engine and cars from the original train, dating from 1880, are on display. The terminal also houses several shops and restaurants and a Holiday Inn.

■ **LOCATION:** The Choo-Choo is in downtown Chattanooga, at 1400 Market Street, just off Interstate 24. ■ **HOURS:** Monday through Saturday, 10–10; Sunday, 12–9:30. ■ **ADMISSION:** Free ■ **TELEPHONE:** (615) 266-5000

ROCK CITY

When the era of automobile travel began, some entrepreneurs were quick to realize that the highway was a splendid advertising medium. Burma

The restored railroad station in Chattanooga. *(Courtesy of the Chattanooga Choo-Choo)*

Shave was the best known example. The company erected rhyming signposts, usually five in a row, everywhere along the nation's roads, making its product posted more frequently than the speed limit.

Rock City's special medium was barns. Starting in 1932, all along the major highways leading south, ads for this attraction atop Lookout Mountain were painted on the sides of barns. Most of them counted down the mileage to this wonder, promising that you could see seven states from its viewpoint. It made lots of farmers happy because of the unanticipated extra income that came their way. After all, their barn was just standing there anyway and what did they care if someone wanted to pay to paint a sign on it? It also gave motorists something to read on the long drive south. Since two of the major highways from the Midwest to Florida funnelled through Chattanooga, Rock City became a big-time tourist attraction. It even merited a 1950s Duke Ellington record, "The Rock City Rock."

In reality, Rock City Gardens is a ten-acre grouping of sandstone formations, given fanciful names, and enhanced with plantings and bridges. And, when the weather is clear, you can still see seven states and a whole lot of sky.

■ **LOCATION:** On the Lookout Mountain Highway, Tennessee 58, above Chattanooga. (Technically, Rock City is across the Georgia state line, but it is most easily accessible from Tennessee.) ■ **HOURS:** Daily 8 to dusk, June

21–Labor Day; 8:30 to dusk, rest of the year. ■ **ADMISSION:** $7.50 ■ **TELEPHONE:** (404) 820-2531

DAYTON

SCOPES TRIAL COURTHOUSE MUSEUM

For a few sweltering weeks in July 1925, this pleasant town in the Cumberland foothills was transformed into a world-class carnival. A local high school biology teacher, John Scopes, was placed on trial for violating a new state law by teaching the theory of evolution. To some Americans, it seemed the perfect place to make a stand against those who would try to tear down the religious beliefs of Fundamentalist Christians. To others, it was a battle for intellectual freedom and protection of the Constitutional guarantee of separation of church and state.

The bill had whipped through both houses of the Tennessee legislature and was signed by the governor. No state politician dared oppose it in the face of its religious sponsors. A local businessman in Dayton decided that the law had to be challenged immediately and contrived with Scopes to get the teacher charged with its violation.

William Jennings Bryan, three times a presidential candidate and a Fundamentalist hero, volunteered to assist the prosecution. Upon hearing this, the great attorney Clarence Darrow agreed to join the American Civil Liberties Union in the defense. With such issues and celebrities involved, the trial became the focus of world attention. It was one of the first events to be covered by radio. Most major American papers and several from Europe sent correspondents. Preachers set up revival tents all along Dayton's main street and ongoing religious meetings kept the faithful stirred up.

In one of the most moving orations of his long career, Darrow summarized why the charges should be thrown out of court. "If today you can take a thing like evolution and make it a crime to teach it in the public schools," he said, "tomorrow you can make it a crime to teach it in the private schools. And the next year you can make it a crime to teach it in the church. And the next session you may ban books and newspapers. . . . If you can do one you can do the other. Ignorance and fanaticism is ever busy and needs feeding. Always it is feeding and gloating for more."

Despite the eloquence of the plea, the trial continued. The prosecution won and Scopes was fined $100. But in the court of public opinion, Darrow destroyed Bryan. He put him on the stand as an expert witness to answer questions about the literal truth of the Bible. Bryan was reduced to a sputtering mass of indignation and contradictions. He died five days after the trial concluded. The story was retold in the award-winning play and film, *Inherit the Wind.*

The Rhea County Courthouse in which the trial was held (it concluded, because of the heat, on the courthouse lawn) has been restored to its appearance of 1925. The courtroom is still in use. A museum on the lower floors traces the history of the trial and displays mementos of the time when the world came to Dayton.

■ **LOCATION:** Dayton is on U.S. 27, about 35 miles northeast of Chattanooga. The courthouse is on New Market Street, near the center of town. ■ **HOURS:** Monday through Friday, 8–4. ■ **ADMISSION:** Free ■ **TELEPHONE:** (615) 775-7801

HENNING

ALEX HALEY HOUSE

Young Alex Haley once sat on the front porch of this house and listened to his aunts tell him stories about his family. About the terrible days of slavery. About a remote, almost mythical figure, called "The African," who was brought to America in a slave ship almost two centuries before and was the founder of their family.

Years later, Haley, having become a famous writer, decided to see if he could track down the facts behind the family stories. As he later recalled, he had just completed his work on *The Autobiography of Malcolm X.* The experience had left him drained, both emotionally and mentally. He was at a loss for a project that would seem as significant. Walking through the streets of Washington, D.C., he wandered into the National Archives. Recalling the stories about his family's past residence in North Carolina, he looked up the census records and found his great grandfather's name listed. The discovery tapped into a need to learn more about the old stories—a hunger finally satisfied with the publication of *Roots.*

This novelistic history, a distillation of one African-American family's experience, was brought to network television in 1977. It made TV history, racking up unprecedented ratings for a dramatic series and turning the saga of Kunte Kinte into a national phenomenon. Two years later Haley bought his childhood home. It had been built in 1918 by his grandfather, Will Palmer, a successful lumber dealer. It has been restored to the way it was during Haley's childhood in the 1920s, and well-informed local guides lead the visitor through the rooms, telling old family stories much like the ones he once heard. Haley died in 1992.

■ **LOCATION:** Henning is about 45 miles north of Memphis by way of U.S. 51 and Tennessee 209. Follow the signs to the house, at South Church Street and Haley Avenue. ■ **HOURS:** Tuesday through Saturday, 10–5; Sunday, 1–5. ■ **ADMISSION:** $3 ■ **TELEPHONE:** (901) 738-2240

The Director of Tourism for The Gambia, Samba M. B. Fye with author Alex Haley. *(Courtesy of Schomburg Center for Research in Black Culture, The New York Public Library, Astor, Lenox & Tilden Foundations)*

HURRICANE MILLS

LORETTA LYNN MUSEUM

She was the Coal Miner's Daughter—the title of one of her songs, her autobiography, and the 1980 movie based on her life. Raised in crushing poverty in Butcher Hollow, Kentucky. Married at thirteen. Driving around the South with her husband, trying to persuade any radio station to play her songs. A dependence on pain pills once she knew success. Loretta Lynn is country music's ongoing soap opera, the toughest and also the most vulnerable of its stars.

Critics say that the statements in her songs helped introduce feminism to an entirely new audience. "Don't come home a'drinkin' with lovin' on your mind" says one song. "You ain't woman enough to take my man," declares another. Her on-stage dress is feminine and demure; "all dressed up pretty for the big dance," as one observer put it. But there is no mistaking the straightforward honesty of what she sings about.

"I put it out there for them all to see it," she said in a 1980 interview. "Life is not that pretty. It has its up and its downs. Life is ugly sometimes. But, big deal, Lucille. It's all life, ain't it?"

Many of the exteriors for *Coal Miner's Daughter* were shot at her ranch in Hurricane Mills. The Butcher Hollow sequences were reconstructions. "It was just too hard to get a camera up in there," she says. There is a simulation of her birthplace at Hurricane Mills, along with tours of her home, and displays from her long singing career.

■ **LOCATION:** The ranch is off Interstate 40, at the Tennessee 13 exit, about 70 miles west of Nashville. ■ **HOURS:** Daily, 9–5, April to October. ■ **ADMISSION:** $10.50 ■ **TELEPHONE:** (615) 296-7700

JACKSON

CASEY JONES HOME aND MUSEUM

On the last day of April 1900, the crack Illinois Central Cannonball Express, rounded a curve near Vaughn, Mississippi (*see* Mississippi) and collided with a parked freight train. The collision killed the Cannonball's engineer, John Luther Jones. Nicknamed Casey, he was a popular figure on the railroad and was famous for his deft hand with the locomotive whistle, eliciting mournful sounds from it that no other engineer could match.

Mournful as one of his whistle calls, the ballad written about that crash made Jones the most famous railroad man of the century. Jackson was his hometown, and it was where his widow continued to live for years after his death. Incidentally, she detested the song because it made Jones out to be a bit of a womanizer, an implication she vehemently denied.

A sister engine to the one he was riding at the time of his death is on display, as are family memorabilia, and other exhibits on early railroading in Tennessee.

■ **LOCATION:** At the U.S. 45 Bypass exit of Interstate 40. ■ **HOURS:** Monday through Saturday, 9–5; Sunday, 1–5. Weekday hours are 8–8, June to September. ■ **ADMISSION:** $2.50 ■ **TELEPHONE:** (901) 668-1222

MEMPHIS

BEALE STREET

Beale Street means the Blues. There may be no other thoroughfare in the country whose name is so inextricably mixed with a form of music. Coming from the Mississippi Delta, the blues arrived in Memphis during the first decade of the twentieth century. There it was first affixed to a musical score by W. C. Handy (*see* Florence, Alabama). He published the "Memphis Blues" in 1905 and a few years later penned his tribute to Beale Street, the main business avenue of the city's black neighborhood.

"I'd rather be there," went the song, "than any place I know." It was the most exciting street in the South, reaching its peak during the 1920s. Millionaires, musicians, and gangsters walked along its length to shop at the city's sharpest stores, flout Prohibition, and listen to the blues. It succumbed, however, to the familiar cycle of urban decay, and, by the 1950s, Beale Street was a dying strip with barred-up windows and vacant storefronts.

Starting in the late 1970s, Memphis dedicated itself to bringing Beale Street back to life. Several blocks have been restored as an entertainment district and historic area. Once again the blues is played in the clubs, and the Daisy Theatre, which once booked the top black entertainers in the country, puts on musical shows once more. Schwab's, the city's oldest department store, where Elvis Presley shopped for his wardrobe after signing his first contract with Sun Records, is still in business on Beale. And, from a small park in front of his former house, a statue of Handy looks across the street he immortalized.

■ **LOCATION:** Beale Street is on the southern edge of downtown Memphis, running east from the Mississippi River.

DANNY THOMAS PAVILION AT ST. JUDE'S HOSPITAL

He was television's quintessential nice guy. The star of the 1950s hit, *Make Room for Daddy,* he helped pioneer the situation comedy format. He primarily played himself, a comedian and singer, trying to raise a family while working crazy hours, frequently on the road. The warm-hearted show lasted eleven years and made Danny Thomas into one of the medium's most enduring stars.

He was born Amos Jacobs outside Toledo, Ohio. He learned the business playing in local and nearby Detroit small clubs. Then, in the late 1930s, he hit it big as the emcee of the Chez Paree nightclub in Chicago.

Louis B. Mayer, the head of MGM, invited him West with the intention of making him a film star. But, as Thomas told the story in later years, "he told me that Americans go to the movies to live in a dream world. They wanted to see beautiful people with perfect faces. So he wanted me to have my nose fixed. That night my agent called me at eleven o'clock and said: 'Don't do it. There'll be plenty of work for you anyway.' Turned out he was right."

When he was broke and got his first job in show business, Thomas vowed to built a shrine to St. Jude—the patron of hopeless causes—in gratitude. He never forgot the promise, and at the height of his success toured the country tirelessly to raise funds for the St. Jude's Children's Hospital in Memphis. It opened in 1962 and for the rest of his life he continued making appearances to help support it and to make sure no child would be denied treatment for lack of funds.

"He never just lent his name to the hospital," his actress daughter Marlo Thomas recalled after his death, "He gave his life to it. He was the genuine article."

Thomas died in 1991 and, at his request, was buried in the hospital rotunda. The pavilion reflects the architecture of Thomas's Middle Eastern ancestry and was modeled after the Dome of the Rock, in Jerusalem. It contains exhibits on Thomas's career, the history of the hospital, and the American Lebanese Syrian Associated Charities, which operates it.

■ **LOCATION:** St. Jude's is just across Interstate 40 from downtown Memphis, at 332 North Lauderdale Street. ■ **HOURS:** Monday through Friday, 10–4; Saturday, 11–4. ■ **ADMISSION:** Free ■ **TELEPHONE:** (901) 522-0327

GRACELAND AND ELVIS UP CLOSE

No other singer ever defined a musical style or an era like Elvis Presley. Between 1956 and 1969, he had seventeen number-one records. His look, his walk, his guitar licks, his sideburns, his pout were copied by millions of young men around the world, while as many million young women's hearts palpitated. Ministers fulminated, editorial writers condemned, teachers warned. All to no avail. Elvis was rock 'n' roll to the generation that passed through high school in the late 1950s—the first mass audience this music hit like a thunderbolt.

Many of these 1950s kids could not reconcile themselves to "the King's" death in 1977. In fact, if anything, Elvis's following has magnified. Sightings are reported, fantastic conspiracy theories are spun to explain that Elvis is actually alive and in hiding. Some tabloid newspapers have even claimed that Elvis has answered prayers. Such is the measure of the effect he had on his times. As the title to one of humorist Louis Grizzard's books notes, "Elvis Is Still Dead, and I Don't Feel So Hot Myself."

Elvis came out of Memphis on the tiny Sun Records label run by Sam Phillips. He had gone into the studio in 1953 to record a present for his mother. Phillips's secretary recalled her boss saying that "If I could find me a white boy who can sing like a Negro, I'll make a million dollars." When she heard Presley, she was convinced that he was the one. But Phillips was harder to persuade. He didn't like any of the country repertoire that Presley recorded. But when he heard him roar into "That's All Right, Mama," by black artist Arthur Crudup, he heard what he had been waiting for.

Sun released five Presley singles, none of which were major hits. In the fall of 1955, his contract was purchased by RCA Victor for an unheard of $40,000 and within five months he released "Heartbreak Hotel," his first chart-topping song.

Fifteen of his top songs were recorded in the next five years. Although he was never quite the same musical force after that, he never lost his importance

Tour guides catch their breath on August 17, 1987, the day after fans crowded Graceland on the tenth anniversary of Elvis's death. *(AP/Wide World Photos)*

as a rock symbol. He grew into a major Las Vegas attraction and his movies, while never critically acclaimed, all made money.

Presley's generosity was legendary. He surrounded himself with family members and a retinue of hangers-on in Graceland, the mansion he built in his hometown. The pressure to maintain the youthful image in an aging body and an addiction to a pharmacopeia of drugs were eventually too much for him and led to his death at age forty-two. Graceland almost immediately became a place of pilgrimage for his fans. They came to tour his home, pay respects at his grave, and on the anniversary of his death, simply to show up and remember what it was like to be young in the 1950s when they first heard him sing.

Elvis Up Close, which is located right across the street and is part of the Graceland complex, displays personal memorabilia, including Presley's clothing, portraits, and family items.

■ **LOCATION:** Graceland is located on Elvis Presley Boulevard. (U.S. 51) south of Interstate 55. ■ **HOURS:** Daily, 8–5, April to August; 9–5, March, September, and October; Closed Tuesday, November to February. ■ **ADMISSION:** Combination ticket to Graceland Elvis Up Close, $15.95; Graceland alone, $7.95. ■ **TELEPHONE:** (901) 332-3322

NASHVILLE

COUNTrY MUSIC HALL OF FAME

In 1961 the National Broadcasting Company decided to drop the oldest show on radio from its network lineup. *Grand Ole Opry,* never missing a beat nor a broadcast, was relegated to its home base, Nashville's clear-channel WSM, and a few other stations in the South. It looked very much like the end of an era, the slow fade of country music from the national spotlight.

Instead, the 1960s became country's biggest decade, when it burst out of its regional base to capture the greatest audience in its history. By 1969, the number of stations carrying this style of music had increased almost eight-fold, from 81 to 610. That year the Opry had to cut off the invitation list at six thousand for the annual birthday bash it throws for itself. Major country artists were crossing over to the pop charts, while rock artists dipped into country techniques.

"Nashville cats play clean as country water," sang the Lovin' Spoonful, "Nashville cats play wild as mountain dew." Recording studios suddenly popped up everywhere in central Nashville. With costs much lower than in other recording centers and with such an enormous reservoir of musical talent, Nashville suddenly became Music City, U.S.A.: Country, rock, and pop records were made here. So were commercials. But country music traditionalists didn't like the changes that came over their music. They especially disliked the introduction of the snare drum, since it betokened rock's influence. The city and the music were transformed to such an extent that afterward, artists would state: "I was country when country wasn't cool."

The Country Music Hall of Fame is a tribute to the history and style of both the music and the city that nurtured it. A visitor will find displays relating to virtually every major figure in country, from Roy Acuff to Bill Monroe to Garth Brooks. Rhinestone costumes. Guitars. Old radio gear. Minnie Pearl's hats and Elvis Presley's solid gold Cadillac. In addition, admission to RCA Victor's local studio, for a behind-the-scenes look at the record business, is part of the admission price.

■ **LOCATION:** Take Exit 209B from Interstate 40 in central Nashville and follow the signs to 4 Music Square, East. ■ **HOURS:** Daily, 9–5; 8–8, in summer. ■ **ADMISSION:** $6.50 ■ **TELEPHONE:** (615) 255-5333

OPRYLaND USA

In 1974 when the Grand Ole Opry moved to its elaborate new quarters and became the central attraction of a whole entertainment complex named for the show, anyone could see that country music had gone from down home to Disney. George D. Hay, a former newspaper reporter, founded the radio show in Nashville in 1925. It was called the *WSM Barn Dance,* but Hay was tickled by the fact that it followed a program of grand opera. So, in his radio persona of the Solemn Old Judge, Hay took to introducing his show as the Grand Ole Opry, and that's the name that stuck.

For forty-nine years it broadcast from various venues in central Nashville, the last thirty-one of those years in a former church tabernacle, the Ryman Auditorium (*see* next entry). But with the explosion of country music in the 1960s, the Opry made the decision to go upscale. While holding on to its older, predominantly small town and rural base, it expanded its appeal to families and the theme park crowd. The park celebrates various American musical styles. There is a hotel on the grounds. The cable studios of The Nashville Network. The Acuff Theatre, presenting Las Vegas style musical reviews. Riverboat rides aboard a paddle wheeler.

But the performances of the Opry are still at center stage. That's what continues to bring in the crowds all year long, when all the roller coasters are shut down. No longer a regional attraction, the Opry's fans come from Canada and every state in the Union. Tickets must be purchased months in advance.

There is no advance word on who will be performing at any given show. Just being at the Opry, in the presence of country's legends, is enough.

■ **LOCATION:** Opryland is northeast of central Nashville and is accessible from the Briley Parkway (Tennessee 155) exit of either Interstate 40 or 65. ■ **HOURS:** Dates and times vary for different attractions. Broadcasts of the Opry and TNN shows go on all year. Opryland theme park operates on a daily schedule Memorial Day to Labor Day; weekends in late spring and early fall, and is closed from mid-November to late March. It is best to call in advance for times. ■ **ADMISSION:** The three-day Opryland USA Passport includes admission to the theme park, a cruise on the General Jackson paddle wheeler, a matinee performance of the Opry and two other shows. Last available price was $80, but that is subject to change. For tickets to an Opry broadcast, write to Grand Ole Opry Tickets, 2808 Opryland Drive, Nashville, Tennessee, 37214. ■ **TELEPHONE:** (615) 889-6700 is the customer service number. Representatives can answer your questions or direct your call to the proper section of the park.

RYMAN AUDITORIUM

During the last days, the paint was peeling and plaster was falling off the walls. Yet when Grand Ole Opry star Minnie Pearl gave her final comedy

The Grand Old Opry began as the WSM Barn Dance (left) and for thirty-one years occupied a former church tabernacle, Ryman Auditorium (right). *(Courtesy of Opryland, USA)*

performance at the Ryman Auditorium she broke down and cried. "I hate to leave," she sobbed to the audience, "It's killing me."

Ryman Auditorium, a onetime religious tabernacle, had been home to the Opry from 1943 to March 1974. From this base, country music expanded from a regional sound to a national phenomenon. So big that it required an entire entertainment complex (*see* previous entry) to hold it. "The thought of leaving really hadn't bothered me until tonight," said singer Hank Snow at the closing performance, "But you've got to realize that for the last ten years this place has been a fire hazard."

But country doesn't forget. The building, which dates to 1891 and was noted for its fine acoustics, has been given a facelift and turned into a small museum. Many veteran performers still recall the muggy summer evenings as the audience endured stifling heat while musicians ran across the alley to Tootsie's Orchid Lounge for the refreshment to carry on. Visitors can now go backstage at the Ryman and visit the dressing rooms and prop storage area.

■ **LOCATION:** The Ryman is located in a downtown area, several blocks to the east of where most of the music business is now centered. It is at 116 Fifth Avenue, North, most easily reached by the eastbound Broadway exit from Interstate 40. ■ **HOURS:** Daily, 8:30–4:30. ■ **ADMISSION:** $2.50 ■ **TELEPHONE:** (615) 254-1445

PALL MALL

SERGEANT YORK MEMORIAL PARK

In 1941, as America was preparing for war, a movie was released to celebrate a hero of the previous conflict. By that time, World War I—the war to end all wars—was already receding in memory, replaced by the far more immediate menace of Nazi Germany and Japan. Most of the films made about the earlier war, had dealt with its waste and the disillusion of those who fought in it. One of them, *They Gave Him a Gun,* even blamed the war for training the future gangsters of the 1920s in the use of firearms.

But *Sergeant York* was another kind of war movie. Alvin York was a sincerely religious man who had applied for conscientious objector status to avoid the draft. When he was turned down, he went off to France and found himself in the middle of the terrible battle in the Argonne Forest, in October 1918. With his platoon trapped by a German machine gun nest and taking horrific casualties, York charged the enemy position. He wiped out the gun crew and captured four officers and 128 men. General John Pershing called it "the most conspicuous act of heroism in the entire war."

York then returned to his home in the eastern Tennessee hills, celebrated in his home state, but almost forgotten in the rest of the country. Until he was portrayed in an Oscar-winning performance by Gary Cooper. It was almost a career-defining role for Cooper, a showcase for his relaxed demeanor and his slow-to-anger-but-then-watch-out persona. The movie also made York a symbol of American heroism.

The gristmill York operated on the Wolf River has been restored as a memorial park. It is a tranquil spot, now run as a state historic area. York and other members of his family are buried in the Wolf River Cemetery, four miles south of the park.

■ **LOCATION:** On U.S. 127, about 10 miles north of Jamestown. ■ **HOURS:** Daily, dawn to dusk. ■ **ADMISSION:** Free

PIGEON FORGE

DOLLYWOOD

This little town on the main road to Great Smoky Mountains National Park was a significant tourist stop before its local star came home. But the return of Dolly Parton, born nearby in a cabin on the Little Pigeon River, made Pigeon Forge a slice of Nashville in the mountains.

Parton moved away as soon as she graduated high school in 1964. "I got my diploma on Friday night and was in Nashville on Saturday morning," she recalled later, "Relatives used to tell me that I started singing about the same time I started talking." She had already appeared on the Grand Ole Opry and was fiercely ambitious about making a career in country music. She got by on hot dogs and the help of friends until getting her big break— singing with the Porter Waggoner band in 1967. Her remarkable voice and even more remarkable pulchritude made her an immediate hit with country fans. She shrewdly parlayed that into a career in pop music and movies, getting both a starring role and a number one hit song out of the movie *9 to 5* in 1981.

She made the decision to return to the mountains a few years later, after extensive hospitalization for a bleeding ulcer. Dollywood, the theme park she built, is a far more ambitious project than the numerous tourist operations founded by other country performers. While musically-based, it celebrates the virtues and crafts of mountain life in its shops and exhibits, besides containing the usual theme park thrill rides. Major concerts are held throughout the season. There is also a small museum of Parton's life.

■ **LOCATION:** Dollywood is just north of town, on U.S. 441. ■ **HOURS:** Daily, 9–9, June to August; Friday through Wednesday, 9–6, May, September and October; Friday through Sunday, 9–6, November to December. ■ **ADMISSION:** $20 ■ **TELEPHONE:** (615) 428-9488

Virginia

ARLINGTON

MARINe CORPS WAR mEMORIAL

How different the capital area memorials to this century's two most costly wars appear. For the Vietnam War, the memorial is black granite covered with the names of the dead (*see* Washington, D.C.). For World War II, a moment of triumph and pride is depicted in a reproduction of the famed newspaper photograph of the flag-raising on Mount Surabachi, Iwo Jima. One represents an inexpressible sadness, the other a great victory.

The five-week battle for Iwo Jima in the late winter of 1945 was the bloodiest single engagement of the Pacific War. The death toll was 4,917 Americans, overwhelmingly Marines, and about eighteen thousand Japanese defenders. The ferocity of the resistance was astonishing. As the Marines assaulted the defenses on Surabachi, an extinct volcano rising sheer from the ocean, they were forced into hand-to-hand combat in caves and pillboxes. Finally, on the morning of February 23, they reached the summit, littered with the bodies of enemy dead. Using a long piece of pipe, the Marines raised the American flag. It was clearly visible to the forces below and as the banner caught the breeze, ship's horns blared and cheers resounded.

About two hours later, with the mountain secured, a much larger American flag was raised by six Marines. This was the picture snapped by Associated Press photographer Joe Rosenthal. He wired it back to New York in time to make Sunday deadlines. Printed on the front page of newspapers across America, the picture became the most famous photo of the war. Historian John Toland called it "unforgettable, symbolizing simultaneously heroism, suffering and accomplishment." Three of the Marines in the picture were killed later on Iwo Jima, as the fighting on the island did not end for another month. An admiral who witnessed the flag-raising said at the time that the picture "guaranteed that there will be a Marine Corps for another 100 years."

The memorial stands at the northern end of Arlington National Cemetery. The seventy-eight-foot-high bronze reproduction of Rosenthal's photograph was cast by Felix de Weldon.

■ **LOCATION:** Near the Virginia side of the Theodore Roosevelt Bridge (U.S. 50), it is most easily accessible by shuttle bus from the Arlington Memorial

The Marine Corps War Memorial, in June 1989: President Bush urges passage of an amendment to ban flag burning. *(AP/Wide World Photos)*

Cemetery visitor center. ■ **HOURS:** The cemetery is open daily, 8–5; until 7 P.M. from April to September. A Marine Corps color ceremony is held at 7 P.M., Tuesday, from the last week in May to the third week in August. ■ **ADMISSION:** Free

DANVILLE

WRECK OF THE *OLD '97* MEMORIAL

Train wrecks were hardly unusual events in the America of 1903. Safety regulations were indifferently enforced and the annual toll in deaths and injuries routinely topped fifty thousand. So the wreck of the *Old '97* on September 27 of that year, in which about two dozen people lost their lives, hardly rated a blip on the disaster charts.

But someone witnessed it, and was moved enough to write a song. Whoever it was borrowed the melody from a ballad written in the 1860s by Henry

C. Work, "The Ship That Never Returned." Work was a fairly well-known composer in his time and also wrote the Civil War classic, "Marching Through Georgia." Fitted out with the new lyrics, his old song became a classic country ballad as "The Wreck of the Old '97."

In 1924, RCA Victor put the tune on the B side of one of the year's biggest hit records, "The Prisoner's Song." Since the record was such a big-seller, RCA didn't want to take any chances on lawsuits. It asked the lyricist of the "Old '97" song to come forward and pick up his royalties. About fifty claimants emerged but most were quickly uncovered as frauds. One of them, however, proved that he was present at the scene of the wreck. Even though the manuscript he offered as evidence of his authorship was clearly written at a later date (it was the version, in fact, on the RCA record) lower courts decided in his favor. The judgement was later reversed on appeal and the writer of this song is still officially unknown.

Even those unfamiliar with the "Wreck of the Old '97" may recall the tune from its reappearance in the 1950s with yet a third set of lyrics. It was the melody used for the Kingston Trio's classic tale of the man who rode forever 'neath the streets of Boston, "The M.T.A."

■ **LOCATION:** The memorial is west of Danville, on Riverside Drive (U.S. 58). ■ **HOURS:** Daily, dawn to dusk. ■ **ADMISSION:** Free ■ **TELEPHONE:** None

RICHMOND

STAIRCASE OF THE JEFFERSON HOTEL

The Jefferson, grand hotel of Virginia's capital, opened its doors in 1895 and was an immediate sensation. It featured fish and alligator ponds, public areas that were described as the most beautiful in America. And a magnificent staircase ascending from the main lobby.

It was not until forty-five years later, though, that this staircase became famous. According to Richmond lore, it was the model for the staircase in Tara, up which Clark Gable carried a struggling Vivien Leigh, in one of the classic scenes in *Gone with the Wind.* Just as there are dozens of houses in Georgia that claim to be the model for the Tara depicted in the film, there are probably other claimants to the original staircase. This one certainly looks the part, though. Moreover, the entire hotel has been designated as a National Historic Landmark.

■ **LOCATION:** The Jefferson is located in downtown Richmond, at the corner of Franklin and Adams streets, 10 blocks west of the State Capitol. ■ **TELEPHONE:** (804) 788-8000

ILLINOIS

INDIANA

MICHIGAN

MINNESOTA

OHIO

WEST VIRGINIA

WISCONSIN

The Automobile in American Life exhibit at Henry Ford Museum. *(Courtesy of the Henry Ford Museum and Greenfield Village)* See page 186.

GREAT LAKES/OHIO VALLEY

ILLINOIS

1 Statue of Popeye, Chester
2 Biograph Theatre, Chicago
3 Ed Debevic's Restaurant, Chicago
4 Museum of Science and Industry, Chicago
5 Pizzeria Uno, Chicago
6 Sears Tower, Chicago
7 Second City, Chicago
8 Untouchable Tours, Chicago
9 Wrigley Field, Chicago
10 McDonald's Museum, Des Plaines
11 Superman's Hometown, Metropolis
12 John Deere Center, Moline
13 Frank Lloyd Wright Studio, Oak Park
14 Billy Graham Center, Wheaton

INDIANA

15 Auburn-Cord-Duesenberg Museum, Auburn
16 Ernie Pyle Memorial, Dana
17 James Dean Memorial, Fairmount
18 Indianapolis Motor Speedway, Indianapolis
19 Louisville Slugger Factory, Jeffersonville
20 John Dillinger Museum, Nashville
21 Indiana Basketball Hall of Fame, New Castle
22 Cole Porter Birthplace, Peru
23 Holiday World, Santa Claus
24 Notre Dame University, South Bend
25 Studebaker Museum, South Bend

MICHIGAN

26 Fair Lane, Dearborn
27 Henry Ford Museum and Greenfield Village, Dearborn
28 General Motors Building, Detroit
29 Joe Louis Memorial, Detroit
30 Motown Museum, Detroit
31 Edsel and Eleanor Ford House, Grosse Pointe Shores
32 International Skiing Hall of Fame, Ishpeming
33 George Gipp Memorial, Laurium
34 Curwood Castle, Owosso

MINNESOTA

35 Mall of America, Bloomington
36 Paul Bunyan Amusement Center, Brainerd
37 Judy Garland Collection, Grand Rapids
38 Greyhound Origin Center, Hibbing
39 Charles A. Lindbergh Home, Little Falls
40 Sinclair Lewis Home, Sauk Centre
41 Laura Ingalls Wilder Museum, Walnut Grove

OHIO

42 Goodyear World of Rubber, Akron
43 Center for the Study of Popular Culture, Bowling Green
44 Professional Football Hall of Fame, Canton
45 Rock 'n' Roll Hall of Fame, Cleveland
46 Thomas-Oakley Collections of the Garst Museum, Greenville
47 Malabar Farm, Mansfield
48 Popcorn Museum, Marion
49 Bob Evans Farm, Rio Grande
50 Tony Packo's Cafe, Toledo
51 Neil Armstrong Museum, Wapakoneta
52 Zane Grey Museum, Zanesville

WEST VIRGINIA

53 Mother's Day Shrine, Grafton
54 Homer Laughlin China Co., Newell

WISCONSIN

55 Circus World Museum, Baraboo
56 Packers Hall of Fame, Green Bay
57 National Fresh Water Fishing Hall of Fame, Hayward
58 Pabst and Miller Brewery Tours, Milwaukee

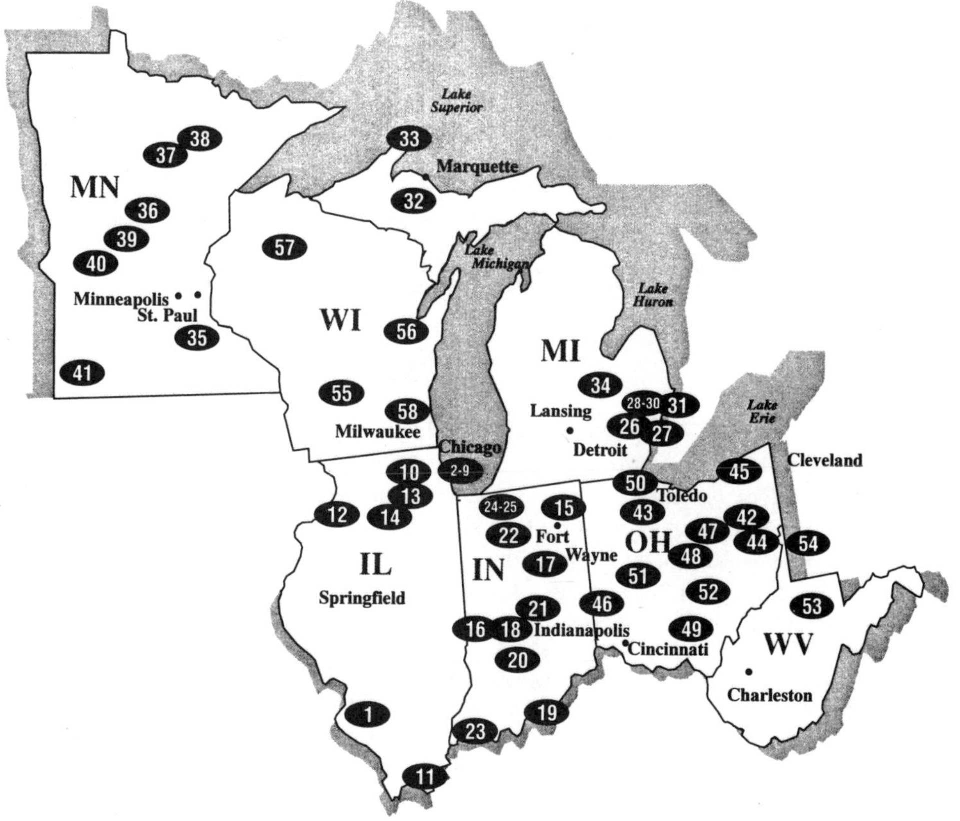
Lake Superior
Marquette
MN
Minneapolis
St. Paul
WI
Lake Michigan
Lake Huron
MI
Lansing
Detroit
Lake Erie
Milwaukee
Chicago
Cleveland
Toledo
Fort Wayne
OH
IL
IN
Springfield
Indianapolis
Cincinnati
WV
Charleston
1
2-9
10
11
12
13
14
15
16
17
18
19
20
21
22
23
24-25
26
27
28-30
31
32
33
34
35
36
37
38
39
40
41
42
43
44
45
46
47
48
49
50
51
52
53
54
55
56
57
58

ILLinoiS

CHESTER

STATUe OF POPEYE

The spinach-loving, pipe-smoking, powerhouse of a cartoon sailor, Popeye was created almost by accident. Elzie Segar was drawing a comic strip called "Thimble Theater" for the King Newspaper Syndicate and in 1929 he decided to send his leading characters, Olive Oyl and her brother Castor, on a sea voyage. "I needed a navigator for the plot line," he explained later, "so I came up with the idea of Popeye. The first thing he was asked was: 'Are you a sailor?' And his response was: 'Do I look like a cowboy?'" It was a typical Popeye line.

Segar was born in this Mississippi River town. He was working as a movie projectionist and house painter when he saw a magazine ad claiming there was big money to be made as a cartoonist. He sent an application to the correspondence school, paid $20 to learn to draw through the mail, and went to Chicago to land a newspaper job. "The editor hired me and because he did nobody could fire me," Segar said later. "Then he told me I could probably do better in New York so I went there and he was right. Things just sort of happened."

In addition to Popeye, Segar was also the creator of a strange little animal with a bright red nose and long tail that moved unstoppably over everything in its way. He called it a jeep, although he never got around to explaining why. When the U.S. Army developed its all-terrain vehicle, some observers felt it bore a strong resemblance to the cartoon figure. So it, too, became a jeep, the name it still bears today.

Segar never lived to see that. He died in 1938 at the age of forty-four from a spleen ailment and the strip was carried on through the years by his associates. The originator of Popeye is remembered in his hometown in a park named after him, with a statue of his best-known character overlooking the river.

■ **LOCATION:** Chester is about 65 miles south of St. Louis, Missouri, by way of Illinois 3.

BIOGRAPH THEATRE

The movie was *Manhattan Melodrama.* It was a gangster film. When John Dillinger, the most wanted man in America, emerged from this theatre after seeing it on the evening of July 22, 1934, the FBI was waiting for him. Tipped off by his landlady, Anna Sage, who was identified then only as "the woman in red," the federal agents brought Dillinger down with shots through the neck and side as he tried to pull his gun. Women dipped their handkerchiefs in his blood.

Dillinger was only 5'-7" and every inch was mean. "The most ruthless butcher of human beings in all the jungles of gangland," opined one newspaper in the obituary. Dillinger indignantly denied such aspersions on his character. "I don't smoke very much," he once said, "and I drink very little. I guess my only bad habit is robbing banks." To many Depression-era observers he was someone to root for, as he continually outwitted police and broke out of their jails. They were willing to overlook the sixteen killings credited to his gang of bank robbers.

There is a museum dedicated to him (*see* Nashville, Indiana) near his hometown. A plaque attached to the wall of the Biograph, which is still in use as a movie theater, describes how he met his end in Chicago.

■ **LOCATION:** The Biograph, a National Historic Landmark, is at 2433 North Lincoln Avenue, on the near North Side.

ED DEBEVIC'S RESTAURANT

Sometime around 1972, it was decided that the 1950s was a "way cool" decade. No one wanted to let go. *Grease* had become a musical smash on Broadway. *Happy Days* was getting huge ratings on TV. Radio stations began switching their formats to play all "Golden Oldies." Elvis was packing 'em in at the big Las Vegas showrooms.

This nostalgia is a familiar phenomenon: The generation that grew up about twenty years ago becomes adults and looks back on the time of their youth as being the best there ever was. It happens every decade. But this was one decade that refused to die: The 1950s nostalgia craze went on far longer than the 1950s did. The sense of a lost world—secure and happy and with a beat you could dance to—was strong.

Then in 1984 people began eating as they had in the 1950s, too. Ed Debevic's, a faithful reconstruction of a genuine fifties diner, was an immediate hit in this city. The inspiration came from Richard Melman, who operates several Chicago eateries with his Lettuce Entertain You Enterprises. The name was made up and "is supposed to sound like the name of a guy back in the kitchen slinging potatoes," said a onetime waitress. "When people ask me where Ed is, I just tell them that he's out playing Bingo or at the VFW."

Ed Debevic's: A "fifties roadside revival." *(AP/Wide World Photos)*

The menu, decor, personnel are all done up in fifties gear and the place has inspired dozens of imitators in every major city in the nation. But with its overstuffed vinyl booths, cherry Cokes, and gum-popping waitresses, Debevic's seems to pull it off best. As one early customer said in astonishment: "Hey, I think I worked here in high school."

■ **LOCATION:** 640 North Wells. ■ **HOURS:** Monday–Saturday, 11 A.M.–midnight; Sunday, 10 A.M.–11 P.M. ■ **TELEPHONE:** (312) 664-1707

MUSEUM OF SCIENCE AND INDUSTRY

The idea for a museum celebrating America's technological and scientific progress began with Julius Rosenwald, president of Sears, Roebuck. Chicago had a great art institute, a museum of natural history, an aquarium, a historical museum. But this was, after all, the "city of the big shoulders." There should be a display of what those shoulders made.

Rosenwald began floating his idea in the early 1920s. He even put up $1 million to finance the project. There were no takers. At this time the former Fine Arts Building of the 1893 Columbian Exposition, the last remaining structure from that world's fair, became vacant. The Field Museum of Natural History had moved into the structure when the fair closed. But when its new home on the lakefront farther north was completed, this model of an ancient Greek temple was left to decay.

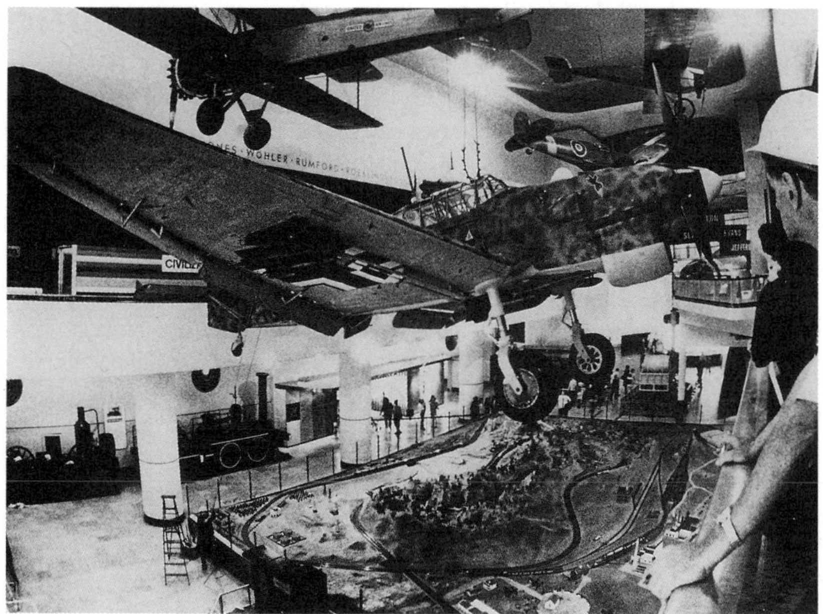

A 1939 German Stuka dive-bomber is hoisted into place at the Museum of Science and Industry (1980). *(AP/Wide World Photos)*

In 1925, Rosenwald agreed to up his offer to $3 million if the voters of Chicago would approve a $5-million-bond issue to rehabilitate the old structure. They did and he did. It took eight years to get the work done (some of the work even dragged on until 1940) but the new Museum of Science and Industry opened just in time for Chicago's second world's fair, the Century of Progress of 1933.

Sally Rand was the star attraction and her fan dances made the headlines, but the museum's exhibits fit the mood of the times. It was the Depression and people were eager to think of the better days ahead and the forces technology would surely bring them. Corporations had been enlisted to underwrite the costs of the displays, leading some to criticize the museum as an advertising mechanism for big business. Nonetheless, the displays are spectacular and the exhibit area is vast. The most popular exhibits are a working coal mine, a captured German submarine, the daily hatching of chicks, and actress Colleen Moore's expansive doll house. But there are also exhibits on biotechnology, agronomics, space flight—all made understandable by good design. Most of all the museum is a monument to America's faith in science and its belief in better living through progress. In that, it is the most American of museums.

■ **LOCATION:** The museum is in Jackson Park, at South Lake Shore Drive and 57th Street. ■ **HOURS:** Daily, 9:30–4. ■ **ADMISSION:** Free ■ **TELEPHONE:** (312) 684-1414

PIZZErIA UNO

Ike Sewell's original intent was to open a Mexican restaurant. He came to Chicago in the late 1930s and began looking for investors. But one guy who had the cash and the interest tried to talk Sewell into a different enterprise. He had just made a visit to Sicily and was impressed with a new dish he sampled there. It was a pizza, but not the pie-shaped kind that was becoming popular in a few American cities with big Italian populations. This kind of pizza was a deep-dish variety, an entire meal in a couple of slices.

Sewell began experimenting and in 1943 he opened Pizzeria Uno, specializing in the new deep-dish pizza. That style now has become a Chicago institution, and through the wonder of franchising has spread across the country.

Pizza was part of the fast-food revolution that swept across America in the 1950s, as more women entered the work force and did not have time for elaborate home-cooked dinners. Pizza was inexpensive and filling. Its growth paralleled that of the hamburger chains (*see* McDonald's Museum, Des Plaines, Illinois). By the 1970s, chic California restaurants had introduced "gourmet" pizzas, with extremely thin crusts and exotic toppings that thrilled the Beverly Hills crowd. Dominos began delivering pizza right to the house, an innovation that vaulted the Michigan company from obscurity to a position as one of the top players in the business. When Dominos owner sold the Detroit Tigers baseball team, the team was bought by another pizza magnate—Mike Ilitch, the owner of chief rival Little Caesar's. Pizza has become big business.

But Chicago still lays claim to being the pizza capital of America. Pizzeria Uno (and its auxiliary operation one block away, Pizzeria Due) are culinary landmarks and the deep-dish variety is recognized as the local standard of excellence. While some entrepreneurs actually did open one or two Mexican restaurants in town, Sewell never regretted his switch.

■ **LOCATION:** 29 East Ohio, just off State Street. ■ **HOURS:** 11:30 A.M.–1 A.M.; Sunday to midnight. ■ **TELEPHONE:** (312) 321-1000

SEARS TOWER

It has always been important in America to be the biggest. In Japan, people say "The nail that sticks out gets hammered down." But in American culture, the competition to be first and tallest and widest has energized the way of life. So when Sears announced in 1971 that it was about to build the highest office building in the country, the statement was treated with some significance.

The World Trade Center in New York was already under construction. Just a few years earlier, its builders, the New York Port Authority, announced that the twin towers would rise to 1,350 feet, thus replacing the Empire State Building (*see* New York, New York) as America's number one skyscraper. Before the Trade Center even could be topped off, Sears raised the ante by 104 feet. The Empire State had argued that its TV tower boosted its height to 1,414 feet, still taller than the Trade Center. But Sears rendered even that point moot with its 1,454-foot construction.

The question of height is a symbolic exclamation point. The Woolworth Building, in New York, was the country's first "cathedral of commerce." Finished in 1913, its height of 792 feet was intended as a celebration of its dime store origins and a towering ad for the company. Woolworth held the title for only sixteen years. By the end of the 1920s, two new New York skyscrapers were competing for the title. Both the Bank of the Manhattan (now known as 40 Wall Tower) and Chrysler Corporation announced plans for Manhattan's tallest tower. When Chrysler topped things off at 925 feet, the Bank of Manhattan went two feet higher and called it a building. What the bank didn't know was that Chrysler had secretly assembled its innovative spire, the building's visual signature through the years, that would elevate its total height by another 123 feet. When the spire went into place, the mortified Bank of the Manhattan found itself relegated to second place.

Chrysler's triumph lasted only two years, until the Empire State Building was completed in 1931 at a height of 1,250 feet. Its reign would run more than forty years. Sears emphasized its role as the new hallmark of height by placing its observation deck on the building's 103rd floor—one floor higher than the Empire State's total of 102. Even though a building's height is measured in feet and not in stories, it did underline the passing of the crown.

The Sears Tower, built by the firm of Skidmore, Owings and Merrill, occupies an entire city block and encloses 3.9 million feet of floor area. The structural steel frame is coated with black aluminum and bronze-tinted glass. The observation deck affords unmatchable views of the Loop, Lake Michigan, and the Illinois prairie, stretching off to the horizon.

■ **LOCATION:** The Sears Tower is situated between Wacker Drive and Franklin Street, Jackson Street and Adams Street. ■ **HOURS:** 9 A.M. to midnight. ■ **ADMISSION:** $3.75 ■ **TELEPHONE:** (312) 875-9696

SECONd CITY

In 1959, a group of young performers occasionally gathered at the Compass Bar, near the University of Chicago campus, to try out new ideas about comedy. They were convinced that improvisation within the framework of a dramatic sketch, dealing with topical matters and sex in all its zaniness, was the way to a fresher and funnier comic sense. At that time, comedy was frozen in traditional patterns. Veterans of theater and vaudeville, many of them with radio shows that had been aired for decades, performed carefully scripted routines, tested over and over again. Older audiences seemed to like the predictability. But wild, new patterns were emerging in the culture.

In New York, Lenny Bruce took the stage with improvisational bits that stretched the boundaries of comedy beyond its breaking point, landing him in legal trouble for violation of obscenity laws. In San Francisco, Mort Sahl was finding laughs simply by free-form commentary on the news. Like the young Chicagoans, these comedians' sensibilities were shaped by jazz, improvisational music that depended on free-form riffs. That's the sense that the Compass Players brought to comedy.

Looking for a permanent home for their performances, they turned to a more northern section of the city. At that time, North Wells Street was just beginning its transformation from a district of broken-down storefronts and boarding houses into Old Town. One of the first examples of restoration of an entire urban neighborhood, Old Town was starting to draw a hip, young, crowd—American rebels who felt the suburbs were spiritual death and turned to the city of Chicago for sustenance. Chicago had always taken a backseat to New York, in population as well as cultural matters. But the regeneration of Old Town seemed to herald a civic rebirth that could challenge the dominance of Manhattan. So the ironically named Second City Company moved to Old Town and proceeded to redefine American comedy.

The list of major stars who emerged from Second City goes on forever. Mike Nichols, Elaine May, and Barbara Harris were in the first wave. A later bunch, led by Gilda Radner, John Belushi, and Bill Murray, went on to win wider fame on *Saturday Night Live.* A Second City adjunct in Toronto produced John Candy, Martin Short, Andrea Martin and brought Canada into the comic mainstream. Other companies, dedicated to the same tenets of improvisational and topical humor, opened throughout the country. Even in New York.

Second City is still doing business at the old stand. Tickets can be hard to come by on weekends and must be reserved several weeks in advance. The cast may be unknowns, but if the past is any guide, you'd be advised to remember their names. In five years, you'll say that you saw them when.

■ **LOCATION:** Second City is at 1616 North Wells, north and slightly west of central Chicago. ■ **HOURS:** Check by phone for performance times. ■ **ADMISSION:** Ticket prices vary; call ahead. ■ **TELEPHONE:** (312) 337-3992

UNTOUcHABLE TOURS

Fedora hat. Spats. Wide-striped suit. Tommy gun. Your basic Chicago gangster. And while the wild nights of gin and gore pretty much ended with the repeal of Prohibition and the subsequent conviction of Al Capone for income tax evasion, this city's image was already fixed.

Even today, among Europeans who know little else about America, the words Chicago and gangster are usually inseparable. As recently as 1974, a British singing group, Paper Lace, had a chart-topping hit record with a number called "The Night Chicago Died," which recounted an entirely fictitious battle between cops and Capone. (The song irritated Chicagoans because it referred to the "east side" of Chicago, of which there is none.)

Wrigley Field in 1990 after a renovation *(left, AP/Wide World Photos)* and a view of the outfield, stands, and neighboring houses *(right, courtesy of Roger Matuz)*.

The Untouchables, as a long-running television series and later as a movie, reinforced the image of this city. So the curiosity remains, maybe stronger than ever, about the sites associated with the bad men of the 1920s. Capone and Frank Nitti and Machine Gun Kelly. The Valentine's Day Massacre, probably the most chronicled and depicted event in the history of American crime. The emergence of Eliot Ness and his stalwart band as a force for good.

Untouchable Tours run bus excursions to the old hot spots: former brothels, speakeasies, hideouts, shootout sites, and places where the end came for a dozen would-be Little Caesars. It's all done in fun, but the tours are a good introduction to this part of the city's history and the violent past that still lingers just below the contemporary veneer.

■ **LOCATION:** The tours leave from Here's Chicago, located in the Old Water Tower pumping station, at 163 East Pearson at Michigan Avenue. They also depart from Capone's Chicago, at 605 North Clark Street, at Ohio Avenue. ■ **HOURS:** From Here's Chicago: 10 A.M., Monday through Saturday, and 11 A.M. Sunday. From Capone's Chicago: 1 P.M., Thursday through Saturday, and 2 P.M. Sunday, with evening tours at 7:30 P.M. Friday and 5 P.M. Saturday. Reservations are needed. ■ **ADMISSION:** Varies with time and tour. Call in advance. ■ **TELEPHONE:** (312) 881-1195

WRIGLeY FIELD

To the baseball purist, this is the way it should be. Grass on the field, ivy on the walls, most games in the daytime, a real city neighborhood all around. Along with Boston's Fenway Park, this is baseball at its nostalgic best.

Wrigley Field doesn't have the stylistic peculiarities of Fenway (*see* Boston, Massachusetts). And, heaven knows, it doesn't have the clouds of glory that hover over Yankee Stadium (*see* New York, New York). It isn't even as old as Tiger Stadium in Detroit, but it retains much more of an old-time feel. Still, the home of the Chicago Cubs is a beloved baseball shrine. When the city finally broke down and permitted light towers here for night games in the late 1980s, there was almost a sense of loss—of something special going out of the game for good.

At the behest of the ballpark's residential neighbors, Cubs management had the sense to limit the number of night games. Since many of these neighbors climb to the roofs of their apartment houses to peer over the outfield walls and watch the games for free, they really can't complain too much.

The team, the park, and the fans are all part of a unique institution. As political columnist George Will put it: "Being a Cubs fan teaches you that man was not born to pleasure." The adjective most often used to describe them is "long-suffering." Long, indeed. The Cubs won consecutive World Series in 1907–8, and have not won another since. Their last pennant came in 1945 and the fifty-year wait for another (as of this writing) is the longest in professional sports history.

The Cubs have become a national treasure, followed with compassion by fans across the country. The adulation is inspired in no small part by the wonderful old ballpark in which they play. It is the second-smallest park in the majors (only Fenway seats fewer) and sellouts are a regular occurrence during the summer months. Weekend tickets especially must be procured several months in advance.

■ **LOCATION:** Wrigley Field is at Clark and Addison streets, on the city's North Side. ■ **TELEPHONE:** (312) 281-5050

DES PLAINES

McDONaLD'S MUSEUM

Some cultural historians say the 1950s really began on July 9, 1955, when "Rock around the Clock" became the first rock hit to top the music charts. But maybe the date should be pushed back about twelve weeks, to April 15, 1955. That was when Ray Kroc opened the first McDonald's franchise, in this Chicago suburb. "You deserve a break today," sang the McDonald's commercial, and the restaurant came to be regarded as just that—a little reward for working parents and their kids. Almost 100 billion burgers later, that event can be recognized as a watershed in American life. McDonald's made dining out, a rare and special event for most families before the 1950s, an everyday experience. The food was served fast and inexpensively, using the principles of assembly-line mass production with high standards of efficiency and quality control.

The pace of life was accelerating in the mid-1950s and most people didn't have time to linger over their meals. Americans were also on the road more often and looked for familiar places to eat, places where they knew what they would be getting. Kroc, an authentic marketing genius, somehow sensed all this when he happened upon Dick and Mac McDonald's operation in San Bernardino, California. Theirs was a very successful business and something of a local institution. The brothers were quite happy right where they were and had no wider ambitions. But Kroc saw the future and it was filled with fries and hamburgers. He negotiated franchising rights with the McDonalds, and then came back to the Midwest to start it up.

With its golden arches and deliberately limited menus, self-service, and young, cheerful staff, McDonald's became a familiar presence across the country. It began as a suburban institution, but expanded into city centers and small towns. Picking a site on the highway just outside of town, McDonald's usually managed to drive the old soda shop and cafe down on the square right out of business. Ironically, in the 1980s McDonald's ads began incorporating the nostalgic and communal symbols that had formerly belonged to these old-style restaurants. McDonald's had become so big it could create its own nostalgia.

That is the purpose of this museum, a nostalgic restoration of Kroc's original drive-in. It is outfitted just the way it would have been in 1955, from the equipment in the kitchen to the wrappings on the burgers to the cars in the parking lot. The actual restaurant had closed in 1983, but the corporation decided to keep it standing for sentimental reasons. It was reopened as a museum two years later.

■ **LOCATION:** The original McDonald's is at 400 North Lee in this northwest Chicago suburb. Take Interstate 90 west, beyond the turnoff to O'Hare Airport, to northbound Lee. ■ **HOURS:** Tuesday through Saturday, 10–4, and Sunday, 1–4, June–August. Wednesday, Friday, and Saturday, 10–4, April, May, September, October. Closed November–March. ■ **ADMISSION:** Free ■ **TELEPHONE:** (708) 297-5022

METROPOLIS

SUPERmAN'S HOMETOwN

William A. McBane was a dreamer of dreams and planner of towns. He came to southern Illinois in 1839 and located what he felt would be the best place for the last railroad bridge across the Ohio River before its meeting with the Mississippi. There already was a community nearby, Massac. McBane ignored it and platted his own town. He saw it as the great metropolis of the West. So he called it Metropolis City.

We now jump ahead ninety-nine years. Two Cleveland high school students, Jerry Siegel and Joe Shuster, had conceived the idea of the Man of Steel—the Caped Crusader, Superman. Although he was faster than a speeding bullet, more powerful than a locomotive, it still took the two young cartoonists several years to find a publisher. In 1938, Superman made his debut in the first issue of Action Comics. Within a year, it became the top-selling comic in America and an entirely new Superman Comic was created just for him. He was a super star.

Superman could fly and he could see through things. He was indestructible and kind. His powers were godlike. But he had certain vulnerabilities that were endearing. A little chunk of Kryptonite, the planet on which he was born, could render him helpless as an infant. And he also had to keep ducking into phone booths to change clothes and become super again.

The concept thrilled America. By 1940, Superman was a network radio star and appeared as a newspaper comic strip. There were movie serials and a TV show. He was the star of a Broadway musical and when a feature film was finally made about him in 1979 it was so successful it spun off two sequels. Superman sold more than one million issues of Action Comics monthly at his peak. He was far and away the most potent comic book force in history.

However, after half a century, sales dwindled and Superman's publishers tried to kill him off in 1992. The outcry was so fierce that he was resurrected a few months later, amid tremendous national publicity. One year later he returned triumphantly to network television in the series *Lois and Clark: The New Adventures of Superman,* as a more sensitive superguy for the 1990s.

Superman and his alter ego, mild-mannered reporter Clark Kent, live in a place called Metropolis. From the tall buildings and nasty individuals depicted in the strip, it is obvious this was intended to represent New York City. But the good folks of Metropolis, Illinois, were having none of that. In 1972, Metropolis officially designated itself as Superman's Hometown. Its weekly paper changed its named to the *Metropolis Planet,* just like Kent's employer. It put up a billboard on the outskirts, painted Superman's likeness on the water tower, erected his statue on the square and even put up a telephone booth where little visitors could duck in and practice changing clothes. They could also hear a recorded message from Superman.

It may not be the fate that William McBane foresaw for his city. But could he leap tall buildings at a single bound? Hardly.

■ **LOCATION:** Metropolis is located just west of Interstate 24, about 12 miles northwest of Paducah, Kentucky. All attractions are free and are open daily.

MOLINE

JOHN dEERE CENTER

In 1836, when John Deere arrived in Illinois, he noticed something about the soil. It was moist, sticky, much harder to work after being broken than the rocky soil of his native Vermont. The loam would stick to the blades of the plows, accumulate into mushy mounds, and make it impossible to drive a straight furrow.

Deere, a blacksmith, spent much of his time repairing iron plows broken by the pull of the horse teams in the heavy loam. He understood that another material was needed and on a visit to the sawmill of a former Vermont neighbor he saw what it was; a blade made of Sheffield steel.

"I carried it back to my shop, cut off the teeth with a hand chisel, and then heated the remaining steel on the forge, shaping it as best I could," he would later recall. That, in short, was how America's first steel plow was invented, a discovery that revolutionized agriculture in the nation's breadbasket. It was self-scouring, durable, and light enough to be carried on a man's shoulder. Within ten years Deere was selling enough of them to move his shop from its original location in Grand Detour, on the Rock River, to Moline, where the river flowed into the Mississippi.

Deere died in 1886 and for the next two generations farm implements continued to be the company's lone product. But after World War II, a subtle change came over the company. America had long since changed from a farming nation to an urban nation. Now it was slowly becoming a suburban nation. Little homes were sprouting on former farm fields outside the big cities, and all those homes had a patch of lawn out in front. Deere became the leading manufacturer of machines to mow those lawns. Today, while the company continues to manufacture heavy farm equipment, most of its advertising is concentrated on the suburban customers, who tend their piece of green as assiduously as John Deere's neighbors looked after their crops in his day.

The Deere Center, designed by noted architect Eero Saarinen, contains exhibits that show off company products, past and present. They trace the advances in agricultural machinery, from Deere's first plow to the latest combines, and the evolution of the power lawn mower.

■ **LOCATION:** The Deere Center is on the southern edge of the city, on Illinois 5 (John Deere Road). ■ **HOURS:** Daily, 9–5:30. ■ **ADMISSION:** Free ■ **TELEPHONE:** (309) 765-8000

OAK PARK

FRANK LLOYD WRIGHT STUDIO

Asked in a courtroom whether he was the world's greatest architect, Frank Lloyd Wright responded: "I am." When questioned about that statement later, he said: "Well, I was under oath." Wright was a man who never doubted his own genius and he became the best-known architect America ever produced. "Early in life," he said, "I had to choose between honest arrogance and

Frank Lloyd Wright's studio entrance at Oak Park. *(Photograph by Jon Miller, Hedrich-Blessing, courtesy of The Frank Lloyd Wright Home and Studio Foundation)*

hypocritical humility. I chose honest arrogance. No coward ever did creative work." Even when he was awarded a gold medal by the American Institute of Architects in 1948, he was so resented by members of the profession that they protested the honor, claiming that his qualifications were open to "serious question."

Wright never claimed he was easy to get along with. He came to Chicago to study with Louis Sullivan, regarded as the father of the skyscraper, then turned on his mentor and declared the skyscraper "inhuman." In 1893, at the age of twenty-four, Wright opened his Oak Park studio and set to work developing his theories of domestic architecture. This came to be known as the "prairie style," because the lines of the houses he built here reflected the horizontal planes of the surrounding flat landscape. "Why are houses so alike all over America," he demanded. "Let inspiration come to us the natural way. Why plant more Oxford Gothic on the plains of Oklahoma? Let us mimic no more. If we build in the desert, let the house know the desert and the desert be proud of the house by making the house an extension of the desert."

Wright's Oak Park homes were regarded as shocking in their time. In this prosperous suburb, filled with Victorian homes of lacy woodwork and dormer windows and high chimneys, he built low-slung structures. They looked like intrusions from another era, which, in some regards, they were. The low ceilings annoyed many of his clients, and so did the final bills, which frequently came in at twice the original estimates. The conservative residents of Oak Park were also outraged when Wright left his wife and ran off to Europe with a neighbor's wife. She was later murdered by a deranged servant and Wright then moved to Japan with a sculptress before finally obtaining a divorce. Oak Park never really forgave him.

Still, there is no denying genius. After Wright's death in 1959, when passions were well cooled, the Chicago suburb began taking stock of what it had—the greatest concentration of Frank Lloyd Wright buildings in the world. There are more than twenty-five of them here and architectural tours leave daily from the Oak Park Visitors Center. His home and studio, where he worked until 1911, has also been restored and is open to visitors.

■ **LOCATION:** Oak Park is west of central Chicago by way of Interstate 290 (Eisenhower Expressway). The studio is at 951 Chicago Avenue and the visitors center is at 158 North Forest. ■ **HOURS:** Tours of the studio are given Monday through Friday, at 11, 1, and 3, and on weekends, 11–4. The visitors center is open daily, 10–5. ■ **ADMISSION:** To the studio, $5. Self-guided architectural walking tour cassettes are available for $5 at the visitors center. ■ **TELEPHONE:** (708) 848-1500

WHEATON

BILLY GRAHAM CENTeR

He grew up in Charlotte, North Carolina, by all accounts a typical teenager of the 1930s. He liked fast cars and pretty girls and used to throw spitballs at friends during Sunday church services. But while still in high school, Billy Graham attended a revival conducted by the Reverend Mordecai Ham and was "saved." Graham began delivering street-corner sermons in his hometown, chastising friends for cursing, and making plans to attend Christian colleges. He had embarked on a life that would make him the best-known evangelist in the world, a confidante to presidents, and a regular on the list of America's most admired men.

He was strong in condemning Communism during the Red scares of the 1950s, but later preached in the (then) Soviet Union and called for reconciliation. "Billy doesn't have the capacity to preach to people and not fall in love with them," said the editor of an evangelical publication in a 1986 interview. "He preached to those people who before were nothing but ideological images and he felt their lives." His books, newspaper column, and televised crusades have influenced more people than any minister in contemporary times.

Graham graduated from Wheaton College in 1943 and became pastor of his first church in the nearby Chicago suburb of Western Springs. Six years later, he was heading rallies nationwide as an evangelist of Youth for Christ. In one Los Angeles appearance, he made six thousand converts. This so impressed newspaper publisher William Randolph Hearst that he directed his chain to give Graham the all-out celebrity treatment. Hearst liked Graham's uncompromising stand against Communism. In a 1953 crusade in Tennessee, Graham ordered the ropes dividing the black and white sides of the audience be taken down or "you can have the revival without me."

By the mid-1950s, he was the country's top religious personality. A brilliant speaker, passionate but controlled, with a knack for projecting a simple sincerity to massive audiences, Graham was made for the television age. He was invited to the White House by Dwight D. Eisenhower and later developed a close relationship with Lyndon Johnson. When Richard Nixon was under fire during the Watergate hearings, Graham staunchly defended him. But when he heard some of the tapes made in Nixon's office, Graham was appalled. "What comes through in these tapes is not the man I had known for many years," he said. Afterward, Graham was reluctant to be pulled into political life, although he did speak at President Clinton's inauguration in 1993.

The figures of the fictional Elmer Gantry and the very real Jim Bakker and Jimmie Swaggart—charlatans brought down by greed and sex—have become the dominant images of the evangelist in America's popular culture. Yet Graham has remained an image of rectitude, untouched by scandal or fiscal impropriety. The Billy Graham Center, at his alma mater, has exhibits on the history of evangelism in America, as well as personal memorabilia from his ministry and travels.

■ **LOCATION:** The Billy Graham Center is on the Wheaton campus, at 500 East College Avenue. Wheaton is about 30 miles west of Chicago by way of Interstate 290 and Roosevelt Road (Illinois 38). ■ **HOURS:** Monday through Saturday, 9:30–5:30; Sunday, 1–5. ■ **ADMISSION:** Free ■ **TELEPHONE:** (708) 260-5909

InDianA

AUBURN-CORD-DUESENBERG MUSEUM

They were American classics. They roared out of the 1920s, with their low, sleek lines and their massive engines. The Auburn, the Cord, and the Duesenberg were the preferred vehicles of international playboys and rakish movie stars, tearing up the racing competition and the highways. And for a few years, just before their extinction in the Depression economy of the 1930s, the cars were all made in this northeastern Indiana town.

The first clutch-driven car with electrical ignition was built in Indiana and during the early days of the auto industry, the state was a leading manufacturing center. Studebaker remained a major player until the 1950s (*see* South Bend, Indiana, further on). But it was a young auto executive in Auburn, Indiana, E. L. Cord, who captured the country's heart: Joining the Auburn Company as a salesman, in 1926, at the age of thirty-one, Cord became the head of the company. Almost immediately he acquired Duesenberg, the Indianapolis-based car company. Its cars were so glamorous and fast that they contributed a slang phrase to the language: "It's a doozey."

Cord was famous for driving around the country and stopping at service stations and garages, asking mechanics and motorists what they wanted in a car and how they thought a great car should look. By 1929, Auburn's line of luxury sedans had become a force in the industry. His stock car model was the first American machine to exceed one hundred miles an hour by stop watch.

But Cord was after something more, an ultimate driving machine. He teamed with a young designer, Gordon M. Buehrig, and in 1935 they brought forth the Cord 810. It had front-wheel drive, retractable headlights, a supercharged V-8 engine that was capable of 115 miles an hour. A total of thirty-seven engineering firsts were in the car, twenty-seven of which were adopted in standard production by the industry. But with a selling price of $2,700, the Cord 810 was $800 more expensive than the Cadillac, the luxury car standard. In 1937, very few people were in a position to spend that kind of money for a car. It went out of production after two years and 2,320 models. A few months later the Auburn and Duesenberg lines shut down, too.

The country never forgot, though. Thirty years later, companies attempted—unsuccessfully—to build modern versions of the design. Among collectors, no American-made cars are more highly prized. At his 1965 retirement, Buehrig (who had subsequently gone on to Ford and helped design the Continental) said the comment about the Cord that pleased him most was: "It looks as if it was born on the road."

The museum is located in a former company showroom, built in 1930, and displays 150 classic cars, with special emphasis on those assembled in Auburn.

■ **LOCATION:** Auburn is located off Interstate 65, about 20 miles north of Fort Wayne. The museum is off the Indiana 8 exit, at 1600 South Wayne Street. ■ **HOURS:** Daily, 9–6. ■ **ADMISSION:** $5 ■ **TELEPHONE:** (219) 925-1444

DANA

ERNIE PYLE MEMORIAL

About two weeks before he was machine-gunned by a sniper, in the World War II battle for Okinawa, Ernie Pyle got the full celebrity treatment in *Life* magazine: "America's favorite war correspondent," read the headline. The story touched upon his shyness, his reluctance to play the role of the Pulitzer-Prize-winning reporter whose dispatches from the front lines were carried in the Scripps-Howard newspapers. It also mentioned his premonition of death and his dread of returning to the battleground.

"Instead of becoming used to danger," he had told a friend, "I become less used to it as the years go by. I've begun to feel as if I've about used up my chances. I'd give anything if I didn't have to go back. But I feel I have no choice. I've been with it so long I feel a responsibility, a sense of duty towards the soldiers. I've become their mouthpiece, the only one they have. And they look to me. I don't put myself above the other correspondents. But I've got a device in my column that they haven't got. So I've got to go again."

After leaving Indiana University in 1922, Pyle had kicked around the newspaper business, mostly as an inside man, an editor. He started doing an aviation column for Scripps-Howard and eventually was made managing editor of the chain's Washington, D.C., paper. But his writing talents were too big to be restricted to administrative work. He was appointed a correspondent-at-large and when war broke out, Pyle, already in his forties, went overseas in 1942.

His knack for telling the story of the war through the words and emotions of the young men who were fighting it won him enormous popularity. He covered the North Africa campaign. He landed in Normandy the day after D-Day and wrote: "It was a lovely day for strolling along the seashore. Men were sleeping on the sand, some of them sleeping forever. Men were floating in the water, but they didn't know they were in the water, for they were dead." He was revolted by the killing, sickened by what he had seen, embarrassed when he returned home and found himself embraced by movie stars. Then he went to the Pacific and on April 18, 1945, on the island of Ie Shima, he was killed.

President Truman, only in office a few days, said, "No man in this war has told the story of the American fighting man as American fighting men wanted it told." Pyle was buried next to the men who had fallen in battle, with a sign reading, "At this spot, the 77th Infantry Division lost a buddy, Ernie Pyle." A movie that was already in production about his work, *The Story of GI Joe,* was released posthumously.

The farmhouse in which he was born in 1900 has been restored to its appearance of that time and is filled with memorabilia of Pyle's life and journalism career.

■ **LOCATION:** Dana is on U.S. 36, just east of the Illinois border and about 25 miles north of Terre Haute. The museum is north of town on Indiana 71. ■ **HOURS:** Monday through Saturday, 9–5, and Sunday, 1–5, May–October; closed all day Monday and on Tuesday mornings, rest of the year. ■ **ADMISSION:** Free ■ **TELEPHONE:** (317) 665-3633

FAIRMOUNT

JAMES DEAN MEMORIaL

He made only three movies and died at the end of the first rock and roll summer, in 1955. But along with Elvis Presley and Marilyn Monroe, James Dean survives as an icon of the 1950s, the image of youthful rebelliousness that would change America forever.

Dean's image seems to grow stronger as the years go by. "He's more popular now than he was 20 years ago," said a marketing executive in a 1986 interview, as a new line of James Dean sunglasses was introduced. His acolytes have turned this Indiana village into a place of pilgrimage, showing up each year on September 30, the anniversary of his death in a speeding Porsche on a California highway.

The story of the fatal accident rated ten paragraphs or so from the wire services. Dean had just finished work on *Giant.* But he had already found his audience that year with his performance in *Rebel without a Cause.* It was the movie of a new generation. His screen presence—lonely, misunderstood, alienated—was the first expression of postwar angst among young people, and they flocked to see that angst personified on the big screen.

Dean's death, at the age of twenty-four, only solidified the image. Nobody really grasped that though until the first anniversary of the crash. Letters began pouring into the Warner Brothers offices. His co-stars began getting them, too.

Expressions of grief. Inquiries about personal glimpses of the actor. Those who knew him best said he was nothing like his film character. He was shy, found it difficult to relate to new acquaintances, and was shattered by the breakup of his romance with actress Pier Angeli. Instead of flickering out, though, the Dean phenomenon just keeps going. Even those born twenty years after his death respond to him and identify him as a symbol of their generation, too.

Fairmount is also the home of cartoonist Jim Davis, creator of "Garfield." Local men are credited with inventing the hamburger and the ice cream cone (although they have many rivals for those claims). But it is Dean who draws the crowds. There is a memorial to him in the small cemetery and the town museum has displays of his career—his boots and chaps from *Giant,* his high school letter sweater, and a soil experiment he did for the 4-H Club. And so the image of the eternal rebel, forever young and forever alone, endures.

■ **LOCATION:** Fairmount is west of Interstate 69, on the Indiana 26 exit. The Fairmount Museum is at 203 East Washington Street. ■ **TELEPHONE:** (317) 948-4555

INDIANAPOLIS

INDIANAPOLIS MOTOR SPEEDWAY

They ran it the first time in 1911 when Ray Harroun tore around the oval track at an average speed of 74.602 miles an hour. The country was aghast. Since then, the Indianapolis 500 has become the ultimate test of man and machine, a Memorial Day racing ritual.

It is the richest auto race in the world. More than a quarter of a million spectators attend, many of them buying their tickets on the day after the previous year's race just to make sure they get in. The Speedway is nicknamed The Brickyard, and every last brick on its two-and-a-half mile track is regarded as holy ground. The race was located here as a measure of the auto industry's importance in Indiana during the industry's early years. The track's avowed purpose was as a testing ground for innovations. Engineers once claimed that 70 percent of the improvements put in family cars and tires originated in the machines that raced here. Among them are rear view mirrors and balloon tires.

The cars go ever faster. By the race's eightieth anniversary, Arie Luyendyk's winning speed was almost exactly two and a half times as fast as Harroun's. But it has also become an American original, a carnival at which speed-loving auto fans lose their inhibitions and rock this sedate midwestern city to its roots. It has been suspended only six times, during the two world wars.

The greatest names in the sport's history—most of them recognized as great by their triumphs here—are memorialized in the Speedway Museum: Gaston Chevrolet, who won in 1920; A. J. Foyt and Al Unser, who won it four times apiece; Bill Vukovich, who won twice in a row and died trying to make it three. The museum shows off several of the winning cars, as well as exhibits of made-in-Indiana automobiles. There are also bus tours of the track, when no events are scheduled.

■ **LOCATION:** The track is 7 miles west of downtown, at 4790 West 16th Street, in the suburb of Speedway. ■ **HOURS:** Daily, 9–5. ■ **ADMISSION:** $2 for museum and bus ride (separate tickets may be purchased for $1). ■ **TELEPHONE:** (317) 241-2500

JEFFERSONVILLE

LOUISvILLE SLUGGEr FACTORY

In 1884 Pete Browning was having a great year with the Louisville Eclipse ball club. He had led the league in hitting as a rookie and now, in his third season, the hometown boy was a tremendous hero, on his way to yet another .300 year. One day, Bud Hillerich, a local wood turner whose family's business specialized in making butter churns, came out to see a game. As luck would have it, that day Browning broke his bat, a special favorite. Hillerich came down from the stands after the game and invited the player to accompany him to the family workshop, where he promised to make him another bat to his specifications.

Browning was delighted with the new club, which was dubbed the Louisville Slugger in his honor. Word of the bat-maker's skill spread and in 1893 a Saint Louis hardware company agreed to nationally distribute the new bats. In a few years, most major leaguers were using the Slugger. Hillerich would supply them for free in return for endorsement rights. The arrangement profited both sides. The autographed bats were soon a familiar sight on sandlots across the country, with Louisville Slugger becoming almost a synonym for baseball bat.

Veterans of the company can still recall delivering new shipments to "Splendid Splinter" Ted Williams, who could detect a variance of half an ounce in his bats. "Other big stars couldn't tell any difference," said a company spokesman in a 1960 interview. "Once Al Simmons was in a slump and demanded a change in the model we made for him. We didn't have time to make the adjustments and instead we just sent him a new batch of the old ones. He got three hits and wired us back to congratulate us on the new model."

Since 1973, the Sluggers have actually been made across the river from Louisville, in a new plant in Jeffersonville, Indiana. Visitors are given a tour of the manufacturing process. A museum at the plant site displays the bats used by many of the best-known players in the game, past and present.

■ **LOCATION:** The plant is on Indiana 62, at 1525 New Albany Road. ■ **HOURS:** Monday through Friday, 8–12 and 1–3:30; tours at 10 and 2.

Closed the first three weeks in July. ■ **ADMISSION:** Free ■ **TELEPHONE:** (812) 288-6611

NASHVILLE

JOHN DILLINGER MUSEUM

It is a familiar tale. Small town boy from Indiana goes to the big city of Chicago in search of a career, becomes famous, meets the wrong kind of woman, and comes to a bad end. In John Dillinger's case, the end was especially nasty. He was gunned down by FBI agents outside Chicago's Biograph Theatre on July 22, 1934 (*see* Chicago, Illinois).

But Dillinger is a bad guy whose legend grows with the years. He fascinates screenwriters, historians, journalists, all of whom can still find profit in retelling the facts of his life. He was the original Public Enemy Number One, so designated by J. Edgar Hoover and the Federal Bureau of Investigation. During 1933–34, he was the object of the most intensive manhunt in the annals of American crime. He had been captured once and incarcerated in the "escape proof" Lake County jail, in Crown Point, Indiana. But Dillinger managed to fashion a toy gun out of wood and used it to bluff his way past guards. Then he waved it in front of a passing driver, took the car, and was gone. The daring escape made him a national celebrity, even winning a degree of sympathy for a man who was thought to have killed sixteen people during a string of bank robberies. More than any other criminal (with the possible exception of Jesse James) Dillinger has become part of national folklore. Even the way he died seemed part of legend: At the age of thirty-three he was betrayed to the FBI by a mysterious "lady in red."

There are stories of secret treasure caches left by Dillinger, another indication of his legendary status. The most well-known of these has it that $25,000 he'd taken from an Indianapolis bank is stashed in a western suburb of that city.

When Dillinger was returned to Indiana for burial, other treasure hunters got in on the act. The trousers he was wearing at the time of his death, along with a death mask, several letters, and other personal belongings were put up for sale. Many of them ended up in this small museum in the middle of scenic Brown County. It may be a bit incongruous for a memorial to a gangster to be situated in what is generally regarded as an artists' town. But there it is, and the town is proud of it.

■ **LOCATION:** The museum is near the center of town, at Van Buren and Franklin streets. Nashville is 15 miles east of Bloomington, by way of Indiana 46. ■ **HOURS:** Daily, 10–6, April–October. Hours are irregular during the rest of the year, and it is best to call first. ■ **ADMISSION:** $3 ■ **TELEPHONE:** (812) 988-7172

NEW CASTLE

INDIANA BASKETBALL HALL OF FAME

It is known in this state as "Hoosier Hysteria." The grip that basketball, especially high school basketball, has upon the minds and emotions of Indiana is legendary. In fact, that's the nickname of the greatest player to come out of the state, Larry Bird. He took Indiana State, a college team that had never before advanced in the tournament, to the finals of the NCAA championships. Then he went on to become one of the top forwards in pro basketball history, winning three championships with the Boston Celtics. So they called him Larry Legend.

But there are plenty of legends in Indiana lore. The popular movie *Hoosiers* was based on an actual small town team that won the state's open-class high school tournament, competing against big city powerhouses. Moreover, the program at Indiana University is regarded as among the most consistent in the country, annually turning out teams that contend for conference and national titles.

This facility, which opened in 1990, recounts the importance of the sport in the life of Indiana. There are historical displays of the game's development, mementoes of outstanding games and players, taped interviews with great stars, and an Honor Wall for those who made exceptional contributions.

■ **LOCATION:** New Castle is about 45 miles east of Indianapolis. Take the northbound Indiana 3 exit from Interstate 70. The museum is in town, at 408 Trojan Lane. ■ **HOURS:** Daily, 9–5. ■ **ADMISSION:** $1.50 ■ **TELEPHONE:** (317) 529-1891

PERU

COLE PORTER BIRTHPLACE

His name is synonymous with the most sophisticated American popular songs. The brilliant lyrics, complex yet melodic tunes, mastery of the symbols of popular romance made Cole Porter a legend of the musical theater. Yet he seemed to achieve fame almost off-handedly. Unlike the majority of songwriters of popular music's golden age, he didn't have a New York background. Instead, Porter was born and chose to be buried in the little town of Peru in the Hoosier Heartland.

Porter's maternal grandfather, James Cole, became a millionaire as a California merchant during the Gold Rush and an owner of West Virginia coal mines. He returned to his boyhood home of Peru in 1867. James always felt that his daughter, Kate, made a mistake in marrying impecunious druggist

Samuel Porter. But as their only child who survived to adulthood, Cole Porter was pampered and adored. When he displayed musical talent he was sent East to study and then enrolled at Yale University.

A small town Midwesterner, even one who was heir to a sizeable fortune, was somewhat out of place at the Yale of 1910, then the very center of America's old money aristocracy. But Porter's bright personality, quick wit, and musical talent made him one of the most popular men on campus. After a few unsuccessful attempts to write commercially in New York, he and his wife, Linda, lived in Europe for most of the 1920s. His songwriting was limited mostly to private parties and the amusement of friends and family. His talent was regarded as far too sophisticated for American tastes.

But by the end of the decade, tastes had changed. Under the influence of such composers as George Gershwin, Jerome Kern, and Richard Rodgers popular music had been transformed from the predictable "moon-June" formula tunes. Porter returned to the reinvigorated New York stage in 1929 with the show *Wake Up and Dream,* which contained the darkly haunting ballad, "What Is This Thing Called Love." It became his first hit and Porter was established as a major musical voice. Throughout the 1930s, his songs and shows set the pace for popular music, dozens of them entering the ranks of standards. Even a riding accident in 1937, which left Porter with shattered legs for the rest of his life, did not diminish his creativity. His 1947 show, *Kiss Me Kate,* is regarded as a high point in the musical theater.

A biographer, in summing up his career, said that Porter never compromised his own tastes to achieve popular success, but instead lifted up popular taste to match his own. Upon his death in 1964, his remains were returned to Peru for burial in the family plot. There are several sites associated with Porter in the Peru area and the Chamber of Commerce puts out a small folder locating them. Among the most important are his birthplace, at 102 East 3rd Street; the home of his grandfather, James Cole, at 27 East 3rd Street; Westleigh, the home of his mother and the mansion featured in the opening scenes of Porter's film biography *Night and Day,* and the burial site in Mt. Hope Cemetery.

■ **LOCATION:** Peru is at the junction of U.S. 24 and U.S. 31, about 70 miles north of Indianapolis. The Chamber of Commerce is at 20 North Miami Street. ■ **HOURS:** All the homes are private and may not be visited. The Chamber is open Monday through Friday, 9–5. ■ **TELEPHONE:** (317) 472-1923

SANTA CLAUS

HOLIDaY WORLD

You want Christmas every day? This is the place. Well, almost. The adjacent theme park is closed during the winter, including Christmas Day.

The sculptor of this stone statue of Santa Claus dedicated it to the children of the world.
(UPI/Bettmann)

This little village originally wanted to call itself Santa Fe. It was 1846 and the Mexican War was on everybody's mind, so it seemed apt to pay tribute to the faraway city that was part of America's newest addition. But when the application was turned in, the U.S. Post Office informed the town that another Indiana municipality and beat them to it and already claimed the name. That setback stopped the locals temporarily. They really liked the rhythmic flow of the name. Because it was the holiday season, they decided on Santa Claus instead.

You really can't say the town has prospered because of its cheery name. It has only a few more than five hundred residents. But in December, its post office is among the busiest in the country as sacks of mail pour in to be remailed with this postmark. For a while the only other evidence of the town's unusual name was a granite Santa Claus that was placed on a nearby hillside and a school for training department store Santas that briefly operated here.

Holiday World changed that. An amusement park with a holiday theme, it has rides and attractions related to Fourth of July, Halloween, and Christmas.

Santa himself is always found in the Toy Store. Although he has no particular connection with Christmas, Abraham Lincoln is also saluted here (the family farm where he grew up is just a few miles northwest). Christmas celebrations have become such an intrinsic part of the American cultural fabric, that having Abe around almost seems natural.

■ **LOCATION:** Santa Claus is in the southwestern corner of the state, about 40 miles east of Evansville. Holiday World is at the junction of Indiana 245 and 162, just north of town. ■ **HOURS:** Mid-May through August Holiday World opens daily at 10 A.M. and closing hours vary from 6 P.M. to 8 P.M., with Saturday closing time as late as 10 P.M. in mid-summer; weekends only, 10–5, from mid-April to mid-May and September–October. ■ **ADMISSION:** $15.95; $11.95 for children under 48 inches tall and senior citizens; children under 2 years of age, free. ■ **TELEPHONE:** (812) 937-4401

SOUTH BEND

NOTRE DAME UNIVERsITY

Its academics are distinguished, consistently ranking it among the highest quality Catholic schools. Its research facilities in biotechnology are among the nation's best. And it is famous as a center for the study of constitutional law.

They also play football at Notre Dame. To the American sports fan, that tends to overwhelm all other perceptions about the university. This is the symbol of the college game. Its subway alumni, those who never have been anywhere near South Bend but follow the Fighting Irish avidly, are famous. They are why Notre Dame has never joined a conference. It prefers instead to play a national schedule, allowing its teams to perform before crowds from Los Angeles to New York. When coach Lou Holtz told a recruit who turned him down, "Son, you didn't just make a four-year mistake, you made a 40-year mistake," everyone knew exactly what he meant. Nothing can compare with the prestige of playing football for the Fighting Irish. The 1993 movie *Rudy* portrays the mythical aspects of Notre Dame football and it was a surprise hit.

The myth began in the fall of 1913, when Notre Dame, then regarded as an obscure school, went east to play the mighty Army team. All during the previous summer, Notre Dame quarterback Gus Dorais had worked as a lifeguard at the Ohio beach resort Cedar Point. Accompanying him, was an end on the football team, Knute Rockne. The two of them practiced the forward pass on the beach. The pass was seldom used in those days, with teams stocking up on beefy linemen and preferring to grind out yardage with superior size. But when Dorais and Rockne went into action on the field, Army was astonished. Notre Dame won 35–13 and in one stroke redrew the strategy of the game, elevating their school to the highest ranks.

In 1918, Rockne took over as coach and, with the aid of stars like George Gipp (*see* Laurium, Michigan) and the Four Horsemen, turned Notre Dame into the dominant football team in the country. Rockne's formations, strategy, and even the way he redesigned the team uniforms were innovative and fresh. It was the birth of the Notre Dame legend. Since 1924, the Irish have won eleven national championships, more than any other college program.

Its stadium is only medium sized as college facilities go. Seating slightly less than sixty thousand, it is dwarfed by the stadiums at places like the University of Michigan and the University of Tennessee. But it is a place that football fans approach in awe. The best way to see the stadium is to go on a tour of the campus, which will include such landmarks as the Golden Dome and "Touchdown Jesus." The Hesburgh Library also contains an extensive collection of materials relating to games.

■ **LOCATION:** Notre Dame is just north of South Bend, at the U.S. 31 exit of the Indiana Toll Road. ■ **HOURS:** Tours of the campus are given by reservation, Monday through Friday during the summer months and by appointment during the academic year. ■ **ADMISSION:** Free ■ **TELEPHONE:** (219) 239-7367

STUDEBAKER MUSEUM

Right after World War II, when Americans were ready to burst loose after years of pent-up demand for new cars, Studebaker came up with one of the most remarkable vehicles ever designed. The automaker had hired the famous packaging expert, Raymond Loewey, to rethink the appearance of the automobile. The result was The Hawk. Comics joked that you couldn't tell whether it was coming or going, since its front and rear ends were identically shaped. But consumers loved its low, sporty lines, different than any other car on the road, and its low price tag, too. By 1951, Studebaker was employing twenty-one thousand workers at its plant here, the highest number in its history.

The Studebaker name goes all the way back to 1852 in South Bend. Two brothers, Henry and Clement Studebaker, arrived here from Ohio and went into business building wagons. Their products became known as the best in the country. Presidents Ulysses S. Grant and Benjamin Harrison used Studebaker carriages, as did many other famous and wealthy men of the day. In 1899, the company tentatively entered the new auto business, making bodies for electric cars. Three years later, it began manufacturing its own electric runabouts, and continued doing this for ten years. By the 1920s, Studebakers were an established part of the industry and by the end of the Depression, South Bend was the last significant independent center of auto production outside of Detroit.

But even with the success of the Hawk, the company simply could not compete with the giant economies of Big Three. In 1963, just twelve years after its peak, the Studebaker plant shut its doors for good. A consortium of local manufacturers continued to build the sporty Avanti at the old plant but even that limited production ceased in 1987.

Studebaker memories are preserved in a museum here, in the city's downtown Century Center. Displays go all the way back to wagon-making days and run through a complete line of the company's best-known models. "More than we promised," was its slogan. And after seeing the still-striking lines of the Hawk, you may be inclined to agree.

■ **LOCATION:** The museum and Century Center is located at 120 South Saint Joseph Street, downtown. ■ **HOURS:** Monday through Saturday, 10–4; Sunday, 12–4. ■ **ADMISSION:** $3 ■ **TELEPHONE:** (219) 284-9714

Michigan

DEARBORN

FAIR LANE

He may very well have been the man of the century. He transformed American industry, the way we travel, where we live and work, the very texture of our lives. For a time, Henry Ford was also probably the richest living American. But he was a complex man of simple tastes. A farmer's son who went out and licked the world. A backyard shed tinkerer who had a clearer economic vision than any Wall Street wizard. A man who preached world peace but hated any part of the world that wasn't just like him.

Ford was born in this western Detroit suburb. He moved his company here as soon as he could, assembled his enormous museums here (*see* next entry, Henry Ford Museum and Greenfield Village) and died in the home he built here. Fair Lane is a surprisingly simple house for a man of such stature. Built in 1915, it was dwarfed by the mansions built by some of his contemporaries and his offspring (*see* Edsel and Eleanor Ford House, Grosse Pointe Shores). But surrounded by hundreds of acres of forests and gardens, it offered the seclusion Ford wanted. As he lay dying, in 1947, the Rouge River overflowed its banks in a spring storm and cut off all electrical power to the home. So the man who was the leading industrial innovator of his time drew his last breath in an upstairs bedroom here by flickering candlelight.

There were several other inventors who were tinkering with gas-powered vehicles around 1900. Ransom Olds already had a car in production by the time Ford came crashing through the garage of his own workshop in downtown Detroit (he forgot to make the door wide enough for the car) and made his first successful run down Detroit's Bagley Avenue. History and geography conspired to make Detroit the center of the new industry. Many local companies experienced in assembling carriage bodies were there and it was the center of Great Lakes transportation, with access to both the iron mines of the north and the energy fields of the east. There was also an excess of investment capital, as the lumber industry was exhausted in Michigan and former timber barons were seeking new outlets for their money. All of this combined to bring autos and the men who dreamed about them to Detroit.

Henry Ford's estate, Fair Lane Manor, is surprisingly simple for the man who transformed American industry. *(AP/Wide World Photos)*

But Ford's major importance was not as an inventor. It was his ability to expand production by using the assembly line, and then to expand his market by raising wages to the then incredible level of $5 a day, that earned him a place in history. He was the first industrialist to understand that unless his workers could afford the products they were making, the possibilities for expansion were limited. This was the miracle that shook the world, changed the lives of working people forever, and put America on wheels.

Much of the Fair Lane property that Ford owned has been developed in recent years. A regional shopping center, office towers, and a college campus now occupy land that once surrounded his home. But Fair Lane preserves some of the seclusion Ford treasured and the house and grounds still let visitors capture some sense of the man who lived there.

■ **LOCATION:** Fair Lane is at 4901 Evergreen Road, just north of Michigan Avenue (U.S. 12). ■ **HOURS:** Tours are given on the hour, Monday through Saturday, 10–3 and Sunday, 1–4, April–December. Monday through Friday at 1:30, rest of the year. ■ **ADMISSION:** $6 ■ **TELEPHONE:** (313) 593-5590

HENRY FORD MUSEUM AND GREENFIELD VILLAGE

As Henry Ford began approaching old age, he made an unnerving discovery. The rural America he had grown up in and loved was disappearing. The little farm towns, the pace of life measured by the seasons, the traditions, the simple virtues. Vanishing before his eyes. And in no small measure what had destroyed them was Ford's automobile.

The evolution of the automobile—on view at the Henry Ford Museum. *(Courtesy of the Henry Ford Museum and Greenfield Village)*

It was because of the automobile that people had greater freedom of mobility than at any other time in the history of the world to date. They were using it to live, work, and shop in ever more widely dispersed patterns. Why patronize the little country store when you could get in the Model T and drive to the county seat? Why go to the husking bee when you could drive to the movies? So Ford resolved to preserve what he could, gather all the elements of the ideal small town of his memory in one setting. But Ford was also an admirer of great men. So the buildings he concentrated on acquiring were those associated with some of the great names of the American past. Noah Webster. Stephen Collins Foster. His friend and mentor, Thomas Edison. The Wright Brothers. He bought their homes and their workshops and transported them to his own town, Greenfield Village, named for the rural township in which he was born, a few miles away.

For all that, Ford was a believer in technology—the American know-how that was changing the world. So he also set about to create a vast museum of these machines. Washing machines. Vacuum cleaners. Phonographs. Bicycles. From the very earliest models to the most contemporary examples. The Henry Ford Museum is a huge repository of everything that helped relegate neighboring Greenfield Village to the history texts. Its most interesting section, perhaps, is the Automobile in American Life. It details the changes that the car worked on our culture, from where we eat, to what we buy, to where we sleep. Even Henry himself might be astonished at the scope.

Signs of the time: The drive-in's 1950s heyday is captured at Henry Ford Museum. *(Courtesy of the Henry Ford Museum and Greenfield Village)*

There are traditional crafts displays in both facilities and special exhibits throughout the year.

■ **LOCATION:** The Village and Museum are at 20900 Oakwood Boulevard, just south of Michigan Avenue (U.S. 12). ■ **HOURS:** Daily, 9–5. ■ **ADMISSION:** Separate $11.50 admissions are required. A $20 combination ticket is good on two consecutive days. ■ **TELEPHONE:** (313) 271-1620

DETROIT

GENERAL MOTORS BUILDING

When plans for this massive structure were announced in 1919 it was called the Durant Building. The building was to be a tribute to the founder of General Motors, William Durant. He came from Flint, Michigan, and succeeded in unifying several Michigan-based auto producers to form GM. While the company could not compete with Ford when it came to supplying basic transportation, it discerned early that there was a growing market for the buyer who wanted to move up. Ford made only the Model T. There was no way for a Ford customer to show his neighbors that he was getting ahead and was able to afford a more expensive car. GM gave him a way.

Durant, however, would not be around to finish the work on the building. By the time construction actually began on his intended monument, he had been booted out of the chief executive's office by the GM board of directors. Although he developed Chevrolet as a low-end model to go head-to-head with Ford, he was also over-extended in the stock market. The DuPont family had quietly bought up a controlling interest in the corporation and decided Durant was not their man. It would be left for Alfred Sloan to lead GM to dominance in the industry. All that remained of Durant were the large letter Ds, already carved into the stone above the main entrance to the new building, and which were never removed.

But GM's location for its new company headquarters was even more significant than what the building was called. The company announced that it was creating a "New Center." For the first time, a major business development was to be built outside the historic downtown area of a city. It was the success of GM's New Center that encouraged the planning of Rockefeller Center in the next decade (*see* New York, New York). The choice also was a tacit acknowledgement that the automobile had changed the shape of the American community. With the nation on wheels, it was now possible to decentralize the urban commercial pattern. People were no longer limited to a single downtown business district. The New Center was the first step on the road to the suburban office park.

The company chose Albert Kahn as its architect. His Detroit-based firm had risen to prominence as the designer of the modern auto factory. When he turned his attention to this office building, he made a statement of unforgettable

In 1919, General Motors announced plans to build its new headquarters: It was the first time a major business center was built outside a city's historic downtown. *(AP/Wide World Photos)*

power. His repeated pattern of windows and setbacks, extending an entire city block in length, was the architectural embodiment of the assembly line, the visual image of the work its tenants directed. The building opened in 1923 and drew as much attention for its spacious ground-floor showrooms as anything else. Detroiters still flock here to see the latest line of GM cars. But the curiosity can't compare to the levels of the 1940s and 1950s, when car models changed annually.

The New Center grouping was completed in 1928 with the opening of the Fisher Building, directly across the street. Built by the company that supplied GM's chassis (Fisher Body), this building was another Kahn project. While he went for power at GM, Kahn designed grace into the Fisher Building. Its slender central tower and, especially, the rich decor and mosaic panels in its lobby, made it the most beautiful office building of its time and the perfect complement to its massive partner across the way.

■ **LOCATION:** The GM Building is located at 3044 West Grand Boulevard (at 2nd Avenue), about three miles north of downtown Detroit. ■ **HOURS:** Monday through Friday, 9-5. The lobby of the Fisher Building, across the street at 3011 West Grand Boulevard, is also open on weekends. ■ **TELEPHONE:** (313) 556-5000

JOE LOUIS MEMORIAL

It seemed that every radio in America was turned to the fight. On the night of June 22, 1938, heavyweight champion Joe Louis entered the ring to face the only man who had ever beaten him, former champion Max Schmeling. The German fighter had been adopted by the Nazis as their ideal Aryan specimen. Although Schmeling himself was a decent man, he had come to stand for a racist

Sculptor Robert Graham's tribute to late great heavyweight champion Joe Louis is one of the most controversial pieces of civic art in the country. *(AP/Wide World Photos)*

ideology that Americans found repellent. For what was, perhaps, the first time in the nation's history, the entire country was rooting fervently for a black man.

Louis didn't disappoint them. In a one-round display of unleashed fury, he battered Schmeling into a helpless pulp, while the country went wild with joy. The real battles were still ahead but on this one night a hateful dogma had been defeated, and Louis was America's hero. The celebration was especially keen in Detroit, the fighter's hometown. Joe Louis Barrow grew up on the city's east side and learned to fight in its gyms. As he rose through the heavyweight ranks, his victories in the ring turned into civic celebrations in the black neighborhood of Black Bottom. The Schmeling fight topped them all.

Louis held the boxing title longer than any other man, retiring in 1949 after twelve years at the top as the most popular champion the fight game ever saw. Detroit never forgot. After Louis' death in 1981, the city started planning a suitable memorial. Former Mayor Coleman A. Young was one of those who had celebrated the fighter's victories in the old days and he was especially eager for a commemorative work. So when the magazine *Sports Illustrated* donated $350,000 to the Detroit Institute of Arts, plans for a Louis memorial began.

The result is one of the most controversial pieces of civic art work in the country, mirroring the racial differences that polarize many urban areas. In 1986, sculptor Robert Graham unveiled a huge clenched fist at the end of a muscled forearm. To some it was the perfect symbol of the fighter's power. To others it spoke more to a salute to Black Power and a reminder of violence. It came to be nicknamed The Big Fist, and remains one of the city's most discussed landmarks.

■ **LOCATION:** The Louis Memorial is situated at the foot of Woodward Avenue, at Jefferson Avenue, in downtown Detroit.

MOTOWn MUSEUM

Berry Gordy bought an old house on Detroit's west side in 1959 and put up a sign that said: "Hitsville, USA." It was a bold claim on the part of a record industry novice whom no one ever heard of. But Gordy, a former auto plant worker, believed he was on to something big—a new urban sound, with a pounding beat and lyrics to reflect the realities of Black city life.

And it all came true. With an almost flawless ear for musical talent and fresh ideas, Gordy built his little seat-of-the-pants operation into a giant. Motown Records dominated American popular music in the 1960s, breaking down racial delineations in the record industry. White stations previously had been reluctant to play Black artists, preferring "cover" versions of the same songs by white performers. They pleaded that they didn't want to "offend" their audiences. But the Motown Sound was irresistible. At a time when civil rights barriers were coming down in the South, Motown had the country "Dancing in the Streets," accomplishing the same goals with music.

In 1961, "Please, Mr. Postman," became the label's first number-one hit. From then on, a steady stream poured out of the studios in this old house. Performed by Diana Ross and the Supremes, The Temptations, The Four Tops, Smokey Robinson, Marvin Gaye, Stevie Wonder. Eventually, the Jackson 5 found their way here and started a whole new chapter in the company's history.

By 1972 Gordy felt that Motown had outgrown Detroit. His ambitions extended to the movie industry. So the company left for Los Angeles, leaving behind the house that was once Hitsville. The company preserved the house as a museum. The studio is kept just as it looked when the songs America danced to were recorded here. The museum also has mementoes of many of the top Motown stars, including several who still make their homes in the Detroit area.

■ **LOCATION:** The Motown Museum is at 2648 West Grand Boulevard, west of the Lodge Freeway (U.S. 10). ■ **HOURS:** Monday through

Saturday, 10–5; Sunday, 2–5. ■ **ADMISSION:** $3 ■ **TELEPHONE:** (313) 875-2264

GROSSE POINTE SHORES

EDSEL AND ELEANOR FORD HOUSE

The lakefront palace, with its elegant avenue of trees leading from the entry gate to the main house, is the sort of baronial residence one associates with the automotive giants. Built in 1929 for Henry Ford's oldest son, Edsel (yes, the one for which the ill-fated car was named) and his wife, the former Eleanor Clay, it is a huge Cotswold cottage, designed by Albert Kahn, the architect who put up the GM and Fisher buildings (*see* Detroit). The home was deliberately built at the opposite end of the Detroit metropolitan area from Henry's estate in Dearborn.

Edsel, a quiet and thoughtful man, was a disappointment to his father. Henry wanted a hard driver, a forceful leader to head the company he founded. While he groomed Edsel for leadership, he handed over more actual power to Harry Bennett, Henry's onetime bodyguard and a former sailor with ties to the underworld. After Edsel's death in 1940 it appeared that Bennett would be able to edge out Henry's grandson, Henry Ford II, from taking over the company.

But in a domestic drama played out in this home, Eleanor Ford confronted the old man and threatened to sell her stock unless Bennett was dismissed and her son named to head the company. Faced with loss of control over everything he had built, Henry acquiesced, then bitterly retired to Fair Lane. Bennett was stunned. "You're taking over a billion dollar organization that you haven't contributed a thing to," he allegedly told Henry Ford II upon his departure. But under the young Ford's leadership, the company entered its greatest period of expansion and prosperity.

The echoes of that great battle still resound in this house. It was furnished with a connoisseur's eye by Edsel and Eleanor. The bedrooms of their children, Henry II and William Clay, are regarded as some of the finest surviving examples of original Art Deco interior decoration in the country. The home's great hall is also used for special exhibits by the Detroit Institute of Arts.

■ **LOCATION:** The house is at 1100 Lake Shore Road, about 9 miles northeast of downtown Detroit. Take Interstate 94 (the Edsel Ford Freeway) east to Nine Mile Road, then right to Jefferson and right again. The home is on the left. ■ **HOURS:** Wednesday through Sunday, 1–4. Tours given on the hour. ■ **ADMISSION:** $4. Grounds only, $2. ■ **TELEPHONE:** (313) 884-3400 (tours); 884-4222.

ISHPEMING

INTERNATIONAL SKIING HALL OF FAME

The ski resort has become the epitome of winter glamour. Places like Aspen and Vail and Sun Valley attract the wealthy and the chic. They stay in luxurious condos and shop in international boutiques. But this is not quite what they had in mind when the whole thing began in Ishpeming. The first national ski tournament in America was held in this old iron-mining town in Michigan's Upper Peninsula in 1904.

Of course, back then skiing meant ski jumping. The downhill variety didn't really catch on in this country until it was imported from Austria in the 1930s. The first version was Scandinavian, in which skiers leaped off the sides of mountains to see who could soar the farthest. When the iron mines opened in this area, employers were keen on hiring workers from northern Europe, people who were used to long, tough winters. They sent recruiters to Norway and Finland. The immigrants brought with them a love of ski jumping and began organizing competitions here in 1887.

Carl Tellefsen, a well-known jumper in his hometown of Trondheim, Norway, arrived the following year and quickly became a local champion. He took the lead in organizing several ski clubs from the upper Midwest. This group is recognized as the forerunner of the U.S. Ski Association, which is still the sport's governing body. Tellefsen finally managed to put together the first national meet and ten thousand skiers and spectators crowded into the little town.

Ski Association headquarters eventually moved to Denver but Ishpeming is still recognized as the U.S. birthplace of the sport. The hall of fame was founded here in 1954, and was recently expanded and modernized. Displays trace the history of skiing back to its Nordic roots and are fairly heavy on the jumping aspects of the sport. But the more familiar names of downhill stars are well represented, too.

■ **LOCATION:** Ishpeming is about 13 miles west of Marquette, by way of U.S. 41. The Ski Hall of Fame is on the highway, between Second and Third streets. ■ **HOURS:** Daily, 10–5. ■ **ADMISSION:** $3 ■ **TELEPHONE:** (906) 485-6323

LAURIUM

GEORGE GIPP MEMORIAL

He came out of this copper mining town, a tough kid, already in his early twenties by the time he attracted the attention of baseball scouts from the University of Notre Dame.

George Gipp's baseball career lasted until Knute Rockne saw the young athlete kick a football during his first autumn on campus. Gipp could play any sport, but his gift was football. He went on to play just twenty-seven games for Notre Dame, from 1917 until his death from pneumonia in 1920. But he led the team in rushing and passing for three of those seasons and his career rushing total of 2,341 yards held for more than fifty years. Rockne called him the most versatile athlete he ever coached and in Gipp's last two years, Notre Dame went undefeated.

Many college athletes accumulated gaudy records and impressive numbers in those years. What made Gipp the player who was never forgotten is something that happened after his death. According to some sports historians, it was at halftime of the 1928 Army game that Rockne first used the phrase that immortalized Gipp. Rockne told his team how he had visited Gipp as he lay dying and was told that some day "when the team is up against it, tell them to go in there with all they've got and win one for The Gipper." The record shows that Notre Dame won that game, 12–6.

But the legend went on. In 1940, Hollywood filmed the story of Rockne's life and a young actor named Ronald Reagan played Gipp and got to make the deathbed speech. It became part of Reagan's persona when he entered politics. He sometimes referred to himself as "The Gipper" and some Americans may have wondered if he even believed that a former All-American halfback had become U.S. president. To "Win One for The Gipper," has entered the American language as a plea to perform the impossible.

Gipp's body was returned to his hometown and at the main entrance to the business district, Laurium built a small memorial park with a bright fountain, dedicated to his memory.

■ **LOCATION:** Laurium is 11 miles north of Hancock, off U.S. 41. The memorial is on the cutoff to the town, Michigan 26.

OWOSSO

CURWOoD CASTLE

For a time he rivaled Zane Grey (*see* Zanesville, Ohio) as the country's best-selling author of adventure novels. But while Grey's province was the West, James Oliver Curwood looked to the North. His stories about the Canadian wilds and Alaska sold so well during the twentieth century's first two decades, that Curwood was able to build his own castle in his hometown.

He was an ardent conservationist whose mission was to inform readers about the importance of preserving the harsh beauty of the north. He adopted a pantheistic outlook, a worship of nature and all its creatures, which led him to oppose hunting. Several of his books even were written from the viewpoint of wild animals. Most of Curwood's works are unread today. But while they lack a degree of literary subtlety when they deal with human conflict, they remain powerful studies of the north and how it affects those who venture into its wild places.

Curwood was an indifferent student. In fact, a local teacher once admitted he felt the boy should be awarded the prize for stupidity "if the school gave out such an award." But he got into the University of Michigan by writing his way through the entrance exam and worked for a while as a reporter on the *Detroit News.* With the publication of his first novel, *Captain Plum,* in 1908, Curwood returned to Owosso, using it as the base for his trips into the northern wilderness.

He built his castle, in the form of a thirteenth-century Norman chateau, in 1924. Even his closest friends couldn't explain why he chose that style of architecture, since he had no special interest in European history. But he worked every morning in an upstairs room, writing on the top of his mother's old sewing machine, and then went out to shoot pool with old pals the rest of the day.

Curwood died of pneumonia in 1927. The Castle was almost lost to taxes, came close to being torn down, and then was used as a school recreation center for many years. It is now a museum of his life and works. The castle also contains displays of other Owosso historical figures, including two-time Republican presidential candidate, Thomas E. Dewey, who was born in Owosso.

■ **LOCATION:** Owosso is about 25 miles west of Flint, by way of Michigan 21. The way to the castle is well-marked once you get to town. ■ **HOURS:** Monday through Saturday, 10–4; Sunday, 1–4. ■ **ADMISSION:** Donation ■ **TELEPHONE:** (517) 723-8844

MiNNEsOta

BLOOMINGTON

MALL oF AMERICA

There is something about the suburbs of Minneapolis that seems to nurture historic shopping malls. It was in nearby Edina, after all, that Victor Gruen designed Southdale, the first fully enclosed mall in history. That was in 1956. Since then, the mall has become America's retailing standard. Many downtowns have folded, their stores abandoned. But the enclosed mall, with its acres of free parking and its passageways that shield shoppers from the weather, thrives as never before. From the bitter winters of Minnesota to the stifling summers of Arizona, the indoor mall has transformed shopping as surely as the Astrodome changed baseball.

Until the Mall of America opened in the summer of 1992, no one fully comprehended how great the phenomenon had grown. This 4.2-million-square-foot, four-hundred-store, seventy-eight-acre, self-contained city is the biggest shopping center in history. *The New York Times* headlined its story on the opening: "The Shopping Mall That Ate Minnesota." Within days it became the state's top tourist attraction and was immediately nicknamed the Mega-mall. Special one-day excursion flights to the mall from other Midwestern cities were run through the Christmas shopping season. There was even an amusement park, Camp Snoopy, with trees and plants and a four-story waterfall. It was situated in what was once the outfield of Metropolitan Stadium, former home of baseball's Minnesota Twins. The whole ballpark would have occupied only a corner of the mall. The mall was so huge, its distances so daunting, that some observers referred to it as "mega-death" and went back to their cars in defeat. . . if they could find their cars in the parking lot.

The shopping mall, as Gruen predicted, has become the country's new community center. People come to them for entertainment and recreation, as well as shopping. They are convenient, predictable, and reassuring in all seasons. But something has been lost as well. Eccentricity, spontaneity, character. The very things that once made each urban downtown individualized are erased in the malls. With access strictly controlled by private ownership, there is no room in the millions of square feet for the unplanned moment or the surprising shop. Yet the Mall of America is doing business beyond its developers' brightest expectations.

"The Mall That Ate Minnesota": The Mall of America is a measure of how important suburban shopping centers have become to American life. *(AP/Wide World Photos)*

■ **LOCATION:** Mall of America is located at Interstate 494 and Cedar Avenue, about 10 miles south of downtown Minneapolis. ■ **HOURS:** Monday through Saturday, 10–9; Sunday, 11–6. ■ **TELEPHONE:** (612) 883-8800

BRAINERD

PAUL BUNYAN AMUSEMENT CENTER

Who knows where the stories came from? Some folklorists find a French-Canadian origin to the tales of the giant lumberjack Paul Bunyan and his great blue ox, Babe, seven ax-handles wide between the eyes. Others say that there are parallels in old Viking legends, so the stories must have been imported with the Scandinavian lumbermen. Wherever men told tall tales amid the tall timber, Bunyan turned up. Across the north woods of Maine, and when the big trees gave out there, into Michigan. Then Wisconsin and Minnesota, and on into the lumbering states of the Pacific northwest. Picking up bits of local color on the way, but always the same story in the essentials.

In other times, Americans commemorated the legend by putting up giant statues to Paul and Babe. But travelers demand more than that now. So in Brainerd, an old lumber camp in an area thick with Bunyan associations, Paul turns up in a theme amusement park. His twenty-six-foot high statue greets visitors and tells them a pre-recorded tale as he perches on a tree stump. In this way, nineteenth-century folklore meets twentieth-century popular culture.

■ **LOCATION:** Brainerd is about 110 miles west of Duluth. The Paul Bunyan Amusement Center is at the junction of Minnesota 210 and 371. ■ **HOURS:** Daily, 10–dusk, Memorial Day to Labor Day. ■ **ADMISSION:** $5.95 ■ **TELEPHONE:** (218) 829-6342

GRAND RAPIDS

JUDY GARLAND COLLECTION

"I was born in a trunk at the Princess Theatre in Pocatello, Idaho." So sang Judy Garland, to an Ira Gershwin lyric, in the classic Hollywood musical *A Star Is Born.* The big number in that 1954 film, "Born in a Trunk" was an almost autobiographical rendering of Garland's career. But it wasn't Pocatello in which she took her first bow. It was as Frances Gumm, in Grand Rapids, where her parents operated a vaudeville house.

Many critics regard Garland as the greatest musical talent ever put on film. From her debut as a teenager in *The Wizard of Oz* (*see* Liberal, Kansas) to her triumph in *A Star is Born,* she made a succession of appearances "about which," in the words of one British critic, "not enough can ever be written." Her life also became a cultural archetype: the star who can never come to terms with her success. Personally unhappy, fighting alcohol and drug addiction, trying to locate her own identity in a world that covered her in make-believe, Garland became an even greater symbol than she was a star. Making one comeback after another, she became a particular favorite of the gay community, which identified with her struggles.

"Over the Rainbow," the song that became her theme, was turned into a personal statement over the years. The song was almost cut from *The Wizard of Oz* by MGM executives who thought it slowed the narrative pace. But the search for a better place was an intrinsic part of the America of the 1930s, when E. Y. Harburg wrote the lyric. One end of the rainbow was in Oz, a make-believe land. The other end may have been in Grand Rapids, where little Frances Gumm had her childhood taken away from her by the demands of her family's show business career. She lived here only as an infant, but the town remembers Garland's career with a collection of personal memorabilia in the old Central High School building.

■ **LOCATION:** Grand Rapids is about 80 miles west of Duluth, by way of U.S. 2. The Central High School Heritage and Arts Center is at the junction of U.S. 2 and 169. The Garland Collection is on the third floor. ■ **HOURS:** Monday through Saturday, 9:30–5. ■ **ADMISSION:** $3 ■ **TELEPHONE:** (218) 326-6431

HIBBING

GREYHOUND ORIGIN CENTER

It was the lifeline of small town America. The trains had stop running many routes. The airlines only landed in big cities. But all across the rural portion of the country, the Greyhound bus was how you got out and how you came home. "Thank God and Greyhound you're gone," said a Country music hit of non-love. But the words were true. Of the country's national transportation systems, only Greyhound linked the towns to the cities.

The line began in the Minnesota iron range in 1914. There was no trolley service to carry workers from the town of Hibbing to the surrounding mines. Eric Wickman took an old touring car that he had been unable to sell and began running a scheduled jitney service. Soon he added a second car and, eventually, he built a twelve-passenger bus on a truck chassis. Within two years, Wickman had taken in some partners and formed the Mesaba Transportation Co., the line that grew into Greyhound. By 1918 his fleet had grown to eighteen buses running all across the iron range.

Wickman, thinking of expansion, moved his base to Duluth and began acquiring small bus lines and incorporating them into his network. He began service between Duluth and Minneapolis, a 160-mile trip that was the longest scheduled run in the country at the time. When Wickman found that it could be operated profitably he was encouraged to move on. By the mid-1920s, he was running buses to Chicago. Among the lines he bought was a small company named Greyhound. He liked the sound of it so much he used it for his entire system.

In recent years, the company, now based in Dallas, has gone through a leveraged buy out and bankruptcy. Its rock-bottom fare structure (the typical Greyhound passenger has an income of just $18,000, or 60 percent of the national average) leaves little room for error. While it still makes 2,600 stops, it has severely cut back its rural service because of its lack of profitability. Nevertheless, the image of the young person waiting for the bus to leave the old homestead for college or the military is an American classic. The Greyhound Center tells the story of how the company was organized and has models of its first vehicles on the iron range.

■ **LOCATION:** Hibbing is about 75 miles northwest of Duluth. The Greyhound Center is in the Hibbing Memorial Building, at 23rd Street and 5th Avenue East. ■ **HOURS:** Monday through Saturday, 9–5, mid-May to late September. ■ **ADMISSION:** $1 ■ **TELEPHONE:** (218) 263-5814

LITTLE FALLS

CHARLES A. LINDBERGH HOME

We will probably never see his equal as a hero again. Dances were named for him. Songs were written for him. Parades were held in his honor. He was mobbed wherever he went. On two continents, people went mad to catch a glimpse of him. Even in the age of mass media celebrity, there was no one quite like "The Lone Eagle," Charles A. Lindbergh.

In 1927 there were still great adventures that could be accomplished by an individual. The achievements of the Astronauts was a tribute to the efficacy of the team. But Lindbergh flew alone. Other aviators had flown the Atlantic, but always with someone else in the cockpit. The image of this tall, shy Midwesterner, alone against the night and the water and the sky, captured the imagination of the world.

He was born in Detroit, but grew up in this small town "where he was allowed to run wild outdoors," in the words of one biographer. His father was a U.S. Congressman, with the Progressive Party, and became highly unpopular when he spoke out bitterly against American involvement in World War I. Young Lindbergh dropped out of college in 1921 and rode off on a motorcycle, looking for someone to teach him how to fly. He succeeded.

But it all turned to ashes, and faster than for most heroes. When his infant son was kidnapped and murdered in 1932, Lindbergh, who had always been a private man, became almost a recluse. Even sixty years after the event, controversy still swirls around it. Although Bruno Hauptmann was executed for the crime, a book published in 1994 purports that the baby was actually killed by his wife's (Anne Morrow Lindbergh's) sister, and that the family kept silent to protect their reputation.

During the 1930s, Lindbergh spoke out, as had his father a generation earlier, against involvement in a European war. When he was decorated by German Field Marshal Herman Goering in 1938, Lindbergh was denounced as a Nazi sympathizer. Others claimed that he was actually spying on Germany during his visits there. He served with distinction as a combat pilot during the war. His public appearances grew increasingly rare afterward and he died in 1974, still regarded as one of America's greatest heroes.

The house in Little Falls contains audiovisual displays relating to three generations of the Lindbergh family. The aviator's recorded voice is heard describing his flight and other family memorabilia are exhibited.

■ **LOCATION:** Little Falls is about 30 miles north of Saint Cloud, on U.S. 51. The Center is west of town by way of Minnesota 27. ■ **HOURS:** Daily, 10–5, May–Labor Day. Monday through Friday, 10–5; Saturday, 10–4; and Sunday, 12-4, rest of the year. ■ **ADMISSION:** $3 ■ **TELEPHONE:** (612) 632-3154

SAUK CENTRE

SINCLaIR LEWIS HOmE

For a long time, Sauk Centre found it hard to forgive Harry Lewis. They felt he had held his hometown up to ridicule, drawn it as a pack of bigots and hicks. His 1920 best-seller, *Main Street,* became one of the most influential

The stucco house in Sauk Centre where author Sinclair Lewis was born in 1885: The Nobel laureate wasn't always well-loved by the townspeople.
(UPI/Bettmann)

novels of its time. It turned away from the idyllic depiction of small town America. Lewis's Gopher Prairie, Minnesota, was a drab place, without imagination or grace, and without even the wit to understand how terrible it was.

Even in 1928, when Sauk Centre was visited by a national correspondent, the town was seething. "It is my belief that Harry Lewis is sincere," said a local minister. "He means to make the world a better place. But it wasn't our idea to annoy him. He doesn't care much about us and we don't think much about him." Added a town doctor: "Oh, he's all right. He just can't help it. He's a freak."

Lewis's own father was the Sauk Centre doctor when the future writer was growing up here. He left to attend Yale in 1903 (dropping his first name shortly afterward and going by his middle one, Sinclair) and embarked on a writing career. He failed at a succession of newspaper jobs, before turning to literature in 1914. *Main Street* was his first success and turned Lewis into a national figure.

He followed that up with a succession of books portraying various aspects of American life. Lewis was a merciless social critic, with a sense of the ridiculous and a wicked ear for dumb remarks. His portrait of service club boosterism, *Babbitt,* contributed a new word to the language. He turned down a Pulitzer Prize, but then became the first American to receive the Nobel Award for Literature in 1930. Nothing he wrote afterward matched the impact of his earlier books. His marriage to foreign correspondent Dorothy Thompson ended unhappily when he felt her fame had begun to out-shadow his own. He lived in Europe for the last years of his life, dying in Italy in 1951.

Sauk Centre has put aside old grudges. Lewis's boyhood home has been restored as a memorial to his work and an information center outside of town tells the story of how this Minnesota community won immortality as Gopher Prairie.

■ **LOCATION:** Sauk Centre is just off Interstate 94, about 40 miles west of Saint Cloud. The Sinclair Lewis Interpretive Center is at the U.S. 71 exit of the Interstate. The home is in town, three blocks off Main Street. The route is well marked. ■ **HOURS:** The Center is open daily, 8:30–5, Memorial Day to Labor Day; weekdays only, 8:30–3, rest of the year. The home is open daily, 9:30–5, Memorial Day to Labor Day. By appointment, rest of the year. ■ **ADMISSION:** The Center accepts donations. $2.50 at the home. ■ **TELEPHONE:** (612) 352-5201

WALNUT GROVE

LAURA INGALLS WILdER MUSEUM

In 1932, an older woman sat down in her farmhouse in the Missouri Ozarks and began to write about her childhood. She remembered her family's homes across the upper Midwest, as she moved from Wisconsin to Minnesota to South Dakota. They were simple and authentic accounts of what it was like to be a child on that long-vanished American frontier. Laura Ingalls Wilder was already sixty-five years old she began her literary career. But the success of the "Little House" books, as they came to be called, made her one of the most honored children's authors of the century. The books won an immediate audience and the Children's Library Association established an award named for her. She was the first recipient in 1954, three years before her death.

But that was only the first chapter. In 1974, the National Broadcasting Company (NBC) began a weekly television series based on her works. To the surprise of almost everyone, the sentimental family show ran for ten years and won a whole new audience for her books. By 1992, they had accumulated total sales of thirty-five million copies. For convenience sake, the action of the books was compressed on TV into the setting of Walnut Grove.

"It was an expensive show to put on," said its star Michael Landon in a 1983 interview, when it finally went off the air. "Because it didn't happen in modern times, you had to build a set for the town, wardrobe the actors. I never thought it would go 10 years."

The set for the show was actually in Simi Valley, California, northwest of Los Angeles. It happened that as the show was winding down, its child actors outgrowing their roles, the producers lost their lease on the land. So they decided to go out with a bang. The series finale involved land developers buying the site of the fictitious Walnut Grove and the townsfolk blowing up their little houses so that they wouldn't fall into their hands. In that way, the destruction of the TV set was filmed as the show left the air. Walnut Grove, Minnesota, however, is still around and a museum in town contains memorabilia of Wilder's life and the history of the town when she lived here.

■ **LOCATION:** Walnut Grove is located in the southwestern corner of the state, about 160 miles southwest of Minneapolis. The museum is off U.S. 14, at 330 8th Street. ■ **HOURS:** Daily, 10–7, Memorial Day to Labor Day; daily 11–4, April, May, September, October. By appointment, rest of the year. ■ **ADMISSION:** Free ■ **TELEPHONE:** (507) 859-2358

Ohio

AKRON

GOODYEAR WORLD OF RUBBER

The strange bounces of the rubber industry have always been a bit confusing. For example, the similar names of tire giants Goodyear and Goodrich have puzzled so many people that the latter company based an ad campaign on it: "No, we're not the ones with the blimp." Not only that, the man who invented vulcanized rubber, Charles Goodyear, had no real connection with the company that bears his name, having died thirty-eight years before it was formed.

Still, after a period in which most American tire-makers were acquired by foreign firms, Goodyear remains a strong presence in the industry's hometown. Goodyear was organized by local businessman Frank Seiberling in 1898. His family had been a major backer of B. F. Goodrich when he went into the rubber business in 1870. It may be that the canny Seiberling was deliberately trying to muddy the waters in going back to the long-deceased Goodyear for his company name; the turn of the century was an especially competitive time to enter the business. Pneumatic tires had enjoyed a steady, if unspectacular market in the bicycle and carriage industries. But there were stories coming out of Detroit about an experimental gas-driven automobile that would send the market for tires off the charts. When the automobile entered mass production and required something to ride on, Akron and its rubber companies grew almost as quickly as Detroit.

During World War I, Goodyear also entered the aircraft industry. It built 1,150 balloons and blimps for the war effort and, as a public relations strategy, maintained its connection with these aircraft. Overhead shots from a Goodyear blimp are a familiar part of every major sporting event on television.

The World of Rubber exhibit, at the Goodyear plant site, presents a historical overview of tires and of the company. Goodyear's laboratory, in which he worked out the formula for vulcanization, the heating process that gives rubber its flexibility and strength, also has been recreated here.

■ **LOCATION:** World of Rubber is on the plant site, at 1201 East Market Street (Ohio 18). ■ **HOURS:** Monday through Friday, 8:30–4:30. ■ **ADMISSION:** Free ■ **TELEPHONE:** (216) 796-2044

BOWLING GREEN

CENTER FOR THE STUDY OF POPULAR CULTURE

This is the academic mother lode for serious students of American popular culture. Bowling Green State University began awarding undergraduate and Master's degrees in popular culture in 1973, under the guidance of the program's founder, Professor Ray Browne. Its library is used by about ten thousand researchers every year, and in its stacks they can find material on everything from comic books to Gothic novels to greeting cards to matchbook covers.

While opposed by some traditional historians, Browne's staff can point to some significant successes in the field. A female student, for example, researched Barbara Stanwyck's movie roles during and after World War II. During the war, she was most often cast as a strong, independent woman, who was taking the place of men who were fighting. Afterwards, she became a femme fatale, a woman in the background, dependent upon men. The conclusion was that such casting helped perpetuate the gender stereotypes that led to the feminist movement of the 1960s.

"If you want to see our society as its most revealing, for better or for worse," said Browne in a 1990 interview, "you find it in popular entertainment, rather than the elite, canonical stuff. What I want to study are the real forces that are shaping the world around us; television, movies, books, word of mouth, buildings, automobiles, fast food. There is nothing I'm not interested in."

■ **LOCATION:** Bowling Green State is located just off Interstate 75, at the Bowling Green exit, about 25 miles south of Toledo. ■ **HOURS:** Call for an appointment. ■ **TELEPHONE:** (419) 372-2531

CANTON

PROFESSIONAL FOOTBALL HALL OF FAME

The first man who played football for money—or the first who admitted to it—was Yale's great lineman, Pudge Heffelfinger. The Allegheny Athletic Association gave him $500 to play against the arch-rival Pittsburgh Athletic Club. That was in 1892. Just three years later, two Pennsylvania communities, Jeannette and Latrobe, met in what is regarded as the first professional football game. That may be stretching the point, though. Only the winning Latrobe players were paid. Jeannette's losers kept their amateur standing, albeit unwillingly.

But the idea caught on and spread through many industrial towns in the Ohio Valley. The local YMCA or major employer would recruit college stars and sponsor the team against neighboring communities. Sometimes entire college squads turned up to play for a town right after graduation. By 1914, the pro game was big enough to be seen as a threat by the colleges, who feared that it would steal their best players and coaches. Collegiate groups spread the word that the games were dishonest and the players susceptible to bribes. Nonetheless, the pro game continued to grow.

In September 1920, representatives from the major pro teams met in an automobile showroom in Canton. For a franchise fee of $100, the American Professional Football Association was officially formed. It was such a roaring flop that in 1921 the entry fee had to be cut to $50. But in that same year, the Decatur team moved to Chicago and renamed itself the Bears, the first time pro football entered a major city. The league also decided on a new name, the National Football League.

The Canton Bulldogs became one of the early powers, winning consecutive championships in 1922–23. By 1925, New York had acquired a franchise and soon the smaller towns were losing their teams to the more profitable metropolitan areas. (The only exception being the Green Bay Packers.) By the 1960s, with a powerful assistance from television, the NFL was recognized as the most profitable athletic enterprise in the country. But it never forgot its origins in the small towns of Middle America. So that's why in 1963 it placed the sport's Hall of Fame in Canton, a few miles from the Hupmobile car dealership where the league began.

Every summer, new players are inducted into the hall and two professional teams play an exhibition game on the adjacent high school field, just as it was when it was all brand new. The displays of the game's history, its great games, and famous names are innovative and interesting. Many of the exhibits are interactive.

■ **LOCATION:** Off the Fulton Road exit of Interstate 77. ■ **HOURS:** Daily, 9–5; between Memorial Day and Labor Day, 9–8. ■ **ADMISSION:** $5 ■ **TELEPHONE:** (216) 456-8207

CLEVELAND

ROCK 'N' ROLL HALL OF FAME

Many social historians give 1955 as the beginning of the rock era. That was the summer "Rock Around the Clock" made it to the top of the *Billboard* sales charts, the first rock recording to be number one. In Cleveland, they trace the genesis of rock to three years before. Local disc jockey Alan Freed scheduled the world's first live rock concert in a hall that seated ten thousand—and thirty thousand kids showed up. That's one of the main reasons Cleveland wound up as the home of rock's hall of fame and museum.

Freed was credited with naming the music. It had been known as "race music," or sometimes rhythm and blues. It was directed toward an African-American audience and was rarely, if ever, heard on mainstream radio stations. But white kids listened, and liked what they heard. The music evolved out of several southern strains and first became identified as a distinct sound in Chicago after World War II. It was raw, frankly sexual stuff. Listeners were implored to "Work with me, Annie" and told that "My baby rocks me with a steady roll." Freed had a nightly show called "Moondog" and became the first white personality to put the music on the air. Consequently, Cleveland became a rock hotbed.

Adults felt immediately threatened, as they usually do when a new musical form appears, from ragtime to rap. But rock was something different—not a variation on the familiar but an altogether new kind of music. They didn't like it. Freed moved on to New York in 1954 and staged the first concert in which Black and white acts appeared on-stage together. His TV show was canceled when the camera picked up a black performer dancing with a white girl. One of his Boston shows ended in a riot when the police tried to close it prematurely.

Freed was later forced from the air during the payola scandals of the late 1950s. He admitted accepting money to play songs on the radio, a common practice at the time. He got a six-month suspended sentence, but never returned to the air. He died in 1965. But when the Rock and Roll Hall of Fame Foundation selected its place for a museum, it remembered Freed, and in 1986 Cleveland got the nod. Several rock legends already have been elected to the facility, even though it is not scheduled to open until 1995.

■ **LOCATION:** Downtown, just off the lakefront, at 1040 East 9th Street. ■ **HOURS AND ADMISSION:** Call in advance. ■ **TELEPHONE:** (216) 781-7625

GREENVILLE

THOMAS-OAKLEY COLLECTIONS OF THE GARST MUSEUM

After he became a famous radio newscaster, Lowell Thomas liked to claim that he was born right next door to Annie Oakley's birthplace. Not quite, but close. Both came from tiny villages in Darke County and both have mementoes of their lives displayed in the county seat of Greenville.

Oakley, whose real name was Phoebe Annie Oakley Mozee, was born near North Star in 1860. By the age of fifteen she was touring the country as a marksman, defeating Frank Butler, whom she later married, in a celebrated competition. That contest supplied the plot for the acclaimed musical show, *Annie, Get Your Gun.* As a member of Buffalo Bill's Wild West Show, she toured the world, astonishing audiences with her shooting. Proficiency with guns was believed to be an exclusively male preserve. But Oakley's shooting became legendary. Her name even became a slang term for a complimentary ticket: many free passes were perforated, resembling the playing cards from one of Oakley's best-known tricks—shooting several holes through a playing card after it was thrown into the air and before it fell to the ground. She was injured in a train wreck during the 1901 tour and never performed in show business again. She returned to Greenville and resided here until her death in 1926.

Thomas's hometown was nearby Woodington, but his physician father moved the family to the mining camp of Cripple Creek, Colorado, when the future journalist was still a child. His father insisted that he rise above his rough surroundings by speaking clearly enunciated and grammatically impeccable English, an attribute that served him well when he sat down in front of a microphone. Thomas acquired a reputation as an excellent free-lance reporter. The U.S. Department of the Interior sent him to Europe to write a history of American involvement in World War I. Instead, he traveled to the Middle East to hook up with the British Army for a major campaign. It was in Jerusalem that he met a brilliant young Englishman who was trying to unite the various Arab factions against the Turks. Thomas joined the campaign and his writings are the origin of the legend of Lawrence of Arabia.

The book Thomas wrote on Lawrence made the young newsman's reputation. He lectured widely, and when network radio began he was one of the first news commentators put on the air. As the narrator for Fox Movietone News, Thomas's voice became one of the most widely recognized in the country during the 1930s and 1940s. He is even credited with giving the first televised newscast, in 1939.

A crusty, irreverent individual into his retirement, Thomas is also fondly recalled for stalking out of the theater when the television show *This Is Your Life* attempted to use him as a subject. He was too much of a journalist to stand still for such sentimentality. Thomas died in 1981 and many of his personal items were returned to this museum near his birthplace.

■ **LOCATION:** Greenville is about 22 miles west of Interstate 75, by way of U.S. 36. The museum is located at 205 North Broadway. ■ **HOURS:** Tuesday through Sunday, 1–4:30. ■ **ADMISSION:** Free ■ **TELEPHONE:** (513) 548-5250

MANSFIELD

MALABaR FARM

In the early 1940s, there was a brief, nostalgic period in which moving to a farm was regarded as the highest form of sophistication among the New York smart set. Cole Porter even satirized the celebrity hayseeds with the song

"Farming," which was performed by Danny Kaye and others in the revue *Let's Face It.* Still, many well-known writers and show business personalities bought farmland out of a sincere love for the land. Among them was Louis Bromfield.

A Pulitzer Prize-winning novelist of the 1920s, Bromfield was known for his portraits of life in a small midwestern city. It was patterned after Mansfield, his hometown. It was his 1933 work, *The Farm,* a novel about rural life in the same area, which he wrote while he was living in France, that became a national best-seller. Six years later, as war in Europe became imminent, he returned to the Mansfield area and purchased Malabar Farm.

Bromfield entertained a steady stream of celebrity guests. One visit in 1945 turned the place into a landmark. This is where Humphrey Bogart and Lauren Bacall chose to get married. They had met the previous year while filming *To Have and Have Not.* Bacall rose to stardom in the film as the possessor of The Look. She explained later that she was very nervous during the filming and that "one way to keep my trembling head still was to keep it down, chin low, almost to my chest, and eyes up to Bogart." Although she was still a teenager, a legendary romance began. Even a generation later, when a popular song said, "We had it all, just like Bogie and Bacall," the association was immediate.

While Malabar Farm, now a state park, is worth a visit for many reasons, from horticultural to literary, it is the exhibits in the Big House, related to the Bogart-Bacall nuptials, that make it a big tourist attraction.

■ **LOCATION:** The farm is located southeast of Mansfield and is most easily reached from Interstate 71 by taking the Bellville exit south on Ohio 97, then north at Butler on Ohio 95. ■ **HOURS:** Daily, 10–4:15. ■ **ADMISSION:** $1.75 ■ **TELEPHONE:** (419) 892-2784

MARION

POPCOrN MUSEUM

It is the most American of snacks. Archaeologists found ears of popcorn in New Mexico caves dating back 5,600 years. Historians believe that it was part of the Native American contribution to the first Thanksgiving feast at Plymouth in 1621. It was called popped corn then and the phenomenon of each kernel expanding thirty times its original size when moistened and heated was regarded as slightly less than miraculous.

During the Chicago Columbian Exposition of 1893, the firm of F. W. Rueckheim and Brother got the idea of coating the kernels with caramel. Three years later this was marketed nationally as Cracker Jacks and became the most popular snack food of the era. The famous line from the song "Take Me Out to the Ballgame," written in 1907, which goes: "Buy me some peanuts and Cracker Jacks" is an indication of how closely it was tied to baseball. By the end of World War I, popcorn machines, colorfully decorated and, in many cases, musical became a familiar part of the urban street scene, located outside department stores and theaters.

Then in 1929 came the turning point. Popcorn moved inside the movies. Theater owners had resisted this for many years, claiming that the machines were too noisy and too messy. Then they started seeing the effect popcorn sales had on their revenues and they welcomed popcorn machines into the lobby with both arms. Since then, popcorn has become identified as the quintessential movie food. There are millions of people who can't get through a feature without a bag.

Popcorn really took off, however, during the era of healthy eating, beginning in the 1980s. It was noted that popcorn, when not drenched in melted butter or covered with salt, is a low-calorie food with few nutritional drawbacks. (Although in 1994, some nutritionists claimed that the liquefying agents used by movie poppers were taking away most of the benefits.) Sales increased by more than fifty percent during the 1980s, to $2 billion a year—enough to feed every person in the country fifty-six quarts annually. Gourmet brands, introduced in 1976 with Beatrice Food's Orville Redenbacher Popcorn, brought it into the upscale market.

The Popcorn Museum, near the center of America's popcorn growing belt, concentrates on vintage popping machines, especially those used in the entertainment industry. There are movie poppers from the 1920s and even an example of a drive-through popping machine from the 1950s.

■ **LOCATION:** The museum is part of Marion's Heritage Hall Museum Center, at 343 South State Street. ■ **HOURS:** Wednesday through Sunday, 1–4. ■ **ADMISSION:** Free ■ **TELEPHONE:** (614) 387-4255

RIO GRANDE

BOB EVANS FARM

In 1946, West Virginia passed a law prohibiting auto companies from sending cars through the state on double-decked trucks. That was the unlikely origin of the Bob Evans restaurant empire. Evans owned a small diner on a major federal highway in Gallipolis, right across the Ohio River from West Virginia. Auto companies suggested that a storage depot where cars and trucks could be kept for loading and unloading for the West Virginia passage could be a prosperous venture for that property. And if Evans wanted to serve meals there, too, so much the better.

The Bob Evans truck stop became a landmark. So did the home-style country meals, featuring the special blend of sausage devised by his wife, Jewel. Even after the West Virginia state law was rescinded, truckers made it a point to stop there. Evans's first love was farming and he owned a 3,500-acre place a few miles away, near the town of Rio Grande. In 1963, he opened a restaurant there, too, and its rustic setting was enormously popular with families.

"We never had any ambition for the business to be as big as it is today," Evans said in a 1979 interview. "It just grew. There wasn't anybody making the kinds of food we served on a national scale. People who wanted country-style sausages, fried mush, country ham, biscuits and gravy came to us." Using the Rio Grande restaurant as a prototype, Evans opened a place in Chillicothe, Ohio, in 1968. It became the first in the national chain.

Company headquarters is now in Columbus, but the company motto, "Down on the farm," is still a reality in Rio Grande. There are craft displays, a restored log cabin village, wagon rides, farm animal exhibits, and weekend festivals all through the summer and fall.

■ **LOCATION:** Bob Evans Farm is just off U.S. 35, about 12 miles west of Gallipolis and the West Virginia border. ■ **HOURS:** Daily, 9–5, April–October. ■ **ADMISSION:** Free, except during Farm Festival, a major exhibit of rural crafts, held on the second weekend in October. Then the price is $4 per car. ■ **TELEPHONE:** (614) 245-5305

TOLEDO

TONY PACKO'S CAFE

For years it was just a neighborhood place, in kind of an aging neighborhood, locally known for its Hungarian hot dogs. Then one night in 1976, Toledo-born actor Jamie Farr, who was playing a major role on the television series *M*A*S*H,* ad-libbed a reference to it. The character he portrayed, Klinger, was noted for dressing in women's clothing in the hopes of getting a discharge from the Korean War. Klinger also yearned for his hometown, which the show's writers made Toledo. So the mention of Tony Packo's was a natural.

Suddenly the place, founded in 1932, was nationally famous. Inquiries poured into the show, asking whether the restaurant really existed. When assured that it did, *M*A*S*H* fans made it a point to visit when passing through Toledo. The cafe now has a souvenir shop and glass cases filled with hot dog buns that are autographed by visiting celebrities.

Tony Packo, Jr., confessed afterward, though, that there was nothing especially Hungarian about the hot dogs, except the ethnic background of the proprietor. "It's just a smoked sausage split down the middle with chili on top," he says. "They split the sausage because it was the Depression when they opened up and they could charge only a nickel for it. Otherwise, it would have been a dime."

Tony Packo's: The autographed hot dog buns are inside. *(Courtesy of Dana Hansen)*

■ **LOCATION:** Tony Packo's is just east of the Front Street exit from Interstate 280, at 1902 Front Street. ■ **HOURS:** Monday through Thursday, 11 A.M.–10 P.M.; Friday and Saturday, 11 A.M.–11 P.M.; Sunday, 1–8 P.M. ■ **TELEPHONE:** (419) 691-6054

WAPAKONETA

NEIL aRMSTRONG MUsEUM

On July 20, 1969, this Ohio town, like most of the world, was gazing up at the moon. A team of American Apollo 11 astronauts had landed at the Sea of Tranquility and were about to take the last step on an almost unimaginable journey. They were about to set foot on the moon.

The culmination of decades of research and testing and probes, the moon landing, carried live on television, was the pinnacle of the space program's technological achievement. A trip that science fiction novelists and moviemakers had speculated about endlessly was finally coming true, right before our eyes.

"That's one small step for a man; one giant leap for mankind," said Neil Armstrong, as he made the jump from the Gemini 8 landing craft to the lunar surface. And in his hometown of Wapakoneta, people remembered him through their pride and tears. Kenneth Weber remembered how he and Armstrong began taking flying lessons together in 1946, when Armstrong was sixteen. He had to ride his bike home from the airport because he couldn't drive a car. Jacob Zint remembered how he let Armstrong, his young neighbor, look through his telescope. Armstrong would always talk about astronomy and the possibility of habitation in space. His mother remembered when he was asked if he wasn't afraid to be a test pilot. "God is up there the same as down here," he replied.

Six weeks after the moon walk, Armstrong was welcomed home by cheers and a parade led by the governor and Bob Hope. Visitors poured into town and lined the street to watch him pass. "Some of you have a favorite song about the Age of Aquarius," he told the students at Wapakoneta High, from which he had graduated in 1947. "I want to tell you I'm a fan of that song, too, because we used the main star of Aquarius as our guide in making our rendezvous with the spaceship."

Through this museum, the town remembers the glory of its native son and the triumph of that day. The capsule in which the first moon landing was made is on display. There is also an exhibit on the history of flight—from balloons to the moon missions. A theater simulates the sensation of being in space.

■ **LOCATION:** Wapakoneta is on Interstate 75, about 55 miles north of Dayton. The museum is at Exit 111, Business Loop 75. ■ **HOURS:** Monday through Saturday, 9:30–5; Sunday, noon–5. ■ **ADMISSION:** $3 ■ **TELEPHONE:** (419) 738-8811

ZANESVILLE

ZANE GREY MUSEUM

With a new degree in dentistry on his wall, a young Ohioan, Zane Grey, went into practice in New York City in 1898. But the work didn't satisfy him and he was constantly haunted by the idea that somehow he had made the wrong choice. He remembered growing up in Zanesville, and the stories he heard about his ancestors, who were among Ohio's first settlers. In particular, he recalled Betty Zane. During the Revolutionary War, she had run from a fort that was being besieged by the British and Indians, to get a supply of gunpowder in a nearby house. There was a monument to her at the cemetery in the little town of Martins Ferry.

The idea of writing about her planted itself in Grey's mind and wouldn't go away. So in 1904 he brought out a novel, *Betty Zane,* which he paid to have published himself. It sold moderately well, and that was enough for him. He abandoned dentistry and from then on considered himself a writer. But he felt that Ohio themes would never get a national audience. Besides, he was fascinated by the West, which was in the process of passing into legend. It would be six long years, however, until Harper's agreed to publish *The Heritage of the Desert.* In 1912, *Riders of the Purple Sage* became a best-seller, with rights sold to the movies. Grey became the most popular novelist in the country.

His westerns were assured hits and many of them were filmed two and three times, as silents and talkies. A 1935 news article estimated that every major western star in the movies got his start playing Zane Grey characters. He originated many of the basic western themes, redone in various forms over the decades. The mysterious stranger rides into town. The greedy land barons. The clash of Indians and settlers. It was his images of the Old West that dominated American popular culture until long after his death in 1939.

Grey lived in California during his most successful years, but his family returned many of his personal belongings to Zanesville. It is appropriate that this facility shares quarters with another state museum, dedicated to the National Road. That was one of the first great overland routes West. His forebears would have traveled on it to reach Zanesville. Wagons and implements used by pioneers on the road are displayed.

■ **LOCATION:** At the U.S. 40 exit of Interstate 70; 8850 East Pike. ■ **HOURS:** Monday through Saturday, 9:30–5; Sunday, noon–5, May–September. Closed Monday and Tuesday, rest of the year. ■ **ADMISSION:** $3 ■ **TELEPHONE:** (614) 872-3143

West Virginia

GRAFTON

MOTHER'S DAY SHRINE

Mother's Day was the special project of a Philadelphia woman, Anna Jarvis. When her mother died in 1905, Jarvis embarked on a campaign to win an annual expression of gratitude to all mothers. In 1908 she convinced Grafton's Andrews Methodist Church, in her mother's hometown, to hold a memorial service. Jarvis built on that and petitioned tirelessly for national recognition. Six years later, by proclamation, President Woodrow Wilson established Mother's Day as the second Sunday in May, the date on which Jarvis's own mother had died.

This is the story of the holiday's origin observed in the Grafton church building. But it is not the only version. Rev. Royal Pullman, brother of the inventor of the Pullman car, reportedly observed an annual Mother's Day service at his church in Baltimore after the death of his mother in 1893. Frank Hering, a onetime captain of the Notre Dame football team, claimed that he had proposed the idea in South Bend in 1904 and showed off a medal proclaiming him to be "the Father of Mother's Day." On the fortieth anniversary of the day's establishment, the National Association of Greeting Card Publishers announced that it was actually Mary Sasseen of Henderson, Kentucky, who started it all. Documentation was produced indicating that she had conducted Mother's Day celebrations in her classroom going back to 1887. Sasseen eventually convinced all public schools in the state to join in and also spread the idea at national educational conferences.

Nonetheless, Grafton still clings to its claim. As for the two women primarily credited with establishing the day for mothers, Sasseen died in labor with her first child in 1904 and Jarvis never married.

■ **LOCATION:** The former Andrews Methodist Church, now the Mother's Day Shrine, is located in central Grafton, about 23 miles south of Interstates 68 and 79, by way of U.S. 119. ■ **HOURS:** Monday through Friday, 9:30–3:30, Saturday, 12–4. ■ **ADMISSION:** Donation ■ **TELEPHONE:** (304) 265-1589

NEWELL

HOMER LAUGHLIN CHINA COMPANY

The clay beds of Hancock County, at the tip of West Virginia's northern panhandle, are among the richest in America for the minerals that go into chinaware. Accordingly, there have been pottery factories in the state since Revolutionary times. The first in Newell was set up around 1830, using local clay to make a crude yellow ware. It was an important product in terms of frontier psychology. In rural America, most families still ate from wooden tableware. The arrival of china plates marked an ascendance into the middle class and the coming of civilized values.

Homer Laughlin started manufacturing his china in this Ohio River town in 1871 and for most of the twentieth century it was the largest such company in America. There was a time, in fact, when you could turn over any cup or plate in an American restaurant or hotel and chances were excellent that it was a product of the Laughlin works. It claims to have produced more than one-third of all the china ever made in this country.

Tours are offered through the factory and an audiovisual presentation explains the historic setting of the china industry in America.

■ **LOCATION:** The factory is on West Virginia 2, about one mile south of the Ohio River bridge. Newell is located right across from East Liverpool, Ohio. ■ **HOURS:** Guided tours Monday through Friday, 10:30 and 1. Outlet store opened Monday through Saturday, 9:30–5, and Sunday, 12–5. ■ **ADMISSION:** Free ■ **TELEPHONE:** (304) 387-1300

WISCONSIN

BARABOO

CIRCUS WORLD MUSEUM

The circus came to town in 1882 and never left. That's the year that five local boys, the Ringling Brothers, organized their first traveling show. They advertised it as "moral, elevating, instructive, and fascinating." It was certainly all that and more. It played to fifty-nine people on its first night.

The Ringlings had show business in their blood. They hadn't been the same since a circus riverboat steamed into their boyhood home of McGregor, Iowa, on the Mississippi. Although their father had a prosperous harness-making business, which he moved to Baraboo, the boys wanted no part of it. Instead, they put their show on wheels and spent the summer touring the upper Midwest. Within six years they were able to afford thirty railroad cars, a wild animal show, and a big tent.

The arrival of the circus in these rural communities, long before the age of cheap transportation and mass communications, was an event of such magnitude that the entire calendar seemed to be shaped around it. The parade, the bands, the clowns, the midway. The Ringlings were masters at building up a sense of anticipation by sending in advance men to crank up the locals. By the turn of the century, they had, in effect, divided the country with their chief rival, Barnum and Bailey. The Ringlings took the western half. Then in 1907, Bailey's widow sold her share of Barnum and Bailey to the Ringlings and the two shows combined to form "The Greatest Show on Earth."

Baraboo remained the winter home of the circus for eleven more years until the Ringlings became involved in Florida real estate and transferred their headquarters to Sarasota. Many of the former circus warehouses were converted to other uses. Other original buildings form the core of Circus World, a look at the historical development of the shows. And in summer, the excitement of an old-time traveling circus is magically recreated at the place where this slice of Americana was born.

■ **LOCATION:** Baraboo is about 50 miles northwest of Madison, by way if U.S. 12. Circus World is located at 426 Water Street. The route is well marked.
■ **HOURS:** Circus performances are given daily, May through mid-September, 9–6; with shows extending until 10 P.M. mid-July to mid-August. Museum

The Giant Musky is a Walk-Thru Fish Museum, a half city block long and 4½ stories tall. *See* page 220. *(Courtesy of National Freshwater Fishing Hall of Fame)*

exhibits are open year round. ■ **ADMISSION:** $10.95 in summer. Lower rates at other times of year. ■ **TELEPHONE:** (608) 356-0800

GREEN BAY

PACKERS HALL OF FAME

Immediately after World War I, when professional football began, it was played in towns like Green Bay and Canton (*see* Ohio) and Portsmouth and Decatur. But places like this couldn't compete with the advantages offered by the big cities. So one by one all the original franchises of the National Football League abandoned their cradles.

All but the Green Bay Packers. They stayed put and won their first championship in 1929. The Packers have repeated that victory ten times since, a record unmatched by any other franchise. It is, in fact, the only pro football team to win the championship three years in a row, and it accomplished that twice. From its first coach, Curly Lambeau, to the man regarded as the greatest coach of the modern era, Vince Lombardi, the Packers have been a force to reckon with.

There is nothing in American sports quite like the love affair between this small city and its football team. On football Sundays, Green Bay comes to a standstill. Those who cannot get into the stadium (which has been sold out for a generation) avidly watch on television. When the Packers battered the New York Giants for the title two years in a row, it was almost as if a national morality play was being carried out on the gridiron. Small town virtue won. So did the stronger offensive line.

The team's nickname reflects its beginnings, when it was sponsored by a local packing house and the players were actually part of its payroll. The Packers are now a publicly-subscribed civic enterprise, and none of the players are required to load hogs. Two home games a year are played in Milwaukee, but the rest of the time the Packers are Green Bay's own. Memories of the team's place in the community are displayed at the Packers Hall of Fame, located directly across from the stadium in the Brown County Expo Center. There are trophies, old photographs, hands-on exhibits, and a collection relating to the career of Lombardi. Tours of the stadium leave from here, too.

■ **LOCATION:** On U.S. 41 at Ridge Road. ■ **HOURS:** Daily, 10–5. Tours begin half an hour after opening, until half an hour before closing, except on home game weekends. ■ **ADMISSION:** $5.50 ■ **TELEPHONE:** (414) 499-4281

HAYWARD

NATIONAL FRESH WATER FISHING HALL OF FAME

Michigan calls itself the "Water Wonderland." Minnesota boasts of "10,000 Lakes." Wisconsin is the "Land o' Lakes." So you get the idea that fishing is on a lot of peoples' minds in this part of America.

This tremendous concentration of fresh water, both in the Great Lakes and a myriad of inland bodies, makes fishing the top recreational pastime in summer. When the water freezes, the hearty natives simply set up their shacks, or tip-ups as they are sometimes called, and cut a hole through the ice.

The top fish in these waters is the muskellunge. They are the biggest and meanest members of the pike family. Specimens routinely top over fifty pounds and some are taken every year that exceed sixty pounds. Muskies are renowned as fighters, aggressive, and almost savage in their resistance to being taken. Many unwary fishermen have had fingers opened up by a musky when their hand got too close to its teeth. So when the Fresh Water Fishing Hall of Fame was built in this northern lake resort, it seemed fitting to design it in the shape of a musky. There is even an observation deck built inside the mouth of the four-and-a half-story-high fish.

Inside are displays of historic equipment as well as dozens of mounted specimens of record catches from around the world. Also included are exhibits on the development of the outboard motor.

■ **LOCATION:** Hayward is about 75 miles south of Duluth, Minnesota. The museum is in town, on Wisconsin 27; 1 Hall of Fame Drive. ■ **HOURS:** Daily, 10–5, mid-April through October. ■ **ADMISSION:** $3.50 ■ **TELEPHONE:** (715) 634-4440

PABST AND MILLER BREWERY TOURS

In the 1840s, German immigration reached flood levels in Wisconsin. The population of the state multiplied tenfold. Political unrest in the homeland made emigration the only alternative for thousands of German families. The newcomers brought with them a wealth of talent and a sense of liberalism that would dominate the state's politics for generations. They brought, as well, the secret of lagering beer. This was a process that had been perfected in Germany, a method of bottom-fermentation that allowed the beer to last longer and to travel. It revolutionized brewing in America.

The new immigrants provided a huge new market for the product. Wisconsin wheat farmers already were planting hops as a crop supplement, insuring a steady supply source. Both ice and cheap wood for barrels were readily at hand. So throughout the decade, a succession of the new arrivals entered the brewing business. There was Jacob Best, a vinegar maker, who decided to switch to beer in 1844. Eventually, one of his nieces married a Great Lakes ship's captain, Frederick Pabst, who ran the brewery so well that its name was changed in his honor.

John Braun got into the business two years after Best and hired as his brew master a newcomer from Mittenberg-on-the-Main, named Valentin Blatz. When Braun passed away, his widow married Blatz and another legendary Milwaukee name appeared. August Krug opened his brewery in 1849, and he, too, left a widow who married a company employee, bookkeeper Joseph Schlitz. Finally, one of Best's nephews sold out his small operation in 1855 to Frederick Miller, adding another name to the brewing pantheon.

All of these remained small, local businesses until right after the Civil War. Then two things happened. A change in federal tax policy made beer a more affordable drink for workingmen than hard liquor. And Chicago burned down. The great fire of 1871 wiped out most of the city's breweries and Milwaukee quickly moved to satisfy the thirst. The breweries never lost their lock on that market and it made their reputation national. By 1890, the whole country knew that Schlitz was "the beer that made Milwaukee famous," and the Wisconsin city became synonymous with brewing. Because their home base was small, the breweries competed fiercely in going after a national market. They outdid each other in ads and promotions, becoming identified as the sponsors of sporting events even before the advent of television. Capt. Pabst even hired actors to walk into bars and order a round of his favorite beer to drink the captain's health.

Prohibition wiped out all but the very biggest breweries, who were able to diversify until Repeal came in. But even the strongest of them were hard pressed to survive the consolidation of the 1970s. Leadership in the industry passed to St. Louis-based Anheuser-Busch, while the Schlitz and Blatz labels were purchased by outsiders. But Pabst and Miller, the nation's number two brewer, are still strong presences in their hometown. Both companies offer tours of their breweries (parts of the Pabst plant date back to the 1840s and resemble a Medieval German fortress), with tasting and snacks at the end. They're the tours that make Milwaukee famous.

■ **LOCATION:** The Pabst Brewery is at 915 West Juneau, immediately west of the central business district. The Miller Brewery, at 4251 West State, is also west of downtown, but a few miles further out. ■ **HOURS:** The Pabst tours are given on the hour, Monday through Friday, 10–11 and 1–3; Saturday, 10–11 and 1–2, June to August; Weekdays only, rest of the year. Miller offers tours Tuesday through Friday, 10–3:30; Saturday, 12–3:30. ■ **ADMISSION:** Free ■ **TELEPHONE:** Pabst (414) 223-3709; Miller (414) 931-2337.

GREAT PLAINS

IOWA

KANSAS

MISSOURI

NEBRASKA

NORTH DAKOTA

OKLAHOMA

SOUTH DAKOTA

TEXAS

Dodge City's reconstructed Front Street. *(UPI/Bettmann)*
See page 235.

GREAT PLAINS

IOWA

1 Surf Ballroom, Clear Lake
2 Field of Dreams, Dyersville
3 Meredith Willson Footbridge, Mason City
4 Maytag Historical Exhibit, Newton
5 Starship Enterprise, Riverside
6 Bridges of Madison County, Winterset
7 John Wayne Birthplace, Winterset

KANSAS

8 Amelia Earhart Memorial, Atchison
9 Martin and Osa Johnson Museum, Chanute
10 Historic Front Street, Dodge City
11 William Allen White Exhibits, Emporia
12 Wizard of Oz House, Liberal
13 The Garden of Eden, Lucas

MISSOURI

14 Country Music Shows, Branson
15 Arthur Bryant's Barbecue, Kansas City
16 Country Club Plaza, Kansas City
17 Hallmark Center, Kansas City
18 The Gateway Arch, St. Louis
19 National Bowling Hall of Fame, St. Louis
20 Ragtime Archives, Sedalia

NEBRASKA

21 Carhenge, Alliance
22 Roller Skating Museum, Lincoln
23 Boy's Town, Omaha

NORTH DAKOTA

24 Roger Maris Baseball Museum, Fargo

OKLAHOMA

25 Lynn Riggs Memorial, Claremore
26 Will Rogers Memorial, Claremore
27 National Cowboy Hall of Fame and Museum, Oklahoma City
28 Pawnee Bill Museum, Pawnee

SOUTH DAKOTA

29 Crazy Horse Memorial, Custer
30 Ingalls Home, DeSmet
31 Cheryl Ladd Room, Huron
32 Mt. Rushmore National Memorial; Rushmore-Borglum Story, Keystone
33 National Motorcycle Museum, Sturgis
34 Wall Drugs, Wall

TEXAS

35 Babe Didrikson Zaharias Memorial, Beaumont
36 Spindletop Boomtown, Beaumont
37 *The Alamo* movie set, Brackettville
38 Neiman Marcus Department Store, Dallas
39 The Sixth Floor, Dallas
40 South Fork Ranch, Dallas (Plano)
41 Audie Murphy Exhibit, Greenville
42 National Cowgirl Hall of Fame, Hereford
43 The Astrodome, Houston
44 Space Center, Houston
45 Tex Ritter Museum, Nederland
46 Texas Ranger Hall of Fame, Waco
47 Mary Martin as "Peter Pan" Statue, Weatherford

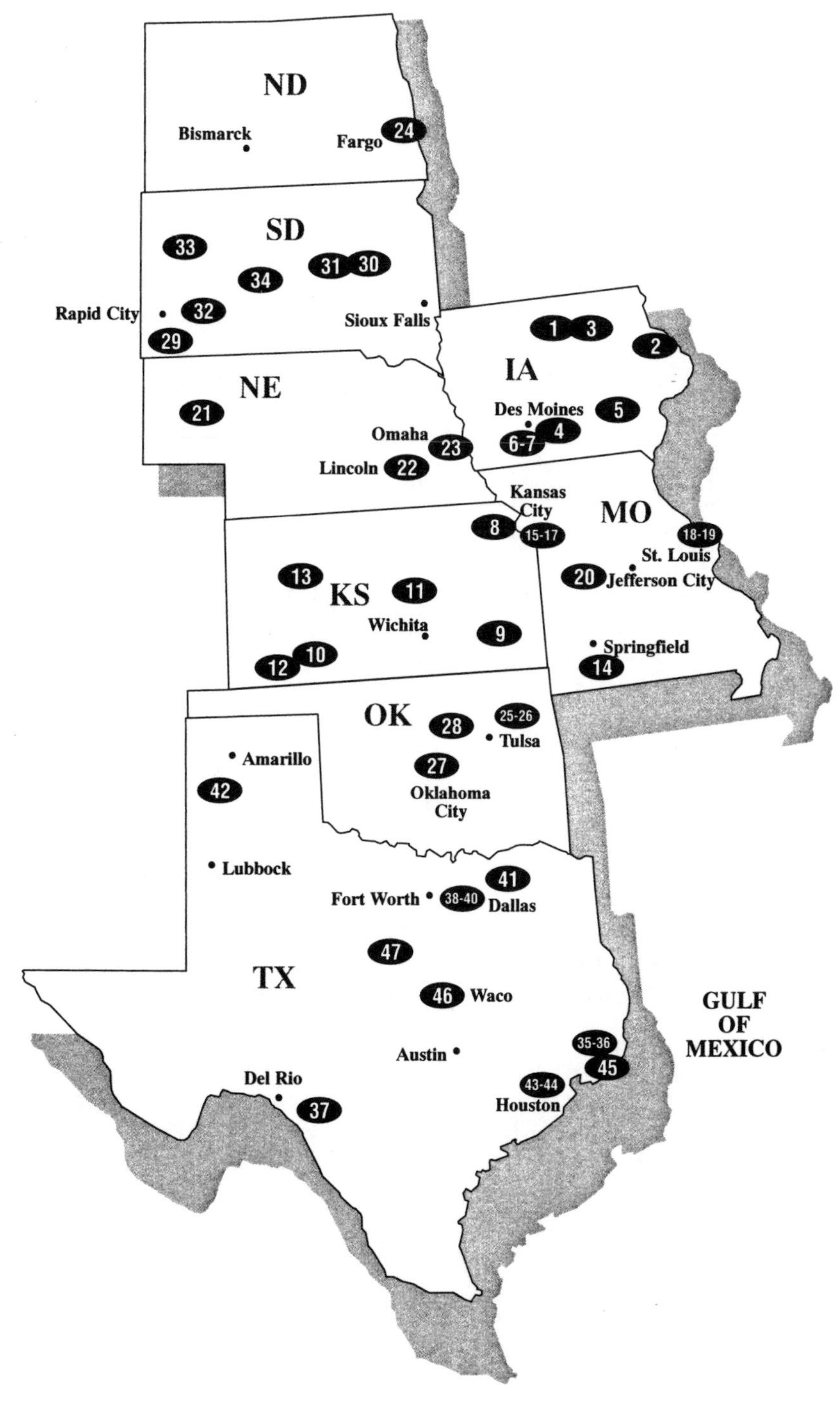
ND
Bismarck
Fargo
24
SD
33
34
31
30
Rapid City
32
29
Sioux Falls
IA
1
3
2
Des Moines
5
4
6-7
NE
21
Omaha
23
Lincoln
22
Kansas City
MO
8
15-17
18-19
St. Louis
20
Jefferson City
KS
13
11
Wichita
9
12
10
Springfield
14
OK
28
25-26
Tulsa
27
Oklahoma City
Amarillo
42
Lubbock
41
Fort Worth
38-40
Dallas
47
TX
46
Waco
GULF OF MEXICO
35-36
45
Austin
Del Rio
37
43-44
Houston

CLEAR LAKE

SURF BALLROOM

The concert was held on February 3, 1959—in the dead of winter, but 1,100 fans showed up at this summer resort to see performances by Buddy Holly, Richie Valens, J. P. Richardson (who was known as The Big Bopper), as well as Dion and the Belmonts. The performers rushed out afterward to catch the bus to their next stop, in Moorhead, Minnesota. But Holly, Valens, and Richardson boarded a single-engine Bonanza aircraft to fly ahead. All had personal business to attend to: Holly wanted to get a suit cleaned, Valens needed a haircut, and Richardson was fighting a cold and wanted some extra sleep.

The plane crashed a few minutes after takeoff, killing the three performers and the pilot. The event was memorialized as "The Day the Music Died" in the 1972 hit song "American Pie." It has become the symbol of the day rock lost its innocence and first looked straight on at death. Two movies, *La Bamba* (in 1987) and *The Buddy Holly Story* (1978), have been made about the performers who died in the crash.

At the time of the crash, a wire service described the seventeen-year-old Valens as "the next Elvis Presley." Holly, twenty-two, was an established star, just beginning to record as a solo act, apart from his longtime group, The Crickets. According to legend, Richardson was supposed to take the bus but had prevailed upon a fill-in musician with Holly's group to give up his seat on the plane. That musician was Waylon Jennings, who would become a major country artist.

Rock fans have made pilgrimages to the Surf on the date of the crash every year since 1979, when *The Buddy Holly Story* occasioned a twentieth-anniversary commemoration event. The ballroom itself was built during the big band era and remodeled in 1947. Its 6,600-square-foot dance floor is regarded as one of the finest in the Midwest and is flanked by soda shop booths that can seat 960. Its walls are decorated with musical memorabilia, including personal items of the stars who played their final concert here.

■ **LOCATION:** Clear Lake is just off Interstate 35, about 10 miles west of Mason City. The ballroom is on the lake front, at 460 North Shore Drive. ■ **HOURS:** Monday through Friday, 9–5. Saturday hours vary, depending

The farmhouse overlooking the "Field of Dreams" (left) and baseball in The Field (right). *(Courtesy of Roger Matuz)*

on whether or not a concert is scheduled. ■ **ADMISSION:** Free on non-concert dates. ■ **TELEPHONE:** (515) 357-6151

DYERSVILLE

FIELD OF DREAMS

Shoeless Joe Jackson was one of the great names of baseball's early years. An almost illiterate South Carolina mill hand, he was a feared slugger with the Chicago White Sox. In 1920, at the peak of his career, he and seven of his teammates were accused of conspiring with gamblers to throw the previous fall's World Series. Jackson claimed he never was paid a dime and, indeed, set a record for hits in the series. Even though a grand jury did not return an indictment, the eight players, who came to be known as the Black Sox, were barred from the big league. Many of the "Black Sox" were outstanding, but Jackson was an unquestioned great.

In a 1982 novel called *Shoeless Joe,* author William Kinsella brought Jackson his redemption. The story is about an Iowa farmer who loves baseball and hears a voice calling to him in the night. It says, "If you build it, he will come." The farmer understands instinctively that what he must do is convert one of his cornfields into a baseball diamond so that Jackson and his teammates can play ball once more and claim the second chance that was denied them in life.

The book, retitled *Field of Dreams,* was a surprise movie hit of 1989, with the "If you build it..." line becoming one of the catch phrases of the year. It was a film also noted for its ability to make male members of the audience cry, a phenomenon noted with wonder by several critics. In its climactic scene, the farmer, played by Kevin Costner, is told that an America hungry for something to believe in and longing for the simple virtues of baseball will find his way to the cornfield to join in the fantasy. And so Americans have. The movie set has been preserved here and is visited by thousands of fans each year. In addition, exhibition baseball games are scheduled during the summer.

■ **LOCATION:** Dyersville is about 25 miles west of Dubuque, on U.S. 20. The Field of Dreams is northeast of town by way of Iowa 136, Northeast 3rd Avenue, Dyersville Road, and Lansing Road. ■ **HOURS:** Daily, dawn to dusk, April–November. ■ **ADMISSION:** Free ■ **TELEPHONE:** (319) 875-8404

MASON CITY

MEREDITH WILLSON FOOTBRIDGE

It may say Mason City on the map. But in our hearts it is forevermore River City, the setting for one of the best loved musicals in American history, *The Music Man.* This was Meredith Willson's hometown and it was on his memories of Mason City that he drew his portrait of small-town Iowa life just before World War I.

Willson left home as a flutist in the John Philip Sousa band. The experience shaped the rest of his life. "I cannot tell you anything appertaining to my career that in some way or another did not involve my leader, Mr. Sousa," he said, in a 1979 interview. "I cannot conceive of even picking up my baton without that experience. And I would never have thought of writing '76 Trombones' if I were not a Sousa man."

He left Sousa to write several popular song hits. His biggest came as musical director of the *Tallulah Bankhead Show* on radio when he composed her signature number, "May the Good Lord Bless and Keep You." Then, encouraged by his friend, composer and publisher Frank Loesser, Willson began to experiment with ideas for a new Broadway show. There would be patter songs. And barbershop quartet harmonies. And a rousing march finale. No one saw much hope in that. But *The Music Man,* which opened in 1958, was a nostalgic triumph and its lead character, Professor Harold Hill, became the very model of the lovable con artist. When—to the strains of "Til There Was You"—Professor Hill chooses between true love and escaping the wrath of the townsfolk he has swindled, audiences melted. Even The Beatles recorded the tune on one of their early albums.

Professor Hill's change of heart takes place on a footbridge. Accordingly, the bridge beside the MacNider Museum, on Willow Creek, has been renamed the Meredith Willson Footbridge. His musical heritage is also celebrated during the North Iowa Band Festival, held here each spring.

■ **LOCATION:** The museum is at 303 2nd Street, Southeast. The bridge is immediately to the east. ■ **TELEPHONE:** (515) 421-3666

NEWTON

MAYTAg HISTORICAL EXHIBIT

In a 1961 interview with *Time* magazine, Fred Maytag II said his goal was to build a washing machine that would require no major repairs for ten years. He said it wistfully, almost as if he realized that he was dealing with an impossible goal. But only five years later, the company began a series of television commercials based on the idea that its repairman was "the loneliest man in town." The ads went on to become the longest-running national commercial in TV history and established the company as a paragon of dependability in the public's mind. At a time when many American companies were having severe problems with quality control, Maytag built a steady reputation.

The company began as a sideline. Maytag's grandfather, who was also named Fred Maytag, had an interest in a firm that manufactured agricultural implements. In 1907, after several years of tinkering, he introduced the company's first washing machine, The Pasttime. It featured an agitator that moved when the handle was turned. Although many other machines were already on the market, the Pasttime was regarded as a true innovation. Maytag began experimenting with gasoline-powered washers and in 1922 brought out the Gyratator, an automatic agitator placed underwater. That concept changed the industry and put the company into the lead in technology. The Master Washer, introduced in 1939, with its exterior wringer, was the most popular machine of its time.

In the 1960s, Maytag began expanding each worker's responsibilities in order to break up the repetitive nature of the assembly line. The company credits these changes, many of which were later adopted by larger industries, with preserving its reputation for well-crafted machines.

A 1987 study concluded that the washing machine really didn't save a significant amount of time in housework. Instead, it expanded the amount of clothes that could be cleaned at home. So the average housewife actually spent more time washing clothes that her grandmother did. But with a good deal less drudgery.

The Maytag Historical Display at the Jasper County Museum traces the development of the washing machine and its role in the life of this Iowa community.

■ **LOCATION:** Newton is about 30 miles east of Des Moines, off Interstate 80. The museum is at the Iowa 14 exit, at 1700 South 15th Avenue,

West. ■ **HOURS:** Daily, 1–5, May–September. ■ **ADMISSION:** $2 ■ **TELEPHONE:** (515) 792-2118

RIVERSIDE

STARShIP ENTERPRIsE

Star Trek went on the air in 1966 and lasted three seasons, fewer than eighty episodes. Then it was canceled. Expensive to produce, so-so ratings, and that was the end of it. Or so thought network executives. In fact, cancellation was only the beginning for a television series that went boldly where no man had ever gone before.

Star Trek in syndication became a TV event. Its imaginative scripts, with their likable characters and unique blend of science fiction and fantasy, attracted a cult following. They became known as "Trekkies" and soon acquired a life of their own. They held conventions and published newsletters. More than a decade after the series went off the air, a Star Trek movie was made and worked so well that five more followed. In addition, an updated version of the original TV program, called *Star Trek: The Next Generation,* also went into TV syndication.

All this was not lost on the town council of Riverside. In one episode, there was a reference to Captain James Kirk's birthplace as being "a small town in Iowa." That was all. But, Riverside figured, why not here? After all, Kirk wasn't even scheduled to be born until the twenty-third century, who could say he wasn't born here? So in 1983 Riverside appointed itself Kirk's hometown. The State Highway Department refused to play along with the gag and made the town take down a sign announcing the fact on the main highway. But the town built a model of Kirk's starship, the *Enterprise,* and called it the *USS Riverside.* The town also celebrates Captain Kirk's birthday every March and holds a Trekkie convention in June.

■ **LOCATION:** Riverside is about 15 miles south of Iowa City on U.S. 218. The starship is on the highway, just south of the Iowa 22 turnoff into town.

WINTERSET

BRIDGeS OF MADISOn COUNTY

One of the early residents of Madison County was Jesse Hiatt. A farmer with an experimental bent, he brought apple seedlings from Vermont and grafted their branches to other varieties. The result was a new kind of apple, juicier and sweeter than any known before. Hiatt called it the Delicious and it has remained an American fruit staple.

Through its settlement, this part of Iowa had strong ties to New England. One of the things the pioneers brought from their former eastern homes was a fondness for covered bridges. There are six still in use in Madison County and for years there has been an annual festival celebrating them. In 1992 these bridges became a national phenomenon: tourists began arriving by the truck-load, Oprah Winfrey and her crew flew in from Chicago to do an entire show here, movie directors arrived to scout out the countryside.

All this because of a thin volume of fiction, *The Bridges of Madison County,* by Robert James Waller, a former management professor at Northern Iowa University. The novel occupied the number-one slot on *The New York Times* best-seller list for more than a year, selling a record four million copies in that twelve-month span. The story of a brief, bittersweet love affair between a photographer (who is assigned to take some pictures of the bridges) and an unhappy but passionate local housewife, the book seemed to connect with the nerve endings of American readers. It was a publishing phenomenon that turned a local attraction into a part of the national culture.

■ **LOCATION:** Winterset is about 35 miles southwest of Des Moines, by way of Interstate 80 and U.S. 169. One of the covered bridges is right in town, in City Park. A map of the others can be obtained at the Chamber of Commerce. ■ **TELEPHONE:** (515) 462-1185 (the Winterset Chamber of Commerce).

JOHN WAYNE BIRTHPLACE

After his death in 1979, a good deal of confusion accompanied the memorial tributes to John Wayne. He had played cowboys and war heroes for so long on the screen, and had become such an international symbol of America, that in his eulogies it was as if the man had become intertwined with the heroes he portrayed—as if Wayne himself were a hero, rather than someone who played heroes for a living. Wayne was born too late to win the West and while others were winning World War II, he stayed behind to make movies about it.

Born Marion Michael Morrison in this Iowa town, Wayne was Winterset's most famous attraction—at least until the Bridges of Madison County frenzy hit (*see* previous listing). A football player at Southern California University, he landed a summer job as a guard on the 20th Century Fox lot and became friendly with director John Ford, who saw something he liked in the young man's face and cast him in westerns. Wayne seemed destined to make a career as a B-movie star, until Ford chose him for the part of the Ringo Kid in the classic 1939 film, *Stagecoach.* Wayne was then thirty-two years old and for the rest of his life he would be among the world's top stars.

He was always the loner, the man with the dark violent secret in his past—never allowing himself to become too close to anyone else, always true to his own code. One critic said the quintessential image of Wayne was in another of his classic roles, in Ford's 1956 *The Searchers.* His character had spent years trying to find his niece and rescue her from captivity among the Indians. In the final frame, as the niece enters the house to be reunited with other family members, the door closes on Wayne, standing alone, always the outsider.

In 1969 Wayne won his only Oscar, for playing what was an affectionate tribute to his own aging image in *True Grit.* He had become an outspoken defender of American involvement in Vietnam and a backer of many conservative causes, causing his popularity to drop among young movie-goers. But at his death he was recognized as the country's most enduring screen hero.

The museum here has restored two rooms in the old family house to their appearance in 1907, the year of Wayne's birth. There are also photographs and other memorabilia of the actor, including his eye patch from *True Grit.*

■ **LOCATION:** 224 South 2nd Street. ■ **HOURS:** Daily, 10–5. ■ **ADMISSION:** $3 ■ **TELEPHONE:** (515) 462-1044

Kansas

ATCHISON

AMELIA EARHART MEMORIAL

On the morning of July 1, 1937, the slight aviatrix from Kansas took off from a dusty airstrip in Lae, New Guinea, and with her navigator, Fred Noonan, vanished into legend. Amelia Earhart was thirty-eight years old and attempting to be the first woman to make an around-the-world flight. She was the first woman to do just about everything else in aviation. Earhart was an American heroine, "Lady Lindy" the press called her. The daughter of a railroad claims attorney, she had gone to private schools and Columbia University and had a degree in social work. But when she first sat down at the controls of an airplane, she had found her true calling.

She became the first woman to fly across the Atlantic in 1928 and from then until her disappearance she was seldom out of the headlines. "Adventure, that's the bug that has bitten this generation," she wrote. "I have tried to play for a large stake and if I succeed, all will be well. If I don't, I shall be happy to pop off in the midst of such an adventure."

She couldn't have scripted it better. The final authenticated message from her plane came the afternoon of July 2, 1937, indicating that the plane was running low on fuel and no land was in sight. A massive naval search was begun. Radio operators insisted they were getting further cryptic messages from her. But one week later, the Navy ended the search and listed Earhart and Noonan as dead. The legend persisted though. There were reports that they had accidentally landed on an island being fortified by the Japanese and were executed as spies. Others that they had gone down on a deserted island and survived until their provisions ran out. What is most likely, however, is that she ran out of gas over the Pacific and simply "popped off."

Her hometown remembers Earhart with a museum at her birthplace, which has been restored and opened for tours. There is also a statue, surrounded by an International Forest of Friendship, at a site adjacent to the town's airport.

■ **LOCATION:** Her birthplace is located at 223 North Terrace, on a bluff overlooking the Missouri River. The airport memorial is west of town, by way of U.S. 73. ■ **HOURS:** The birthplace is open daily, 1–5. ■ **ADMISSION:** Free ■ **TELEPHONE:** (913) 367-4127

CHANUTE

MARTIN AND OSA JOHNSON MUSEUM

About six months before Amelia Earhart's disappearance, (*see* previous entry) another adventurous Kansas woman was involved in a headlined air tragedy. Osa Johnson was on her way to Los Angeles with her husband, Martin, when their passenger plane slammed into a mountain side near Newhall Pass. Martin Johnson was killed, ending one of the most famous film collaborations in history.

The couple's travel and adventure movies had become extremely popular in the 1920s and 1930s. At a time when the world was a lot bigger and mysterious, they made repeated trips to Africa and the South Pacific, to places that were still veiled in myth and seemed unknowable. They brought out movie images that were remarkable, glimpses of places that American audiences had only dreamed about seeing. Martin Johnson, who grew up in nearby Independence, Kansas, had gone on the road as a teenager, traveling to England on a cattle boat. He came home, read that novelist Jack London was looking for a third person to sail the Pacific in his 47-foot boat, and volunteered for the job. "Can you cook," London wired him. "A little," Johnson responded. Johnson went out and worked as a short-order cook in a local restaurant for a week, before joining London for the start of the journey.

In 1910, while lecturing in Chanute about one of his trips, Johnson met Osa Leighty, a high school student who sang at the show. They were married before the year was out and honeymooned in the Pacific. From then on, their life consisted of travel to uncharted places, filming what they saw, and lecture tours. Martin did most of the filming. Osa became his protector, a crack shot who reputedly brought down charging animals, permitting her husband to capture some of the most spectacular footage ever recorded. Barely five feet tall, she was also an asset on the stage, where she dressed in high fashion and leavened her husband's lectures with a lively sense of humor.

After her husband's death, Osa tried to carry on the travels alone. But the formula didn't work. The films they made, however, were a staple of the town hall circuit for years and even resurfaced as an early television feature in the 1950s. But with safari tours becoming commonplace and remote Pacific islands just a jet ride away, the sense of adventure slowly diminished. Osa Johnson died in 1953.

The museum in Chanute contains artifacts from their trips, photographs, exhibits of the equipment they used and extensive displays of village life in West Africa.

■ **LOCATION:** Chanute is about 70 miles south of Interstate 35, by way of U.S. 59 and 169. The museum is at 16 South Grant. ■ **HOURS:** Monday through Saturday, 10–5; Sunday, 1–5. ■ **ADMISSION:** $3.50 ■ **TELEPHONE:** (316) 431-2730

DODGE CITY

HISTORIC FRONT STREET

In its day, which was short and nasty, Dodge City was one of the wildest cattle towns in the Old West. It was one of the primary railheads to the east and massive cattle drives from Texas came here throughout the early 1880s. Cowboys looking for pleasures of any kind after long months on the trail were almost impossible to control. The law was sketchily enforced, frequently by men who were just as wild as the cowboys. Wyatt Earp took a turn as town marshal, as did Bill Tilghman, Luke Short, and Bat Masterson. Legendary names, all of them. But by 1884, other railheads had been established, and the Great Blizzard of 1887 virtually wiped out the herds in this part of Kansas. Dodge City settled down to a quiet anonymity. Front Street, which paralleled the Santa Fe tracks, shut down and the focus of the town's activity moved a few blocks away. Midway through the twentieth century, all that was left was a memory.

And then came television. A steady progression of TV westerns made in the 1950s and set in old Dodge City suddenly rekindled interest in Front Street in all its bawdy and raucous glory. *Wyatt Earp* became a hit and so did *Bat Masterson.* But the biggest of them all was *Gunsmoke.* Billed as the first adult western, the adventures of the fictitious Marshal Matt Dillon was one of the longest-running shows in TV history, launching the careers of several major stars.

It also launched Front Street. Deciding to cash in on the *Gunsmoke* craze, Dodge City rebuilt the notorious thoroughfare, more closely resembling the TV setting than historical fact. The local Rotary already had restored Boot Hill in 1930 and erected spurious gravestones detailing the violent deaths of several unlikely characters. Front Street follows in this tradition. The two-block long restoration does contain some historically accurate exhibits. But what is important is the impact the twentieth-century media had in influencing our ideas of what the nineteenth-century West looked like. And Dodge City is happy to comply.

■ **LOCATION:** Dodge City is at the junction of U.S. 50 (the old Santa Fe Trail) and U.S. 283. It is about 90 miles south of Interstate 70. ■ **HOURS:** The Front Street and Boot Hill complex is open daily, 8–8, late May through August; daily, 9–5, early May, September, and October; Monday through Saturday, 9–5, and Sunday, 1–5, rest of the year. ■ **ADMISSION:** $5. There is a further admission to the nightly variety show at the Long Branch Saloon. ■ **TELEPHONE:** (316) 227-8188

EMPORIA

WILLIAM ALLEN WHITE EXHIBITS

What's the Matter with Kansas?" wrote the young editor of a small Kansas newspaper during the 1896 presidential campaign. The editorial, which ringingly affirmed the moderate Republican position, was credited by many with carrying the Midwest for the GOP candidate, William McKinley. It also brought William Allen White and his *Emporia Gazette* to national attention. In the next fifty years he became a journalism legend, the small town newspaperman, wise and incorruptible, who wrote with greater intellect, grace, and sense than the metropolitan stars.

White's newspaper writings, along with his novels and longer political studies, made him a national force in the GOP. His articles were syndicated across the country and through them Emporia became a paradigm of the American small town, a repository of civic virtues. He was awarded a Pulitzer Prize for editorial writing in 1922. He was the model for countless fictional newspapermen and an inspiration for real editors.

Born in Emporia, White worked briefly in Kansas City before buying the *Gazette* with a borrowed $3,000 in 1895. He died in 1944 but the newspaper is still operated by members of his family. There is a display of newspaper equipment used during White's tenure at the *Gazette* offices, where you can also pick up a driving tour map that identifies other places in the city associated with him. Most notable is the William Allen White Archives at Emporia State University, a large collection of his personal and private memorabilia.

■ **LOCATION:** Emporia is near the junction of Interstate 35 and the Kansas Turnpike, about 60 miles south of Topeka. The *Gazette* offices are at 517 Merchant Street. ■ **HOURS:** Both the *Gazette* and the Archives are open Monday through Saturday, 9–5. ■ **ADMISSION:** Free ■ **TELEPHONE:** (316) 342-1600 for the *Gazette;* (316) 343-1200 for the Archives.

LIBERAL

WIZARd OF OZ HOUSe

"Toto," said Dorothy, "I don't think we're in Kansas anymore." With that observation, the movie screen, which had suddenly gone from black and white to full color, opened out on the Land of Oz. Kansas has since styled itself the Land of *Ahhs* and built a yellow brick road that leads to this community in the southwestern part of the state. Author L. Frank Baum didn't actually specify what part of Kansas he had in mind when he wrote *The Wizard of Oz.* Anyplace with lots of wind would do. So the town of Liberal, which was named for an early resident's generosity in granting water rights, decided that Dorothy may as well live there.

A replica of Auntie Em's house from the 1939 movie (which was shot on a Hollywood back lot), with Dorothy's bedroom fully furnished as it was in the film, is now part of the Coronado Museum here. There are ruby slippers, a stuffed version of Toto, the tiny model of the house that was shown being blown to Oz in the twister, even autographs by some of the Munchkins. Clips from the movie are also shown periodically. Students of popular culture cite the *Wizard of Oz* as the quintessential Depression-era film. Its biggest song, "Over the Rainbow," expressed the desire of millions of Americans to escape the drab struggle of the 1930s for a happier place and time. By the end of the century, most Americans would have probably settled for Kansas.

■ **LOCATION:** Liberal is at the junction of U.S. 54 and 83, on the Oklahoma border. The museum is at 567 East Cedar Street and Dorothy's house is listed at 567 Yellow Brick Road. ■ **HOURS:** Tuesday through Saturday, 9–5; Sunday, 1–5. ■ **ADMISSION:** Free ■ **TELEPHONE:** (316) 624-7624

LUCAS

THE GaRDEN OF EDEN

In the course of American history, many communities have claimed to be the new Eden. Lucas, however, has a distinct advantage. One of its residents, S. P. Dinsmoor, actually carved his version of the Biblical garden—complete with Adam and Eve, serpent, and dozens of other fanciful figures—out of 113 tons of cement. They surround his former farmhouse in this tiny village.

It took Dinsmoor twenty-two years, from 1907 to 1929, to complete this great work, a bit longer than the Almighty's time. A retired veteran of the Civil War, Dinsmoor also built himself a "log cabin," constructed out of concrete, in the middle of the garden. He filled the area with several modern parables of Biblical tales, such as attorneys and bankers rejoicing over the form of the crucified Christ. It is one of the most obsessive attractions on the American roadside, one man's view of a paradise lost.

■ **LOCATION:** Lucas is 15 miles north of the Wilson exit of Interstate 70, by way of Kansas 232. The Garden is at 2nd and Kansas streets. ■ **HOURS:** Daily, 9–6. Winter months, daily, 10–4. ■ **ADMISSION:** $1.50 ■ **TELEPHONE:** (913) 525-6395

MISSOURI

BRANSON

COUNTRY MUSIC SHOWS

One of the basic laws of physics is that for every action there is an equal and opposite reaction. That seems to apply to country music, too. During the 1960s, the music's longtime home base of Nashville (*see* Tennessee) started becoming too urban, too crowded for some tastes. A few performers decided to move to surroundings more in keeping with the spirit of their music. They chose Branson, a little resort town in the Missouri Ozarks.

The place was already known to tourists as the setting of the novel, *Little Shepherd of the Hills,* a tale of life on the Ozarks frontier. An annual theatrical production drawn from the book is still put on here. But with the arrival of the country brigade, Branson suddenly became an entertainment hot spot.

Many of the stars decided to try out their new material in local clubs. These places soon blossomed into full-fledged showrooms, headlining the biggest names in the field. As in Las Vegas, many revues continue playing year after year. Freddy Fender brought his Tex-Mex style to Branson. Boxcar Willie opened a theater in which he performed his songs of the road. The Plummer Family brought gospel to the mix and Roy Clark lined up a changing array of guest stars in his Celebrity Theatre. By the early 1990s, more than sixteen showrooms lined Branson's strip and the place had been transformed into Missouri's greatest music attraction. It now has the most intensive concentration of country entertainment anywhere, including Nashville.

■ **LOCATION:** Branson is about 45 miles south of Springfield by way of U.S. 65. The showrooms are concentrated west of town on Missouri 76. ■ **HOURS:** Opening dates vary, but most places operate from April through October. ■ **ADMISSION:** Price range is usually $6–12. ■ **TELEPHONE:** Branson Lakes Area Chamber of Commerce has information on shows and opening dates at (417) 334-4136.

KANSAS CITY

ARTHUR BRYANT'S BARBECUE

For years, this was an unpretentious neighborhood restaurant, located a few blocks from Kansas City's former baseball stadium. Then native son Calvin Trillin blew its cover. In articles written for *The New Yorker* and other publications that attract sophisticated palates, Trilling described Arthur Bryant's as flat out "the best restaurant in the world."

Trilling presupposes that every red-blooded American loves barbecue, which is not a real stretch. Barbecue has a virtually unanimous culinary appeal. You can get into ugly regional arguments when discussing the merits of its various schools. North Carolina and Texas have been going at each other for years over the issue of which state does barbecue right. But Kansas City is acknowledged as the big city in which barbecue reaches its apogee, and Bryant's is at the very height.

The place is decorated in early formica, and jars of aging barbecue sauce are its primary ornaments. People order up their barbecue and take it over to picnic tables for consumption. As most great barbecue chefs allow, the secret is in the sauce. But Bryant's meticulous preparation, with the meat falling off the bone, marks the place as well.

The restaurant is now a Kansas City landmark, almost unchanged from the days when it was merely a neighborhood eatery. It has local rivals who claim that Trillin might just as easily have named half a dozen Kansas City pits as the world's best. But he didn't, and it may take the visitor many days of assiduous research to determine whether he was right.

■ **LOCATION:** Bryant's is just east of downtown Kansas City. Take The Paseo exit from Interstate 70 south to 18th Street and turn east to Brooklyn. The restaurant is on the corner at 1727 Brooklyn. ■ **HOURS:** Monday through Saturday, 10 A.M. to 11 P.M. ■ **TELEPHONE:** (816) 231-1123

COUNTRY CLUB PLAZA

Jesse Clyde Nichols announced plans for this development in 1922 and was immediately hooted down. No one had ever heard of the idea of building a major shopping area outside the central business district. Everything was up to date in Kansas City's downtown and hardly anyone thought that shoppers would bother to traipse several miles away in order to buy.

But Nichols was one of the first developers to understand and react to a gathering cultural and demographic force. He knew that significant money was moving out of the central cities and into the suburbs. Those customers wanted convenience close to home. He had pioneered an earlier residential development near Kansas City Country Club in 1908 and he saw the enthusiasm with

A planned town center: The J. C. Nichols Fountain splashes in Country Club Plaza. The copy of Seville's Giralda Tower is on the right. *(Courtesy of the Kansas City Area Development Council)*

which his wealthy clients rushed to the more open setting. So he reasoned that he would bring a new kind of downtown to them, too.

If Country Club Plaza actually were the prototype for future developments, America's suburbs would be far more interesting places than they are. This is not a mall. That concept was still thirty years in the future when the Plaza opened. This is, instead, a planned town center, mixing commercial and residential units on fifty-five acres, all unified by a central theme. In this case, the theme is Spanish architecture. A copy of the Giralda Tower, of Seville, is the centerpiece. Throughout the streets, fountains, which are also knock-offs of the Spanish originals, splash merrily over colorful tiles. Kansas City claims to have more fountains than any other city in the country, and the Plaza is certainly the reason for that. Many of the country's most prestigious retailers have outlets here and the Christmas season light show is regarded as one of the finest in the country.

■ **LOCATION:** Country Club Plaza is about 2 miles south of downtown Kansas City, by way of Main Street. The major cross street is 47th. The Country Club Plaza Merchants Associations publishes walking maps of the area. It is located at 4625 Wornall Road. ■ **HOURS:** Stores are generally open Monday through Saturday, 9–6, but hours vary seasonally.

HALLMaRK CENTER

Joyce Hall arrived in Kansas City in 1910, accompanied by two brothers and two shoe boxes filled with a persistent idea. Hall came from Nebraska, where he sold picture postcards. In Kansas City, he intended to expand into stationery. But among the items he had become familiar with in his line of work were greeting cards. They intrigued him. At that time, they were flowery, lacy contrivances, expensive to make and to buy. But Hall wondered what the demand would be for mass-marketed cards expressing sentiments that could apply to thousands of people. That was what he carried in the shoe boxes.

That idea has made Hallmark Cards one of the largest privately held companies in the world. It dominates the greeting card business, which it practically created, with 45 percent of the $5 billion market. It produces eleven million cards every working day, and has expanded into a chain of independently owned card shops. Its slogan, "When you care enough to send the very best" was coined by Hall himself in 1945 and has been more effective than any message carried in its cards. From the early days of television is has sponsored a series of shows, *The Hallmark Hall of Fame,* that consistently draw fair ratings, but sweep the annual award competitions and win acclaim for quality programming. It is part of the Hallmark image.

The company has remained true to its midwestern roots and also is a true barometer of popular culture. It has to be. Its employees describe themselves as being in "the emotion business." "What we say is 'I love you' 10,000 different ways," was how one of them described the work in a 1990 *Wall Street Journal* interview. Hallmark encourages its writers to stay in close touch with developments in popular culture, even paying for movie passes as the occasion warrants. The card messages are frequently drawn from changing tastes or new fads. But Hallmark can also reach back into its memory chest, as it did during the Persian Gulf War, when it brought back a series of cards that had been popular during World War II. It has developed more contemporary, hipper card lines. But messages that come across as too clever, or with too many layers of meaning, or overly cynical, are discarded.

One of its proudest local achievements is the development of Crown Center. An urban redevelopment project that took a decade and half a billion dollars to complete, it underscored the company's commitment to its home base. It has also become one of the prime shopping and entertainment centers in the city, and a model for privately financed urban projects. Part of Crown Center is the Hallmark Visitors Center. The exhibits here relate the history of the company and greeting cards, show how they are made and even feature a make-your-own-bow machine.

■ **LOCATION:** The Center is at Pershing and 25th streets, in Crown Center. ■ **HOURS:** Monday through Saturday, 10–5; Sunday, 12–4. ■ **ADMISSION:** Free ■ **TELEPHONE:** (816) 274-5672

The Gateway to the West. *(AP/Wide World Photos)*

ST. LOUIS

THE GATEWAY ARCH

It has been called a "giant wishbone" and "the world's largest McDonald's stand." One Congressman vowed that it would be financed "over my dead bones" and another called it a "monument to fraud, graft, corruption and waste." Nonetheless, there it stands, 630 feet high, one of the twentieth century's most readily identifiable structures and the signature of St. Louis. Taller than the Washington Monument or the Statue of Liberty, the arch symbolizes the gateway to the promise of the American West.

The proposal for a park to commemorate the Louisiana Purchase of 1803 was first approved by Congress in 1933 and signed by President Roosevelt the following year. But enormous Republican opposition to the project stalled it. The proposal was seen as just another New Deal boondoggle. St. Louis kept at it, though. The city cleared away its riverfront, a tangled thicket of old warehouses and railroad tracks that blocked the water. The project grew into a pioneering urban renewal program, with St. Louis reclaiming a big chunk of its past and opening it to new downtown development. Finally, in 1946, the arch design was approved, drawn up by Michigan architect Eero Saarinen. He described it as an inverted, weighted, catenary curve and worked out the initial design with pipe cleaners. (Catenary, incidentally, means the shape assumed by a chain hanging freely between two points.)

Actual construction had to wait another seventeen years, until federal funding for the project finally came through. At last, in 1967, the first passenger boarded the little train that runs up the arch's interior. By that time, Saarinen had been dead for six years, but his widow attended the opening ceremony and declared it "overwhelming. Of all the things Eero did, this is the most exciting."

Millions of visitors since then, and those who have merely driven across the Mississippi into St. Louis and have seen the arch outlined against the sky, would agree. The arch is now surrounded by a ninety-one-acre park. The Museum of the Western Expansion with exhibits detailing the history of the Purchase and the American frontier, is located beneath it.

■ **LOCATION:** At the foot of Market Street. ■ **HOURS:** Daily, 9:30–5:30; in summer months, 8:30 A.M.–9:30 P.M. ■ **ADMISSION:** Admission to the base of the arch is free. Tram rides to the top are $2.50. During peak times it is sometimes necessary to buy tickets for later in the day. ■ **TELEPHONE:** (314) 425-4465

NATIONAL BOWLING HALL OF FAME

Bowling did not enter the United States with the most savory of reputations. Several state legislatures even banned the sport of nine-pins, which was imported from Germany in the 1840s, as a severe moral threat. The casual European attitudes toward alcohol consumption, especially on Sunday, deeply offended the Protestant clergy of the Northeast and South. They equated the sport with the beer-garden setting in which it was played.

Bowlers got around the ban, however, by simply adding a tenth pin, which created a uniquely American form of the sport. More than three hundred forms of bowling have been traced back to France, and since St. Louis is a city heavily influenced by French and German traditions, the sport was always popular here. The Women's International Bowling Congress was founded in the city in 1917 and Budweiser, which is based locally, has been a sponsor of some of the most formidable teams in the sport's history. So when cities were invited to bid for the Bowling Hall of Fame in 1978, St. Louis came up with a free piece of land downtown and was awarded the facility.

There are historical displays here, the most popular being an old fashioned alley with hand-set pins. There are also exhibits of vintage equipment, memorabilia of some of the sport's greatest figures, and a video show in which top bowlers offer tips to the viewer.

■ **LOCATION:** The museum is located directly across from Busch Stadium, at 111 Stadium Plaza. ■ **HOURS:** Daily, 9–7, Memorial Day to Labor Day. Monday through Saturday, 9–5; Sunday, 12–5, rest of the year. ■ **ADMISSION:** $4.50 ■ **TELEPHONE:** (314) 231-6340

SEDALIA

RAGTImE ARCHIVES

It is hard to imagine the impact with which ragtime hit American music at the opening of the twentieth Century. Subsequent years have produced their successive outrages toward jazz, swing, rock, and rap: Each in its turn was decried as the end of civilization as we know it. By the end of the century, much popular music was deliberately intended to shock. To ears that have known rap, after all, ragtime seems like pretty sedate stuff. But when it came rippling out of the South and Midwest in the 1890s, with its ragged meter that carried an irresistible invitation to dance, it seemed as if American youth was being corrupted beyond recall. It is so evocative of the century's early years, that when E. L. Doctorow sought a motif for his best-selling novel about that historical period he called it *Ragtime.*

It was also the first African-American music to permeate the popular culture, which may have had something to do with all the outrage. The lyrics to Meredith Willson's patter song "Trouble" from *The Music Man* was written many years later. But when that song told parents that ragtime music was "shameless" and that it would wrap their sons and daughters "in the arms of a jungle, animal instinct," Willson was right on target. Contemporary racist attitudes fueled much of the dislike of rag.

The master of the form was Scott Joplin, a Black musician who learned the music while playing the bars of the tough railroad town of Sedalia. His most famous composition, "The Maple Leaf Rag," was composed here in 1897 is a tribute to the saloon in which he performed. It became the biggest selling sheet music composition in history. Joplin later moved to St. Louis and spent the rest of his life trying to prove to an indifferent country that he was also an accomplished classical composer.

The Ragtime Archives were founded as a tribute to Joplin and the Missouri roots of the music. The Archives, which contain old sheet music and memorabilia of some of ragtime's top practitioners, is on the campus of State Fair Community College.

■ **LOCATION:** Sedalia is about halfway between Kansas City and Jefferson City on U.S. 50. From Interstate 70, take the southbound U.S. 65 exit. The college is located on Clarendon Road. ■ **HOURS:** Monday through Friday, 9–5. ■ **ADMISSION:** Free ■ **TELEPHONE:** (816) 826-7100

NebraskA

ALLIANCE

CARHEnGE

Americans seem to have always held the conviction that anything Europeans could do, we could do better. Many U.S. cities pride themselves on their reproductions of famed European landmarks, from the elaborate to the cheesy. There is a strong impulse in our popular culture to improve upon the Old World's handiwork. That is one possible explanation for Carhenge.

Another explanation is that James Reinders simply liked to bury old cars in the ground. The Alliance resident planted twenty-six of them, back end first, in a grouping reminiscent of Stonehenge, the Neolithic monument on England's Salisbury Plain. Seven more vehicles are fastened cross-wise, to simulate the arches in the original. The surrounding treeless plain of western Nebraska even resemble the English moors. Well, kind of.

Scholars feel that Stonehenge was used as a solar observatory for religious rituals. Many people in Alliance feel that Carhenge has no use whatsoever except as a nuisance. Nevertheless, in 1989 the city council defeated an effort to have it dismantled, and granted it a zoning variance as a tourist attraction.

■ **LOCATION:** Carhenge is located north of town, on U.S. 385. ■ **HOURS:** Daily, dawn to dusk. ■ **ADMISSION:** Free ■ **TELEPHONE:** (308) 762-1520

LINCOLN

ROLLEr SKATING MUsEUM

In 1979, a man named Theodore J. Coombs started off from Los Angeles and roller skated all the way to New York. Then he turned around and skated back to Yates Center, Kansas, for a grand total of 5,193 miles. No one ever traveled that far, before or since, on roller skates.

They have traveled faster: Luca Antoniel of Italy managed to propel himself on roller skates at 26.85 miles an hour in 1987. They have traveled more violently: Anyone who has ever watched a roller derby can attest to that. They

Jim Reinders configured cars to the dimensions and specifications of England's Stonehenge—including the Heel Stone (upper right corner). *(Worley Studio)*

have traveled more extravagantly: An entire musical performed on roller skates, *Starlight Express,* was a hit in London and New York in the 1980s. They have traveled hipper: A walk along Venice Beach (*see* California) will verify that. Roller skates are, in fact, the fad that never went away.

When the first public roller skating rink opened in Newport, Rhode Island, in 1866, roller skating was regarded as a temporary craze. Only three years before, James L. Plimpton had patented the four-wheel skate that has remained the most familiar model. Plimpton fared much better than the Belgian, Joseph Merlin, who is credited with being the originator of the wheeled skate. According to the *Guinness Book of Sports Records,* Merlin was demonstrating the contrivance at a London party in 1760 when he was unable to stop and crashed into a large mirror, incurring nearly fatal injuries.

Plimpton's safer model was an immediate hit (it allowed forward motion to be stopped more easily than its predecessor). Rinks were built all over the United States, providing a safe and decorous mode of public entertainment. Even in the West, a skating rink was regarded as a sign of growth and sophistication in frontier communities. It was especially popular in Nebraska, and Lincoln has been the headquarters of the International Roller Skating Federation since its organization in 1924. So, it is a natural location for the museum. There are historic exhibits, tracing the development of the skate through photographs, videotapes, and artifacts.

■ **LOCATION:** The museum is at 4730 South Street, in the southeastern part of the city. ■ **HOURS:** Monday though Friday, 9–5. ■ **ADMISSION:** Free ■ **TELEPHONE:** (402) 483-7551

BOYS TOWN

"There is no such thing as a bad boy." That's what Father Edward J. Flanagan said when he opened Boys Town in 1917 and he went on to preach it for the rest of his life. "The nation could arouse itself to its duty to its children," he insisted as World War II was winding down. "We could provide the spiritual vitamins that would infuse a clearer understanding of child problems in the general public. When this war is over, there will be other Hitlers unless we make sure that the new world is built on faith."

The words sound prophetic in a country that has since been racked by ever-worsening teenage violence, and seems to have no clear idea of how to cope with it. Father Flanagan believed in giving young children responsibility and encouragement, duties and education. "We work and pray and pray and work," he said, describing the routine at Boys Town. "Many of our boys came to us after taking a life. Not one of them ever caused trouble."

Flanagan came to Nebraska in 1912 from his native Ireland and was appointed to a mission in O'Neill. But after several years, he grew tired of ministering to defeated men and decided that the only way to deal with the problems of alcoholism and crime was through children. Transferred to Omaha, he began raising funds for a facility that would be a haven, a school, and an opportunity for incorrigible boys.

The movie based on his work, *Boys Town,* earned an Oscar for Spencer Tracy (who donated the award to Father Flanagan) and won the place national fame. "It brought some problems, too," the priest admitted later, "because many local people assumed we had been paid a fortune for it and donations fell off. Actually, we were given only $5,000. But the tide turned so greatly because of that film that we always considered it a blessing." A sequel, *Men of Boys Town,* was almost as successful.

Although elevated to the rank of Monsignor, he always insisted on being called Father Flanagan. After the war, he was sent to evaluate the problems of youth in the defeated nations. In 1948, while on one of these trips to Germany, he died. Visitors to Boys Town can visit historical displays relating to the school and to Father Flanagan, as well as a shrine dedicated to the priest.

■ **LOCATION:** Boys Town is about 15 miles west of Omaha, at the U.S. 6 exit of Interstate 680. ■ **HOURS:** Daily, 8–4:30. ■ **ADMISSION:** Free ■ **TELEPHONE:** (402) 498-1140

North Dakota

FARGO

ROGER MARIS BASEBALL MUSEUM

For the first four seasons of his big league baseball career, Roger Maris flashed some indications of power. He played briefly for Cleveland and Kansas City, and in three years he totalled fifty-eight home runs. Then he was traded to the Yankees in 1960, hit thirty-nine more homers and was voted the league's Most Valuable Player. But in 1961, the twenty-six-year-old Maris suddenly went off in pursuit of a ghost, and that one season changed his life.

This was the year in which the American League first expanded from eight teams to ten, weakening the pitching on every team. It became apparent in the early part of the year that hitters were going to rack up some extraordinary figures—especially on the mighty Yankees. Mickey Mantle, who already was regarded as the top slugger in the game, was on a tremendous pace. And right behind him was Maris.

By late summer, both hitters were threatening the home run record of sixty in a season, set by Babe Ruth in 1927. Mantle began to falter in the hot weather, but Maris kept right on plugging away. By September it became apparent that he was poised for a run at Ruth. It seemed the entire national media machine was focusing on him. The Yankees had ended the pennant race early that month and the only story anyone cared about was Maris's run.

Always a shy, soft-spoken man, Maris wilted under the spotlight. Every step he took he was surrounded by an army of reporters and television cameras. He couldn't eat. His hair began falling out. He became the target of resentment. How dare anyone of such ordinary talents challenge the mighty Babe! With expansion, eight games had been added to the baseball schedule. The Commissioners office decreed that unless Maris matched Ruth's total in the old 154-game season, an asterisk would be attached to his record in the books. Maris got to sixty within the allotted period, but then hung on that number as the season wound down. Finally, on the last day of the season, he caught a Tracy Stallard fast ball and put it into the right-field seats at Yankee Stadium for number sixty-one.

The record had fallen, asterisk or no. But Maris was haunted by it for the rest of his career. Dogged by injuries, he never again came close to being that kind of dominant hitter again. Always the target of media attention and fan expectations, he seemed to shrink into himself. Finally, in 1967, he was traded to St. Louis and in his last two seasons helped the Cardinals win two pennants. "Baseball is fun again," he told reporters, who marveled at how friendly and affable he was.

A native of Fargo, Maris went on to business success after his retirement from baseball. He died in 1985. A collection of personal belongings and baseball memorabilia is displayed here in a special memorial to a hitter who never carried an asterisk beside his name in this state.

■ **LOCATION:** The Roger Maris Museum is located at the south end of West Acres Shopping Center, at the 13th Avenue South exit of Interstate 29. ■ **HOURS:** Monday through Saturday, 10–9; Sunday, 12–5. ■ **ADMISSION:** Free ■ **TELEPHONE:** (701) 282-2222

OkLahomA

CLAREMORE

LYNN rIGGS MEMORIaL

When Oklahoman Lynn Riggs drew from his state's rich history for a play, the results were not encouraging. The Theater Guild produced the show *Green Grow the Lilacs* on Broadway by in 1931. It ran sixty-one performances to indifferent critical response and closed without making much of a ripple.

One who was charmed by the play was Theresa Helbrun, a director of the Guild. She felt it contained the perfect elements for a musical. In 1942 she was especially anxious to revive it: The Guild was almost broke and she thought a successful musical could put it back on firm financial footing. She called composer Richard Rodgers to see if he was interested.

Rodgers was just ending his long association with Lorenz Hart and told Helbrun that if she could get Oscar Hammerstein II to join the project as the lyricist, he would sign on. Hammerstein, who had written the lyrics for *Show Boat,* was familiar with Riggs's play and shared the belief that it could be a great musical. But it would be a new kind of musical: Both he and Rodgers agreed that it had to be faithful to the spirit of Riggs's text, there would be no chorus girls, no gags, no stars.

When backers heard the plan they didn't give it a chance, especially when they were told the musical would also feature a ballet. But The Guild doggedly held fund-raising parties and managed to come up with the $83,000 necessary to mount the production, which was called *Away We Go.* After several weeks of road previews, it was decided to elevate a minor dance number into a dramatic choral treatment and make that song's title the name of the show. So the show debuted on Broadway in 1943 as *Oklahoma!*

The production transformed the musical play, ushering in its richest and most productive age. Its 1946 premiere in this state was declared a legal holiday. To assess Riggs's contribution to the final form of *Oklahoma!* it is only necessary to read his original introduction. "It is a radiant summer morning several years ago, the kind of morning which the enveloping shapes of the earth—men, cattle in the meadow, blades of the young corn, streams—makes them seem to exist now for the first time, their images giving off a visible golden emanation that is partly true and partly a trick of imagination, focusing to keep alive a loveliness that may pass away."

Hammerstein read those stage directions and found the inspiration for the show's opening song, "Oh, What a Beautiful Mornin'." The memorial at Rogers State College preserves many of Riggs's personal items, including manuscripts, photographs, and the original Surrey with the Fringe on Top.

■ **LOCATION:** The memorial is located inside the college's Thunderbird Library. ■ **HOURS:** Daily, 10–4; Sunday, 12–4. ■ **ADMISSION:** Free ■ **TELEPHONE:** (918) 341-7510

WILL ROGERS MEMORIAL

In many minds, he was the perfect successor to Mark Twain—the homespun philosopher, reeling off profound and wise observations from behind a rustic facade. Will Rogers was, in fact, an admirer of Twain. While on a trip to a Nevada town Twain had written about, Rogers went to the hotel and asked which bedroom his idol had used. "They told me that when he was there he couldn't afford a bed," he said afterward. "So maybe things are gettin' better in the humor game."

Rogers said he never met a man he didn't like. He also noted that all he knew was what he read in the newspapers, and when someone asked if he ever read fiction, he repeated: "I just told you, I read the newspapers." He had Indian blood and proudly stated that his ancestors didn't come over on the *Mayflower* but were there to meet the ship. He described the Depression by saying that America had the "distinction of being the only nation to go to the poorhouse in an automobile." He added: "I am a member of no organized political party; I am a Democrat."

For thirty years he kept America laughing. First with his rope-twirling, wisecracking performances in the *Ziegfeld Follies.* Then with his daily newspaper column. Later it was with his movies, which were the top money-makers in history until Shirley Temple came along. A steadfast family man, a philanthropist, an old cowboy who never took himself too seriously, Rogers was the model of how Americans liked to think of themselves. His topical humor was an innovation that has been copied by other comics. He also was one of the great improvisers, never memorizing dialogue in his movies or plays but simply getting a sense of the plot and making up lines as he went along. It worked for him.

Rogers was an enthusiastic advocate of aviation, talking up its possibilities at every opportunity. On a promotional trip, flying across the North Pole to the Soviet Union, he and pilot Wiley Post were killed in 1935. America mourned for weeks, and even fifty-five years later, his personality was strong enough to provide the core of the Tony-award winning Broadway musical, *The Will Rogers Follies.*

Rogers was born in the town of Oolagah, when Oklahoma was still called the Indian Territory. Later he had residences in Beverly Hills and New York, but he always called Claremore his home. The land on which the memorial to him is situated was his property. Personal memorabilia, including his saddles, ropes, and blankets, fill the galleries here. There are also dioramas portraying episodes in his show business career. Sculptress Jo Davidson's famed statue of Rogers in a cowboy pose stands in the foyer.

■ **LOCATION:** Just west of the town center, by way of Will Rogers Boulevard (Oklahoma 88). ■ **HOURS:** Daily, 8–5. ■ **ADMISSION:** Free ■ **TELEPHONE:** (918) 341-0719

OKLAHOMA CITY

NATIONAL COWBOY HALL OF FAME AND MUSEUM

To much of the world, the cowboy is the figure that symbolizes America—the man of the frontier, unattached to tradition or authority, carrying the law in a side holster, always ready for action. It is the most powerful image this country ever exported, and it surfaces throughout our history: Theodore Roosevelt was called "that damned cowboy" by members of his own party, and eighty years later nervous Europeans referred to Ronald Reagan by the same term. Now "cowboy" is used to refer to renegade artists, to those who refuse to conform to a pin-stripe world, and to anyone who takes chances.

The real era of the cowboy was very short. The great cattle drives lasted about two decades, from a few years after the Civil War to the mid-1880s, when technology and a run of harsh weather put an end to them. Real cowboys have lingered on for another century, performing their rather unglamorous jobs on the vast cattle ranches of the West. Even more profoundly, they live on in the popular culture. Beginning with the very first feature length movie, *The Great Train Robbery,* images of the men of the West have pervaded American entertainment—its films, novels, and music. Every great movie star has played a cowboy at least once in his career. John Wayne played a cowboy so well that he came to be regarded as the real thing, an authentic embodiment of the West.

You'll find all of them in this museum. There are those who lived the historical realities of cowboy life and those who only depicted those realities—all the great stars, from Tom Mix (*see* Florence, Arizona, and Driftwood, Pennsylvania) to Roy Rogers (*see* Victorville, California) to Wayne himself (*see* Winterset, Iowa). They're all assembled in this onetime frontier town in the Indian Territory, many of them represented by displays of their own western collections.

Perhaps, the most moving segment of the museum is the famed sculpture, *End of the Trail.* The eighteen-foot high work by James Earle Fraser, depicting an exhausted Indian slumping on his pony, is shown off in its own hall. Art work by Frederic Remington and Charles M. Russell is also displayed.

Will Rogers: He never met a man he didn't like. *(Courtesy of Will Rogers Memorial)*

■ **LOCATION:** Just off Interstate 35, at 1700 Northeast 63rd Street. ■ **HOURS:** Daily, 8:30–6. ■ **ADMISSION:** $5.50 ■ **TELEPHONE:** (405) 478-2250

PAWNEE

PAWNEe BILL MUSEUm

He was an authentic survivor of the Old West—a buffalo hunter and trapper, a leader of the "Boomers" who came pouring over the state line from Kansas in 1889 and forced Congress to open the Indian Territory to white settlement. Gordon W. Lillie found his greatest fame as a showman, as the rival and later the partner of Buffalo Bill Cody. Lillie joined Cody in 1883, bringing with him a band of Pawnee from the Indian agency where he was working at the time, which earned him the nickname he carried for the rest of his career—Pawnee Bill.

After two years, he broke away from Buffalo Bill's operation and formed his own wild West show. Unfortunately, he wasn't very good at the financial end of it and the show went broke in Maryland. The Boomers, who were then in the final stages of winning approval for their land rush, remembered the young Lillie from a previous affiliation. They took up a subscription to get him back home, where he assumed their leadership. When they burst into Oklahoma, Lillie was at the head.

But Lillie was too fond of show business to become a homesteader. His second entree was far more successful than the first and eventually he united his own show with Buffalo Bill's. It was this partnership that formed the backdrop to the famous musical *Annie, Get Your Gun* (*see* Greenville, Ohio). The entire cast of both shows came together to sing the musical's climax, "There's No Business Like Show Business." It was a sentiment the real Pawnee Bill would have heartily endorsed.

For years, the two men toured the world with their extravaganza, taking the lore and color of the Old West to its first mass audience. The show finally folded in 1919, under the competition of western movies, and Lillie returned here to his ranch. He went on making personal appearances, dressed up in his performer cowboy outfits, until his death in 1942. The ranch still has its original furnishings along with displays of Lillie's long career in politics and show business.

■ **LOCATION:** Pawnee is about 60 miles west of Tulsa, by way of U.S. 64, part of a transcontinental road that Pawnee Bill lobbied for and which was called The Pawnee Trail. The ranch is just west of town, at Blue Hawk Peak. ■ **HOURS:** Tuesday through Saturday, 9–5; Sunday, 1–5, May through October. Closed Monday and Tuesday, rest of the year. ■ **ADMISSION:** Free ■ **TELEPHONE:** (918) 762-2513

South Dakota

CRAZY HORSE MEMORIAL

Korczak Ziolkowski learned about carving mountains at the right hand of the master, Gutzon Borglum (*see* Keystone, South Dakota, further on). He was one of the top assistants on the Mount Rushmore project. In 1940, as work on Rushmore was winding down, Ziolkowski was paid a visit by a Oglala Sioux chief, Henry Standing Bear. He was a nephew of Crazy Horse and asked if the sculptor would undertake the project of carving a likeness of the great warrior in another part of the Black Hills "so the white man will know we had heroes, too."

Work began on the project in 1948. It was still going in 1982, at Ziolkowski's death. As of this writing, it is still being carried on under the supervision of the sculptor's sons. The endless project has become one of the state's greatest attractions, with one million visitors a year showing up to watch the work. The U.S. Post Office even issued a commemorative stamp bearing the likeness of Crazy Horse that will be seen on the memorial, if it is ever completed.

The proposed sculpture will dwarf Mount Rushmore. All four presidents would fit within the chief's head. It will be 563 feet high and 641 feet long, and depict a mounted Crazy Horse with arm extended across the surrounding land. Its title is: "Where My Dead Lie Buried."

Crazy Horse himself was one of the top strategists in the 1876 campaign that resulted in the annihilation of General George Custer's command at Little Big Horn. The following year, while he was a prisoner at Fort Robinson, Nebraska, Crazy Horse was killed, probably murdered by federal troops.

There is a museum of Lakota history and culture at the sculpture site, as well as an audiovisual display on how the project is being carried out.

■ **LOCATION:** The Crazy Horse site is just north of Custer, on U.S. 16, 385. ■ **HOURS:** Daily, dawn to dusk. ■ **ADMISSION:** $7.50 a car. ■ **TELEPHONE:** (605) 673-4681

DESMET

INGALLS HOME

The Laura Ingalls Wilder's *Little House on the Prairie* books were set in several locales around the upper Midwest, following the Ingalls family's movement across the region. For the sake of economy, the popular television series concentrated its action in Walnut Grove, Minnesota, (*see* Minnesota). There is more of the family remaining in DeSmet, though.

The Ingalls family moved to DeSmet in 1877; their first home here is called the Surveyor's House, her father, Charles, having worked in that job for the railroad. The homestead has been refurbished as it would have appeared during the time of their residence and is still surrounded by the cottonwood trees the family planted. Ten years after arriving, Mr. Ingalls built another, substantial home, which still stands.

It was in DeSmet that the writer met her husband, Alonzo Wilder. It was also here that Laura Ingalls Wilder's daughter, Rose Wilder Lane, who would become her editor and collaborator on the books, was born in 1887. The town has preserved other sites associated with the family, including the church and school the author attended.

These Happy Golden Years, a pageant based on the books, is presented during three weeks in late June and early July every year.

■ **LOCATION:** DeSmet is located about 40 miles west of Interstate 29, from the U.S. 14 exit at Brookings. ■ **HOURS:** The Surveyor's House and Ingalls Home are open daily, 9–5, June–mid-September. By appointment, rest of the year. Tours of the local Laura Ingalls Wilder sites leave from the gift shop near the home during the hours it is open. ■ **ADMISSION:** $3 ■ **TELEPHONE:** (605) 854-3383

HURON

CHERYL LADD ROOM

Here's the scenario. Girl is working as waitress in hometown restaurant in South Dakota. Customers tell her she's so pretty she should try Hollywood, which, coincidentally, was her own secret dream. So Cheryl Stoppelmoor headed for the West Coast in 1970.

She landed a job as a singing voice in a TV cartoon series, *Josie and the Pussycats.* There were commercials, bit parts in movies. After seven long years, she was up for a major role in a new television series, *Family,* but lost out in the final cut. She considered giving up and devoting herself to her young family.

Then, one of Hollywood's hot stars, Farrah Fawcett-Majors, walked out of her role on the hit series, *Charlie's Angels,* in a contract dispute. Producers frantically sought a replacement, a presence big enough to step right in and keep the momentum going. Cheryl Stopplemoor, meanwhile, had married well—her husband, David Ladd, was a top executive with 20th Century Fox. She refused to take a screen test, which served to make her distinctive to the *Charlie's Angels'* producers. Cheryl Ladd got the role and she became a star.

Huron didn't forget. The Barn, the place where she once served daily specials and dreamed big dreams, assembled some of her belongings and set aside a Cheryl Ladd Room to honor the hometown girl who went out and did it. Only in America.

■ **LOCATION:** The Barn is located just outside of town on Route 5. ■ **HOURS:** Daily, 8 A.M.–9 P.M. ■ **TELEPHONE:** (605) 352-9238

KEYSTONE

MT. RUSHMORE NATIONAL MEMORIAL/RUSHMORE-BORGLUM STORY

"There is something in sheer volume," said sculptor Gutzon Borglum, "that awakes and terrifies, lifts us out of ourselves. Something that relates us to God and to what is greatest in our evolving universe." No other artist in modern times worked with the mass and volume Borglum assayed. In the thirteen years he spent working on Mount Rushmore, more than four hundred thousand tons of rock were stripped away by a crew of fifty drillers, blasters, and chiselers working under him. The heads of four United States Presidents—George Washington, Theodore Roosevelt, Thomas Jefferson, and Abraham Lincoln—are carved sixty feet high into the mountainside.

Borglum himself didn't live to see the work completed. He died early in 1941. His son, Lincoln, was able to clean up the rough stone around the faces and hands until funds ran out later that year. It was then officially declared completed, although plans for a Hall of Records behind the carvings were never carried out.

Borglum was already famous for his large-scale sculptures when he accepted this job in 1926. He had recently resigned from the Stone Mountain project (*see* Atlanta, Georgia) in a dispute with the planners and smashed all his models for the work. But even after this unhappy experience, the South Dakota project captured his imagination. Funds raised in the state by public subscription were exhausted by the end of the first year of work, but President Calvin Coolidge, a champion of the project, secured federal money for it to be completed.

From then on, it was Borglum against the elements and everybody else. He angrily waved off those who complained that the work was taking too long. "I

Sculptor Borglum's masterpiece: It took thirteen years to complete. *(Courtesy of the Rapid City Convention and Visitors Bureau)*

have no intention of leaving a head on that mountain that in the course of 500 or 5,000 years will be without a nose," he said. When federal officials complained that he was "temperamental," he told them that this was "not a road contractor's job," and suggested they were simply trying to hide their own ignorance of engineering. He fretted for years over whether or not Lincoln should be shown with a beard. Borglum preferred clean-shaven, and would have sculpted him that way, but he knew the public expected the beard and he finally acquiesced. When a fissure developed across Jefferson's face, Borglum had to realign the entire sculpture.

From the moment of its completion, Mount Rushmore became one of the country's most popular symbols, depicted in everything from commercials to movies. The most memorable showing was in Alfred Hitchcock's thriller, *North by Northwest,* in which Cary Grant eludes murderous spies by scrambling across (a replica of) the huge presidential faces.

The Rushmore-Borglum Story, in the nearby town of Keystone, enables visitors to see original models and how the project was planned. Newsreel footage shows the actual construction and samples of Borglum's other works are also displayed.

■ **LOCATION:** Keystone and Mount Rushmore are about 20 miles south of Rapid City, on U.S. 16. The Borglum Studio is on Main Street (U.S. 16 Alt).

■ **HOURS:** The Memorial visitor center is open daily, 8 A.M.–10 P.M., mid-May to mid-September; daily, 8–5, rest of the year. The Rushmore-Borglum Story is open daily, 8–8, mid-June to Labor Day; daily, 9–5, from mid-April to mid-June and Labor Day to mid-October. ■ **ADMISSION:** Mount Rushmore, free; Rushmore-Borglum, $5. ■ **TELEPHONE:** Mount Rushmore, (605) 574-2523; Rushmore-Borglum (605) 666-4449.

STURGIS

NATIONAL MOTORCYCLE MUSEUM

The Jackpine Gypsies were a restless bunch. It was late in the Depression and this local motorcycle club, most of whom owned Indian bikes, decided it would be fun to sponsor a rally at which they could show off their cycles and run some competitive events. So under the leadership of J. C. "Pappy" Hoel, they held the first Sturgis Motorcycle Rally in 1938.

It has grown into the biggest summertime biker event in the country. In some years, crowds of four hundred thousand have jammed into this town, whose year-round population is five thousand. It is predominantly a family affair, with few of the problems the public usually associates with bikers descending on an isolated small town. It isn't Marlon Brando's *Wild One* revisited.

After fifty rallies, Hoel began making plans for a museum and hall of fame for his favorite sport. His intentions were to make it both a celebration and a further counter-balance to the event's negative reputation. The museum opened in 1990, one year after Hoel's death. It displays antique motorcycles, some of them rare machines, and commemorates the top competitive racers in the sport.

■ **LOCATION:** Sturgis is located off Interstate 90, about 30 miles north of Rapid City. The museum is at 2438 Junction Avenue. ■ **HOURS:** Monday through Friday, 9–5; Saturday, 10–4, Memorial Day to Labor Day. Weekdays only, rest of the year. ■ **ADMISSION:** $2 ■ **TELEPHONE:** (605) 347-4875

WALL

WALL DRUG STORE

The whole thing began with ice water. Dorothy Hustead and her husband Ted owned a gas station/drugstore in Wall, a town that got its name because it sits beside rock ramparts at the edge of the Badlands. Parched travelers would emerge from the Badlands, looking for the first place that served something

The ice water is still free at Wall Drug. *(Courtesy of Wall Drug Store)*

cold. (This was in 1931, before cars were air conditioned.) Dorothy's gimmick was free ice water. Once their thirst was satisfied, they would probably step inside and buy a meal or a souvenir. Or a bottle of aspirin. Or, at least, a cup of coffee for a nickel.

Soon Wall became something of a landmark. After driving across miles and miles of miles and miles, here was this Dakota oasis, selling every conceivable sort of western gear and postcard and corny souvenir. The Husteads began putting up signs all along U.S. 16, the main highway from the east, and even more travelers showed up. It became kind of a national gag. "Only 500 more miles to Wall Drug." During World War II, Wall Drug milepost signs were spotted in North Africa, Guam, and Australia, all approximately correct in terms of distance. They covered almost as much territory in that era as the ubiquitous Kilroy.

Wall Drug is still a family enterprise, although it is now Interstate 90 that brings travelers to the store. It extends over the length of an entire block, and it has room for 520 diners, who feast on buffalo burgers and homemade ice cream. There is animated entertainment and a clothing store stocking a complete line of western togs. The ice water is still free and coffee still costs a nickel.

■ **LOCATION:** Wall is due north of the western entrance to Badlands National Park, about 55 miles east of Rapid City. ■ **HOURS:** Daily, 6 A.M.–10 P.M., Memorial Day to Labor Day. Hours vary rest of the year. ■ **ADMISSION:** Free ■ **TELEPHONE:** (605) 279-2175

Texas

BEAUMONT

BABE DIDRIKSON ZAHARIAS MEMORIAL

She was called a real-life Wonder Woman, a feminine counterpart of the fictional Frank Merriwell. One eulogist said that she held a place with Annie Oakley in American folklore. Even her nickname was the same as the country's greatest athletic hero, Babe Ruth. Her records have fallen as a new generation of women athletes, benefitting from better training techniques, have run faster and jumped higher. But no woman ever had a greater impact on American sports than Mildred "Babe" Didrikson.

She came out of Beaumont in the early 1930s as a high school athlete, winning more events and setting more records than any woman in the history of Texas. She went on to Los Angeles in 1932 and won two gold medals at the Olympics, for the javelin and eighty-meter hurdles, setting records in both. In 1935 she switched to golf and in the next eighteen years she won eighty-two championships, totally dominating the field. "I guess I was the first woman to play golf like the men play it," Didrikson said. She could drive the ball three hundred yards off the tee with a long game that most male athletes envied. When the singer Hildegarde asked why she couldn't hit a ball that far, Didrikson replied: "You've got to loosen your girdle, honey, and give it everything you've got."

Her skills didn't end there. She once hit nine home runs and drove in twenty-two runs in a softball doubleheader. She scored 106 points in a basketball game. She pitched for the St. Louis Cardinals in an exhibition game and spent one summer playing with the House of David semipro baseball team. She played championship level billiards, won occasional sets from nationally ranked tennis players, and had a bowling average of 190. *Time* magazine once described her as "a woman whose life is like a constant campaign to astound people." In 1950 when the Associated Press voted for the outstanding female athlete of the first half century, no one else was even close.

She took up golf on a whim, seeing a set of new clubs in a Dallas sporting goods store and wondering how they'd play. After five rounds, she was consistently breaking ninety and when she went into serious training and entered her first tournament she shot a round of seventy-seven. Olympic officials restricted her to just three events in the 1932 Games because at the women's trials she so dominated the rest of the field that it was regarded as unfair to allow her to enter more. In 1938 she married professional wrestler George Zaharias, whom she met at a golf tournament, and they remained together for the rest of her life.

She was operated on for cancer in 1953 while she was still at the top of women's golf. Six months later, she went out and won another tournament. "I guess I'll have to call that the biggest thrill of my life because I didn't think that I'd ever win another one," she said. The struggle was more than even she could overcome and she died in 1956 at the age of 43.

The memorial and museum in her old hometown displays awards won by the Babe as well as personal memorabilia belonging both to her and Zaharias.

■ **LOCATION:** Off Interstate 10, at the Martin Luther King/Magnolia exit; 1750 Interstate 10 East. ■ **HOURS:** Daily, 9–5. ■ **ADMISSION:** Free ■ **TELEPHONE:** (409) 833-4622

SPINDLETOP BOOMTOWN

When the twentieth century began, the U.S. petroleum industry consisted of Standard Oil, a monopoly run with ruthless efficiency by John D. Rockefeller. Most of the country's known reserves were in the East, capacity was low, and Rockefeller limited production to keep prices high. No one had any idea of the wealth sitting beneath the soil of Texas—wealth that would soon transform the economy of the state and turn the Texas oil tycoon into a nationally recognized stereotype.

Only one man believed that he could find oil there and that was a Beaumont character named Pattillo Higgins. A lumberman and Sunday school teacher, Higgins taught himself some geology. He became convinced that a hillock south of town, Spindletop, contained oil. He spent ten years and $30,000, every penny he could get his hands on, to find it, while Beaumont residents jeeringly offered to drink all the oil he could come up with. He was joined by a mining engineer, Anthony Lucas, who agreed with Higgins's assessment. Lucas got in so deep that he sold his furniture to keep the operation going. Finally, they brought in Mellon money from Pittsburgh to secure financing. On January 10, 1901, Spindletop came in, a gusher spouting out of a 1,100-foot- deep hole in the side of the hill. By the end of the next year, 138 wells had been brought in with a combined production greater than the rest of the world. Texaco and Gulf formed to compete with Standard and the American economy was changed forever.

Oil has since been discovered in 195 Texas counties and as late as 1960 the state produced thirty-eight percent of the country's output. "The oil money was so big that it made cattle money look like a tip," said one Texas humorist. A boomtown grew up around Spindletop and a certain cachet developed in the oil industry about tracing your family's fortune back there. "It was like coming over on the Mayflower," said John Bainbridge, in his book *The Super-Americans.*

Happy Shahan in front of the replica he built of the Texas shrine for the John Wayne movie *The Alamo.* (AP/Wide World Photos)

Neither Lucas nor Higgins cashed in, however. Both of them had to give up their rights before the big gusher came through. Lucas returned to engineering, but Higgins roamed the state for the next fifty years, trying to find another field like Spindletop. At his death, in 1955, among his personal effects was a paper attesting to the fact that he was the first man to determine the location of Spindletop. It was signed by forty citizens of Beaumont and stamped by the county clerk, the only recognition he ever received.

The Spindletop community came and went in a rush, with the drills and rigs moving on when the field was exhausted. The historic boomtown has been recreated, along with the sort of vintage equipment that would have been used there, on its original site.

■ **LOCATION:** Spindletop is south of I-10, on U.S. 69, 96, 287 at University Drive. ■ **HOURS:** Tuesday through Sunday, 1–5. ■ **ADMISSION:** $2 ■ **TELEPHONE:** (409) 835-0823

BRACKETTVILLE

THE ALAMO MOVIE SeT

One of the finest achievements of the movies is to recreate great moments from the past, rebuild vanished monuments of American history. The Alamo, however, is still very much with us. The mission that was bravely defended by a handful of Americans before being overrun by overwhelming Mexican forces in 1836 is a revered landmark in San Antonio. It is such a precious piece of history that allowing a movie crew on the premises would amount to sacrilege.

Yet the events surrounding that battle are so dramatic that several movies have been made about The Alamo and the men who died there. In the 1950s, a national fad was touched off when the Walt Disney Studios resurrected Davy Crockett, dressed him in a coonskin cap, gave him a dandy theme song, and put him on television. Some parents were quite disturbed when the final frame of the movie showed Davy about to go down fighting at The Alamo. They petitioned Disney for a happier ending, to no avail.

A few years later, building on that success, John Wayne decided to film his own version of *The Alamo.* A movie set was constructed near the west Texas town of Brackettville, and, in 1959, shooting commenced. Wayne later described it as his favorite picture. Although *The Alamo* did not rank that high with the critics, the set still stands, giving it a unique sort of immortality. An entire Western town has been built around this Alamo replica and entertainment is offered during the summer months. Although gunfights and stagecoach robberies were not really part of the original Alamo story, it all kind of fits in.

■ **LOCATION:** Brackettville is on U.S. 90, about 125 miles west of the genuine Alamo, in San Antonio. The movie set is 7 miles north of town, on Ranch Road 674. ■ **HOURS:** Daily, 9–6, mid-May to mid-September; 10–5, rest of the year. ■ **ADMISSION:** $6 ■ **TELEPHONE:** (210) 563-2580

DALLAS

NEIMAn-MARCUS DEPaRTMENT STORe

Texas' best known store opened its doors in 1907, about six years after the state's first oil gusher came in at Spindletop. The two events are hardly coincidental. From the beginning, Neiman-Marcus had a very specific goal in mind. It was to be the great arbiter of taste and fashion in a part of the country that was growing rich faster than it was growing experienced.

Stanley Marcus, the store's longtime chief executive, once described the process as "authentication." When an item appeared in Neiman-Marcus, with the store's tag on it, it was simply assumed to be "tops in fashion, taste, and quality." The label became a magic tag, conferring goods with "a safe conduct pass."

The store has promoted itself tirelessly in this role. It is famous for its gala parties, for its one-of-a-kind items intended to appeal to the mega-rich, and for its European style boutique approach to merchandising long before it became generally accepted in America. It is also more deeply imprinted with the personality of its owners than any other major department store.

The quintessential Neiman-Marcus company tale concerns a woman who showed up at the store in 1927 in sunbonnet and bare feet to purchase a mink coat. "When she had selected the coat," said the official company history, "she paid for it on the spot with currency. The sales force at Neiman's, sensing an

The Book Depository (left) and nearby Dealey Plaza (right). *(Courtesy of Carl M. Wheeless)*

exceptional opportunity, also sold her a pair of shoes." The store remains the symbol of big Texas money and all the good things it can buy.

■ **LOCATION:** Neiman Marcus's main store is in downtown Dallas, at the corner of Main and Ervay. ■ **HOURS:** Vary seasonally. ■ **TELEPHONE:** (214) 741-6911

THE SIXTH FLOOR

The midpoint of the century is generally given as 1950. But if the twentieth century experience had a pivot, it was surely November 22, 1963. Nothing seemed the same afterward. It was as if all sense of restraint had been removed from American life after President John F. Kennedy was assassinated. After that, any act—no matter how horrifying—was conceivable, and often done.

Even a generation after the assassination, controversy rages over the event. Repeated surveys show that a majority of Americans still believe that Lee Harvey Oswald was only part of a conspiracy. Books and films deepen the conviction that the Warren Commission report did not uncover the truth. On any given day, the topic is debated in classrooms, on talk shows, in public forums. It has passed from the realm of history into that of folklore, an event so shattering to the order of things that it is now woven into the threads of the culture.

The sixth floor of the Texas School Book Depository Building, from which the fatal shots were fired at the president's motorcade, is now a museum of Kennedy's life. (In describing this place, a major guidebook uses the phrase "allegedly fired." Even the Dallas County Historical Foundation's establishment of the museum in this spot is not regarded as convincing evidence of its veracity: Critics of the Warren Commission have cast so many doubts, some fanciful and some demanding a response, on its assassination report that questions still exist in many minds whether Oswald was the actual gunman and the shots were really fired from this location.) There are exhibits on the Kennedy legacy, with self-guiding audio cassettes to the collection of historic photographs and items relating to the day of the assassination.

■ **LOCATION:** In downtown Dallas, at 411 Elm Street. (Dealey Plaza, where the president's motorcade was at the time of the assassination, is nearby on Elm Street.) ■ **HOURS:** Daily, 10–6. ■ **ADMISSION:** $4 ■ **TELEPHONE:** (214) 653-6666

GREENVILLE

AUDIE MURPHY EXHIBIT

"After I left the service," Audie Murphy once said, "I couldn't get a job that would leave me with self respect. I met two kinds of people—those who wanted to use me for my war record and those who wouldn't hire me because of it. It's bad enough that I had to go to Hollywood and make pictures."

He was the most decorated American soldier of World War II, a teenaged radio repairman who had been turned down by the Marines for being undersized. The five-foot-five-inch Murphy joined the Army, instead, and fought through Italy and into France. In one engagement, outside of Colmar, he climbed atop a burning tank and although wounded himself fought off advancing German troops with a machine gun. He was credited with 240 enemy kills.

When his picture was placed on the cover of *Life* magazine, the movies took notice. He was signed to a studio contract right after he was discharged, and every ounce of publicity was squeezed out of it. He was cast in a succession of bad westerns ("I made the same movie over and over again and just changed horses," he said). His most popular role was when he played himself in the film made from his autobiography, *To Hell and Back.*

A TV series failed, and so did a marriage. In 1968 he declared bankruptcy when his oil business went down the drain. He died three years later in a Virginia plane crash while on a business trip.

He said that he gave away all his medals to relatives and admirers. "I've been fed up with that 'most decorated' business for a long time," he said in a 1950 interview, "I gave away my medals because I never felt they belonged to me. My whole unit earned them, but I didn't know how to give them to my whole unit." Some of the medals Murphy won, his uniform, along with some other personal items, are on display in a special room in his hometown library.

■ **LOCATION:** Greenville is about 50 miles east of Dallas, by way of Interstate 30. The W. Walworth Harrison Public Library is at 3716 Lee Street. ■ **HOURS:** Monday through Saturday, 10–4. ■ **ADMISSION:** Free ■ **TELEPHONE:** (903) 457-2992

HEREFORD

NATIONAL COWGIRL HALL OF FAME

Out in the middle of Texas cattle country, in the seat of Deaf Smith County, an historic wrong has been addressed. In popular culture, the winning of the West has traditionally been depicted as an all-male affair. The female role has been limited to the supportive and suffering wife and mother (as in the Madonna of the Trail monuments erected in many states) or the barroom trollop. It really wasn't until Dale Evans rode after the bad guys beside Roy Rogers in a succession of late 1940s western films that western heroines began to emerge.

One area in which women always found a niche in Western lore was the rodeo. Many events do not rely on strength as much as agility and durability, and women excelled at them. Hereford puts on the country's largest all-women rodeo each year and was a natural choice for a facility to honor the stars of that competition, as well as other women who figured in the development of the West.

■ **LOCATION:** Hereford is on U.S. 60, about 45 miles southwest of Amarillo. The hall of fame is at 515 Avenue B. ■ **HOURS:** Monday through Friday, 9–5. ■ **ADMISSION:** $3 ■ **TELEPHONE:** (806) 364-5252

HOUSTON

THE ASTRODOME

On April 10, 1965, the first domed stadium in the history of American sports opened its doors. According to some observers, it immediately rendered every other ballpark obsolete. "One of the great wonders of the world," marvelled Dr. Billy Graham when he saw it, "A magnificent dream coming true before our eyes. The boundless imagination of man transformed to reality."

The dome was the inspiration of Judge Roy Hofheinz, owner of the Houston baseball team. When the city was granted a National League franchise in 1962, it was apparent that the local climate presented certain problems. Abundant rain and hot, sticky summer days would make it unlikely that the team could ever attract a large fan base. Unless they somehow could watch baseball while under an air-conditioned roof.

So for $31.6 million, Hofheinz built the Astrodome. With its 208-foot-high roof, the equivalent of eighteen stories in an office building, it modestly billed itself as "The Eighth Wonder of the World." But a few kinks in the plan quickly became apparent. When the Houston outfielders took the field for their first practice, they found it impossible to follow fly balls in the structural supports and lights at the roof of the dome. Every pop fly became an adventure. It was

The Astrodome. *(AP/Wide World Photos)*

decided that the dome had to be darkened. But that made it impossible for sunlight to penetrate the place and for grass to grow. So a new sort of artificial surface had to be devised. It was called Astroturf in the stadium's honor. That single development changed much of baseball and football, almost beyond recognition. It made the games faster and a good deal more dangerous. Football injuries, especially, increased enormously.

The domed stadium is now a fixture in sports. Four other baseball teams—Seattle, Minnesota, Toronto, and Montreal—now play under a roof, with Atlanta scheduled to move into its dome after the 1996 Olympic Games. Yet it has not proven to be the wave of the future. In fact, a reaction against domes has set in. Several cities have built determinedly old-fashioned-looking new stadiums featuring real grass. Many other ballparks that put down Astroturf have switched back to a natural surface.

Through the 1994 Super Bowl, no professional football team that plays its home games in a domed stadium had ever won the NFL championship. Still, in Houston, the concept has been a success and the Astrodome remains a landmark.

■ **LOCATION:** On Interstate 610, the South Loop Freeway. ■ **HOURS:** Daily tours are given at 11, 1 and 3, except when afternoon events are scheduled. ■ **ADMISSION:** $4, with an additional $4 parking fee. ■ **TELEPHONE:** (713) 799-9595

SPACE CENTER

The drama of America's adventure in space was at Cape Canaveral, where television cameras caught the slender rockets bursting from their pads in a tail of flame. But the brain was in Houston, at Mission Control. In fact, "Houston" became the abbreviated way of referring to the space industry, much as

"Wall Street" came to mean the financial community, and "Detroit" is shorthand for the auto industry. The name alone defines the enterprise.

Political log-rolling by the strong Texas Congressional delegation won the National Aeronautic and Space Administration for this state. Houston in the 1950s then became the home of the astronauts—the best and brightest of America—scientists with the bodies of athletes who would lead the country into outer space. They became the very symbol of the community, giving the name to Houston's baseball team and the stadium in which they play (*see* previous entry). Astronauts were the mid-century's ultimate national heroes; the possessors, according to writer Tom Wolfe, of *The Right Stuff.*

Much of the mystique has worn off space flight and the agency must now fight for its share of federal funds from an increasingly dubious Congress. But the romance of what NASA accomplished and the men and women who made trips out of this world still burns brightly at the Space Center. It is an educational facility, detailing the inner workings of the agency, its great feats, and some of the stuff it brought back from the moon. There are also flight simulators, films, and a giant-screen showing of *To Be an Astronaut.*

■ **LOCATION:** The Space Center is 25 miles southeast of central Houston by way of Interstate 45. ■ **HOURS:** Daily, 9–7. ■ **ADMISSION:** $8.75 ■ **TELEPHONE:** (713) 244-2100

NEDERLAND

TEX RITTER MUSEUM

It was while he was a pre-law student at the University of Texas that Maurice Woodward Ritter first started to sing. He was taking a class in Texas folklore from the famed historian J. Frank Dobie and became fascinated with the wealth of musical material from his home state's past. So he put together a show called "The Texas Cowboy and His Songs." Soon he was performing on the radio in Houston and, by 1930, in Chicago. Then he went to Hollywood and became one of the cowboys he sang about.

"I shot the same actor from behind the same rock about twenty times," Ritter recalled in a 1972 interview, "I guess I was pretty tough. Roy Rogers and Gene Autry sang more and I did more shooting." He was among the first of the "singing cowboys" who thrilled matinee audiences in the 1930s and 1940s. But he was never actually seen in his best-known movie role. It was his voice that was heard in the title theme to the Academy Award winner, *High Noon.* The 1952 movie is legendary. After it was edited the first time, viewers thought it was one of the dullest westerns ever made. Too much exposition, not enough action. So someone hit upon the bright idea of letting the theme song explain

Southfork: J. R. doesn't live there anymore. *(AP/Wide World Photos)*

what was going on and concentrating on the characters and gunplay. The result was an Oscar for star Gary Cooper and Ritter's biggest record.

Tex Ritter became one of the original inductees into the Country Music Hall of Fame (*see* Nashville, Tennessee). He died in 1974 and was buried beside the Neches River, in a site he had chosen himself. Nederland's Windmill Museum displays some of his costumes, his guitar, and memorabilia.

■ **LOCATION:** Nederland is about 10 miles south of Beaumont by way of U.S. 96, 287. The displays are part of the Dutch Windmill Museum, in Tex Ritter Park, at 1500 Boston Avenue. ■ **HOURS:** Thursday through Sunday, 1–5, Labor Day to March 1; summer hours, Tuesday through Thursday, 1–5. ■ **ADMISSION:** Free

PLANO

SOUTHFORK RANCH

On a November evening in 1980, an estimated eighty-three million Americans sat transfixed before their television sets to learn the answer to the question that had baffled the nation: Who shot J. R.? It was a TV phenomenon, the highest rating for a regular series episode in history (since exceeded by the final installment of *M*A*S*H*). More people watched *Dallas* that night than had voted in the presidential election three weeks earlier.

Dallas went on the air in 1978 and became an instant hit as the first prime time soap opera. J. R. Ewing, played by Larry Hagman with a sneer and a Stetson, became a symbol of the Texas businessman. He was greed in cowboy boots and lust in a string tie. The show's ongoing financial double-dealings and sexual switcheroos seemed to strike a chord. It was a major hit not only in the

United States, but around the world. *Dallas* was denounced by the Vatican and just about every other religious organization, but the masses still watched with fervent anticipation.

"The only one I never slept with during the course of this show was Barbara Bel Geddes, and she played my mother," said Hagman in a 1991 interview, shortly before the show went off the air, "Have you seen daytime soap opera? They would do it!" It was one of the few taboos *Dallas* wouldn't touch. The producers didn't shy away from other shenanigans: An entire season, in which a major character died, was later revealed to be a dream, perplexing many fans.

In the 1991 interview Hagman also said he felt that when the show was aired in Eastern Europe it helped topple Communism: "I think the opulence, the consumerism, the food, the cars—these things made people want more than their government provided them. You take people who don't have any food into a supermarket, they're going to want to stay."

The ranch at which some of the show's exteriors were shot became a major tourist attraction. At the peak of its popularity, Southfork Ranch was the ninth most visited attraction in the state. Since then it was foreclosed, but has reopened for tours, which show off items associated with its fictional owners, the Ewing family. It is also used as a conference center.

■ **LOCATION:** Southfork is near the suburb of Plano; north of Dallas on U.S. 75, east at exit 30 for 6 miles to Farm Road 2551, then right. ■ **HOURS:** Daily, 9–5. ■ **ADMISSION:** $6 ■ **TELEPHONE:** (214) 442-7800

WACO

TEXAS RANGER HALL OF FAME

The most famous law-enforcement agency of the Old West, the Rangers were heroes of hundreds of movies and books. "One riot, one Ranger," was their credo. Tough and fearless. Ruthless in confronting their enemies. And the truth wasn't far off.

They were formed in 1823 as a paramilitary outfit of mounted irregulars, supported by local communities rather than the government. Their main responsibility was maintaining order on the wild Texas frontier. "West of the Pecos," was a synonym for lawlessness in the mid-nineteenth century. The Rangers were expected to face down Comanche raiders, Mexican soldiers and outlaws. One historian wrote that the history of west Texas after 1836 was no more than the history of the Rangers. The Ranger could "ride like a Mexican, trail like an Indian, shoot like a Tennessean, and fight like a devil." Sam Houston urged the federal government to keep its troops out of Texas. "We don't want regular troops," he told the U.S. Senate, "Just give us 1,000 Rangers."

Their paragon was Jack Hays, who joined the Rangers in 1840. He is credited with being the first to understand the advantages of the new Colt revolver. The six-shooter revolutionized combat in the West and whoever owned one had an insuperable advantage. When Hays and a party of fifteen Rangers armed with the new Colts fought off a force of eighty Comanches, killing half of them, the weapon received national publicity and the reputation of the gun was made. So was that of the Rangers.

In later years, the Rangers were accused of excessive brutality in dealing with non-Anglos and some of their reputation was tarnished. But their place in American popular culture is secure. Almost every major western star portrayed a Ranger at one time or another and the image of The Lone Ranger became the standard of heroism and bravery by which the entertainment industry defined Western history.

The Texas Ranger Hall of Fame is located in Waco, which saw its share of Rangers when it was one of the wildest cow towns in the days of the Chisholm Trail. It is part of Fort Fisher Park. The hall contains a wax museum, dioramas, and some of the original weapons, saddles, and other equipment used by the Rangers.

■ **LOCATION:** The park is located along the Brazos River, off Interstate 35. The museum is housed in Taub Hall. ■ **HOURS:** Daily, 9–5. ■ **ADMISSION:** $3.50 ■ **TELEPHONE:** (817) 750-5986

WEATHERFORD

MARY MARTIN AS PETER PAN STATUE

She came flying out of Texas to delight Broadway for more than half a century. She washed that man right out of her hair as nurse Nellie Forbush in *South Pacific*. She heard the *Sound of Music* as Maria von Trapp (*see* Stowe, Vermont). She played Venus in *One Touch of Venus* and first won attention by performing a sedate striptease and singing "My Heart Belongs to Daddy."

But the role for which Mary Martin is remembered most vividly was as the forever young Peter Pan. It became a television tradition in the 1960s. Already a forty-six-year-old grandmother, Martin gave the role such joyful youth and verve that it was hard to recall anyone else playing it after her. Suspended by cables and soaring across the screen, she proved to a generation of kids that they could fly.

The musical first appeared on Broadway in 1954 and did not do well. When its run ended, she recreated her role on TV the following year. This time it was an instant hit on the small screen. In 1960 when it was redone in color it became a legend.

Martin grew up in Weatherford, the daughter of a lawyer and a violin teacher, and made her stage debut at a fireman's ball at age five. She left in 1930 to attend the University of Texas, where she married Benjamin Hagman. The marriage lasted only a year, but it produced Larry Hagman, the actor who later portrayed the archetypal Texan, J. R. Ewing, on the TV hit, *Dallas* (*see* Plano, Texas).

Weatherford erected the statue of Martin, in eternal flight as Peter Pan, shortly before her death in 1990.

■ **LOCATION:** Weatherford is about 25 miles west of Fort Worth, by way of Interstate 20. The statue is in front of the public library, at 1214 Charles Street.

WEST AND PACIFIC

ARIZONA

CALIFORNIA

COLORADO

HAWAII

IDAHO

NEVADA

NEW MEXICO

OREGON

UTAH

WASHINGTON

WYOMING

The big sign as it looked in March 1924.
(UPI/Bettmann) *See* page 292.

WEST AND PACIFIC

ARIZONA

1 Tom Mix Memorial, Florence
2 Andy Devine Room, Kingman
3 London Bridge, Lake Havasu City
4 Last segment of Route 66, Seligman
5 Big Surf, Tempe
6 O.K. Corral, Tombstone
7 Old Tucson, Tucson
8 Rex Allen Exhibit, Willcox

CALIFORNIA

9 Disneyland, Anaheim
10 Maps of the Movie Stars' Homes, Beverly Hills
11 Rodeo Drive, Beverly Hills
12 Lowest Point in America, Death Valley
13 Lawrence Welk Museum, Escondido
14 Crystal Cathedral, Garden Grove
15 Forest Lawn Memorial Park, Glendale
16 The Big Sign, Hollywood
17 First Studio Museum, Hollywood
18 Mann's Chinese Theater, Hollywood
19 Walk of Fame, Hollywood
20 Tail o' the Pup, Los Angeles
21 Universal Studios Tour, Los Angeles
22 Venice Beach, Los Angeles
23 Cannery Row, Monterey
24 The Rose Bowl, Pasadena
25 Alcatraz, San Francisco
26 Cable Car Museum, San Francisco
27 Chinatown, San Francisco
28 Golden Gate Bridge, San Francisco
29 Hearst Estate, San Simeon
30 Snoopy's Gallery, Santa Rosa
31 Roy Rogers-Dale Evans Museum, Victorville

COLORADO

32 Molly Brown House, Denver
33 Baldpate Key Museum, Estes Park
34 Coors Brewery, Golden
35 Jack Dempsey Museum, Manassa
36 Pikes Peak Highway, Manitou Springs
37 Drive-in Movie-Motel, Monte Vista
38 Red Ryder Museum, Pagosa Springs

HAWAII

39 Waikiki Beach, Honolulu
40 *USS Arizona* Memorial, Pearl Harbor

IDAHO

41 First Planned Ski Resort, Sun Valley
42 Evel Knievel Jump Site, Twin Falls

NEVADA

43 Hoover Dam, Boulder City
44 Ponderosa Ranch, Incline Village
45 Liberace Museum, Las Vegas
46 The Strip, Las Vegas
47 Wedding Chapels, Las Vegas
48 "Biggest Little City," Reno
49 Harrah National Automobile Museum, Reno

NEW MEXICO

50 Smokey Bear Historical Park, Capitan
51 Norman Petty Recording Studios, Clovis
52 Atomic Museum, Los Alamos
53 Town named for a quiz show, Truth or Consequences

OREGON

54 Nike Town, Portland

UTAH

55 Monument Valley Tribal Park, Gouldings

WASHINGTON

56 Set for *Northern Exposure*, Roslyn
57 Museum of Flight, Seattle
58 Space Needle, Seattle
59 Bing Crosby Library, Spokane

WYOMING

60 Buffalo Bill Historical Center, Cody

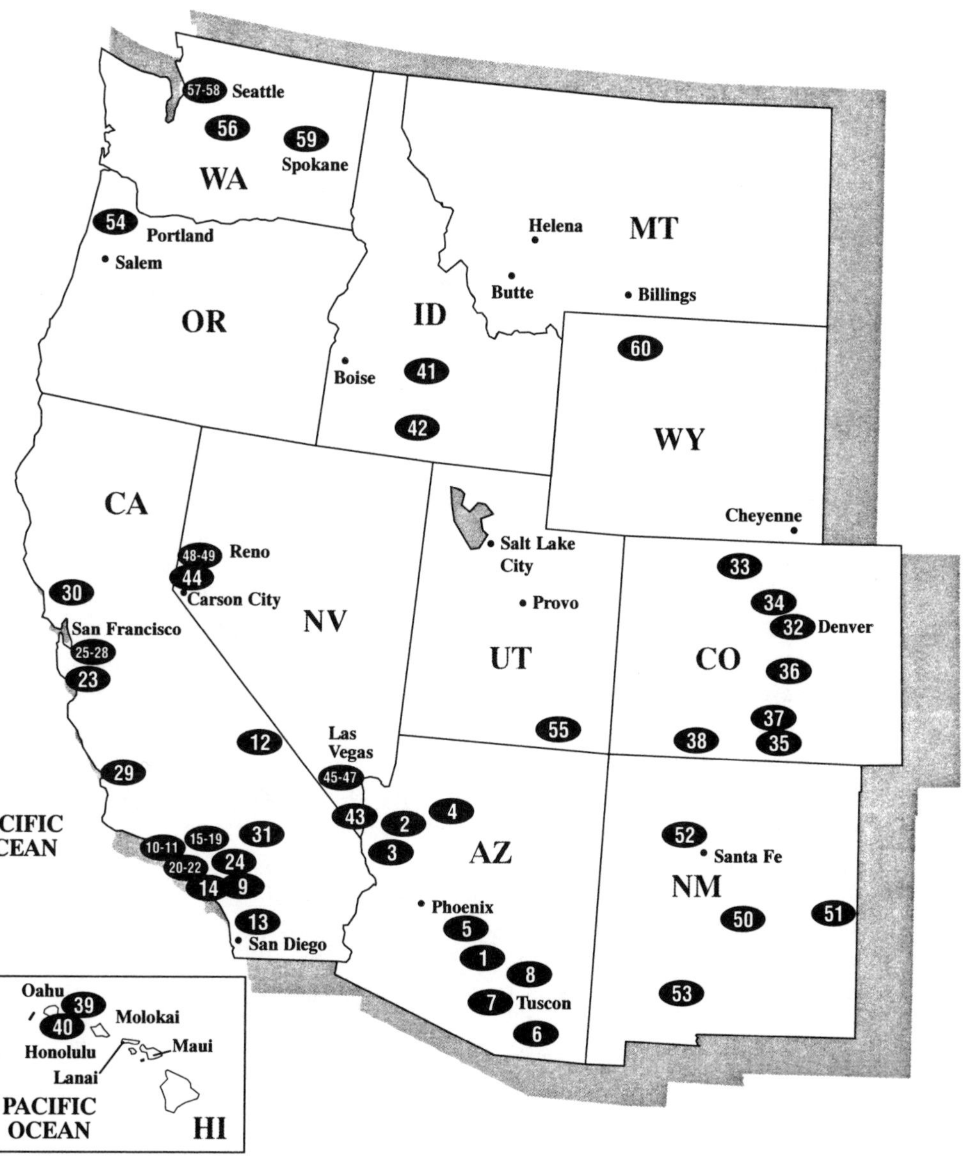
57-58 Seattle
56
59 Spokane
WA
54 Portland
Salem
OR
Helena
MT
Butte
Billings
ID
Boise
41
42
60
WY
Cheyenne
CA
48-49 Reno
44 Carson City
NV
30
San Francisco
25-28
23
Salt Lake City
Provo
UT
55
33
34
32 Denver
CO
36
37
38
35
12
Las Vegas
45-47
29
43
2
4
3
AZ
PACIFIC OCEAN
10-11
15-19
31
20-22
24
14
9
13
San Diego
Phoenix
5
1
8
7 Tuscon
6
52
Santa Fe
NM
50
51
53
Oahu
39
40
Molokai
Honolulu
Maui
Lanai
PACIFIC OCEAN
HI

FLORENCE

TOM MIX MEMORIAL

His birthplace was a source of dispute. Tom Mix claimed it was on a ranch near El Paso, and that he grew up there before setting off to ride with Teddy Roosevelt and fight in the Boxer Rebellion. Unfortunately, that wasn't quite true. He was actually born in Pennsylvania and his military service was a good deal less glamorous than he claimed (*see* Driftwood, Pennsylvania).

But there is no doubt about his death. In October 1940, while driving at about eighty miles an hour, he hit a dirt detour. His car went out of control, flipped over, and broke the cowboy star's neck, killing him instantly. Some editorialists took solace in the fact that he went to his reward in the Old West that he had depicted so many times. He also died with his boots on. (He was wearing the cowboy outfit in which he had appeared in his wild west show, which played Tucson the preceding day.)

Mix was the highest paid actor in silent films during the 1920s and, unquestionably, the best-known cowboy star of the era. Although he made his last movie in 1935, his character was still being portrayed in a television series, *The Tom Mix Program,* twenty years after his death. That was also about as long as it took to straighten out his will. While he had been a wealthy man, claimants to his estate wiped out all its assets and his heirs received nothing. Mix was buried in Hollywood's Forest Lawn Memorial Park, wearing a U.S. cavalryman's uniform. Beside him was his trademark white hat.

A memorial to Mix was placed at the site of the fatal accident.

■ **LOCATION:** The Tom Mix Memorial is just south of Florence, on U.S. 89, at a roadside rest area.

KINGMAN

ANDY DEVINE ROOM

Devine was the consummate movie sidekick, the hero's comical best pal. His voice was compared to the sound of a rusty door hinge. He played professional football in his youth and frequently weighed in at over three hundred pounds for his movie roles.

"I never won an Oscar," Andy Devine once recalled. "But I loaned a lot of money to some guys who did. I never starred. I was always the second man through the door in the Westerns. I never got the credit when the picture was a hit, but I never got blamed for all the crap I was in, either."

Work as a sidekick was steady. He broke into movies in 1926, still wearing his Santa Clara College letter sweater. When sound came in, his raspy voice, the result of a childhood accident involving a coat hanger, turned out to be a distinguishing asset. He played Jack Benny's pal in an ongoing western spoof on radio, during the 1940s was Roy Rogers's chum in several of the star's westerns, and tagged along with Guy Madison in the 1950s TV hit *Wild Bill Hickok*. His gravelly call of "Hey, Wild Bill, wait for me," was a playground staple across America in those years.

Devine grew up in Arizona. He was born in Flagstaff, but his parents were in the hotel business and wandered from place to place. For a while, they owned the Beale Hotel in Kingman, and the actor always considered this town his home. Kingman feels the same. The main road into town from the Interstate was renamed Andy Devine Avenue after his death in 1977. A collection of his personal memorabilia and displays about his long career are exhibited in a special room at the Mohave Museum of History and Arts.

■ **LOCATION:** The museum is in downtown Kingman, at 400 West Beale Street, not far from the Beale Hotel. ■ **HOURS:** Monday through Friday, 9–5; weekends, 10–5. ■ **ADMISSION:** $1 ■ **TELEPHONE:** (602) 753-3195

LAKE HAVASU CITY

LONDOn BRIDGE

The London Bridge of the nursery rhyme was built in 1206. While it never did fall down, it was replaced 625 years later by a rather plain, five-arched structure. The new bridge did its job, carrying traffic across the Thames River, until 1968. Then the city of London decided it could no longer carry its weight, and made plans to tear it down.

Meanwhile, strange events were going on in the Arizona desert. A manufacturer named Robert McCullouch, chafing under California's taxes, decided he would move his power saw business to the far side of the Colorado River. He acquired some Arizona land near Parker Dam, one of the major components of the Los Angeles water system. The dam was built in 1938 under incredibly difficult conditions and the entire region was regarded as uninhabitable. But a man who is mad at the taxman will not be put off by such trivial concerns. McCullouch set about to create a community on his land. Not only

Lake Havasu's London Bridge is a major tourist attraction. *(AP/Wide World Photos)*

a community, but a resort. The dam had also created Lake Havasu, and McCulloch reasoned that a lake in this arid country had tremendous recreational potential. Then he heard about the London Bridge being for sale.

He felt that bringing the structure to Arizona would bring an instant identity to his new town. London Bridge, after all, was a symbol of tradition and permanence. It turned out, he was actually thinking of *Tower* Bridge, London's picture-postcard span with the decorative central towers. McCullouch was a bit disappointed when he realized his mistake. But he went ahead and made the deal for $2.4 million, then had the thing packed up in crates and shipped to Arizona. London was happy to see it go.

"It was a good deal dirtier than our pictures had shown it to be," McCulloch said later. "But, needless to say, I'd do it again. Our lot sales doubled after we put it up here."

Americans have long felt that any monument Europe could build, they could build better. But no one had ever attempted to move an entire stone span from there to here. London Bridge reopened in Lake Havasu City in 1971. Its cables were strengthened and fifty-three feet were chopped from its length. And, as incongruous as it may seem, the old bridge has thrived in its new setting. An entire complex based on a British theme has sprung up around it. A residential community has developed on the other side of the span. (After all, it counts for something to be able to tell guests that you live on the far side of London Bridge.) The bridge itself, as McCulloch intended, has become a major tourist attraction, by one count second only to the Grand Canyon in the state. And it, assuredly, is not falling down.

■ **LOCATION:** Lake Havasu City is about 25 miles south of Interstate 40, by way of Arizona 95. The bridge is in the center of town. Adjacent to the span is English Village shopping plaza and the Ramada London Bridge Resort. The resort offers good views of the bridge area.

SELIGMAN

LAST sEGMENT OF RoUTE 66

John Steinbeck called it the "mother road," in his classic 1930s novel, *Grapes of Wrath.* A 1940's hit song urged travelers to "get their kicks" by driving it from Chicago to Los Angeles. In the 1960s, a television series was built around the adventures of two guys cruising the road in their Corvette. This was U.S. Route 66, the most celebrated federal highway in America.

It started in Chicago and headed southwest, angling across Illinois and Missouri, then straightening out to head due west across the southwestern states. For two generations, it symbolized the promise of California at the end of the road. One state away from that goal, in Arizona, it roared through the city of Flagstaff. Then, near the town of Seligman, it took a jog to the north, to avoid the rugged terrain around the Cottonwood Cliffs and Peacock Mountains. This is now the last remaining segment of the original Route 66. The rest of the route has been usurped by interstates.

Route 66, in the few areas where it survives, is a service drive. In an effort to drum up tourism, some local interests have put up markers identifying these disconnected segments as "Historic Route 66." But the route is not continuous and is no longer marked on most road maps. In Arizona, Interstate 40 runs where U.S. 66 used to, except for this one 119-mile strip, between Seligman and Kingman. Arizona has retained the old number for this last portion of Highway 66 even though it is maintained as a state road, not as a U.S. highway.

The route was originally surveyed by U.S. Army Lt. Edward Beale in 1857. He was charged with plotting a wagon road from Santa Fe to Los Angeles and was famous for importing camels from the Middle East to transport his equipment on this expedition. It was also the route followed by the Santa Fe Railroad when it came through in 1883.

Highway 66 winds through the Hualapi Indian reservation to the town of Peach Springs, which is the departure point for nineteenth-century excursions to the most accessible part of the Grand Canyon. The highway bends back down through a few desert towns until it rejoins Interstate 40. That's all there is. But the drive is a part of history.

■ **LOCATION:** Seligman, where the route begins, is about 75 miles west of Flagstaff.

TEMPE

BIG SuRF

As late as 1950, there were only 750,000 people living in the entire state of Arizona—less than the population of Phoenix alone in 1990. There were more people in either Maine or Rhode Island than there were in Arizona. Now this state has almost twice as many inhabitants as the other two combined.

In terms of percentages, no state grew like Arizona during the rush of the Sun Belt years. The growth of Arizona also marks the growth of the air-conditioning industry. Without it, the torrid summer heat could not support such a population. Arizona, by necessity, is the product of an artificial environment. The most remarkable symbol of that is Big Surf.

Americans have never liked being told they can't have it all. Just because you live in a desert, why can't you have ocean-like waves when you want to go swimming? Big Surf was among the first urban swimming pools to take advantage of new technology permitting the generation of big waves. (Even the name is a pun on the California ocean area, Big Sur.) Since its debut in the 1970s, the Big Surf concept has been imitated in many communities far from the sea. But nowhere is it more striking than among the cacti of Tempe. Here it stands as a definitive statement of Arizona's refusal to accept nature as a limitation.

■ **LOCATION:** Big Surf is at 1500 North Hayden Road. ■ **HOURS:** Daily, 10:30–6; Wednesday and Friday, until 10:30 P.M. ■ **ADMISSION:** $10.95 ■ **TELEPHONE:** (602) 947-2478

TOMBSTONE

O.K. CORRAL

They died the first time in 1881. The Clanton and McLaury brothers were no match for the guns of the Earp clan and Doc Holliday. When the smoke cleared, three of them lay dead on the streets of Tombstone. Since then, they have died a few thousand more times. In the movies, on television, in bimonthly reenactments of the famed shootout in the place where it occurred. The Gunfight at the O.K. Corral is the quintessential Western showdown, a compelling morality play in which good outguns evil. Two completely new versions of the incident were playing America's movie theaters as recently as 1993.

The facts are a bit more ambiguous. The marker over the grave of the three dead cowboys in Boothill Cemetery, in fact, reads: "Murdered on the streets of Tombstone." There were accusations that the Earps were taking payoffs from gambling interests and brothel-owners in town. Allying themselves with Holliday, a notorious gunman, also did their reputation no good. Although a court hearing later cleared the Earps of wrongdoing, both Morgan and Virgil Earp were shot from ambush in the next few months. Wyatt departed hastily for more salubrious surroundings.

Tombstone itself went into a steady decline after 1887. Underground water began seeping into its gold mines, making them unprofitable. Its population dropped from fourteen thousand to fewer than two thousand in less than three years. Still, the community held together, unlike many other western towns that disintegrated when the miners left. Tombstone proudly called itself "The Town Too Tough To Die."

Then in 1963, a Grosse Pointe, Michigan attorney and western buff, Harold O. Love, stopped for a visit and found most of the town was for sale. Over the next twenty years he spent millions of dollars restoring many of Tombstone's famed historic monuments, and returning Allen Street to the look of its frontier days. Tombstone was remade in the image of its Wild West reputation. The Crystal Palace Saloon, the Bird Cage Theatre, the Tombstone Epitaph—all of them looking as they did when the Earps and Doc Holliday slapped leather. So does the O.K. Corral itself, another Love restoration. The legendary gunfight is repeated there two Sundays a month. Wyatt Earp draws his six-gun once more, just as Henry Fonda, Burt Lancaster, Kurt Russell, and Kevin Costner did when they portrayed him on the big screen, and America thrilled in the darkness of a thousand theaters.

■ **LOCATION:** Tombstone is located about 70 miles east of Tucson, by way of Interstate 10 and Arizona 80. The O.K. Corral is on Allen Street, between 3rd and 4th Streets. ■ **HOURS:** Daily, 8:30–5. The gunfight re-enactment takes place at 2 P.M. on the second and fourth Sundays of the month. ■ **ADMISSION:** $1 ■ **TELEPHONE:** (602) 457-3456

TUCSON

OLD TUCSON

Tucson was Arizona's territorial capital for ten years and the biggest city in the state until the 1920s. It was a rip-roaring sort of place during frontier days, cut off for a time by the Apache forces of Cochise and even briefly threatened by Confederate raiders from New Mexico. In 1939 when Hollywood made a movie about that era, it reconstructed frontier Tucson in the desert west of the modern city. The set was regarded as among the most elaborate ever built for a western. When production wrapped, it was decided to preserve the set and make "Old Tucson" a permanent attraction.

The movie itself, *Arizona,* was a formula western that won good reviews for stirring action sequences and a likable pair of stars, Jean Arthur and William Holden. Its climax, in which the two leads get married and she goes home to prepare dinner while he walks off to have a gunfight with the bad guy, was especially applauded.

The set is still used occasionally for film production. The TV series *High Chapparal* was shot there and so are many commercials with an Old West theme. But it is predominantly a tourist park now, with gunfights and brawls staged daily in a vision of authenticity shaped by generations of western movies, including the one for which the whole thing was built in the first place.

■ **LOCATION:** Old Tucson is in Tucson Mountain Park, 12 miles west of central Tucson by way of Speedway Boulevard. ■ **HOURS:** Daily, 9–9. ■ **ADMISSION:** $8.95 ■ **TELEPHONE:** (602) 883-6457

WILLCOX

REX ALLEN EXHIBIT

Rex Allen's first Hollywood movie was called *The Arizona Cowboy,* a true case of art nodding to authenticity. That is exactly what Allen was, growing up on a small ranch outside this southeastern Arizona town. His family had moved here from a more remote location, after his older brother was bitten by a rattlesnake and could be not be taken for medical help in time to save his life.

After high school Allen joined the rodeo but had greater success as a singer entertaining the crowds before the events. So he switched to radio, landing a job in the famous western town of Trenton, New Jersey. Soon he had a permanent spot performing on the National Barn Dance out of Chicago. This was in the mid-1940s, at the peak of the singing cowboy craze. Roy Rogers (*see* Victorville, California) and Gene Autry were at the height of their popularity, and Republic Pictures, the home of the B-western, was looking for actors who could warble as they rode.

Allen filled the bill and was cast in a variety of forgettable films. When he left the studio in 1954, he was the last contract western star there. His singing career was more successful, though, and he had a country hit with "Crying in the Chapel." He had a brief run with a TV series, *Frontier Doctor,* in the early 1950s and went on to narrate a series of Walt Disney Studio nature films. His deep, folksy voice became the signature of these movies.

He maintained his ties with his boyhood home and mementoes of his career in music and film are displayed in a special exhibit at the Cochise County Museum.

■ **LOCATION:** Willcox is off Interstate 10, about 80 miles east of Tucson. The museum is at the Arizona 186 exit, at 150 Railroad Avenue. ■ **HOURS:** Monday through Saturday, 9–5; Sunday, 1–5. ■ **ADMISSION:** Free ■ **TELEPHONE:** (602) 384-2272

CaLifornia

ANAHEIM

DISNEyLAND

He was originally called Mortimer. He looked more rodent-like in the beginning, too, with an elongated nose and pointed ears. But by 1928 when moviegoers first heard his voice, he was good old Mickey Mouse, the most popular animated creature ever created. And the squeaky voice was that of his creator, Walt Disney. That first sound cartoon, "Steamboat Willie," was the foundation of the Disney empire.

Within three years, the mouse had become so popular that twenty-one cartoons were turned out annually. They became a ubiquitous part of moviegoing. One famous magazine cartoon of the period showed a dejected audience trooping out of a theater with the caption "No Mickey Mouse." In 1932, the studio turned out its first color cartoon, "Flowers and Trees." By the end of the decade, the Disney studios were established enough to release the first full-length feature, *Snow White,* one of the most financially successful movies ever made. It also turned out *Fantasia,* so advanced that it took twenty years to find its audience and also featured the first step toward stereophonic sound.

The words "Mickey Mouse" entered the language during World War II to describe a ridiculous bit of discipline or routine. It was also the password during the Normandy landings. Disney welcomed the advent of television and was among the first moviemakers to get into a weekly series, opening the studio vaults for a never-ending supply of material. In 1955 Disney topped it all. He reinvented the amusement park and in so doing redrew the patterns of American travel and entertainment.

The opening of Disneyland was a cultural earthquake. Within months, the terms "Magic Kingdom" and "Fantasyland" had entered the language. As did "Disneyland" itself, as a description of something too imbued with the fantastic to be real. Its imaginative rides—a jungle cruise, a submarine adventure, spinning teacups—were all drawn from Disney movies and created an entire new audience for these films. Old-fashioned roller coasters were cunningly disguised as runaway trains and bobsleds. Walt Disney had created something new—the theme park, with every feature in it referring back to the Disney movies. There was a parade up Main Street every day. Music filled the air and

In early July 1955, two lucky kids get a preview of Disneyland, and their tour guide is Walt Disney himself. *(UPI/Bettmann)*

Disney characters would magically appear to hug the kids. The park celebrated childhood but at the same time it also wrote the textbook on crowd control, cleanliness, and relentlessly upbeat employees. Gone was the sleaze of the carnival-like amusement parks of the past. In Disneyland, nothing nasty or negative intruded.

Within two decades, Disneyland had evolved into its own massive spinoff across the continent (*see* Lake Buena Vista, Florida). Much larger than the original, Walt Disney World eventually dwarfed it in attendance, too. But the original Disneyland remains as the model, and proof of how much can come out of one mouse.

■ **LOCATION:** The park's address is 1313 Harbor Boulevard, just off Interstate 5. ■ **HOURS:** Monday through Friday, 10–6; weekends, 9–midnight. ■ **ADMISSION:** $25.50 a day, with a $4 parking fee. ■ **TELEPHONE:** (714) 999-4565

BEVERLY HILLS

MAPS oF THE MOVIE STARS' HOMEs

A recent guidebook to hangouts of the stars contains this warning in boldface type: "Do not approach or otherwise disturb the occupants of any of the homes in this book. Stay away from the occupants for your own safety!"

Dangerous business, this star-watching. And still they come, from every corner of America, to buy the maps sold from card tables on the streets of Los Angeles, and to look for stars. Most of the maps are hopelessly out of date. Actors move around even more than average homeowners and some of the

On Disneyland's opening day, July 17, 1955, the doors to Fantasyland were finally flung open and the rush was on. *(AP/Wide World Photos)*

material in the guides hasn't changed for fifteen years. Even the information in the spiel on the guided bus tour is not always accurate. Still the tourists dutifully drive up the streets of this city, peering at the home of a furniture manufacturer and hoping to see Madonna.

While many of the big names in Hollywood, especially the older ones, do live in Beverly Hills, the chances of actually catching a glimpse of them near their homes is less than remote. Most of the residences are set well back, with privacy fences and hedges, to protect against just such an intrusion. Nevertheless, the appeal of actually seeing a movie star in person is as strong as ever.

The concept of the movie star goes back to 1914, when film-makers began to understand featured players' impact on audiences. Mary Pickford was the first to have full-length films actually built around her screen persona. The word "star" as applied to an actor, dates from the theater of the 1860s. Until the rise of Pickford, however, it was felt that the novelty and visual effects of the movies in themselves would attract an audience, without the need of big name performers. Her popularity was so enormous, that Pickford was the first to be referred to as a "movie star" and in another few years she would be publicized as "America's Sweetheart."

Since that time, the publicity build-up of film actors has been an intrinsic part of the movie business. As Peter O'Toole wailed plaintively in the film *My Favorite Year:* "I'm not an actor, I'm a movie star." No wonder the maps always have a market.

■ **LOCATION:** The best way to actually see stars is to find where location shooting is going on each day in the Los Angeles area. There are several companies that will furnish you with a list and a road map for a fee. Check with the Hollywood Visitors Information Bureau at 6541 Hollywood Boulevard. ■ **TELEPHONE:** (213) 461-4213

RODEO DRIVE

To an earlier generation, New York's Fifth Avenue was America's most fashionable shopping street. But Fifth Avenue was a long thoroughfare, that also contained offices, churches, clubs—a lot more than just stores. Rodeo Drive is solely the Avenue of Acquisitiveness. Its two-block run, from Wilshire Boulevard to Santa Monica Boulevard, contains all items whose price tags elicit low whistles of disbelief. Some of the stores won't even let you in without an appointment. Others serve champagne or espresso to favored customers. It is the most intensive concentration of wretched excess in America, a sidewalk sale for the rich and famous.

On Rodeo Drive, the emphasis is always on the second syllable, not the first as in the country songs. The root word is the same, though. It is Spanish for "gathering." In this case the word goes back to the original name for Beverly Hills, "Rancho Rodeo de las Aguas," or Gathering of the Waters. When the town was platted in 1906 it was owned by the Rodeo Land and Water Company. The owner of the firm came from Beverly, Massachusetts, however, and he liked the sound of that better. So Rodeo survives only on this street of dreams. By terms of the original plan, commercial development in Beverly Hills was allowed only on this small triangle between the two major boulevards. It did well with the space it had.

■ **LOCATION:** Rodeo Drive runs north from Wilshire Boulevard, about half a mile east of the major intersection with Santa Monica Boulevard.

DEATH VALLEY

LOWEST POINT IN AMERICA

To the pioneers who took a wrong turn in Nevada and found themselves trapped in this wasteland, it truly was a valley of death. In more recent years, however, it functions more as a symbol than a threat. Death Valley is now a National Monument and tourists flock here. Paved roads carry the traveler in and out easily. There are even resort hotels built within its boundaries.

But the name acquired a life of its own. It has been borrowed by sports, to designate a stadium in which it is especially difficult for visitors to win (Clemson University) or a baseball field with an extremely deep center field (Tiger Stadium). Writer Frank Norris set the climax of his novel *McTeague* here, as a

Death Valley's vast wasteland includes the Devil's Golf Course, an expanse of crystallized salt. *(AP/Wide World Photos)*

symbol of the desert to which human greed leads. In American culture, "death valley" has come to mean an impossibly hopeless situation. Because of these associations, many more people probably can identify America's lowest point, than they can its highest. (That is now Alaska's Mount McKinley. But before Alaska joined the union, it was Mount Whitney, which, oddly enough, is less than one hundred miles west of here.)

The actual low point at Badwater is 282 feet below sea level. Nearby, the highest temperature ever recorded in the United States topped out at 144 degrees Fahrenheit in July 1913. Just before that, for the 993 days preceding May 6, 1912, there was no recorded precipitation in the area—the longest dry spell in national history.

■ **LOCATION:** Badwater is located near the center of the National Monument, south of the visitor center at Furnace Creek. ■ **HOURS:** The visitor center, where one should stop before going into the area, is open daily, 8–8, November to Easter Sunday; 8–5, rest of the year. ■ **ADMISSION:** $5 a car. ■ **TELEPHONE:** (619) 786-2331

ESCONDIDO

LAWREnCE WELK MUSeUM

"You'll be back just as soon as you get hungry," his father called after him as he left the family farm in Strasburg, North Dakota. That was in 1924. Lawrence Welk decided he would go on the road as a musician. He played accordion with pickup bands, assembled his own group, occasionally got time on a national broadcast. This was the era of the swing bands, but Welk persisted in playing a more melodic, lilting style. It was hopelessly corny and old fashioned. But swing came and went and so did bop, and Welk just kept right on lilting along. Always wholesome, always schmaltzy, always working. And, despite his father's prophecy, always eating regularly.

The name for his musical style came to him during a series of broadcasts in Pittsburgh in 1938. The show's announcer said that several letters had come in saying that "Listening to your music is like sipping champagne." From then on, he played Champagne Music, with bubbles perking through every chord.

Welk stayed on the road for twenty-seven years, until going on a Los Angeles television station in 1951. The response was enormous, his band became a regular show locally, and two years later was picked up by a national network as a summer replacement. *The Lawrence Welk Show* remained on the air for eighteen years, headed by a cast of unknowns who were rarely paid above the union minimum. The main attraction was the music. Even in the midst of the rock era, in February 1961, Welk managed to chart a number-one record with the song "Calcutta." It was the last number-one hit to feature a harpsichord in the arrangement.

After Welk's death in 1991, a small storm blew up over a Congressional appropriation to restore his birthplace. It was ridiculed, even by President George Bush, as a worst-case example of pork barrel politics, and it was rescinded. But the museum at the Lawrence Welk Resort Theatre here shows off the memorabilia of the champagne bandleader's life.

■ **LOCATION:** About 40 miles north of San Diego, at the Lawrence Welk Drive exit of Interstate 15; 8845 Lawrence Welk Drive. ■ **HOURS:** Daily. It opens at 10 A.M. and closing time depends on whether there is an attraction at the adjacent theater. ■ **ADMISSION:** Free ■ **TELEPHONE:** (619) 749-3448

GARDEN GROVE

CRYSTaL CATHEDRAL

The Reverend Robert Schuller saw the world was changing. Big city churches were fragmenting because of the move to the suburbs. Life was moving at a faster pace. People wanted to know how to use their religion to get ahead in life. The result was the *Hour of Power,* one of longest running religious programs on television, in which Schuller talked about "possibility thinking."

So the ministry that began in 1955 in a parking lot with a congregation of twelve families and $86.87 in the first collection plate, grew into the Crystal Cathedral. This star-shaped church of ten thousand windows, designed by Philip Johnson, is a religious landmark, and a monument to the persuasiveness of Schuller's message.

From the start, he unabashedly declared that a church is a business, "a shopping center for God, part of the service industry." He was among the first to encourage drive-in worship, in which people parked out in the lot and tuned in the service on the radio. Schuller always stressed the importance of a big parking lot. "You can be the greatest preacher in the world, but if people can't find a place to park they won't stop to hear your message," he said in a 1976 interview.

He differed from other televangelists in that his message was pitched more toward personal success rather than religious passion. But while his denomination, the Reformed Church in America, was declining in numbers, his congregation quadrupled in a decade. Traditional theologians criticized his message as "shallow." But Schuller insisted that people did not want to attend church to hear "one-sided bigoted statements." They wanted an optimistic message to apply to their daily lives.

"When faced by a mountain, I will not quit," runs his credo. "I will keep on striving until I climb over, find a pass through, tunnel underneath or simply stay and turn the mountain into a gold mine, with God's help." Or if not gold, then crystal.

■ **LOCATION:** The Crystal Cathedral is off the Santa Ana Freeway (Interstate 5), at Chapman Avenue and Lewis Street. ■ **HOURS:** Monday through Saturday, 9–3:30; Sunday, 1:30-3:30. ■ **TELEPHONE:** (714) 971-4013

GLENDALE

FOREST LAWN MEMORIAL PARK

Hubert C. Eaton felt that cemeteries had the whole thing exactly backwards. They were depressing places, he thought, because "they depicted ends and not beginnings." So when he got the chance in 1917, as his bank foreclosed on an old cemetery on a suburban hillside here, he decided to put his theories into practice. The result is a sculpture park, filled with historic structures, some imported from Europe. It is empty of tombstones but filled with flowers and ponds and Carrara marble.

Forest Lawn became an American original—satirized by some for placing marriage chapels and horticultural displays among the dead, but happily embraced by most Californians. Ronald Reagan and Jane Wyman were married here in 1940 at the Wee Kirk o' the Heather. This old church was Eaton's major coup. It is an exact copy of the church in Glencairn, Scotland, in which Annie Laurie, of the sad ballad, worshiped and was buried. A wishing chair, built of stones from the original, is intended for newlyweds to sit in.

Also on the three-hundred-acre property is a copy of the church at Stoke Poges, England, where Thomas Grey wrote "Elegy in a Country Churchyard." There is a stained glass recreation of Leonardo da Vinci's *Last Supper* in the Memorial Court of Honor. A museum on the premises shows off coins named in the Bible, stained glass, and an exhibit on Michelangelo. There are maps available at the gate but they do not show the burial plots of celebrities, like Will Rogers, who rest here.

■ **LOCATION:** Forest Lawn is off the Glendale Freeway (California 2) at the San Fernando Road exit, then right to 1712 South Glendale Avenue. ■ **HOURS:** Daily, 10–5. "The Last Supper" is shown on the hour, 10–4. ■ **ADMISSION:** Free, donation asked at "The Last Supper." ■ **TELEPHONE:** (213) 254-3131

HOLLYWOOD

THE BIG SIGN

When the sign on Mount Lee first went up in 1923 it read "Hollywoodland." It was intended as a promotion for a new housing development on the hillside right below it. It stayed that way for twenty-six years when the last four letters were taken down and the sign, regarded as a priceless local landmark, was taken over by the Hollywood Chamber of Commerce. It had become a symbol of the film capital, one of the most widely recognized civic emblems in the country.

Each letter is forty-five feet high and the sign extends for a length of three hundred feet. It is even licensed, so that royalties from reproductions go to the Hollywood Sign Trust to support its upkeep. The upkeep is expensive. The sign had to be rebuilt completely in 1978, at a cost of $27,700 per letter (total price tag $249,300). Several show business personalities contributed to the cost. (The original was put up for a *total* price tag of $21,000.) Safety features have also been built into the sign to guard against vandalism, a frequent occurrence throughout its history. Letters were altered to form all sorts of messages, some of them harmless and others mindless. A gate has been installed so that the sign can no longer be approached from above. It is visible, on clear days, all across the valley. Although the Hollywood below is not what it was in the golden era, the sign still keeps the faith that movies are better than ever.

■ **LOCATION:** Best close-up view of the sign is from Mulholland Drive, the hilltop thoroughfare, as it runs west from the Hollywood Freeway (U.S. 101).

FIRST STUDIO MUSEUM

The movies came to California in 1908, when a Chicago production company, hampered by bad weather, arrived to finish shooting on *The Count of Monte Cristo.* They ended up with an entirely different cast than the one they started with, and their set was the back of a Chinese laundry. But it was a start. Other filmmakers got the message quickly and within a year pioneers like Bronco Billy Anderson were grinding out a picture a week, shooting all over the streets and hillsides of Los Angeles. In 1913, a new company, called Famous Players, provided the industry with a geographic focus. Famous Players was organized by vaudeville producer Jesse Lasky, his brother-in-law, Samuel Goldwyn, and playwright-director, Cecil B. DeMille. It was actually the corporate egg that grew into MGM (Metro Goldwyn Mayer) and Paramount. Among its first projects was *The Squaw Man.* Its release in 1914 marked the first feature-length western in history, and its success encouraged other producers to set up shop in the Hollywood area.

DeMille went on to specialize in large-scale Biblical productions. His name became synonymous with the word epic. But like so many other Hollywood figures, his career began with a western. *The Squaw Man* was shot in a barn at Vine and Selma streets. The barn was later moved to the Paramount back lot and doubled as a railroad station in episodes of *Bonanza.* Now it is run as a museum of early film history, operated by Hollywood Heritage, Inc. It contains mementoes of early stars, a reconstructed screening room, and a reproduction of DeMille's office.

■ **LOCATION:** The museum is at 2100 North Highland Avenue, at the edge of the Hollywood Bowl. ■ **HOURS:** Thursday through Sunday. Hours vary throughout the year and it is best to call in advance. ■ **ADMISSION:** $3.50 ■ **TELEPHONE:** (213) 874-2276

MANN'S CHINESE THEATER

According to the legend, construction work was still going on at the new theater of showman Sid Grauman right up until opening night, May 18, 1927. When actress Norma Talmadge arrived for the show, she accidentally stepped in wet concrete. Other witnesses say it was Grauman himself who made the misstep. However it happened, Grauman seized the moment. He persuaded Mary Pickford and Douglas Fairbanks to add their footprints, and so one of the great show business traditions was born.

The theater itself is a magnificent relic of the movies' golden era, when theaters were supposed to look like fantastic palaces. Or, in this case, a Chinese temple. It was built as a follow-up to the Egyptian Theater, which Grauman had opened five years before. But the Chinese Theater and its footprints of the famous became a landmark, the ultimate recognition of movie celebrity.

The prints outside Mann's Chinese Theater are considered a Hollywood treasure. *(UPI/Bettmann)*

Al Jolson put his bended knee in the cement. Eleanor Powell, her tap shoes. Eddie Cantor traced the outline of his famous banjo-eyes. Sonja Henie put in her ice skates, John Barrymore his profile, and Betty Grable her leg. Someone threw an egg at Victor McLaglen when he went through the ceremony and the splatter marks are still visible in the pavement.

The bulk of the prints were made during the 1930s and 1940s, when stars were stars. But although Grauman never liked to admit it, more prints were made than survived. If he guessed wrong, and a rising star slipped back into obscurity, he would have that bit of pavement replaced. He loved his footprints too much to have anyone less than a top star included.

The theater is now owned by the Mann chain. But the prints, with their effusive tributes to Grauman, a man who would otherwise have been long forgotten, are still a treasured piece of Hollywood history.

■ **LOCATION:** Mann's Chinese Theater is at 6925 Hollywood Boulevard. The courtyard (where the prints are) is always open.

WALK oF FAME

As far back as 1928, Hollywood was declared over the hill. A news item from that year said it could no longer be considered the center of the film industry, since studios had dispersed to places like Culver City and Burbank.

But that was a bit premature. Hollywood continues to be one of those rare localities in which the name of the place is synonymous with its main product.

But throughout its history, local businessmen have noticed that Hollywood was starting to look a little seedy, and a push for some kind of spruce-up campaign has begun. The Walk of Fame is a product of such a crusade of the late 1950s.

On the fame chart, it's a few notches down from the footprints at Mann's Chinese Theater (*see* previous entry). More than two thousand stars are now embedded in the sidewalk along Hollywood Boulevard and Vine Street. Moreover, the lucky star has to fork over $4,800 for the privilege. Some have flatly refused and others have ignored the Hollywood Chamber of Commerce's invitations. A few have such devoted fan clubs that members have anted up to get their favorite's star put into place. Many more have paid gladly, happy enough to get their very own star. The installation of a new star is always a major publicity event.

The idea has been copied by other cities seeking to honor famous local people for one reason or another. But Hollywood's Walk of Fame is a genuine attraction, and one of the few chances most Americans will ever get to walk all over a movie star.

■ **LOCATION:** The Walk runs along Hollywood Boulevard, between Gower and Sycamore Streets, and on Vine, between Sunset Boulevard and Yucca Street.

LOS ANGELES

TAIL o' THE PUP

When Los Angeles was younger, the city was famous for its playful attitude toward eating places. The hamburger wasn't invented here, but it could be argued that it was brought to its fullest development here. National chains McDonald's and Big Boy originated in the area. So did the coffee shop, a West Coast adaptation of the traditional diner. One of the city's best-known landmarks was the Brown Derby, a restaurant shaped like a hat. The original stood on Wilshire Boulevard with its motto, "Eat in the hat."

The Tail o' the Pup is one of the last survivors of that era of L.A. glitz and innocence. This fast-food stand, shaped like a hot dog held between two buns, has been a landmark in the west Hollywood area since the early 1950s. It was relocated in 1986 for posterity and its grand reopening was marked by a celebrity-studded affair. It is truly a unique chance to get a taste of the old L.A.

■ **LOCATION:** The Tail is at 329 North San Vicente Boulevard, just north of Beverly Boulevard. ■ **HOURS:** Daily, 11–11. ■ **TELEPHONE:** (213) 652-4517

UNIVERSAL STUDIOS TOUR

Universal has been in the movie-making business since 1912, when several small independents combined to form the studio. Its symbol of a revolving globe is among the most familiar in the industry. But by the 1980s, its movies almost seemed like an incidental means to a greater end. The theme park that Universal constructed around its studios produced more revenue for the company than the movies that were made here.

This is the ultimate backstage tour. It started small back in the 1960s, as kind of a casual stroll through the lot. Universal was the only company that permitted tourists on its property and through word-of-mouth the tours steadily grew more popular. Aspiring actors were hired as tour guides and their glib patter became part of the fun. A tram ride was added showing off some of the most special of special effects. The shark from *Jaws* leaps from a pool. King Kong threatens to turn the tram over. A simulated earthquake hits and then a flood follows. Visitors watch an entire set go up in artificial flames and stunt men battle to a make-believe death.

Famous sets and landmarks from movies of the past are shown off. Technicians explain some of the tricks of making movies. Instead of diminishing the magic, this peek behind the curtain seems to enhance it. Only Disneyland draws more people in southern California, and like that enterprise, Universal opened another park and production facility in central Florida.

■ **LOCATION:** At the Lankersheim Boulevard exit of the Hollywood Freeway (U.S. 101). ■ **HOURS:** Opening is at 8 A.M. in summer; 9 A.M., the rest of the year. Closing times vary. ■ **ADMISSION:** $24, plus a $4 parking fee. ■ **TELEPHONE:** (818) 508-9600

VENICE BEACH

This is where Los Angeles remains forever young. The laid-back southern California way of life may be only a memory in this city. It has become a difficult place to live: The freeways are clogged, the cost of living is high, crime is frightening, the air is unbreathable, and cultural diversity strains nerves. But on the beach, there are no problems. Only surf, sand, and sun, the way it was when the Beach Boys sang and the 1960s were coming in on the next big wave.

It is a byword in the advertising industry that every national fad begins among the kids of Los Angeles. Most of them start right here, at the edge of the continent. Venice Beach is an endless summer—a circus of skateboarders, tee-shirt shops, surfers, basketball players, body builders, street musicians. All of them flung together on this ocean walk, like characters in some poorly written but visually fascinating scenario.

Venice was founded with high intentions. Its developer, Abbott Kinney, sought to rebuild the grandeur of its Italian namesake, right down to the canals. But by 1906 the beach front had become an entertainment district with a

Universal Studios tour then and now: What began as a ride through the back lot in a peppermint-striped tram (left) is now a full-fledged amusement ride (right). *(AP/Wide World Photos)*

distinctly bawdy American texture that flavored the rest of the community. Most of the canals were filled in and Venice turned into a snug little beach town.

There are other beaches on the golden crescent that runs from Malibu down to Long Beach. Many of them are a lot richer. But Venice is California a la mode. It is a potpourri of all the fantasies that once made L.A. a magnet for dreams.

■ **LOCATION:** North from Washington Boulevard to the ocean.

MONTEREY

CANNErY ROW

John Steinbeck chronicled the dark side of the California dream. He told of migrant workers from Mexico and Oklahoma who broke their backs in California's fields. The debris of the golden state. Drifters and losers. *Grapes of Wrath* is one of the most powerful and influential works in the history of American fiction, and it sparked a national outrage at the plight of "the Okies" in the 1930s. Steinbeck was denounced as a Communist. The book was banned in some places and even burned. But the author was awarded the Pulitzer Prize and the country was moved as never before to look at those who had been defeated by the economic system.

Steinbeck also had a lighter side. *Cannery Row* appeared in 1945. It was a slim volume about a group of eccentrics and dreamers, presided over by a philosophical marine biologist, living amid the empty sardine factories on the Monterey waterfront. The book developed a tremendous cult following, especially among college students who were drawn to its anti-establishment attitude. The setting and characters were so popular that Steinbeck wrote another book about them, *Sweet Thursday.* They defied translation to the musical stage and movies. What was amiably weird on the printed page became simply goofy when enacted. The books remain essentially literary experiences, timeless and enchanting.

Cannery Row, however, has been utterly transformed. Local entrepreneurs, realizing that tourists were interested in the area because of the Steinbeck associations, began fixing up the empty canneries in the early 1960s. They were turned into jazz spots and shops. Soon art galleries and upscale restaurants moved in. The biggest attraction in Monterey, the Aquarium, is situated right in the midst of it all. Cannery Row now is long on imported salmon and brie, but short on sardines and any hint of Steinbeck. The California dream got the last laugh after all.

■ **LOCATION:** Cannery Row is on the waterfront, several blocks west of Monterey's Fishermen's Wharf area.

PASADENA

THE ROSE BOWL

First there were burro races. That was the featured event on January 1, 1890, the first time the people of Pasadena gathered in a park and held a parade with flower-bedecked carriages. The affair went over so well that in five years it was named the Tournament of Roses, complete with queens and floats. Then in 1902 someone got the idea of playing a football game. The University of Michigan was invited to come west and play Stanford. The game was not an artistic success. Michigan was too good and racked up the California school by a score of 49–0. After that, they went back to simply holding a parade and a few chariot races for the next fourteen years.

In 1916 they tried football again. Washington State was matched against Brown from the Ivy League and the West Coast team won. The people of Pasadena liked that. Seven years later, the game was officially titled the Rose Bowl. Except for one year during World War II when the venue was switched to Durham, North Carolina, for security reasons the game has been played in Pasadena ever since.

Television announcers are fond of describing it as "the granddaddy of the bowl games," and they are right. Until 1935, in fact, it was the only college bowl game. The champion of the Pacific Coast Conference was matched against the best team from the rest of the country. Even Notre Dame paid a visit in 1925, the only postseason bowl game that school permitted its team to play in for the next forty-five years. The Rose Bowl's prestige was such that few schools could decline an invitation.

Some of the games became legendary. In 1929 Roy Riegle, playing for the University of California, ran the wrong way to score a safety for Georgia Tech's 8-7 win. After quarterbacking his Alabama team to victory Johnny Mack Brown went straight into the movies as a cowboy star. In 1934 an underdog Columbia team beat favored Stanford with a trick play in the fourth quarter. Since 1947, the game has matched the winners of the Pac 10 and the Big 10 conferences. Other bowl games now determine the national champion more often. But none of them has the luster of the original bowl.

The stadium was built in 1922 in an arroyo at the foot of the San Gabriel Mountains, a setting more scenic than any other stadium in the country. With a seating capacity of more than one hundred thousand, it has also hosted several Super Bowl games. The stadium may be visited throughout the year, except on days when events are scheduled.

■ **LOCATION:** Off the Foothills Freeway (Interstate 210) at Arroyo Boulevard. ■ **HOURS:** Monday through Friday, 9–4. ■ **ADMISSION:** Free ■ **TELEPHONE:** (818) 577-3106

SAN FRANCISCO

ALCATrAZ

The original occupants were pelicans. That's what the name means in Spanish, *alcatraces.* Then odd birds of a very different nature took up residence there. They had names like Machine Gun Kelly, Al Capone, Creepy Karpis, and Robert Stroud, better known as "the Birdman of Alcatraz."

The prison has been closed since 1963 when Attorney-General Robert Kennedy decided it was too expensive to maintain. The cost was $48,000 a year per inmate. But these were not the usual prisoners. This was the end of the road in the federal penal system. This was where the incorrigibles, the top-security risks were sent. While it has been a tourist attraction since 1973, the name can still send a chill down the spine. Alcatraz still means The Rock, the most forbidding prison in American history. The place had a reputation, though, for good food and plentiful cigarettes. The wardens felt that those items would keep even the worst prisoners content.

Its history as a prison went back to the Civil War, when military prisoners were sent here to sit out the conflict in a fort constructed in the 1850s. The present buildings were put up with convict labor around the beginning of the twentieth century. The mystique of Alcatraz is its location. Just a twenty-minute boat ride from the heart of one of the country's largest cities, it was, by all accounts, escape-proof. A few tried to leave. Fourteen drowned, seventeen were recaptured, and five went on the records as missing (but they never turned up and are presumed dead). Only one man, John Paul Scott, is known to have reached the mainland, but he came ashore exhausted at the foot of the Golden Gate Bridge and was arrested without resistance.

Much of Alcatraz remains just as it was when the last prisoner was removed. The cell blocks and corridors have been kept in lock-down condition. One of the cells is furnished just as it would have been then. Its last "occupant" was Burt Lancaster during the filming of the movie, *Birdman of Alcatraz.*

■ **LOCATION:** The boats for Alcatraz leave from Pier 41, at Fisherman's Wharf. During the summer months, one-month advance reservations are suggested through Ticketron, (415) 392-7469. Two days is usually enough leadtime the rest of the year. Only same-day tickets can be bought at the boat landing, but all tickets must be picked up there. ■ **HOURS:** Boats leave daily every 45 minutes from 8–3; with longer hours in summer. ■ **ADMISSION:** $5 ■ **TELEPHONE:** (415) 546-2896

CABLE CAR MUSEUM

They vanished for two years in the 1980s and most of the city went into mourning. And when they began running again, on June 3, 1984, San Francisco celebrated with a spirit that some newspapers described as "frenzied." Columnist Herb Caen said: "Take the cable cars away and we pay a price that this city can no longer afford—the price of ordinariness."

As everyone knows, these are the cars that "climb halfway to the stars"—which may be the only instance of a city's transit system being celebrated in a popular song. There has been scattered sentiment in favor of getting rid of the cars by those who view them as antiquated, dangerous, uneconomical. But San Francisco has refused. When the system needed to be renovated (the reason for the two-year shutdown) more than $10 million of the $58 million total cost was raised by public and corporate contributions.

The cars began running in 1873 and at the system's peak it extended over two hundred miles. But a lot of it never reopened after the earthquake of 1906 and other parts could not compete with electric railways and private cars. The two lines that survive, however, on Powell and California streets, are institutions. As former mayor Diane Feinstein put it: "Their address is San Francisco, but America is their home."

The Victorian charm of the little cars is part of the fun. They were built to seat thirty-five people each, but crowds of ninety, many of them hanging on the outside step, are common. The ringing bells, the upbeat personalities of the specially selected conductors and brakemen, the air of being on an amusement park ride instead of urban transit is all part of the fun too.

Visitors can see how the system works and get a view of the actual operating machinery at the Cable Car Barn Museum. The first cable car is on display as is historic equipment. Displays also show how the little trolleys figured in the city's past.

■ **LOCATION:** The museum is at the corner of Washington and Mason streets. ■ **HOURS:** Daily, 10–5. ■ **ADMISSION:** Free to the museum. Cable car fare is $2. ■ **TELEPHONE:** (415) 474-1887

CHINATOWN

This is perhaps the most famous ethnic enclave in America. Other cities have their Chinatowns. The Chinese were noted for settling in compact, tightly integrated economic units. But none is as large as San Francisco's, which with an estimated population of more than 80,000 is the biggest outside of Asia. Its markets and restaurants, architecture, and crowds make it a true city-within-a-city.

The Chinese presence in San Francisco is older than American title to the land. The first recorded arrival was in 1840, when this was still a Mexican provincial town. The official statehood parade ten years later included fifty representatives of this community. The Chinese gold miner, and later, the railroad worker, were an intrinsic part of California's early history. While facing severe discrimination and racial hatred, the Chinese managed to prosper. Their communities are models of self-help—raising and investing capital to build their own institutions.

Most of the original Chinatown was wiped out by fire resulting from the 1906 earthquake. After rebuilding, Grant Avenue remained at its heart and the street is one of the most evocative in the country. A walk up its length, from Bush Street to Broadway, is as dazzling an eight blocks as there are in America.

■ **LOCATION:** The Chinese Cultural Center, on the third floor of the Holiday Inn, at 750 Kearny Street, contains exhibits on the community and a shop; it also offers walking tours of the Chinatown area. Reservations must be made in advance. ■ **HOURS:** Tuesday through Saturday, 10–4. ■ **ADMISSION:** Free ■ **TELEPHONE:** (415) 986-1822

GOLDEN GATE BRIDGE

It is much more than a bridge. If there was any doubt of that, it was erased entirely in 1987 when the Golden Gate turned fifty. A celebration was planned, but no one was prepared for the form it took. An estimated 350,000 people showed up on May 24 to walk across the span. Traffic was clogged in all directions, but it was a festive, almost jubilant gathering. Because on the West Coast, the Golden Gate Bridge had become the symbol of America. To arriving immigrants from Asia it meant hope. To servicemen returning from wars in Japan, Korea, and Vietnam it meant home. It had become the West's Statue of Liberty. So when the bridge turned fifty they came out to rejoice and turned a modest event into an overwhelming celebration of America.

The Golden Gate: It has become a symbol of the American West.
(The Bettmann Archive)

The bridge was talked about for years before being built. The treacherous waters and the changeable weather made the construction a dangerous project. It took four years and cost eleven lives to place the span across the mouth of San Francisco Bay. It is as high as a forty-story skyscraper and 4,200 feet across at the main span (sixty feet shorter than the Verranzano Narrows Bridge in New York, which is the longest suspension bridge in the country). Its reddish orange color was chosen for visibility as well as for its resistance to wind and sea spray.

From the beginning, it has been an accessible bridge. At any given time its pedestrian lane is filled with joggers, walkers, bikers, and skaters.

And sometimes there are jumpers. For some reason, the bridge has attracted an extraordinary number of suicides—an average of sixteen a year. That is the confirmed number. An additional 350 are listed as possibles (although no bodies were found) and through the years, another two thousand were stopped just in time. "The public myth is that it is a glamorous way to die," said a medical director at a nearby hospital. But that is the other side of the Golden Gate.

■ **LOCATION:** The Golden Gate carries U.S. 101 from San Francisco to Marin County. The best view is from Fort Point, directly below the support on the San Francisco side. Watch for the turnoff going down and to the right, about half a mile before the entrance to the bridge toll plaza.

William Randolph Hearst called it "the Ranch." During its heyday, an invitation to this San Simeon estate was Hollywood's hottest invitation. *(AP/Wide World Photos)*

SAN SIMEON

HEARST ESTATE

On this hilltop in California, high above the pounding Pacific, fantasy and reality become intertwined. This is the estate of the greatest newspaper mogul of the twentieth century. William Randolph Hearst, with his blend of sensationalism and populist crusades, celebrity coverage, and splashy headlines practically created the modern newspaper. Already a wealthy man from his family's share in the Comstock Lode, Hearst also grew into one of the most powerful men in the world. His company was sought out by politicians, princes, and movie stars. They knew that a word from him in his newspapers had the ability to make or break careers. So on this hilltop property (originally purchased by his father, George Hearst), a parcel of land half the size of Rhode Island, he built the most fantastic palace of the age, San Simeon.

But Hearst's story has become inextricably bound up with that of *Citizen Kane,* the classic Orson Welles film that is, in the estimation of many critics, the greatest American-made movie of all time. In the film, newspaper magnate Charles Foster Kane's estate was called Xanadu, after the "stately pleasure dome" of Samuel Taylor Coleridge's poem "Kubla Khan." Kane's life and career were obviously modeled on Hearst's, and the film went unreviewed in all the chain's newspapers. Hearst lived until 1951, almost a decade after the movie was released. But for anyone who has seen *Citizen Kane,* it is almost impossible to think of Hearst's life and works without getting an image of the other.

Hearst set about to gather treasures from around the world for San Simeon. He was a tireless buyer of art work from Europe, traveling almost half the year to seek out new acquisitions. "Pleasure is worth what you can afford to pay for it," he once said, and Hearst could afford plenty: A ceiling from an Italian palazzo, tapestries from Belgium, the bed of Cardinal Richelieu, Egyptian statues, bas-reliefs from Florence—an endless profusion of riches. The project began in 1919 and was still not finished at his death.

An invitation to the baronial great house, "the Casa Grande," was the ultimate A-list for more than thirty years. (Hearst always referred to the estate simply as "The Ranch.") In 1957, his heirs, facing ruinous taxes and upkeep, decided to donate the entire property to the state of California. Located on the Pacific Coast Highway, almost precisely halfway between Los Angeles and San Francisco, it has become one of the state's top attractions. Access to the house is only by guided tour (four different ones are offered) and visitors are advised to obtain tickets far in advance. No cars are allowed on the grounds. Visitors park their cars and take shuttle buses up the hill.

Try as they might, however, in going through all the treasures here, no one has been able to come up with any trace of a sled.

■ **LOCATION:** San Simeon is off California 1, about 40 miles north of San Luis Obispo. ■ **HOURS:** Daily, 8–3:30; to 8–5, in summer. Tours last one and three-quarters hours. Tour One is recommended for first-time visitors; it takes in the gardens, one guest house, pools, and the main floor of the great house. ■ **ADMISSION:** Each tour costs $12. Advance reservations are strongly recommended and can be made by calling 800-444-7275. ■ **TELEPHONE:** (805) 927-2020

SANTA ROSA

SNOOPy'S GALLERY

The cast of characters hardly ever changed. A bald-headed kid who kept getting a football yanked away from him every time he went to kick it. A girl with naturally curly hair. Another boy who kept a bust of Beethoven on his toy piano. A beagle who imagined that he was a World War I aviator, or a star goal-scorer for the Montreal Canadians, or college guy Joe Cool.

"Peanuts" was the most popular comic strip in the history of newspapers, run by more than two thousand of them in sixty-eight countries. It inspired a successful musical show, numerous television specials, an exhibit at The Louvre, and a half-time show at the Super Bowl. Pretty good for a self-confessed shy guy from Minnesota, who didn't think he could draw especially well and who, as a kid, experienced almost as much rejection as his alter ego, Charlie Brown.

Charles Schulz began drawing a strip called "L'il Folks" for the *St. Paul Pioneer Press* in 1947 and three years later it went into syndication. In his biography, published in 1989, Schulz recalled how that big break occurred just three weeks after his ultimate rejection, a turndown of a marriage proposal. "It's heartbreaking," he said, "something you never get over. But I think the only purpose in recounting the story was to show how experience prompts a cartoonist's ideas." The object of Schulz's affection became "the little red-haired girl," who is never seen in the strip but is the flame of Charlie Brown's life.

Schulz has made his home in the Santa Rosa area since the mid-1950s, and there are often references to it in his strip. The wrist-wrestling championships in nearby Petaluma. His love for the San Francisco Giants. He even built the Redwood Ice Arena here so that he'd have a place to play his favorite sport, hockey.

An intensely private man who declares himself an agoraphobic (one who fears crowds and open places), Schulz is still a familiar figure in this area. His most visible presence is at Snoopy's Gallery, a little shop he licensed that contains many of his original drawings as well as displays about the history of "Peanuts."

■ **LOCATION:** Santa Rosa is about 60 miles north of San Francisco on U.S. 101. The gallery is at 1665 West Steele Lane. ■ **HOURS:** Daily, 10–6. ■ **ADMISSION:** Free ■ **TELEPHONE:** (707) 546-3385

VICTORVILLE

ROY ROGERS-DALE EVANS MUSEUM

One of Ronald Reagan's favorite stories involves a stop he made with his wife, Nancy, at a rural farmhouse during his first presidential campaign. An elderly man answered without any sign of recognition. Reagan told him he was running for president. No response. He said that he came from Hollywood. Still nothing. Finally, he said that his initials were R. R. The man's face broke out in a big grin. "Come here, momma," he called to his wife. "It's Roy Rogers and Dale Evans and they're running for President."

An apocryphal tale, surely. But an indication of how much a hold this husband-and-wife western team had on the imagination. They made three dozen movies together, starred for years in their own TV series, and made more personal appearances at fairs and rodeos than anyone can count. He was the "King of the Cowboys," the undisputed star of the western movie box office throughout the 1940s and 1950s. Originally a singer with the Sons of the Pioneers, the Ohio-born Leonard Slye had boyish good looks combined with the squinty-eyed ruggedness of a genuine cowhand. Nice voice, too. Riding the splendid palomino, Trigger, he was the epitome of the big screen hero.

Rogers was already established as a western hero when he first teamed up with Dale Evans in 1941. She had been a big band singer and had aspirations toward the Broadway stage. After her first western with Rogers, she hated it. "Who wanted to be billed behind a horse," she said later. Only the threat of legal action persuaded her to stay with Republic Pictures and make more westerns. The two were married in 1946.

At the start, not only was Evans billed behind Trigger, but behind Rogers's sidekick Gabby Hayes, as well. Evans's billing soon rose and so did her status. Long before the era of gender equity, she became known as "Queen of the West," a title she held almost without competition.

The Rogers-Evans team favored westerns that were short on violence and always contained a morally uplifting message. By the end of the 1950s, as tastes changed, their popularity started to wane, and the couple has lived on a ranch near this southern California town ever since. Trigger died in 1966 at the age of thirty-three and a grief-stricken Rogers had him mounted. "I just couldn't bury him," he said. "I had a request from the Smithsonian wanting to know if they could have him when he passed away. But I'd rather not part with him. I never rode another horse in a movie."

Trigger is the centerpiece of the museum here. Memorabilia of the careers of the two western stars is displayed. Both Rogers and Evans make frequent visits to the place and enjoy mingling with the crowds.

■ **LOCATION:** The museum is located at the Palmdale Road exit of Interstate 15, at 15650 Seneca Road. ■ **HOURS:** Daily, 9–5. ■ **ADMISSION:** $3 ■ **TELEPHONE:** (619) 243-4547

COLORADO

DENVER

MOLLY BROWN HOUSE

For years it was just an old house on an old street, once inhabited by an almost forgotten local eccentric. But in 1960, Molly Brown suddenly reared up and started kicking again, the title character of a new Broadway show by Meredith Willson (*see* Mason City, Iowa). *The Unsinkable Molly Brown* was later turned into a movie with Debbie Reynolds in the lead role. And the old house, not even mentioned in the guidebooks, suddenly became one of the biggest attractions in Colorado.

The place was built in 1889 by J. J. Brown, who had hit it big in the gold mines of Leadville. His wife, Molly, had gone through the lean years in the mining camp with him and now she wanted to make a splash in Denver society. Her snubbing move to Europe and triumphal return as a heroic survivor of the *Titanic* disaster of 1912, for which she received her nickname, was the stuff of the musical show. She died in the 1920s and the house passed through a variety of owners.

After Molly's restoration to the rank of international celebrity, the house was acquired by a Denver historic preservation group and was also restored to its look at the time of her residence. None of the furnishings are original, but a small museum in back has some exhibits on the real Molly Brown. Unfortunately, she didn't look much like Debbie Reynolds.

■ **LOCATION:** The house is east of downtown and south of U.S. 40, at 1340 Pennsylvania Street. ■ **HOURS:** Monday through Saturday, 10–4; Sunday, 12–4, June–August; Closed Monday and final tour at 3 P.M., rest of the year. ■ **ADMISSION:** $3 ■ **TELEPHONE:** (303) 832-4092

ESTES PARK

BALDPATE KEY MUSEUM

Two elderly caretakers arrive at a summer resort in the middle of a howling winter storm. They have instructions to open the place up for a mysterious guest. That's how *Seven Keys to Baldpate* opens, in the best "dark and stormy night" tradition. The comedy-mystery became one of the most popular plays of this century's early years and was turned into a movie several times.

Novelist Earl Derr Biggers was inspired to write the original novel after a visit to this inn in the Colorado Rockies. Biggers was then in his twenties, a recent Harvard graduate, and this novel would be his first major success. He went on to even greater fame as the creator of the great fictional detective Charlie Chan.

Baldpate was turned into a play by George M. Cohan and was one of the biggest non-musical works of the entertainer's career. It opened on Broadway in 1913 and was acclaimed as the hit of the season, "shining like a brilliant on a dirty finger," as one critic phrased it. The work is dated now and is seldom performed. Still, Baldpate Inn relishes its past literary associations and has put together what it claims to be the largest collection of noteworthy keys in the world.

■ **LOCATION:** The Inn is 7 miles south of Estes Park, on Colorado 7. ■ **HOURS:** Daily, Memorial Day to Labor Day. ■ **ADMISSION:** Free ■ **TELEPHONE:** (303) 586-6151

GOLDEN

COORS BREWERY

It was a regional brew, the symbol of the Rocky Mountain states, impossible to find east of the Mississippi. That was part of the Coors mystique. People tended to first sample it on a trip to Colorado and ever afterward they associated its taste with the beauty of the high country. Its popularity seemed to rise with that of singer John Denver, whose songs about Colorado topped the charts in the 1970s and brought the state to the center of the country's pop culture. Coors was only too happy to go along for the ride.

The beer had been made in this mountain town since 1873 and its brewery was (and remains) the largest in the world. Still, there were problems. The Coors family was outspoken in its political conservatism and its anti-union stance. It was a frequent target of labor boycotts and libel suits. Things also began to change in the brewing industry in the 1980s. Advances in technology had enabled the brewer to sell its product, which is not pasteurized, on a national market. But the expansion was not entirely by choice. It had become a matter of expand or die. With industry giants Miller and Anheuser-Busch dominating the market, there was little room left for the number-three slot. Coors considered a merger with Detroit-based Stroh's, a move that would have given the new company about 18 percent of the market. But the merger was challenged under the anti-trust laws by several smaller brewers, and eventually, Coors decided to keep its own strong identity and go it alone. It is now ensconced in third place.

Coors continues to maintain a strong identity with its setting. Advertisements emphasize Coor's sense of place in the pristine Rockies and its use of spring water from the mountains. Miller has its strong identity with athletes and the Milwaukee brewing heritage. Anheuser-Busch has its Clydesdales. But Coors has the mountains. A fair exchange.

■ **LOCATION:** Golden is in the western suburbs of Denver, about 12 miles from downtown, by way of U.S. 6. The brewery is at 13th and Ford streets. ■ **HOURS:** Monday through Saturday, 10–4. ■ **ADMISSION:** Free ■ **TELEPHONE:** (303) 277-2337

MANASSA

JACK DEMPSEY MUSEUM

He was a brawler out of the Colorado mining towns, riding freight cars in search of fights. In tank towns he fought against a series of stiffs and earned a reputation as a dirty fighter who wouldn't hesitate to foul. His one venture into New York City earned him $16 for ten rounds of work. But Jack Dempsey had a punch that could paralyze a giant and when he finally found Jack Kearns as a manager, he became one of the biggest draws in the history of boxing.

Dempsey defeated the 6-foot-6-inch Jess Willard for the title in 1919, knocking him down four times in the first round, in an attack that left the hulking champion a bloody wreck. He opposed French champion Georges Carpentier in the first million-dollar gate in boxing history. In 1923, he had one of the most memorable battles in ring lore with the Argentinean Luis Firpo, in which Dempsey was knocked right out of the ring before charging back and knocking his man out in the second round.

He lost the title to Gene Tunney, a "scientific" fighter, who outboxed the stronger Dempsey. Their rematch was one of the most famous bouts in history. A crowd of almost 105,000 packed Chicago's Soldier Field in 1927 to see it. Tunney again battered Dempsey for six rounds. Then in the seventh, the former champion suddenly erupted with a flurry of punches that sent Tunney to the canvas. But he insisted on hovering over his fallen opponent, ignoring a newly adopted rule that mandated him to go to a neutral corner. The referee had to push Dempsey away before counting over Tunney. By some estimates, Tunney was on the floor for a full fourteen seconds. But the official count only reached nine, and he was able to get up and out-point Dempsey the rest of the way. Oddly enough, the "long count" fight made Dempsey more popular than ever. He retired from the ring, took up a brief acting career, and spent many years as a successful New York restaurant owner. At his death in 1983, he was among the best-loved champions who ever fought.

Pikes Peak symbolizes the mystery and power of the Rockies. *(AP/Wide World)*

His nickname was "The Manassa Mauler," after this little mining town where he was born to a Mormon schoolteacher and his wife. The family moved on in a few years but Manassa remembers its champ with displays relating to Dempsey's childhood years and exhibits of his later fighting career.

■ **LOCATION:** Manassa is in the south-central part of Colorado, about 25 miles south of Alamosa, by way of U.S. 285 and Colorado 142. The museum is between 4th and 5th streets, on the state road. ■ **HOURS:** Monday through Saturday, 9–5, May–September. ■ **ADMISSION:** Free ■ **TELEPHONE:** (719) 843-5207

MANITOU SPRINGS

PIKES PEAK HIGHWAy

Its first recorded sighting by a European was in 1806, when an American expedition led by Zebulon Pike caught a glimpse of it from far out on the Colorado plains. Standing apart from any other peak, it seemed to symbolize the mystery and power of the Rockies. Pike estimated its height at eighteen thousand feet, described it as the highest mountain he had seen, and wrote that it would never be conquered. Actually, he was off by almost 4,000 feet and Pike's Peak is only the twenty-eighth highest mountain in Colorado. Still, its lonely grandeur is a compelling sight and through the years of the western expansion, the motto "Pikes Peak or Bust" was a familiar sight on prairie wagons.

By the end of the century, the peak would be so tamed that a passenger train would run to its summit. Katherine Lee Bates stood there in 1893 and was moved to write a song that would become an alternate national anthem, "America, the

Beautiful." Yet, the lonely peak remains a symbol of romance. It is the western frontier and the American Dream, attainable to those who dare to climb.

Since 1915 the climb has been achievable in an automobile. The eighteen-mile toll-road ascends to the 14,110-foot peak and every July cars race to the summit in the annual Pikes Peak Hill Climb. The highway actually begins its ascent from an altitude of 7,773 feet above sea level but the drive still holds a grip on the American imagination. Climbing Pikes Peak is unlike any other mountain trip. Those who think they have driven to the roof of the Rockies have, like Pike, overestimated their peak. The road up Colorado's Mount Evans, in the Arapaho National Forest, actually ascends 150 feet higher. But no one ever said Mount Evans or Bust.

■ **LOCATION:** The Pikes Peak Highway branches off U.S. 24, west of Manitou Springs, about 12 miles west of Colorado Springs. Summit House, at road's end, has lookout points and U.S. Forest Service displays. ■ **HOURS:** The road is open daily, 7–6:30, June-August; 9–3, May, September, and October. ■ **ADMISSION:** Toll is $5. ■ **TELEPHONE:** (719) 684-9383

MONTE VISTA

DRIVE-IN MOVIE-MOTEL

The first drive-in movie opened in Camden, New Jersey, on a June night in 1933. Richard Hollingshead devised a system of ramps that enabled occupants of one car to see the screen over the roof of the one ahead of it. But the drive-in's golden age was the postwar period. During the late 1940s and early 1950s, the drive-in movie became an economic force. Almost one-quarter of all the movie screens in the country were located in drive-ins. They were economical and allowed young families to get out for the night. While mom and dad watched the double feature, the kids could drop off to sleep in the back seat. Among teenagers, the back seat was put to other uses. The drive-in became a generation's introduction to sex education long before it was taught in the classroom.

At about the same time, the motel was changing America's habits in overnight accommodations. People liked the convenience of driving right to their door without having to go to the bother of parking and carrying their bags through a hotel lobby. Because of this ability to avoid the fish eye of the clerk at the front desk, the motel also became a part of the sexual revolution.

Time passed. By the 1980s, the drive-in was an endangered species. Built in formerly far-flung suburbs in the 1950s, their land value escalated as the city rushed out to surround them. It made more sense for owners to shut them down and sell the property to developers. By 1991, drive-ins made up less than 4 percent of the country's movies. And while the motel fared a little better, many of them had grown into motor hotels, with full service and a lobby entry. But in this Colorado town, two of the 1950s cultural icons live on.

The Movie Manor Motor Inn, part of the Best Western chain, allows patrons to sit in their rooms and watch movies on an outdoor screen. George Kelloff, who operates the facility, started off with the drive-in in 1955 and opened the motel with a view nine years later. The adjacent restaurant, the Academy Award Room, follows through on the 1950s movie theme.

■ **LOCATION:** The Movie Manor is west of town, on U.S. 160. ■ **HOURS:** The motel is open all year. Make sure you specify that you want a room facing the screen. ■ **TELEPHONE:** (719) 852-5921

PAGOSA SPRINGS

RED RyDER MUSEUM

Fred Harman grew up as a cowboy. His family moved to a ranch in southwestern Colorado in 1902, when he was two years old and this country was still flavored by the frontier. Harman's closest friends were cowhands and Indians from the nearby Ute and Apache tribal lands. He was also quick on the draw, but with a pencil rather than a revolver. By the time he was in his twenties, he resolved to somehow make a living as an artist.

One winter he got a job in a Kansas City newspaper pressroom and then managed to line up a position with a company that made commercial cartoons. He and a fellow artist there hit it off and decided to go into business together. The venture flopped, Harman returned to ranching and his ex-partner, Walt Disney, headed for California to seek work.

Harman could never shake the drawing bug. He tried to syndicate several comic strips with a western theme. Finally, in 1938, he came up with the idea of Red Ryder. In a 1948 interview, he said that all the characters were based on people he had known as a cowhand in Colorado. Even Ryder's Indian sidekick, Little Beaver, was modeled after a childhood friend, although he had to concede to popular taste in dressing the character in traditional Indian garb. "The romantic idea is sort of foreign to fact," he said.

Harman's original western art work is now displayed in a small museum not far from his lifelong home. Western memorabilia and movies relating to his famous cowboy character are also exhibited.

■ **LOCATION:** The Fred Harman Museum is 2 miles west of Pagosa Springs, on U.S. 160. ■ **HOURS:** Daily, 10–4, Memorial Day to early October. ■ **ADMISSION:** Donation ■ **TELEPHONE:** (303) 731-5758

Hawaii

HONOLULU

WAIKIKI BEACH

One guidebook calls this "the most famous stretch of beach in the world." That is no exaggeration. People who know little else about Hawaii, know about Waikiki. One guide refers to it as "a major disappointment." This is also true. A beach, after all, no matter how renowned, is only a beach. It is crowded. The sand is a sort of dirty white, having been imported from other locations to fill in what was once a swamp.

Nonetheless, it has been the symbol of romantic Hawaii since the 1898 annexation of the islands by the United States. Five years before that, Hawaiian dancers performed at Chicago's Columbian Exposition. It was the first time most Americans saw the hula and the shows touched off a craze for the islands. A second wave of Hawaii mania occurred during World War I when the ukulele began turning up in popular music. "On the Beach at Waikiki," in which the instrument was prominently featured, was one of the big hits of 1915. In the next decade, the uke and Hawaiian songs became a part of the college boy image. Radio shows broadcast from Waikiki heightened this sense of romance.

The name Waikiki means "spouting water," although this is the safest beach on Oahu. The sweeping view from the rock wall of Diamond End back to the middle of Honolulu also contributed to its popularity. Most of the buildings that now line the beach are modern high-rises, but a few of the vintage hotels remain. Most prominent is the pink palace, the Royal Hawaiian, built in the Spanish Colonial style by Matson Cruise Line in 1927. It looks like a piece of Beverly Hills dropped onto the islands. Even more evocative is the Sheraton Moana Surfrider. This was the first of the grand hotels on Waikiki, dating from 1901. Under the banyan tree in its beachfront courtyard the program *Hawaii Calls* was broadcast live for decades. A major restoration project was completed in 1987, bringing the exquisite teak and mahogany surfaces back to their original sheen. The view from its lounges out to Diamond Head is the Waikiki of all the postcards.

■ **LOCATION:** Waikiki is immediately east of central Honolulu, along Kalakaua Avenue. The Royal Hawaiian is at 2259 Kalakaua and the Moana Surfrider is at 2365 Kalakaua.

Thousands bask in the sun at Waikiki, on the day before Christmas 1986.
(AP/Wide World Photos)

PEARL HARBOR

USS ARIZONA MEMORIAL

Never has the changing of the world been marked so decisively as here. Nothing was ever the same after December 7, 1941. The United States and its role in the world was altered forever when Japanese aircraft made the surprise attack that brought America into World War II, a conflict from which it would emerge as the unquestioned leader of the Free World.

Even half a century after the event, the words Pearl Harbor ring like an alarm. Every American who was alive on that date remembers precisely where they were when they heard the news. In recent history, only the assassination of John F. Kennedy compares in impact. And like that event, investigators still strongly disagree about what really happened. Did America know that an attack was planned? Was Japan baited into making a strike as a way of marshalling public opinion behind entry into the war? Did massive blunders leave the country unprepared? Or was it truly a surprise, an all-or-nothing gamble on the part of Japan to knock America's navy out of the war before it began?

The debate still rages, while Pearl Harbor remains a central part of American cultural awareness. Dozens of movies and novels have been written about the event. From the fictional *From Here to Eternity* to the semi-documentary *Tora! Tora! Tora!* Even in the 1980s, a science fiction picture, *The Final Countdown* used the attack as the basis for its time-travel plot: What if a contemporary American aircraft carrier encountered the Japanese planes on the way to their bombing mission? The raid still colors American relationships with Japan: For years almost any surprise move by the country, which is among the USA's largest trading partners, would be described as "a Pearl Harbor" by angry politicians and commentators.

The *USS Arizona* Memorial houses the historical record of the attack on Pearl Harbor. *(UPI/Bettmann)*

One of the most moving trips in the country is the short boat ride to the submerged *USS Arizona,* which went to the bottom with 1,177 men aboard. The battleship sunk in less than nine minutes. The fatalities accounted for almost half of the Americans killed during the attack. The memorial has been built above the spot where the *Arizona* rests. It displays the historical record of the attack. Moored alongside is the *USS Bowfin,* a submarine from the World War II era, which can be boarded by visitors.

■ **LOCATION:** Pearl Harbor is immediately west of Honolulu International Airport, by way of the Kamehameha Highway. Shuttle boat tickets may be purchased at the Visitor Center, off the highway. No advance reservations are accepted, so it is best to obtain tickets immediately upon arrival. ■ **HOURS:** Daily, 7:30–5. ■ **ADMISSION:** Free ■ **TELEPHONE:** (808) 422-0561

Idaho

SUN VALLEY

FIRST PLANNED SKI RESORT

Downhill skiing first began figuring into America's winter vacation plans in the 1930s. Much of that impetus was furnished by the 1932 Winter Olympics. They were held at Lake Placid, New York, and trains loaded with ski enthusiasts made daily trips to the resort from New York City.

Averell Harriman, a former governor and diplomat, then chairman of the board of the Union Pacific Railroad, was impressed. He reasoned that if special trains could be filled to Lake Placid, why not to a resort that could be served by his railroad? He hired an Austrian ski expert with a title, Count Felix Schaffgotsch, and told him to find the perfect place for a ski resort. The only proviso was that it had to be somewhere the Union Pacific ran. The count searched the West and finally came up with a valley in the Sawtooth Range of Idaho. It had a good snow record, open terrain, mild weather. Publicity man Steve Hannagan is credited with giving it the name Sun Valley. He reasoned that even skiers like to be warm.

There were other ski resorts before Sun Valley. They were set up in already established communities in New England and Colorado. This was the first time anyone ever thought of starting a self-contained resort from scratch. It set the standard for both winter and summer resorts: Find the right geographical factors and then build. When Sun Valley opened in 1936, it was unique.

Downhill skiing quickly became the most glamorous pastime for the rich and famous. A Hollywood director took a punch at a Chicago socialite at the resort's opening party. Notoriety never hurts. The railroad arranged for several movies to be filmed in the area, which also added to Sun Valley's aura. The resort was sold by the railroad and given a massive overhaul in the late 1960s. While newer resorts in Colorado have taken away much of Sun Valley's celebrity trade, they can never take away its claim to have been first. The original lodge is now surrounded by a complex of shops, restaurants, and galleries.

■ **LOCATION:** Sun Valley is near the town of Ketchum, about 80 miles north of Interstate 84, by way of U.S. 93 and Idaho 75. ■ **HOURS:** Sun Valley Lodge is open year-round. ■ **TELEPHONE:** (208) 622-4111

TWIN FALLS

EVEL kNIEVEL JUMP SITE

When his name was Robert and he was growing up in Butte, Montana, he got into many scrapes with the law. Knievel felt he was just being adventuresome, but a few judges thought otherwise. Once he landed in a cell with a guy named Knoffel, whom the guard nicknamed "Awful." It was just a short jump to calling young Bobby "Evil" Knievel. Only the spelling changed over the years.

He was the self-styled king of daredevils—propelling his motorcycle over parked cars, shark tanks, and double-decker buses. Well, sometimes over, sometimes *into.* He managed to break every major bone in his body, claimed to have fourteen steel plates in various parts of his anatomy to replace missing pieces of himself, once spent thirty days in a coma, and suffered more concussions than he could recall. Someone asked him once if he had ever consulted a psychiatrist. "I wouldn't have anything to do with them crazy buzzards," Knievel replied.

His top stunt, the one that may go down as either the most daring scheme or the biggest con job in history, came in September 1974. He said he would jump the Snake River Canyon, one mile wide and six hundred feet deep, in a jet-powered motorcycle. He charged admission. He sold television rights. The national media flocked to Idaho to watch this wild man. Then as the cycle soared into space, he bailed out, riding a parachute to the ground and laughing all the way to the bank. "When I was a kid, I wanted to drive at Indianapolis," he said later. "The Snake River took its place."

Later he beat up a former manager with a baseball bat when he said "insulting things about me" in a book. He put out a line of toys and also made advertisements, including public service announcements about safety. But the Snake River jump was the pinnacle of his career and of America's fascination with him.

■ **LOCATION:** The jump site is north of town and one mile east of the Perrine Memorial Bridge on U.S. 93. The takeoff ramp he used is still in place. ■ **HOURS:** There is a visitor center with information on the jump at the bridge. It is open daily, April–October. ■ **ADMISSION:** Free

NevadA

BOULDER CITY

HOOVEr DAM

It isn't the largest dam in America. Oroville Dam is thirty feet higher. It isn't even among the top twenty-five in the water volume it carries. But more than any other such project in American history, Hoover Dam shaped the future of a region and took hold of the popular imagination.

The dam was built in the middle of the Great Depression, when the country was looking to massive public works projects as a way of reasserting America's confidence in itself. Its opening in 1936 became a source of tremendous national pride. It also made possible the enormous postwar expansion of southern California, Arizona, and Nevada. Without the electric power and water generated by this facility, that growth would have been extremely difficult, if not impossible. The bright lights of Las Vegas, just a few miles to the north, were turned on by the impetus from this dam.

The project was first planned because of a flood. In 1905, the Colorado River went on the greatest of its spring rampages. The river was a thin lifeline for the entire Southwest and utterly unpredictable. That year it inundated southern California, forming the Salton Sea and taking sixteen months to return to its banks. That prompted the formation, in 1922, of the Colorado River Compact, an agreement to allot water from the proposed dam among the affected states. Most of the negotiations were carried out under the direction of then Secretary of Commerce, Herbert Hoover. Actual construction began during his presidency. So the dam was named for him.

By the time the dam was finished, Hoover the public regarded Hoover as the man who had brought on the Depression. The name was quickly changed to Boulder Dam. There was a problem with that, too. Original plans had called for the project to be built at Boulder Canyon. Later surveys determined that Black Canyon would be the better site and that's where it was constructed. There was no sentiment for calling it Black Dam, which sounded vaguely like cussing. In 1947, when political passions had cooled, the dam was once again named in Hoover's honor.

The dam site is now the second most popular tourist attraction in Nevada, trailing only the Vegas Strip. Its reservoir, Lake Mead, has become one of the

Hoover Dam changed the future of the Colorado River Valley and took hold of the popular imagination. *(Courtesy of the Las Vegas News Bureau)*

top recreational areas in the region. The view from the canyon top, with its stark desert vista broken by a bright band of water, is one of the most memorable in the country. Because parking is severely restricted at the dam itself, a system of satellite parking lots and shuttle buses has been set up. (You can usually get a bit closer to the dam if you cross over and look for parking on the Arizona side.) Besides the tour of the dam, be sure and take in the Exhibit Building, on the Nevada side, with its scale model of the Colorado River Valley. Only then can you appreciate the magnitude of the dam's impact on this area.

■ **LOCATION:** About 25 miles south of Las Vegas, by way of U.S. 93. ■ **HOURS:** Daily, 8–6:45, Memorial Day to Labor Day; 9–4:15, rest of the year. ■ **ADMISSION:** $1 for the dam tour; the Exhibit Building is free. ■ **TELEPHONE:** (702) 293-8367

INCLINE VILLAGE

PONDEROSA RANCH

In the middle 1960s, when the country seemed to be coming apart, with revolution right around the corner, the top-rated show on network television was pulling in precisely the opposite direction. *Bonanza* ruled the ratings from 1965 to 1967. It was a family western—a story about a Nevada rancher and his three sons trying to do the right thing on the Western frontier.

The first dramatic series to be broadcast in color, *Bonanza* ran for fourteen years and 428 episodes, from 1959 to 1973. It turned around the most enduring heroic Western images. No solitary gunslingers or tough sheriffs. This was the adventure of the four Cartwright men, bound by blood and concerned with family matters and domestic problems. There was no shortage of action and adventure but long before "family values" became a political catchword it was celebrated by the Cartwrights.

The show's galloping introductory music became instantly identifiable as one of the great Western themes. It launched the career of Michael Landon, who would return to television as the star of another landmark family series, *Little House on the Prairie* (*see* Walnut Grove, Minnesota).

On a hill above Lake Tahoe, the Ponderosa Ranch, used as the setting for the series, is now a Western theme park. Many of the sets used in the production of the series are still standing, as is the Cartwright ranch house. There is also a petting zoo, saloon, and playground.

■ **LOCATION:** Ponderosa Ranch is on the north shore of Lake Tahoe, in the Crystal Bay area, off Nevada 28. ■ **HOURS:** Daily, 10–5, April to October. ■ **ADMISSION:** $6.50 ■ **TELEPHONE:** (702) 831-0691

LAS VEGAS

LIBERACE MUSEUM

When he got into show business as a teenaged piano player in Chicago, he went under the name of Walter Busterkeys. But at the age of eighteen, when he debuted with the Chicago Symphony, the orchestra wanted no part of the Busterkeys business. It billed him by his real name, Wladziv Liberace.

He decided to keep it. For the next forty years, Liberace was one of the great names in show business, and one of the few identified by one name alone. His act bridged the gap from pop standards to the classics and always featured a lot of friendly interaction with some of the most devoted fans any performer ever had.

He was famous for the candelabra that was always placed on his piano. "I got the idea from the movie about Chopin, *A Song to Remember,*" he explained. He was famous for his dimples and curly hair, a look that drove older women in the audience wild. He was famous for his incredible wardrobe. He wore ten costumes in his act, one more glittering than the last, and topped it all off with a 136-pound Norwegian blue fox cape.

At the end of his life, however, he was famous for being one of the first major celebrities to die of AIDS. The question of sexual orientation had followed him throughout his career. He had won a 1959 libel judgement against a London paper that described him as "fruit flavored." In 1982 a $113-million palimony suit filed against him by a male dancer was thrown out of court. Almost alone among major entertainers of the time, his homosexuality was an open secret, but one that never seemed to detract from his appeal.

"So many people depend on me for a livelihood," he said in a 1984 interview, three years before his death. "I can't think of retirement. I would like to be like Cary Grant, be a sex symbol at 80."

He made Las Vegas his home and played there half the year. His museum, in which he displayed his clothing, jewelry, and musical memorabilia, was an especially important project to him. It contains pianos once owned by two of his idols, Chopin and George Gershwin, as well as a uniform worn by Czar Nicholas II. When a neighboring mall complained of the traffic jams the museum was causing, he simply bought the mall and lowered everybody's rent. Liberace knew how to keep an audience happy.

■ **LOCATION:** The Liberace Museum is at 1775 East Tropicana. ■ **HOURS:** Monday through Saturday, 10–5; Sunday, 1–5. ■ **ADMISSION:** $6.50 ■ **TELEPHONE:** (702) 798-5595

THE STRIP

Its real name is Las Vegas Boulevard. But only the mailman calls it that. To the rest of America, it is The Strip, a stretch of outlandish signs, incredible hotels, and unbelievable claims, most of them having something to do with "liberal slots." Since the early 1960s, it has also been the center of America's entertainment industry. Veteran vaudevillians always dreamed of playing the Palace; the mark of stardom today is headlining the showroom of a Strip hotel.

Some people would say that this stretch of highway is the definition of American popular culture. It is where dreams of avarice go to die. Where hoteliers try to outdo one another in creating dreamlike environments—from ancient Rome to medieval England to Hollywood—in the middle of the desert. Where America's most desperate hopes are reflected, magnified tenfold.

The Strip is the Mob's gift to the nation. This was just sand and scrub until Benjamin Siegel arrived in 1946. Some people referred to him as Bugsy. A few who did even lived. He was a member of the New York mob's innermost circle,

The Strip. *(Courtesy of the Las Vegas News Bureau)*

its West Coast operative. And it was his vision that created The Strip. In those years, Las Vegas consisted of a small group of casinos clustered in the downtown area. Prosperity had arrived with the construction of nearby Hoover Dam (then called Boulder Dam) and many celebrities already visited to gamble. Siegel thought he could do much better.

A handsome, dapper man, he had many friends in the show business community. He knew that a new, luxurious hotel, with top names playing its showroom, would draw more business than any of the existing facilities had ever dreamed. He convinced the money men in New York and work began on the Flamingo Hotel. Unfortunately, there were cost overruns. Siegel was something of a perfectionist as well as a visionary. The Flamingo started racking up bills double the original estimates. Nevertheless, he managed to open Christmas week, 1946, much of the work still unfinished. Bad weather also kept most of the celebrities away. One month later, the place closed for remodeling.

Siegel's associates were unhappy. On June 20, 1947, he was shot to death in his Beverly Hills home. Half his face was blown away. "Live fast, die young and have a good looking corpse," was one of his favorite sayings. At least, he got the first two right. In 1981, when a TV series depicted Siegel he was shown as violent and dumb. One of his former business partners said someone should be sued. "What are you going to sue them for," said Meyer Lansky, financial wizard of the mob. "In real life he was much worse." In 1991, a highly sanitized version of Siegel was portrayed by Warren Beatty in the film *Bugsy*.

The Flamingo reopened (a few months after it had closed) and became the anchor of The Strip. New hotels, more elaborate than even Siegel had envisioned, opened in succession. After a slight slump in the early 1980s, Las Vegas rebounded by appealing to the family market. New Strip hotels opened since then have all been heavy on children's activities and recreational facilities, while giving the adults ample opportunity to blow their paychecks. According

The Wee Kirk o' the Heather is one of two surviving wedding chapels from the pre-World War II days when marriage was Las Vegas' flourishing industry.
(AP/Wide World Photos)

to the Las Vegas Chamber of Commerce, when three massive new hotels opened at the corner of The Strip and Tropicana Avenue in 1993, the single intersection contained more hotel rooms than there were in the entire city of San Diego. If only Siegel had lived to see it.

■ **LOCATION:** The Strip extends south from downtown Las Vegas, paralleling Interstate 15 on the east. Its parameters are usually given as Sahara Avenue on the north and Tropicana Avenue on the south, but in recent years it has extended farther to the south. Las Vegas, incidentally, may be the only city in the world that names streets after the major Strip hotels located on them.

WEDDInG CHAPELS

In 1950, the total population of the state of Nevada was 160,000 people. It was very much the last American frontier, the last refuge of the unbridled individual. Nevadans had a traditional distrust of any kind of government interference in their lives. There was plenty of room for everyone in this near-wilderness and everyone was free to conduct their life as they wished. As Nevada has grown, Alaska has replaced it in frontier image. But there is still much of the old attitude in this state. Brothels were permitted. Gambling was legalized in 1931, (giving official sanction to a practice that was almost universal). The country's most liberal divorce law required just six weeks residence—this at a time when divorce was a process that could require many years, several lawyers, and repeated legal deceptions in most eastern states. And getting married in Las Vegas was simplicity itself. No waiting. All you had to do was show up with someone to love.

Californians have flocked across the border for decades to wed on impulse in Las Vegas. Since the city is the top tourist destination in the country, a Las Vegas wedding has become a common occurrence among vacationers from all parts of the country. The concentration of wedding chapels are an attraction in themselves. The profusion of heart-shaped signs, neon bells, and cupids is almost as impressive as the glitter of the big hotels a few blocks away. This is the epicenter of Love, American Style. And since most states have caught up with Nevada in granting easy divorces, a Vegas wedding is much more easily negated than is a loss at the Vegas craps tables.

■ **LOCATION:** The chapels are found throughout the area, but the most intensive concentration is along Las Vegas Boulevard, just north of The Strip.

RENO

"BIGGEST LITTLE CITY"

When Nevada legalized gambling in 1931, Las Vegas was still a dusty little burg. It wouldn't begin to grow for another decade, until cheap electric power from Hoover Dam came on line (*see* Boulder City, Nevada). But Reno was positioned to take advantage of the new law. Already an established community and the biggest city in the state, it moved quickly to transform its downtown into a neon canyon. Reno became, as a horseshoe-shaped sign still proudly proclaims, "The Biggest Little City in the World."

Reno did not develop a Strip, as did Las Vegas. So the casinos and hotels are still concentrated in the center of town. The intensive display of lights and action is, if anything, more astonishing than its southern rival's. Many of the major hotel companies that grew up along The Strip in Las Vegas opened their Reno branches downtown. Bally's, Circus-Circus, Flamingo, Sands are all here—albeit in smaller versions than the originals. In addition, Harrah's, the oldest established casino-hotel in Reno, remains a strong presence.

■ **LOCATION:** The intersection of Virginia and 2nd Street is usually regarded as the center of Reno's downtown casino district.

HARRAH NATIONAL AUTOMOBILE MUSEUM

William Harrah got into gambling by running a blackjack club for his father in Venice, California. It was profitable but there was one small problem: It wasn't legal. So in 1937 he moved to Reno and with a borrowed $500 opened a bingo parlor. He parlayed that small beginning into the largest gambling operation in northern Nevada. In 1955 he opened another casino on the south shore of Lake Tahoe. The lake had been a summer resort for generations. But Harrah figured that with his position on the California border if he

Reno in 1963. *(AP/Wide World Photos)*

could invest in a fleet of snowplows to keep the roads clear from San Francisco, allowing him to run the resort year round. He was right, and between the Tahoe and Reno operations he became a very wealthy man.

Before all of this, Harrah had attended the University of California to study mechanical engineering and he became fascinated by cars. "I was always interested in anything that moved, and if it moved fast so much the better," he said in a 1963 interview. His first buy was a 1908 Maxwell. At least, the seller told him that's what it was. When he started restoration work on it, he found that it was actually a 1911 model, worth far less. But after that initial misstep, Harrah became known as one of the shrewdest buyers of historic cars in the world. His collection grew into the largest in America. Many of them were not even displayed "because they can still be seen too often on the street," he said. He admired Henry Ford and had a complete inventory of every model the company ever made. But he kept models in a garage until they were twenty years old.

Harrah began the car collection as a promotional tool for his casinos. But when the casino operation went public in 1971 and was run by full-time managers, Harrah turned full-time to collecting cars. In 1975, he saw the opening of the museum, which permanently displays only 200 cars—a small portion of his 1,100. The Harrah collection is still the fullest expression of the country's infatuation with the automobile, and one man's passion for it. Its research library is regarded as the most complete resource of its kind in the world. Many of the cars are displayed in authentic historic street scenes, with mannequins dressed in vintage driving wear. Among the rare cars is a Bugatti Royale, which had been hidden in the sewers of Paris during World War II to avoid capture by the Germans.

■ **LOCATION:** The Harrah Museum overlooks the Truckee River, downtown, at Lake and Mill streets; 10 Lake Street, South. ■ **HOURS:** Daily, 9:30–5:50. ■ **ADMISSION:** $9.50 ■ **TELEPHONE:** (702) 333-9300

New Mexico

CAPITAN

SMOKEY BEAR HISTORICAL PARK

A terrible fire roared through the Lincoln National Forest in 1950. Shortly after fire fighters put it out, a game warden went into the devastated area to assess the damage. Among the things he found was a forlorn little bear cub, clinging to a tree and crying for its mother.

There already was a Smokey the Bear. He was a cartoon figure in a Forest Ranger hat who gruffly reminded people that "Only you can prevent forest fires." He had been created by a Los Angeles advertising agency as a symbol for the U.S. Forest Service. But here was a living, breathing Smokey. It was after the discovery of the little survivor here, and his taking up residence in the National Zoo, in Washington, D.C., that Smokey became a star.

He began appearing on lunch boxes, tee shirts, comic books, TV ads, with all fees licensed by the Forest Service. When the Tournament of Roses parade wanted Smokey to appear, it was the little cub from New Mexico who rode on the float. He became one of the National Zoo's most popular attractions. More important, he was an effective salesman. The number of forest fires dropped in absolute numbers from the time he began making his pitch.

The real Smokey died in 1976 and was returned here for burial, not far from where he was first found. The historical park has displays about his career in show business, as well as exhibits on fire-fighting and the forest lands of the state.

■ **LOCATION:** Capitan is about 75 miles west of Roswell, on U.S. 380. The museum is in the center of town. ■ **HOURS:** Daily, 9–4. ■ **ADMISSION:** 25 cents ■ **TELEPHONE:** (505) 354-2748

CLOVIS

NORMAN PETTY RECORDING STUDIOS

It was 1957 and there was music in the air in west Texas. Rock and roll was still regarded with suspicion in this part of the country. It was race music, not the sort of thing white musicians played. But in towns across the southern

The main store in Los Alamos: In 1945 it was still a "mystery town," where the allied nations' top scientists pooled their labors.
(AP/Wide World Photos)

plains, the rock beat was starting to infuse the country sound, creating something people were calling rock-a-billy. For a few months, a small recording studio just across the New Mexico line was the center of it.

Musician and producer Norman Petty had set up shop here in his hometown, hoping to get some of the sound on record. His first customer was Buddy Knox. With two friends from West Texas State College, Knox showed up with $60 in his pocket, wanting to cut a record. Petty heard their song and improvised a production. A cardboard box was stuffed with cotton to fill out the drum sound. A member of the local high school marching band was called in to play cymbals. Knox's sister and two girlfriends were recruited to sing back-up. The session lasted three days and at the end they had "Party Doll," one of the top hits of the year and the first chart-topper to come out of Clovis.

The second was six months later. A group out of Lubbock, Texas, showed up to redo a song that had already been turned down by Decca. Members of the group had written it the previous year, inspired by a John Wayne line in the movie *The Searchers:* "That'll be the day," said Big John. Although Buddy

Holly was the lead singer, the record couldn't be released under his name because of his contract with Decca. So it went out credited to The Crickets.

The finger-snapping, rocking sound was so infectious that New York record producers came down to Clovis to study how Petty was doing it. They copied his technique, redid the entire arrangement for a new McGuire Sisters record, and found the beat traveled well. They had another top hit with "Sugartime."

The old studios now have been restored to their late 1950s look, complete with sound equipment and memorabilia of the artists who recorded there. Kenneth Broad is co-administrator of the studios and leads guided tours, by appointment only.

■ **LOCATION:** Clovis is on U.S. 60, 70, just west of the Texas border, and about 110 miles northeast of Roswell. ■ **TELEPHONE:** (505) 356-6422

LOS ALAMOS

ATOMIc MUSEUM

For more than two years, it had no name in the outside world. It was simply: P.O. Box 1663, Santa Fe, N.M. There was no indication that a community called Los Alamos even existed and that almost six thousand people lived there. Of course, not all of them were using their real names. One resident, for example, was called Henry Farmer. But he was actually one of the top scientists in the world, Enrico Fermi, whose specialty was nuclear physics.

There were two other secret American communities at that time: Oak Ridge, Tennessee, and Richland, Washington. But it was in Los Alamos that the actual work on a nuclear bomb was taking place. From 1943 until August 1945, when the bombs were dropped on Hiroshima and Nagasaki to end World War II, only a handful of Americans knew of Los Alamos' existence. And it was another twelve years before any outsider—anyone without top security clearance—was permitted inside, as work on thermonuclear devices continued.

Its isolation was what appealed to the Manhattan Project planners. In 1943 when the scientists moved in, this was just scrub and mountain, the former home of a boy's ranch. The Atomic Energy Commission built a completely planned community, looking like any other American suburb. But, as one resident put it, "without any urb." The AEC turned the place over to private ownership in 1965.

The laboratory here, an arm of the University of California, is still engaged in nuclear research and many facilities and roads are closed to the public. It continues to boast the highest concentration of PhDs in the country and is now an attractive community of nineteen thousand, in a high-growth part of the country. But the result of what was done here shaped the second half of the twentieth century and the cloud of Los Alamos continues to influence virtually every major decision in world politics.

Its effect on music, films, and books was equally profound. The realization that human beings had it within their power to destroy themselves by the slightest miscalculation cast doubt on the whole concept of optimism and progress that had animated popular culture up to then. From the early 1950s on, the doomsday scenario became a standard of popular entertainment, from *Dr. Strangelove* to *On the Beach* to *Planet of the Apes* to *Fail-Safe.*

The Science Museum contains exhibits on the history of nuclear research, as well as the casings of "Fat Man" and "Little Boy"—the first two nuclear devices. The actual site of the first A-bomb test is open to the public twice a year. The Trinity Site is several hundred miles south of here, however, in the appropriately named desert of Jornada del Muerto (the "Journey of Death" got its name because several parties traveling between Mexico City and Santa Fe in colonial times perished there from lack of water).

■ **LOCATION:** Los Alamos is 35 miles northwest of Santa Fe, by way of U.S. 285 and New Mexico 502. The museum is just south of Los Alamos Canyon Bridge, on Diamond Drive. ■ **HOURS:** Tuesday through Friday, 9–5; Saturday through Monday, 1–5. ■ **ADMISSION:** Free ■ **TELEPHONE:** (505) 667-4444 ■ **NOTE:** Trinity Site is open to visitors only on the first Saturdays of April and October. For information on making the trip, contact the Alamogordo Chamber of Commerce at (505) 437-6210.

TRUTH OR CONSEQUENCES

TOWN nAMED FOR A qUIZ SHOW

It first went on the air in 1940. Emcee Ralph Edwards asked a question, failed to get the right answer, and as a result, the hapless contestant had to do a recitation while holding a lollipop in his mouth. Of such inspiration were radio hits born in a more innocent time. *Truth or Consequences* became the top quiz show on the air throughout the 1940s. But the emphasis was never on the prizes that were offered. It was on the bizarre stunts that losing contestants were made to perform.

One man had to hop twenty-four miles on a pogo stick to see if he could beat an airliner's time of circling the world, a trip of 24,000 miles. Another had to get in a canoe and accompany a sea lion on a swim across the English Channel. Yet another unfortunate soul had to wear leg irons until someone mailed in the key that would open them, a project that required 32,744 letters before the right key was found. In 1945 when listeners were asked to identify the voice of Mr. Hush, after being given a set of cryptic clues to the celebrity's identity, the country flooded their local stations with entries for the $20,000 prize. (It was Jack Dempsey.)

One of the more inventive stunts was the 1950 offer to do the show from an American community if it agreed to change its name to Truth or Consequences. The town of Hot Springs, New Mexico, took Edwards up on it. So the entire troupe showed up, did the broadcast from the high school gymnasium and went home. The show, subsequently, tried to make the switch from radio to television, but something was lost in the translation. Its old gags fell flat. Sample material: Question: "Who is the only man President Truman has to take off his hat for." Answer: "His barber." The show soon left the air and Edwards devoted his attention to another of his radio concepts that did turn into a TV hit, *This Is Your Life.*

While *Truth or Consequences* may be only a memory in broadcasting, it is still very much on the map in New Mexico. The Geronimo Springs Museum contains displays on the town's week as a radio hot spot as well as mementoes of Edwards's career.

■ **LOCATION:** Truth or Consequences is off Interstate 25, about 70 miles north of Las Cruces. The museum is at 325 Main Street. ■ **HOURS:** Monday through Saturday, 9–5. ■ **ADMISSION:** $1.50 ■ **TELEPHONE:** (505) 894-6600

Oregon

PORTLAND

NIKE TOWN

I thought this was just another store, said a shopper at Nike Town at its 1990 opening. "But this is like the Oregon Museum of Science and Industry. *The New York Times* described it as a shoe store that is "part Disneyland, part MTV"—a fifteen-thousand-square-foot facility dedicated to turning the purchase of athletic shoes into a family adventure. There is music and multi-media images and sports memorabilia in the display cases. Shoe boxes shoot from storage areas to the selling floors in see-through tubes.

The country's largest manufacturer of athletic shoes had shown that it wasn't just selling sneakers anymore. The humble gym shoe, devised in the 1890s, had developed one century later into a cultural artifact. Nike, in fact, came under fire from some African American groups for promoting the sale of high-priced shoes to a black, urban culture that could not afford it. Many crimes of violence had been traced to the acquisition of shoes.

That was not the sort of thing anticipated by Nike founder Philip Knight. An Oregonian by birth, he was intrigued by the possibilities of the athletic shoe market. In the 1960s the high-quality end of it was dominated by German manufacturers. Knight thought, what if he could imitate their shoes and have them manufactured in Japan for sale in America? He did a paper on the topic while working for an MBA at Stanford and after graduation went to Japan to size things up. Wangling a meeting with a Japanese manufacturer, he was asked what company he represented. "Blue Ribbon Sports," he replied, making up the name on the spot. He struck a deal and the company evolved into Nike.

Most athletic shoe companies at the time were getting endorsements from pro athletes. Nike was the first to understand that the larger market was in the gyms and playgrounds. They approached college coaches and signed them to contracts to promote the shoes at summer basketball camps. Nike caught on as the shoe of choice in the urban, basketball-mad playground culture. The company also hit the wave of a new passion for physical fitness and tailored its ads to appeal to this emerging lifestyle, with every activity demanding a different kind of shoe.

The company is based in suburban Beaverton and decided to open its first shoe supermarket in Portland to test the concept. It served as both a laboratory, at which Nike executives could get quick consumer feedback to new products, and as a showcase. "We were spending $100 million in advertising," said Knight, "and most of our accounts would just take the product and throw it up on a store wall. This way we can show our retailers and consumers who we are."

Shopping as entertainment also fit in with the concept that Nike had defined for itself—that shoes are a personal statement. Within two years, the company had opened a thirty-thousand-square-foot store in Chicago, and several others of various sizes in other major urban areas. But Portland's was the first.

■ **LOCATION:** Nike Town is at 930 Southwest 6th Avenue, downtown. ■ **HOURS:** Monday through Saturday, 10–7; Sunday, 11–6. ■ **TELEPHONE:** (503) 221-6453

Utah

GOULDINGS

MONUMENT VALLEY TRIBAL PARK

When film director John Ford first came to Gouldings in 1938, Monument Valley was one of the wildest and most remote corners of the West. Usually, when Hollywood westerns were shot on location that meant traveling a few miles from Los Angeles. Several southern California sites were used repeatedly by production companies. The ease of access to the studios and the comforts of home made them the preferred locales.

But Ford was not a man who cared much for comfort, and he didn't expect his cast and crew to be concerned about such matters, either. He was bored with the same old vistas, used in so many films, and he sensed that audiences were too. As he planned to film his major western epic, *Stagecoach,* he was looking for authenticity. That's how he came to Monument Valley.

This was the West of towering mesas and rocks twisted into dramatic shapes. Vast distances and endless sky. The majesty of the landscape became part of a movie's texture, a silent presence that dwarfs the human activity around it. It was as if Ford understood that the landscape created the legends. Ford returned to the area again and again, shooting many of his best-known films. One film critic called Monument Valley "the Yankee Stadium of westerns."

It is still an out of the way place. Interstates do not come close. But visitors often get an eerie sense of déjà vu when they come here for the first time. They have seen these mesas and rocks so many times on the screen that for many of them it is almost like returning to a scene recalled from childhood.

■ **LOCATION:** Monument Valley lies along the Utah-Arizona border, within the Navajo Indian Reservation; the area is administered by the tribe. Best access is from U.S. 163, about 170 miles northeast of Flagstaff, Arizona. ■ **HOURS:** Daily, 7 A.M.–8 P.M., mid-March to September; 8–5, at other times. ■ **ADMISSION:** $1 ■ **TELEPHONE:** (801) 727-3287

Monument Valley, looking across Ford's Point. *(AP/Wide World Photos)*

Washington

ROSLYN

SET FoR NORTHERN eXPOSURE

For a little more than a century after its founding in 1886, the town of Roslyn enjoyed a pleasant sort of obscurity. In the Yakima Valley, across Snoqualmie Pass from the urban areas on Puget Sound, surrounded by coal fields. It was a nondescript little place with a lot of flavorful buildings from the 1920s, when the nearby mines brought in its greatest degree of prosperity.

Then, for a few seconds each Monday night, scenes of Roslyn were shown during the opening credits for the Columbia Broadcasting System hit TV show, *Northern Exposure.* Roslyn was actually standing in for the fictitious town of Cecily, located much further north. But shooting in Alaska presented too many problems in logistics for the show's producers. Their scouts thought Roslyn kind of looked the way they wanted a town in Alaska to look. So the show came here to shoot its exteriors.

The move touched off a tourist boomlet in Roslyn (population seven hundred). With its offbeat characters and free-spirited plot lines, the show attracted a sort of cult following; the kind of viewers who would not hesitate to get in the car and drive to Washington just to drop in for a visit and walk the streets they saw on the tube. If you want to get a feel for the real Roslyn, however, the town has an historic museum, with displays explaining how the place got to look so much like Alaska.

■ **LOCATION:** Roslyn is about 80 miles east of Seattle on Interstate 90. The museum is at 28 Pennsylvania Avenue. ■ **HOURS:** Daily, 1–4:30. ■ **ADMISSION:** Donation ■ **TELEPHONE:** (509) 649-2776

SEATTLE

MUSEUm OF FLIGHT

Thirteen years after the first successful flight by the Wright Brothers at Kitty Hawk, North Carolina, a lumberman at the other end of the continent was struck by a great notion. He would build airplanes. Fleets of them. He already

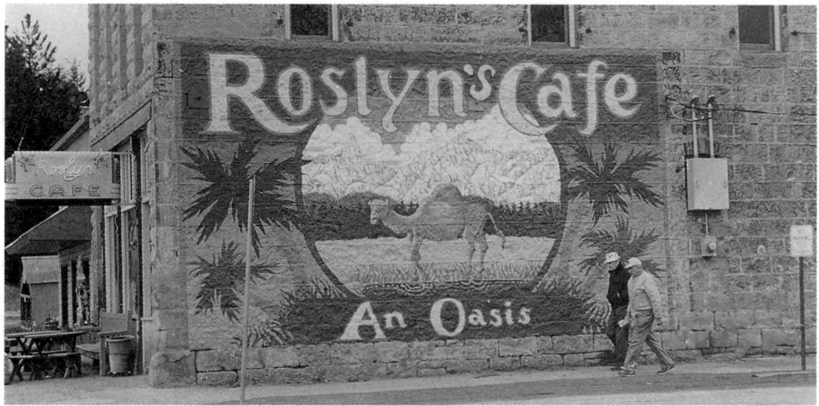

Roslyn offers familiar sites for *Northern Exposure* fans. (AP/Wide World Photos)

had part of the process at his disposal, all the spruce wood he could ever want. With some linen fabric to cover the wings and piano wire to hold the thing together, William Boeing, Sr., assembled a crew and went into business.

The original 1916 factory grew into a massive installation called the Red Barn. Since 1987 this structure has been the Museum of Flight, a tribute to the pioneering aviators of America. When Boeing started production, airplanes were already being used in warfare in Europe. The first scheduled passenger service had started up in 1914, carrying one paying customer from Tampa to St. Petersburg, Florida, for five dollars a trip. That service lasted only four months.

Eventually, Boeing would excel in both the commercial and military aspects of the field. In 1939, the Boeing 314 Clipper, a seventy-four-passenger seaplane, became the first craft to be used in regularly scheduled service across the Atlantic. During the war, the company developed the B-17, the famed *Flying Fortress.* The design enabled U.S. bombers to fly further and faster, while carrying heavier payloads, than any enemy craft. The Boeing 707 became the first jet passenger service to Europe in 1958. Just twelve years later, Boeing introduced the 747, the first of the jumbo jets, capable of carrying more than five hundred passengers. In 1971, however, the company suffered its most bitter defeat, when government funding was withdrawn from development of the Supersonic Transport, a project led by Boeing. (The project lives on, oddly enough, in the name of Seattle's pro basketball team. They were known as the Supersonics, but are now usually referred to as simply the Sonics.)

Boeing has become the leading employer in the Seattle area and the top airplane producer in the country. It presided over an era when air travel transformed the world, shrinking time and distance, bringing impossible voyages within the reach of people of average means. In the popular culture, the train whistle that once symbolized departure has been replaced by the roar of jet engines and "Leaving on a Jet Plane" became the anthem of sad farewells.

The Space Needle dominates the skyline in Seattle, the symbol of the 1962 World's Fair. *(AP/Wide World Photos)*

The museum, located right on the Boeing airport, traces the history of commercial aviation, from its beginnings in French hot air balloons. Among the rare models on exhibit are a 1929 Boeing 80 A-1 and a Curtiss-Jenny biplane, stripped down to show how its wing structure was put together back in 1917.

■ **LOCATION:** The museum is located south of downtown, off Interstate 5, at exit 158; 9404 East Marginal Way, South. ■ **HOURS:** Daily, 10–5. ■ **ADMISSION:** $5 ■ **TELEPHONE:** (206) 764-5720

SPACE NEEDLE

Some world fairs leave a lasting mark on their cities. The Eiffel Tower, after all, was built for the Paris Exposition of 1889 and Chicago's Museum of Science and Industry (*see* Illinois) was left over from the Columbia Exposition of 1893. The Space Needle left the same sort of legacy to Seattle and the rest of the country.

The 605-foot-high Space Needle, built for the World's Fair of 1962, was erected as a symbol of the fair and intended mainly as a curiosity. Organizers hoped for an attendance of one million at the needle. Visitors could ride to its observation deck for the view of the city, Puget Sound, and Mount Rainier (on days when it was visible), and maybe have a meal in its innovative revolving restaurant. Instead, the needle drew more than three million visitors and became a permanent part of the Seattle skyline.

The rotating restaurant idea was a winner. It was copied in high-rise buildings across the country. The concept that diners would be willing to pay big bucks for an ever-changing panorama of the surrounding countryside was a revelation to developers, and by the 1970s even suburban motor inns were promoting them. Meanwhile, the Space Needle has become such an intrinsic part of Seattle that in 1989 it was paid the supreme tribute. A local TV station announced it had collapsed as part of an April Fools broadcast and was inundated by calls from tearful viewers who didn't get the gag. There are some things you just don't joke about in Seattle.

■ **LOCATION:** Seattle Center is one mile north of downtown and is reached most easily by the monorail also built as part of the fair. The terminal is at 4th Avenue and Pine Street. ■ **HOURS:** Daily, 9 A.M.–midnight. ■ **ADMISSION:** $5.50, free if you eat at the restaurants. ■ **TELEPHONE:** (206) 443-2100

SPOKANE

BING CROSBY LIBRARY

"You could warm your hands on the sound of that voice," wrote *Washington Post* media critic Tom Shales upon the death of Bing Crosby in 1977. "I always feel a little better when I hear Bing Crosby," *Detroit News* columnist Bill Gray recalled his grandmother saying. Other writers said how much he symbolized a different America, the musical voice of the Depression and World War II eras.

His mellow baritone was made for the microphone. Before its invention, singers had to be belters, shouters, capable of being heard in the last row of the balcony. But the mike changed all that, allowed an intimacy that was impossible before. Crosby was among the first to master the new technique. It came to be called crooning; a soft, almost off-handed delivery that surrounded songs in a glow of romance. When he injected each performance of his theme song, "Where the Blue of the Night Meets the Gold of the Day," with a few lines of hummed "buh-buh-buh-boos," music critics howled. But record buyers loved it. Although balding and jug-eared and far from a conventionally handsome man, Crosby became a romantic symbol of his generation because of the warmth of that voice.

Harry Lillis Crosby got his first break singing with the best-known 1920s jazz band, the Paul Whiteman Orchestra. He was part of a side group called the Rhythm Boys. But he really hit it big on the radio, a medium made for his style. It was said that his voice resonated with reassurance, and while his early efforts in movies were awkward he soon developed a corresponding screen persona. Always relaxed and in control, displaying a surprising comic touch at the right moment.

All through the 1930s and 1940s, there was a steady succession of number one hit records, from "Swingin' on a Star" (performed in his Academy-Award winning role in the 1944 film, *Going My Way*) to "Don't Fence Me In." But all of them were topped by "White Christmas," a song that became the musical symbol of the American observance of the holiday.

Crosby was born in Tacoma and moved to Spokane as a child. He attended Gonzaga University and retained strong ties with his old school for the rest of his life. He insisted at one point on having the school produce a TV special he starred in. Gonzaga is now the repository of twenty-four thousand artifacts relating to Crosby's life and career, ranging from original sheet music to monogrammed pajamas to a first edition volume of Charles Dickens.

■ **LOCATION:** The Gonzaga campus is northeast of downtown Spokane, and the Crosby Library is at 502 East Boone. ■ **HOURS:** Daily, 9–5, September to April. Weekdays only, rest of the year. ■ **ADMISSION:** Free ■ **TELEPHONE:** (509) 328-4220

Wyoming

CODY

BUFFALO BILL HISTORICAL CENTER

"Buffalo bill's defunct," wrote lower case poet e. e. cummings upon the occasion of Colonel William F. Cody's death in 1917, "how do you like your blue-eyed boy, mr death?"

It is difficult to comprehend the grip that this showman and frontiersman had on early twentieth century America. The country was already on wheels, in planes, watching movies about the winning of the West. And here was one of the men who had actually won it, reenacting the legend, bigger than life.

Partially, he was the creation of dime novelist Ned Buntline. But he was partially the genuine article, too. As a young man, he hunted buffalo for the railroads as they moved across the plains. He killed Cheyenne chief Yellow Hand in personal combat and then scalped him. He was a scout with the 5th Cavalry.

But when the West Cody had known as a young man began to die, he went on reliving it as the star of his own Wild West show. Cody toured America and Europe for more than thirty years, until the extravaganza finally went broke in 1911. In the process, he became a living legend, the embodiment of a glorious era.

Cody is associated with many places in the West. He owned ranches in several states. But it was with Cody, Wyoming that he became most closely identified. It actually was platted in 1895 and its developers were among the first to recognize the tourist potential of an Old West atmosphere. Especially, since it was situated on the main road to Yellowstone National Park. Cody was invited to become president of the development company "since he was the best-advertised man in the world." When he insisted the new town be named after himself, the partners agreed that "it did no harm to us and highly pleased the Colonel."

The Irma Hotel, one of the great historic inns of the West, was built by Buffalo Bill and named after his daughter. This is also where he gathered a lifetime of personal effects. Old guns, awards given to him by royalty, posters for his traveling show, memorabilia of those who had worked for him, such as Annie Oakley and Sitting Bull. The town is now a resort village and the Buffalo

The young scout on his horse: The Buffalo Bill Statue is on Sheridan Avenue's west end. *(AP/Wide World Photos)*

Bill Museum forms the centerpiece of an historical center. The complex also includes museums of Western art, Plains Indians and firearms.

■ **LOCATION:** Cody is about 55 miles east of the entrance to Yellowstone, on U.S. 14, 16, 20. The museum complex is in the center of town, at 720 Sheridan Avenue. ■ **HOURS:** Daily, 7 A.M.–10 P.M., June to August; 8–5, April, May, September, October; Tuesday through Sunday, 10–3, March and November. ■ **ADMISSION:** $7 ■ **TELEPHONE:** (307) 587-4771

Selected events that are part of or have influenced American popular culture.

1742 Faneuil Hall Marketplace is established in Boston, Massachusetts.

1789–97 George Washington serves as the first U.S. president.

1792 The first formal trading agreement is drawn up and the stock exchange opens for business at what will become 40 Wall Street.

1797–1801 John Adams serves as U.S. president.

1801–09 Thomas Jefferson serves as U.S. president.

1806 Zebulon Pike discovers "Pikes Peak" in the Rocky Mountains.

1809–17 James Madison serves as U.S. president.

1816 Cultivation of the cranberry begins in Cape Cod, Massachusetts.

1817–25 James Monroe serves as U.S. president.

1823 To maintain order on the wild frontier, the Texas Rangers is formed as a paramilitary outfit of mounted irregulars.

1825–29 John Quincy Adams serves as U.S. president.

1826 In Boston, Quincy Market is built next to Faneuil Hall.

1829–37 Andrew Jackson serves as U.S. president.

1836 The Alamo is bravely defended by a handful of Americans before being overrun by Mexican forces during the Texas war for independence.

1837–41 Martin Van Buren serves as U.S. president.

1839 Abner Doubleday is said to invent baseball in Cooperstown, New York.

1840s Bowling is imported from Germany. Protestant clergy who equate the sport with a beer-garden setting, induce several state legislatures to ban the sport, which is seen as a severe moral threat.

German immigrants flood into Wisconsin.

1840	San Francisco, still a Mexican provincial town, first records a Chinese presence.
	Frenchman Antoine Alciatore opens a New Orleans restaurant, Antoine's.
1841	On April 4, William Henry Harrison dies of pneumonia, one month after taking office as U.S. president.
1841–45	John Tyler serves as U.S. president.
1844	The first bathhouse is erected at Coney Island.
	Jacob Best, forerunner of Pabst, begins brewing beer in Wisconsin.
1845–49	James K. Polk serves as U.S. president.
1846	Alexander Cartwright draws up the first generally accepted rules for hardball for the New York Knickerbocker Ball Club.
1849	August Krug opens his brewery (which later becomes Schlitz Brewing) in Wisconsin.
1849–50	Zachary Taylor serves as U.S. president.
1850s	The development of bright-leaf tobacco triples production, making it North Carolina's leading cash crop, a position it still holds in the late twentieth century.
1850–53	Millard Fillmore serves as U.S. president.
1853–57	Franklin Pierce serves as U.S. president.
1855	The Frederick Miller Brewing Company is established in Wisconsin.
1857	What will become U.S. Route 66 is originally surveyed by U.S. Army Lieutenant Edward Beale.
	The first of the official Mardis Gras parade organizations, the Mystic Krewe of Comus, is formed in New Orleans.
1857–61	James Buchanan serves as U.S. president.
1858	Archbishop John Joseph Hughes lays the cornerstone for New York's St. Patrick's Cathedral. It will take twenty-one years to complete.
1860	Phoebe "Annie Oakley" Mozee, is born near North Star, Ohio.
1861–65	Abraham Lincoln serves as U.S. president.
	Jefferson Davis serves as president of the Confederacy.
1863	President Lincoln officially establishes the fourth Thursday in November as Thanksgiving Day. This act also gives the nod to

Massachusetts' Plymouth Rock as the landing site of the pilgrims; the other claimed landing site is now in the Confederacy.

1865 On April 14, President Abraham Lincoln is shot and killed by John Wilkes Booth at Ford's Theatre, Washington, D.C.

1865–69 Andrew Johnson serves as U.S. president.

1866 The first public roller-skating rink opens in Newport, Rhode Island; roller skating is regarded as a temporary craze.

1868 In Louisiana Edmund McIlhenny concocts Tabasco Pepper Sauce, using especially hot peppers from Mexico.

1869–77 Ulysses S. Grant serves as U.S. president.

1871 The great Chicago fire rages.

The Homer Laughlin China Company begins manufacturing in Newell, West Virginia.

1872 The Mardis Gras celebration in New Orleans takes form.

1873 In Golden, Colorado, a brewer begins making Coors beer.

The San Francisco cable cars begin running. At its peak, the system extends over two hundred miles.

1874 The first lawn tennis court in America is laid out on Staten Island, New York.

c. 1875 Milk chocolate makes its first recorded appearance in Switzerland.

1875 The first Kentucky Derby is run without much notice.

1876 A U.S. Army campaign against Native Americans results in the annihilation of General George Custer's troops at Little Big Horn.

The first international polo match in America is held at Newport, Rhode Island.

1877–81 Rutherford B. Hayes serves as U.S. president.

1880s The first skyscrapers are built in Chicago.

The flow of European immigration to America steadily swells.

1881 The Clanton and McLaury brothers die at the hands of the Earp clan and Doc Holliday in the Gunfight at the O.K. Corral.

The first U.S. Open Tennis Tournament is held at Newport, Rhode Island.

President James Garfield is assassinated on September 19, six months after taking office.

1881–85 Chester A. Arthur serves as U.S. president.

Created by accident in 1886, now it's consumed 448 million times a day. *(Courtesy of the Coca-Cola Company)*

1882 The five Ringling brothers organize their first traveling circus.

1883 Colonel William F. Cody organizes Buffalo Bill's Wild West Show, which tours Europe and the United States until 1916.

James L. Plimpton patents the four-wheel roller skate.

1884 Wood-turner Bud Hillerick creates the "Louisville Slugger" baseball bat.

1885–89 Grover Cleveland serves his first term as U.S. president.

1886 The Statue of Liberty, the work of Frédéric-Auguste Bartholdi, first lifts her torch in New York's harbor.

Cola syrup is mistakenly mixed with carbonated water at Jacobs Pharmacy in Atlanta, creating the first glass of Coca-Cola.

1887 Helen Keller's parents hire Anne Sullivan to teach their blind and deaf child to communicate.

The Great Blizzard of 1887 virtually wipes out herds in Kansas.

1888 Pushing steadily south down the East Coast, the railroad arrives in Florida. With it comes the first swarm of sun-seekers.

George Eastman markets the first Kodak camera; purchase price is $25.

Thomas Edison files for a patent on what he calls a Kinetoscope, a motion picture camera.

1889 Congress opens Oklahoma to non-Indian settlement.

1889–93 Benjamin Harrison serves as U.S. president.

1890s The musical form ragtime is born.

The original gym shoe is devised.

1890 On January 1, the people of Pasadena, California, hold a parade of flower-bedecked carriages, as one of the events surrounding annual burro races.

1891 Springfield (Massachusetts) College instructor James Naismith invents basketball, using peach baskets hung on the gym wall.

On May 5, Carnegie Hall's opening night features a program of works written by Russian composer Peter Ilitch Tchaikovsky, who also conducts the program.

1892 The new immigration center opens on Ellis Island in Hudson Bay, New York.

Pudge Heffelfinger is the first man to admit playing football for money and is considered the first professional football player.

1893 Henry Ford builds his first automobile.

Katherine Lee Bates stands at Pikes Peak, Colorado, and is moved to write "America, the Beautiful," a song that becomes an alternate national anthem.

Hawaiian dancers perform at Chicago's Columbian Exposition. It is the first time most Americans see the hula and the shows touch off an islands craze.

Frank Lloyd Wright opens his Oak Park, Illinois, studio and begins developing his theories of domestic architecture.

1893–97 Grover Cleveland serves his second term as U.S. president.

1895 On February 6, Babe Ruth is born in a Baltimore row house.

The annual chariot race in Pasadena, California, is named the Tournament of Roses.

The first U.S. Open Golf Tournament is held at Newport, Rhode Island.

Two Pennsylvania communities, Jeannette and Latrobe, meet in what is regarded as the first professional football game.

1896 "What's the Matter with Kansas?" writes William Allen White, editor of a small Kansas newspaper, during the presidential campaign. During the next fifty years White becomes a journalism legend.

The first penny candy, the Tootsie Roll, makes its debut.

General Grant National Memorial is opened in New York City.

1897 The first amusement area, Steeplechase Park, opens at Coney Island.

1897–1901 William McKinley serves as U.S. president

1898 Goodyear Tire Company is organized by businessman Frank Seiberling in Akron, Ohio.

The United States annexes the Hawaiian islands.

Macy's department store is founded by former whaling captain R. H. Macy.

1899 Actor William Gillette brings the famous detective from print to stage in the title role of *Sherlock Holmes,* which opens in New York.

Studebaker tentatively enters the new auto business, making bodies for electric cars.

Ernest Hemingway is born on July 21, in Oak Park, Illinois.

c. 1900 Jazz originates in New Orleans.

1900 The first illuminated sign in New York is put up at 5th Avenue and 23rd Street. (It's for Heinz Pickles.)

In April, railroad engineer "Casey" Jones is killed when the Illinois Central Cannonball Express collides with a parked freight train in Vaughn, Mississippi.

1901 On January 10, Spindletop oil well in Beaumont, Texas, comes in with a gusher. By the end of 1902, 138 wells are brought in with a combined oil production greater than the rest of the world.

On January 19, Guglielmo Marconi sets up his first wireless station on American soil, in South Wellfleet, Massachusetts.

1901–09 Theodore Roosevelt serves as U.S. president.

1902 In Pasadena, California, the annual events surrounding the chariot races—the Tournament of Roses—are extended to include a football game. When the University of Michigan beats the home team, Stanford, by a score of 49–0, the football game is dropped.

At Henry Ford Museum (Dearborn, Michigan): Lasting symbols of Texas' oil-rich soil. *(Courtesy of the Henry Ford Museum and Greenfield Village)*

Studebaker begins manufacturing its own electric runabouts, and continues doing this for ten years.

1903 Michigan automaker Ransom Olds ends a winter-long argument with Cleveland automaker Alexander Winton by racing their cars on a one-mile track laid out on Daytona Beach, Florida. They agree to a rematch the following year. The event is the beginning of Daytona racing.

With $100,000 in hand, Henry Ford founds Ford Motor Co.

In a Milwaukee backyard William Harley and three Davidson brothers build a motorcycle.

Louis' Lunch in New Haven, Connecticut, begins serving hamburgers. The restaurant will claim to be the birthplace of this definitive national dish.

Milton Hershey builds the planned industrial town of Hershey, Pennsylvania, for the sole purpose of manufacturing candy bars.

The New York Times builds its new editorial offices at the intersection of Broadway and 42nd Street, giving its name to the facing square—Times Square.

The first feature length movie, *The Great Train Robbery,* is introduced.

On December 17, Orville Wright pilots the first successful flight in a motor-powered airplane at Kill Devil Hills, North Carolina.

1904 The first national ski tournament in America is held at Ishpeming in Michigan's Upper Peninsula.

1906 An earthquake shakes San Francisco, California, setting off fires and destroying national treasures including the cable cars and much of Chinatown.

Venice Beach, California, whose founder had intended to rebuild the grandeur of its Italian namesake, has become an entertainment district with a distinctly bawdy American texture.

1907 U.S. immigration reaches its peak of 1.3 million European immigrants.

The Plaza Hotel opens in New York City.

Fred Maytag introduces the Pasttime washing machine.

Barnum and Bailey and the Ringling Brothers circuses combine to form "The Greatest Show on Earth."

The first Neiman-Marcus department store opens in Dallas, Texas.

The American baseball anthem, "Take Me Out to the Ballgame," is penned.

1908 Adventure writer James Oliver Curwood's first novel, *Captain Plum,* is published.

The movie industry arrives in California when a Chicago production company is hampered by bad weather in the Midwest and moves to the Golden State to finish shooting *The Count of Monte Cristo.*

The Chicago Cubs win consecutive World Series (1907–08). As of 1994, this is the last time the baseball team will win the series.

1909 Tom Mix catches the eye of movie scouts while traveling with the 101 Ranch touring show. Mix becomes a star of silent westerns.

The first movie cartoon, "Gertie, the Dinosaur," appears.

1909–13 William Howard Taft serves as U.S. president.

1910 Writer Thornton Burgess begins inventing animal tales for the amusement of his young son. The stories are collected and published as *Old Mother West Wind.* Two years later, he begins his syndicated feature, which continues for forty-eight years.

1911 Winsor McCay turns his newspaper feature, "Little Nemo," into the movies' first big animated hit. By the 1920s, the cartoon segment is a familiar part of every movie program.

The Indianapolis 500 is first run, with winner Ray Harroun racing around the oval track at an unprecedented speed of 74.602 miles an hour.

Carry Nation, leader of the temperance movement, dies—not living to see Prohibition.

1912 On March 9, the first group of American Girl Guides meets at the Savannah home of Juliette Gordon Low.

Boston's Fenway Park is built. Because of space constrictions, the left-field barrier is only 315 feet from home plate.

Zane Grey's *Riders of the Purple Sage* becomes a best-seller, with rights sold to the movies, making Grey the most popular novelist in the country.

On her maiden voyage, the luxury ocean-liner the *S.S. Titanic* sinks in the Atlantic after hitting an iceberg; 1,513 drown.

Several small independent filmmakers combine to form Universal Studios in California.

L. L. Bean opens his doors in Freeport, Maine, to sell his Maine Hunting Shoe—a rubber boot on which he sews a leather top.

W. C. Handy publishes the first jazz composition, the "Memphis Blues."

Native American athlete Jim Thorpe wins both the pentathlon and decathlon at the Stockholm Olympic Games.

1913 A long shot named Donerail wins the Kentucky Derby and pays off at better than 90-to-1, giving the little-known race tremendous publicity.

Notre Dame University rises from obscurity when it beats the mighty Army team, 35–13. Notre Dame quarterback Gus Dorais throws a forward pass to Knute Rockne, redrawing football strategy.

The Woolworth Building in New York is finished. At a height of 792 feet, it is the country's first cathedral of commerce.

The Apollo Theater opens in New York City.

In Daytona Beach, Florida, guests mark out a shuffleboard court on the cement walk of the Lynhurst Hotel. Before this, the game has only been played aboard ships.

In July, the highest temperature to be recorded in the United States tops out at 144 degrees Fahrenheit in Death Valley, California.

In Hollywood, California, a new company called Famous Players is organized by vaudeville producer Jesse Lasky, Samuel Goldwyn, and Cecil B. DeMille. This corporate egg becomes Metro Goldwyn Mayer and Paramount.

1913–21 Woodrow Wilson serves as U.S. president.

1914 President Woodrow Wilson officially establishes Mother's Day as the second Sunday in May.

On June 28, the assassination of Archduke Franz Ferdinand, heir of the Austro-Hungarian empire, leads to the outbreak of the First World War in late July and early August.

The first bus passenger service is begun by Eric Wickman in the Minnesota iron range. Within two years, Wickman and partners form the line that will become Greyhound.

Famous Players releases *The Squaw Man,* the first feature-length western.

1915 An eighteen-mile toll-road ascending the 14,110 feet to Pikes Peak enables automobiles to make the climb.

The American Kazoo Company begins manufacturing kazoos in Eden, New York.

The American Girl Guides, organized only three years earlier, has grown so rapidly that national headquarters are moved to Washington, D.C., and the name is changed to Girl Scouts.

Parris Island, South Carolina, is established as a U.S. Marine Corps training facility.

Automobile magnate Henry Ford builds Fair Lane, his private residence, in Dearborn, Michigan.

1916 The organizers of the Pasadena, California, Tournament of Roses try football again: Washington State is matched against Brown from the Ivy League and the West Coast team wins. The game remains part of the annual event.

William Boeing, Sr., begins in the airplane manufacturing business.

The United Daughters of the Confederacy commission a huge sculpture of General Robert E. Lee, General Stonewall Jackson, and President Jefferson Davis at Stone Mountain Georgia.

1917 Hubert C. Eaton begins Forest Lawn Memorial Park in Glendale, California.

In Lincoln, Nebraska, Father Edward J. Flanagan opens Boys Town, a haven and school for difficult young men.

American scout and showman Colonel William F. (Buffalo Bill) Cody dies.

University of Southern California takes on the University of Michigan at the 1989 Tournament of Roses, played every year since 1916. *(Courtesy of George Matuz)*

The Women's International Bowling Congress is founded in St. Louis, Missouri.

Freshman George Gipp begins his football career at Notre Dame.

1918 World War I ends on November 11.

1919 Boxer Jack Dempsey defeats the 6-foot-6-inch Jess Willard for the title. Dempsey goes on to oppose French champion Georges Carpentier in the first million-dollar gate in boxing history.

Newspaper mogul William Randolph Hearst begins work on a lavish San Simeon, California, estate. The project is still not finished at the time of his death in 1951.

1920s Tom Mix is the highest-paid actor in silent films, making $17,500 a week.

The ukelele and Hawaiian songs become a part of the college boy image.

The Jazz Age is on: Ideally suited to the new phonograph, jazz defines the entire decade. Its top artists become national celebrities.

Journalist H. L. Mencken reaches the peak of his popularity. His irreverence seems to match the spirit of the time.

The Auburn, the Cord, and the Duesenberg are the preferred vehicles of movie stars and international playboys.

The traditional folk music of the South slowly evolves into a new musical form—country and western.

The first limited access roads, or parkways, are built around New York City.

1920 The Yankees swing the most notorious deal in baseball history, acquiring Babe Ruth from the Boston Red Sox.

Chicago White Sox slugger Shoeless Joe Jackson and seven of his teammates are accused of conspiring with gamblers to throw the previous fall's World Series. The media dub the players "the Black Sox."

All-American halfback George Gipp dies of pneumonia during his senior year at Notre Dame.

The American Professional Football Association is officially formed in September. The name is changed to the National Football League in 1921.

Sinclair Lewis's best-seller *Main Street* becomes one of the most influential novels of its time—his portrayal of small-town American life is far from the idyllic.

1920–33 Prohibition is enacted in the U.S. The illegal liquor trade becomes violent, with organized crime playing a major role.

1921 Eubie Blake and Noble Sissle co-write the revue *Shuffle Along,* the first Broadway production staged by African-Americans and incorporating jazz in its score.

The Miss America beauty pageant is invented by Atlantic City promoters to extend the resort's summer season beyond the traditional Labor Day closing.

Albert Payson Terhune's first book, *Lad: A Dog,* is published. Terhune's books are huge national best-sellers in the 1920s.

1921–23 Warren G. Harding serves as U.S. president.

1922 Developer J. C. Nichols announces plans to build a shopping area outside Kansas City, Missouri's central business district. Country Club Plaza is the first development to recognize the pull of the suburbs.

Emporia, Kansas, newspaperman William Allen White is awarded a Pulitzer Prize for editorial writing.

More than fifty-seven years after the assassination of President Abraham Lincoln, the Lincoln Memorial is formally dedicated in Washington, D.C.

A land rush is on at Miami Beach, Florida. Formerly worthless lots sell for tens of thousands of dollars and Miami Beach basks in winter warmth and glamour.

Maytag brings out the Gyratator washing machine, with an automatic agitator placed underwater. The concept changes the industry.

It's come a long way since Goodyear acquired manufacture rights in 1923: The blimp as it looked in 1994. *(Courtesy of Linda Nelson Key)*

1923 The annual football game played during Pasadena's Tournament of Roses event is officially titled the Rose Bowl.

The new General Motors headquarters, designed by Albert Kahn, opens in Detroit's New Center.

On Mount Lee, near Los Angeles, California, a sign goes up reading "Hollywoodland"—a promotion for a new housing development on the hillside.

In one of the most memorable battles in boxing lore, Jack Dempsey is knocked out of the ring by Argentinean Luis Firpo. The American returns to the ring to knock out Firpo in the second round.

New York's Yankee Stadium opens its gates.

Goodyear Tire & Rubber Company acquires Zeppelin rights for the manufacture of rigid airships.

1923–29 Calvin Coolidge serves as U.S. president.

1924 Notre Dame University wins the first of eleven national championships, more than any other college program.

Twenty-nine-year-old bureaucrat J. Edgar Hoover is named to head the Federal Bureau of Investigation (FBI).

1925 George D. Hay, a former newspaper reporter, creates the radio show, the *Grand Ole Opry,* in Nashville. It is originally called the *WSM Barn Dance.*

In Dayton, Tennessee, high school biology teacher John Scopes goes on trial for violating a new state law that prohibits teaching the theory of evolution. The case becomes known as the Scopes Monkey Trial.

1926 Andy Devine, who becomes the sidekick for Jack Benny, Roy Rogers, and Guy Madison of TV's *Wild Bill Hickok,* breaks into the movies.

Sculptor Gutzon Borglum accepts the job of carving the heads of four U.S. presidents—George Washington, Thomas Jefferson, Theodore Roosevelt, and Abraham Lincoln—sixty feet high into a mountainside at Keystone, South Dakota.

Annie Oakley dies in Greenville, Ohio.

1927 Charles A. Lindbergh makes the first solo nonstop transatlantic flight from Roosevelt Field, New York, to Le Bourget Air Field in Paris.

In one of the most famous bouts in history, a crowd of almost 105,000 packs Chicago's Soldier Field to see the rematch between boxing powerhouse Jack Dempsey and Gene Tunney.

Best-selling adventure writer and conservationist James Oliver Curwood dies of pneumonia.

Mann's Chinese Theater opens in Hollywood on May 18.

1928 Movie-goers hear the squeaky voice of Mickey Mouse in the first sound cartoon, "Steamboat Willie," which becomes the foundation of the Disney empire. The character's creator, Walt Disney, provides the voice.

At Daytona Beach, Florida, Malcolm Campbell races across the sand at 206.95 miles an hour, setting a land speed record.

Amelia Earhart becomes the first woman to fly across the Atlantic.

In Detroit, the Fisher Building opens in the General Motors New Center, the first major business development built outside the historic downtown area of a city.

During halftime of the Army game, Notre Dame football coach Knute Rockne first uses the phrase that immortalizes All-American halfback George Gipp; "win one for The Gipper."

1929 The Green Bay Packers win their first national football championship. The Packers will take that victory ten more times, a record unmatched by any other franchise.

The U.S. Stock Exchange collapses on October 28.

Elzie Segar, creator of the "Thimble Theater" comic strip sends leading characters Olive Oyl and her brother Castor on a sea voyage. Their navigator is Popeye.

Popcorn machines are introduced inside movie theaters.

Cole Porter's show, *Wake Up and Dream,* hits the New York stage. Its ballad, "What Is This Thing Called Love" becomes the songwriter's first hit.

New York's Chrysler Building is completed, becoming the country's tallest building.

John D. Rockefeller, Jr., announces plans for his "city within a city"—Rockefeller Center. Critics denounce the idea because the location is considered too far uptown to attract tenants or customers.

Auburn's line of luxury sedans are a force in the auto industry. Its stock car model is the first American machine to exceed one hundred miles an hour by stop watch.

1929–33 Herbert Hoover serves as U.S. president.

1930s Downhill skiing is imported from Austria.

The Auburn, Cord, and Duesenberg automobiles meet their extinction in the Depression economy.

Cole Porter's songs and shows set the pace for popular music.

Shuffleboard is the most widely played seniors game in the country and it becomes a Florida signature.

Jazz evolves into swing.

1930 Sinclair Lewis is the first American to receive the Nobel Award for Literature.

1931 In New York, the Empire State Building is completed. At a height of 1,250 feet, its reign as the country's tallest building will run more than forty years.

Nevada legalizes gambling.

With three hundred flamingos in its infield, the Hialeah Park racetrack opens in Florida. The pink birds, imported from Cuba, become the track's signature.

Inventor Thomas Alva Edison dies in West Orange, New Jersey.

Pearl Buck's *The Good Earth* wins the Pulitzer Prize. Between the world wars, Buck is considered the only American writer capable of portraying still-distant China.

1932 The Winter Olympics are held at Lake Placid, New York, and trains loaded with ski enthusiasts make daily trips to the resort from New York City.

Disney studios turn out its first color cartoon, "Flowers and Trees."

Sixty-five-year-old Laura Ingalls Wilder begins writing the remembrances of her childhood on the American frontier—the *Little House on the Prairie* series of novels begins.

Charles and Anne Morrow Lindbergh's infant son is kidnapped and is later found murdered.

Radio City Music Hall, home of the precision-dancing Rockettes, opens and is the largest indoor theater in the world.

Track-and-field athlete Mildred "Babe" Didrikson wins two gold medals and one silver at the Los Angeles Olympics.

1933 The new Museum of Science and Industry opens just in time for Chicago's second world's fair, the Century of Progress.

Jimmie Rodgers, the father of country music, dies from tuberculosis.

Playwright Eugene O'Neill pens his only comedy, *Ah, Wilderness!,* a nostalgic portrait of small-town life.

Fenway Park in Boston is redesigned and the first version of The Wall is erected.

On a June night, the first drive-in movie opens in Camden, New Jersey.

The 21st Amendment to the U.S. Constitution repeals Prohibition.

1933–34 John Dillinger, the original Public Enemy Number One, is the object of the most intensive manhunt in the annals of American crime.

1933–45 Franklin D. Roosevelt serves as U.S. president.

1934 Al Capp begins drawing the comic strip "L'il Abner," creating the village of Dogpatch.

On May 23, six special officers shoot and kill gunman Clyde Barrow and his cigar-smoking companion Bonnie Parker. The couple were accused of killing twelve people and were the objects of a national search.

On July 22, John Dillinger, the most wanted man in America, emerges from Chicago's Biograph Theatre and is gunned down by the FBI agents waiting for him.

1935 E. L. Cord teams up with a young designer, Gordon M. Buehrig, to create the Cord 810, which includes thirty-seven automobile engineering firsts. Twenty-seven of them are adopted in standard production by the industry.

Elvis Presley is born on January 8 in Tupelo, Mississippi.

George Gershwin pens the musical classic, *Porgy and Bess.*

A statue at the Will Rogers Memorial (Claremore Oklahoma): The humorist kept America laughing for thirty years. *(Courtesy of Will Rogers Memorial)*

Humorist and actor Will Rogers and pilot Wiley Post are killed while on a promotional trip, flying across the North Pole to the Soviet Union.

1936 Capitalizing on America's new interest in downhill skiing, Sun Valley, the first planned ski resort in the U.S., opens in Utah.

The Hoover Dam is opened in Boulder City, Nevada, making possible the enormous postwar expansion of southern California, Arizona, and Nevada.

1937 Actor William Gillette, who portrayed detective Sherlock Holmes on stage, dies.

Disney studios release the first full-length feature, *Snow White*, which becomes one of the most financially successful movies ever made.

In June, aviator Amelia Earhart begins her attempt to be the first woman to make an around-the-world flight.

On July 2, the final authenticated message from Amelia Earhart indicates her plane is running low on fuel and no land is in sight. The week of July 9, the Navy lists Earhart and navigator Fred Noonan as dead.

1938 Superman makes his debut in the first issue of Action Comics. Within a year, it is the top-selling comic in America.

A swing concert is performed by Benny Goodman's band at Carnegie Hall, breaking the ground for popular entertainers to appear at this showcase for high culture.

Director John Ford first films at Monument Valley, Utah. The site will long remain the shooting location for Ford's many westerns.

The von Trapp family, later subjects of the musical *The Sound of Music,* flee Austria after voicing opposition to forced unification with Nazi Germany.

Artist Fred Harman comes up with the idea for Red Ryder, which becomes a famous cowboy character.

The originator of Popeye, Elzie Segar dies.

The first Sturgis Motorcycle Rally is held at Sturgis, South Dakota.

On June 22, heavyweight Joe Louis defeats former champion Max Schmeling, a German, in a one-round boxing match.

When they write to a radio station saying, "Listening to your music is like sipping champagne," Pittsburgh listeners dub Lawrence Welk's style Champagne Music

1939 On Easter Sunday, Marian Anderson sings on the steps of the Lincoln Memorial after the Daughters of the American Revolution decide that a black woman may not appear in Constitution Hall.

Little League baseball is founded by Carl Stotz in Williamsport, Pennsylvania.

The Baseball Hall of Fame is opened in Cooperstown, New York.

Ted Williams joins the Boston Red Sox. When he leaves twenty-one years later, after hitting a home run in his last time at bat, he will have stepped across the threshold of legend.

Author Zane Grey, whose images of the Old West dominate American popular culture, dies.

Director John Ford hires B-movie star John Wayne to play Ringo Kid in the film *Stagecoach.*

Hollywood reconstructs frontier Tucson in the desert west of the modern city for the making of the film *Arizona.*

The Wizard of Oz is released. Its biggest song is "Over the Rainbow."

Gone with the Wind, featuring Clark Gable and Vivien Leigh, is released.

Lowell Thomas gives the first televised newscast.

Artist Anna Mary Robertson, "Grandma" Moses, is "discovered" by vacationing Manhattan collector Louis Caldor.

John Steinbeck's *The Grapes of Wrath* sparks a national outrage at the plight of "the Okies." The author is denounced as a Communist, and in some places the book is banned.

The first section of the Pennsylvania Turnpike opens, and becomes the prototype of the interstate system that develops after World War II and transforms American auto travel.

The Boeing 314 Clipper, a seventy-four-passenger seaplane, is the first craft to be used in regularly scheduled service across the Atlantic.

The Second World War begins on September 1 when Nazi Germany invades Poland.

1939–1940s In a series of popular Sherlock Holmes movies, actor Basil Rathbone portrays the famed detective.

1940 Disney releases the cartoon feature *Fantasia,* so advanced it takes twenty years to find its audience.

Superman becomes a network radio star.

Actor Ronald Reagan and actress Jane Wyman are married in Glendale, California.

John Steinbeck's *The Grapes of Wrath* is awarded the Pulitzer Prize.

Truth or Consequences, the most popular quiz show of the decade, goes on the air.

Tom Mix, the greatest of the silent screen's western stars, dies in an automobile accident near Florence, Arizona.

1941 Blues musician Muddy Waters is first brought to public attention when he is recorded by musicologist Alan Lomax.

Red Sox player Ted Williams leaves the team. His record-setting .406 batting average stands for half a century.

Citizen Kane, the film loosely based on the life and times of newspaper mogul William Randolph Hearst, is released.

On December 7, the Japanese launch a surprise attack on the U.S. military installation at Pearl Harbor, Hawaii, bringing the United States into World War II.

Mount Rushmore sculptor Gutzon Borglum dies before seeing the project completed.

1942 For World War II-related security reasons, the venue for the annual Rose Bowl game is switched from Pasadena, California, to Duke University in Durham, North Carolina.

Gordon W. Lillie (Pawnee Bill), master showman and partner of Buffalo Bill Cody, dies.

Cypress Gardens begins its water skiing show, setting the attraction apart from other Florida tourist attractions.

The Atomic Energy Commission establishes the top-secret scientific community at Los Alamos, New Mexico, as part of the Manhattan Project. It is here that the first atomic bomb is designed and built.

1943 The musical *Oklahoma!* debuts, ushering in Broadway's richest and most productive age.

In Chicago Ike Sewell opens Pizzeria Uno, specializing in new deep-dish pizza. The style becomes a Chicago institution and spreads across the country.

Billy Graham graduates from Wheaton College in Illinois and goes on to become pastor of his first church.

1944 D-Day: On June 6, U.S., Canadian, and British forces invade the beaches at Normandy, signalling the Allied invasion of western Europe.

In August, the U.S. drops atomic bombs on Hiroshima and Nagasaki, Japan.

While serving in the military, bandleader Glen Miller's England-to-Paris flight disappears on December 15.

1945 The five-week battle for Iwo Jima is the bloodiest single engagement of the Pacific War. The death toll is 4,917 Americans and about 18,000 Japanese defenders.

On April 18, Pulitzer Prize-winning journalist Ernie Pyle is killed in conflict on the Pacific island of Ie Shima.

VJ-Day: Japan surrenders on September 2, signalling the end of World War II.

John Steinbeck's *Cannery Row* is published. The book develops a tremendous cult following.

Humphrey Bogart and Lauren Bacall marry at novelist Louis Bromfield's Malabar Farm in Mansfield, Ohio.

1945–53 Harry S Truman serves as U.S. president.

1946 Western movie stars and on-screen partners Roy Rogers and Dale Evans marry.

The design for the Gateway Arch in St. Louis, Missouri, is drawn by architect Eero Saarinen.

Gangster Bugsy Siegel arrives in the Las Vegas, Nevada, desert to establish the Strip—a row of casinos and resort hotels.

The American film classic *It's a Wonderful Life,* starring Jimmy Stewart, is released.

1947 Industrialist Henry Ford dies at his residence in Dearborn, Michigan.

The legendary racehorse "Big Red" dies at the age of thirty. More than three thousand mourners attend the animal's funeral.

Baron Georg von Trapp, patriarch of *The Sound of Music* von Trapps, dies.

On June 20, Benjamin "Bugsy" Siegel is shot to death in his Beverly Hills home.

Cartoonist Charles Schulz begins drawing a strip called "L'il Folks" (forerunner of "Peanuts") for the *St. Paul Pioneer Press.*

Cole Porter's show, *Kiss Me Kate,* is regarded as a high point in the musical theater.

1948 Babe Ruth, baseball's Sultan of Swat, dies.

Sculptor Korczak Ziolkowski begins carving a likeness of the great Oglala Sioux warrior Crazy Horse in the Black Hills of South Dakota.

Frank Lloyd Wright is awarded a gold medal by the American Institute of Architects.

Boys Town founder Father Edward J. Flanagan dies.

Humphrey Bogart turns in a career-defining performance in the movie *Key Largo.*

1949 In California, the last four letters are removed from the "Hollywoodland" sign.

After twelve years at the top of the heavyweight boxing world, Joe Louis retires.

late 1940s After World War II, a musical genre formerly categorized as "hillbilly" comes into its own as country and western.

The Overseas Highway is built, connecting Key West to mainland Florida, paving the way for the town's rediscovery.

late 1940s –1950s The motel changes America's habits in overnight accommodations.

The drive-in movie becomes an economic force.

1950s Walt Disney Studios airs the movie *The Adventures of Davy Crockett* on television, setting off a national fad.

The government begins buying up land in Cape Canaveral, Florida. The coastal scrub and sand become a rocket launch site.

The "Golden Age of Television" is on with live studio drama making up much of TV's nighttime programming. The decade begins with an estimated 1.5 million TV sets in the U.S. and ends with about 85 million TV sets in the U.S.

The fast-food revolution sweeps across America.

The Houston Space Center becomes the home of the National Aeronautic and Space Administration (NASA).

Billy Graham is the country's top religious personality.

1950 Wisconsin Senator Joseph McCarthy launches a sweeping anti-Communist campaign in the U.S.

Jim Thorpe is voted the greatest athlete of the half century by the Associated Press.

Charles Schultz's comic strip "L'il Folks" (the forerunner of "Peanuts") goes into syndication.

Mildred "Babe" Didrikson is voted the outstanding female athlete of the first half century by the Associated Press.

At Hollywood Boulevard and Vine Street in Hollywood, California, the Walk of Fame is begun.

The Tail o' the Pup, a fast-food stand shaped like a hot dog held between two buns, is opened in west Hollywood, California.

The Korean War begins when troops from Communist North Korea invade South Korea and President Truman authorizes the use of U.S. land troops.

1951 *The African Queen,* starring Humphrey Bogart and Katharine Hepburn, is released.

William Randolph Hearst, credited with practically creating the modern newspaper and considered one of the most powerful men in the world, dies.

Novelist Sinclair Lewis dies.

After twenty-seven years on the road, Lawrence Welk goes on the air at a Los Angeles television station.

At the height of production, automaker Studebaker employs twenty-one thousand workers at its plant in South Bend, Indiana.

1952 Humphrey Bogart wins an Academy Award for his portrayal of the profane, boozing river boat captain in *The African Queen.*

Superman is featured in his first TV series.

Cleveland disc jockey Alan Freed schedules the world's first rock concert.

1953 Senator Joseph McCarthy opens hearings on alleged Communist infiltration of American life.

Chevrolet first shows off the Corvette at the General Motors Motorama. It is the pet project of GM's legendary design chief, Harley Earl.

Athlete Jim Thorpe dies.

Lawrence Welk and his band are broadcast by a national network as a summer replacement. *The Lawrence Welk Show* remains on the air for eighteen years.

The Korean War ends.

1953–61 Dwight D. Eisenhower serves as U.S. president.

1954 Senator Joseph McCarthy is condemned by the Senate for misconduct related to his anti-Communist hearings.

The Supreme Court rules against segregation of public schools in the landmark case *Brown v. the Board of Education.*

Based on the enduring success of the *Little House on the Prairie* series of novels, the Children's Library Association establishes an award named for Laura Ingalls Wilder; she is the first recipient.

Alan Freed moves to New York and stages the first concert in which black and white acts appear on-stage together.

The Fontainbleau Hotel, the apotheosis of Miami Beach's greatest era, opens.

In New York, the Ellis Island immigration facility shuts down.

1955 What will become the Crystal Cathedral is begun in a Garden Grove, California, parking lot by Reverend Robert Schuller, a congregation of twelve families, and $86.87 in the first collection plate.

On March 7, *Peter Pan,* starring Mary Martin, is first aired. It becomes a television favorite.

On April 15, Ray Kroc opens the first franchised McDonald's, in the Chicago suburb of Des Plaines.

"Rock Around the Clock" makes it to the top of the *Billboard* sales charts, the first rock recording to be number one.

Elvis Presley's first chart-topper, "Heartbreak Hotel," is released.

From hard-packed sand to state-of-the-art speedway: Daytona before the big race in 1994. *(Courtesy of Glenn A. Key)*

On July 17, Walt Disney reinvents the amusement park with the opening of Disneyland in Anaheim, California.

Wernher von Braun—the mastermind behind the German V-2 project who later develops the Jupiter C Rocket for the U.S. government that puts the first American astronauts into orbit—becomes a U.S. citizen.

On September 30, James Dean dies in a speeding Porsche on a California highway.

1956 The Montgomery, Alabama, bus boycott results in a Supreme Court ruling outlawing segregation of public transportation.

Journalist and writer H. L. Mencken dies.

Peyton Place, Grace Metalious's searing portrait of small-town America, is published.

In Edina, Minnesota, Victor Gruen designs Southdale, the first fully enclosed mall.

Athlete Mildred "Babe" Didrikson Zaharias dies.

The International Tennis Hall of Fame and Museum opens at the Newport Casino in Rhode Island.

Harland Sanders hits the road in a ten-year-old Ford, selling fried chicken franchises. Within seven years, the "Colonel" opens six hundred outlets.

1957 The Soviets launch *Sputnik,* the first orbiting satellite.

Musician and producer Norman Petty sets up shop in Clovis, Texas; his recording studio captures the rock-a-billy sound.

Wham-O introduces the Pluto Platter, the precursor to the Frisbee.

Laura Ingalls Wilder, one of the most honored children's authors of the twentieth century and author of the *Little House on the Prairie* series, dies.

1958 Blues musician W. C. Handy dies.

Meredith Willson's *The Music Man* is a nostalgic triumph on Broadway.

Daytona Beach, Florida, holds its last auto race on the sand.

"We're beat, man," says Jack Kerouac in an interview with *Playboy* magazine, the year after his landmark novel *On the Road* was published. "Beat means beatific, it means you got the beat, it means something. I invented it." The author unwittingly gives a name to the Beat generation.

The Boeing 707 is the first jet passenger service to Europe.

1959 Architect Frank Lloyd Wright dies.

The Daytona International Speedway opens in Florida to become one of stock car racing's top venues.

Tenor Mario Lanza dies.

A group of young performers gathers at the Compass Bar, near the University of Chicago campus, to try out new ideas about comedy. It is the beginning of Second City.

The television western *Bonanza* is the first dramatic series to be broadcast in color.

The play *The Miracle Worker,* chronicling Anne Sullivan's work with Helen Keller, opens.

In Detroit, record producer Berry Gordy, Jr., establishes Hitsville, USA, introducing America to a new urban sound, with a pounding beat and lyrics that reflect the realities of Black city life, breaking down racial delineations in the record industry. The label is the precursor of Motown Records.

On February 3, Buddy Holly, Richie Valens, and J. P. Richardson (The Big Bopper) are killed when their airplane crashes en route from Clear Lake, Iowa, to Moorhead, Minnesota.

It's perhaps an all too familiar part of our shared consciousness: the grassy knoll near where President John F. Kennedy was assassinated in November 1963. *(Courtesy of Carl Wheeless)*

1960s–1970s Floridian Don Garlits dominates drag racing.

1960 *The Unsinkable Molly Brown,* a new show by Meredith Willson, opens on Broadway.

U.S. Route 66, the most celebrated federal highway in America, becomes the subject of a television series.

1961 Writer Ernest Hemingway commits suicide on July 2.

Yankee Roger Maris matches and exceeds by one the record sixty-one home runs in one season originally set by Babe Ruth in 1927. Because Maris does not exceed Ruth's record in the old 154-game season, his record is asterisked.

In February, in the midst of the rock era, Lawrence Welk charts a number-one record with the song "Calcutta."

Artist "Grandma" Moses dies at the age of 101.

"Please, Mr. Postman," is Motown's first number-one hit.

American astronaut Alan Shepherd makes a suborbital ride. He is the first American in space.

1961–63 John F. Kennedy serves as U.S. president.

1962 The 605-foot-high Space Needle is built for the World's Fair in Seattle, Washington.

Actor Danny Thomas founds the St. Jude's Children's Hospital in Memphis, Tennessee.

American astronaut John Glenn flies into orbit.

Alcatraz closed as a prison in 1963. Since 1973, it's been a tourist attraction.
(Courtesy of Linda Nelson Key)

The Vietnam War begins.

1963 President John F. Kennedy is assassinated in Dallas on November 22.

Cape Canaveral, Florida, is renamed for President John F. Kennedy a few weeks after his assassination.

Alcatraz prison, long considered the end of the road in the penal system, closes when it is decided that the San Francisco Bay facility is too expensive to maintain.

The Football Hall of Fame is established in Canton, Ohio.

Studebaker, in South Bend, Indiana, is unable to compete with the giant economies of Detroit's Big Three automakers, and closes its doors for good.

The first Bob Evans restaurant is opened near Rio Grande, Ohio.

Dr. Martin Luther King, Jr., delivers his "I Have a Dream" address on the steps of the Lincoln Memorial in Washington, D.C.

Betty Friedan publishes *The Feminine Mystique,* reviving the American feminist movement.

1963–69 Lyndon B. Johnson serves as U.S. president.

1964 The Civil Rights Act bans segregation of public accommodations.

The Free Speech Movement at Berkeley, California, sets the pattern for student protests.

Songwriter Cole Porter dies.

Helen Keller is awarded the Presidential Medal of Freedom.

Part of Opryland's elaborate new home: The old WSM barn dance launched an entire entertainment complex, including a luxury hotel. *(Courtesy of Opryland, USA)*

Martin Luther King, Jr., is awarded the Nobel Peace Prize.

1965 Thornton Burgess, perhaps America's most prolific writer of children's literature dies.

On April 10, the Houston Astrodome opens its doors. It is the first domed stadium in American sports.

The movie version of the 1959 Broadway hit *The Sound of Music* is released, starring Julie Andrews.

In Alabama, Martin Luther King., Jr., leads a march protesting state regulations limiting black voter registration.

Forty thousand march on Washington, protesting escalating U.S. involvement in Vietnam, where there are 184,000 American troops.

1966 Television's *Star Trek* goes on the air.

Walt Disney dies.

The National Organization (NOW) for Women is founded.

The Black Panther Party is founded.

1967 By the end of the year, there are 500,000 U.S. troops in Vietnam. Draft resisters and protesters make headlines around the country.

Richard Petty wins a record twenty-seven out of forty-eight stock-car races, including an incredible ten in a row.

Bobby Gentry's "Ode to Billy Joe" takes the top spot on the charts away from both the Beatles and Motown artists.

The Gateway Arch in St. Louis, Missouri, is completed.

The Frisbee reaches the height of its popularity.

1968 On April 4, Dr. Martin Luther King, Jr., is assassinated in Memphis, Tennessee.

Presidential hopeful Robert F. Kennedy is assassinated.

Helen Keller dies on June 1.

Bob Evans opens the first restaurant in the national chain in Chillicothe, Ohio.

1969 *Sesame Street* is created by the Children's Television Workshop and is aired on public television stations.

The classic biker and counter-culture movie *Easy Rider* is released.

John Wayne wins his only Oscar, for playing what is an affectionate tribute to his own aging image in *True Grit.*

Jack Kerouac, novelist and spokesman of the Beat generation, dies.

On July 20 a team of American Apollo 11 astronauts lands at the Sea of Tranquility and Neil Armstrong becomes the first man to set foot on the moon.

Native American protesters take over Alcatraz Island in San Francisco Bay.

The U.S. begins withdrawing troops from Vietnam.

After fewer than eighty episodes, *Star Trek* is canceled by network executives, but maintains a cult following for many years.

Richard M. Nixon is inaugurated president.

1970s Musician Eubie Blake is rediscovered by musicians when a new appreciation of ragtime develops. He becomes regarded as a national treasure.

Big Surf, in the desert environment of Tempe, Arizona, is among the first urban swimming pools to take advantage of new technology permitting the generation of big waves.

1970 Boeing introduces the 747, the first of the jumbo jets, capable of carrying more than five hundred passengers.

Miami Beach, America's former winter playland, is in economic distress.

1971 In Chicago, Sears announces it will build the highest office building in the country. When it is completed, the Sears Tower ends the Empire State Building's reign as the country's tallest building.

London Bridge is reopened in Lake Havasu City, Arizona, by developer Robert McCullouch, who thought at the time of purchase that he was buying London's Tower Bridge. He pays $2.4 million for the plain, five-arched structure.

World War II hero-turned-actor Audie Murphy dies in a Virginia plane crash.

Walt Disney World opens near Orlando, Florida.

1972 Cape Canaveral, Florida, reverts to its original name. The space center there keeps the Kennedy name.

Metropolis, Illinois, officially designates itself Superman's hometown.

Drag-racer Don Garlits becomes the first man to break the two-hundred-mile-an-hour land speed barrier.

Singer songwriter Don McLean memorializes the passing of Buddy Holly as "the day the music died" in the hit song "American Pie."

J. Edgar Hoover dies, ending forty-eight years as head of the FBI.

1973 Richard M. Nixon begins his second term in the White House.

Georgia's Stone Mountain, the Mount Rushmore of the Confederacy, is completed after fifty-seven years of work.

Pulitzer Prize and Nobel laureate Pearl Buck dies.

Alcatraz prison in San Francisco Bay opens as a tourist attraction.

American involvement in the Vietnam War ends.

1974 The Grand Ole Opry moves to elaborate new quarters in Nashville, and becomes the center of an entertainment complex.

Tex Ritter, one of movies' first singing cowboys, dies.

Charles Lindbergh, one of America's greatest heroes, dies.

After the Watergate scandal and threats of impeachment, Richard Nixon resigns as president of the United States. V.P. Gerald Ford is sworn into office.

The refurbished cable cars: a San Francisco treat. *(Courtesy of Roger Matuz)*

In September, daredevil Evel Knievel claims he will perform his all-time top stunt: jumping Idaho's Snake River Canyon, one mile wide and six hundred feet deep, in a jet-powered motorcycle.

NBC begins a weekly television series based on the works of Laura Ingalls Wilder; the show, *Little House on the Prairie,* runs for ten years.

1974–77 Gerald R. Ford serves as U.S. president.

1975 The Harrah National Automobile Museum opens in Reno, Nevada.

1976 The real Smokey the Bear dies and is buried in Capitan, New Mexico.

1977 President Jimmy Cater pardons most Vietnam War draft dodgers.

After forty-three years, Al Capp, the creator of "L'il Abner," calls it quits. At the height of its popularity, the comic strip was carried in more than nine hundred newspapers.

Entertainer Bing Crosby dies.

Elvis Presley, the "King of Rock 'n' Roll," dies.

Movie sidekick Andy Devine dies.

The miniseries *Roots* scores the highest ratings in television history to date. Its author, Alex Haley, is the first African-American to win a Pulitzer Prize.

1977–81 James "Jimmy" Carter serves as U.S. president.

1978 *Dallas* goes on the air and becomes an instant television hit as the first prime-time soap opera.

Ben (Cohen) and Jerry (Greenfield) scrape together $12,000 and open their first ice cream plant in a converted gas station in Burlington, Vermont.

Paul "Bear" Bryant, coach of the Alabama football team, wins his last national championship.

Artist Norman Rockwell, best known for his classic American art that graced *Saturday Evening Post* covers, dies.

1979 A feature film about Superman is released and is so successful that it spins off two sequels.

Screen legend John Wayne dies.

1980s The drive-in movie becomes an endangered species: Built in formerly far-flung suburbs in the 1950s, they are now sold for development.

1980 Ted Turner puts a 24-hour-a-day TV news station on the air in June; CNN (Cable News Network) beams its signal to only 1.7 million households.

Colonel Sanders dies at the age of ninety. A Coca-Cola executive salutes him as "our last living American symbol."

An estimated eighty-three million Americans tune in to the television series, *Dallas,* to learn the answer to the question, "Who shot J.R.?"

1981–89 Ronald Reagan serves as U.S. president.

1982 The Vietnam Veterans' War Memorial is dedicated in Washington, D.C.

In September, a sitcom called *Cheers,* set in a Boston bar, debuts on NBC.

EPCOT, a Disney-owned science and international travel theme park, opens in Lake Buena Vista, Florida.

Paul "Bear" Bryant, one of the most beloved figures in American sports, retires as coach of the Alabama football team.

1983 American blues musician Muddy Waters dies.

Boxer Jack Dempsey dies. He is among the best-loved champions who ever fought.

Ragtime musician Eubie Blake dies shortly after his hundredth birthday.

Paul "Bear" Bryant dies one month after stepping down as Alabama coach.

1984 After two years of refurbishment, San Francisco's cable cars begin running again on June 3. The city celebrates with a spirit that some newspapers describe as "frenzied."

1985 Three-hundred and sixty-three years after it sunk off the coast of Florida, Mel Fisher finds the *Nuestra Señora de Atocha.* The treasure adds up to a $400 million, the greatest bonanza of the century.

Coca-Cola changes the taste of its product. Public outcry for original Coke makes the new taste a failure, but the original product is as popular as ever.

1986 The U.S. space shuttle *Challenger* explodes on takeoff. The event marks the beginning of difficulties at NASA that last through the decade.

As part of the Statue of Liberty centennial celebration, Ellis Island is restored.

Cleveland, Ohio, is named as the future site of the Rock and Roll Hall of Fame.

1987 San Francisco's Golden Gate Bridge turns fifty. During a May 24 celebration, an estimated 350,000 people show up to walk across the span.

Pianist and showman Liberace dies.

Maria von Trapp, matriarch of *The Sound of Music* von Trapps, dies.

1988 Chevrolet releases the thirty-fifth anniversary model of the 'Vette. It receives so many orders that some disappointed customers have to wait a year for delivery.

1989 Pro-democracy student demonstrators are shot down by Chinese troops in Beijing.

Communist rule of East Germany ends and the Berlin Wall comes down, amid much celebration.

late 1980s Light towers go up at Chicago's Wrigley Field, permitting night games.

1989–93 George Bush serves as U.S. president.

1990s Branson, Missouri, is established as the most intensive concentration of country music entertainment anywhere, including Nashville.

Coca-Cola is consumed 448 million times a day in 160 countries.

1990 Communist governments collapse in East European countries.

Actress Mary Martin dies.

The National Motorcycle Museum opens in Sturgis, South Dakota.

With twenty-one bureaus and satellite links that carry it to ninety countries, cable station CNN is a window on America.

Nike Town opens in Portland, Oregon.

1991 In the Gulf War, UN-authorized forces, including American troops, use force against Iraq after Iraq's 1990 invasion of neighboring Kuwait.

Drive-ins make up less than 4 percent of the country's movie theaters.

Entertainer and philanthropist Danny Thomas dies.

Band leader Lawrence Welk dies.

1992 Superman's publisher announces the end of his comic book. Public outcry is fierce and he is resurrected a few months later, amid tremendous national publicity.

Author Alex Haley dies.

The Mall of America, a 4.2-million-square-foot, four-hundred-store, seventy-eight-acre, self-contained city, opens in Bloomington, Minnesota; it is the biggest shopping center in history.

1993 In May, after eleven years on the air, *Cheers* concludes with a final episode that is the media event of the year.

Superman triumphantly returns to network television in the series *Lois and Clark: The New Adventures of Superman.*

1993– William Clinton serves as U.S. president.

FURTHER READING

A selective bibliography of works that were especially helpful in researching this book.

Barone, Michael. *Our Country.* New York: The Free Press, 1990.

Barth, Jack. *Roadside Hollywood.* Chicago: Contemporary Books, 1991.

Boorstin, Daniel J. *The Americans: The Democratic Experience.* New York: Random House, 1973.

Bronson, Fred. *Billboard Book of Number One Hits.* New York: Billboard Publications, 1985.

Cohen, Hennig and Tristam Peter Coffin. *America Celebrates!* Detroit: Visible Ink Press, 1991.

Davidson, James Dale. *An Eccentric Guide to the United States.* New York: Perigree, 1980.

Encyclopedia of Great Movies. Minneapolis: Woodbury Press, 1985.

Flexner, Stuart Berg. *Listening to America.* New York: Simon and Schuster, 1982.

Green, Abel and Joe Laurie, Jr. *Show Biz from Vaudeville to Video.* New York: Henry Holt, 1951.

Leighton, Isabel, ed. *The Aspirin Age.* New York: Simon and Schuster, 1963.

Lord, Walter. *The Good Years.* New York: Harper and Row, 1960.

Spaeth, Sigmund. *A History of Popular Music in America.* New York: Random House, 1948.

Stern, Jane and Michael Stern. *Jane & Michael Stern's Encyclopedia of Pop Culture: An A to Z of What's What, from Aerobics and Bubble Gum to* Valley of the Dolls *and Moon Unit Zappa,* New York: HarperCollins, 1992.

Stewart, George R. *American Place Names.* New York: Oxford University Press, 1970.

Wellman, Paul I. *A Dynasty of Western Outlaws.* New York: Doubleday, 1961.

Young, Mark, ed. *The Guinness Book of Sports Records.* New York: Facts on File, 1991.

INDEX

Page numbers in *italic* type indicate illustrations

A

B

C

D

E

G

K

L

M

N

O

Q

R

T

U

V

W

Y

Z